X-MEN

FATAL ATTRACTIONS

X-MEN

Mark D. Beazley
COLLECTION EDITOR

Sarah Brunstad
ASSOCIATE EDITOR

Joe Hochstein
ASSOCIATE MANAGER, DIGITAL ASSETS

Jennifer Grünwald
SENIOR EDITOR, SPECIAL PROJECTS

Jeff Youngquist
VP, PRODUCTION & SPECIAL PROJECTS

Jeph York
RESEARCH & LAYOUT

ColorTek & James Emmett
PRODUCTION

Adam Del Re
BOOK DESIGNER

David Gabriel
SVP PRINT, SALES & MARKETING

Axel Alonso
EDITOR IN CHIEF

Joe Quesada
CHIEF CREATIVE OFFICER

Dan Buckley
PUBLISHER

Alan Fine
EXECUTIVE PRODUCER

X-MEN
CREATED BY
Stan Lee &
Jack Kirby

X-MEN: FATAL ATTRACTIONS. Contains material originally published in magazine form as UNCANNY X-MEN #298-300, #303-304 and #315, X-FACTOR #92, X-FORCE #25, X-MEN UNLIMITED #2, X-MEN #25, WOLVERINE #75, and EXCALIBUR #71. Second edition. First printing 2016. ISBN# 978-1-302-90105-9. Published by MARVEL WORLDWIDE, INC., a subsidiary of MARVEL ENTERTAINMENT, LLC. OFFICE OF PUBLICATION: 135 West 50th Street, New York, NY 10020. **Printed in the U.S.A.** ALAN FINE, President, Marvel Entertainment; DAN BUCKLEY, President, TV, Publishing & Brand Management; JOE QUESADA, Chief Creative Officer; TOM BREVOORT, SVP of Publishing; DAVID BOGART, SVP of Business Affairs & Operations, Publishing & Partnership; C.B. CEBULSKI, VP of Brand Management & Development, Asia; DAVID GABRIEL, SVP of Sales & Marketing, Publishing; JEFF YOUNGQUIST, VP of Production & Special Projects; DAN CARR, Executive Director of Publishing Technology; ALEX MORALES, Director of Publishing Operations; SUSAN CRESPI, Production Manager; STAN LEE, Chairman Emeritus. For information regarding advertising in Marvel Comics or on Marvel.com, please contact Vit DeBellis, Integrated Sales Manager, at vdebellis@marvel.com. For Marvel subscription inquiries, please call 888-511-5480. **Manufactured between 7/29/2016 and 9/5/2016 by LSC COMMUNICATIONS INC., ROANOKE, VA, USA.**

10 9 8 7 6 5 4 3 2 1

FATAL ATTRACTIONS

Scott Lobdell, J.M. DeMatteis,
Fabian Nicieza & Larry Hama with Joe Quesada
WRITERS

Brandon Peterson, John Romita Jr., Richard Bennett,
Joe Quesada, Greg Capullo, Jan Duursema, Andy Kubert,
Adam Kubert, Ken Lashley & Roger Cruz with Cliff van Meter, Jae Lee,
Chris Sprouse, Paul Smith, Darick Robertson & Matt Ryan
PENCILERS

Al Milgrom, Dan Panosian, Dan Green, Matt Ryan, Jimmy Palmiotti,
Keith Williams & Josef Rubinstein with Richard Bennett, Cliff van Meter,
Bob Wiacek, Scott Hanna, Kevin Conrad, Terry Austin, Tom Palmer,
Mark Farmer, Mark Pennington, Cam Smith, Randy Elliott,
Randy Emberlin, Mark Nelson, Bud LaRosa & Hilary Barta
INKERS

Marie Javins, Steve Buccellato, Glynis Oliver, Joe Rosas, George Roussos & Mike Thomas
COLORISTS

Chris Eliopoulos, Richard Starkings, Bill Oakley & Pat Brosseau with Dave Sharpe
LETTERERS

Lisa Patrick, Jaye Gardner & Ben Raab
ASSISTANT EDITORS

Bob Harras, Kelly Corvese & Suzanne Gaffney
EDITORS

John Romita Jr., Dan Green & Chris Sotomayor
FRONT COVER ARTISTS

Andy Kubert, Matt Ryan & Matt Milla
BACK COVER ARTISTS

MARVEL® COMICS

THE UNCANNY X-MEN®

$1.25 US
$1.60 CAN/UK 70p
298
MAR
02461

BCPeterson
MILGROM

Acolytes Return!

SOFT-SPOKEN
CONTEMPLATIVE.
CONFINED TO A WHEELCHAIR.
IT IS EASY TO UNDERESTIMATE PROFESSOR CHARLES XAVIER--
--THE RECLUSIVE GENETIC RESEARCHER...
...HEADMASTER OF AN EXCLUSIVE "SCHOOL FOR GIFTED YOUNG-STERS."
EASY... BECAUSE HIS MOST IMPRESSIVE ACCOMPLISH-MENTS CANNOT BE SHARED WITH THE REST OF THE WORLD.

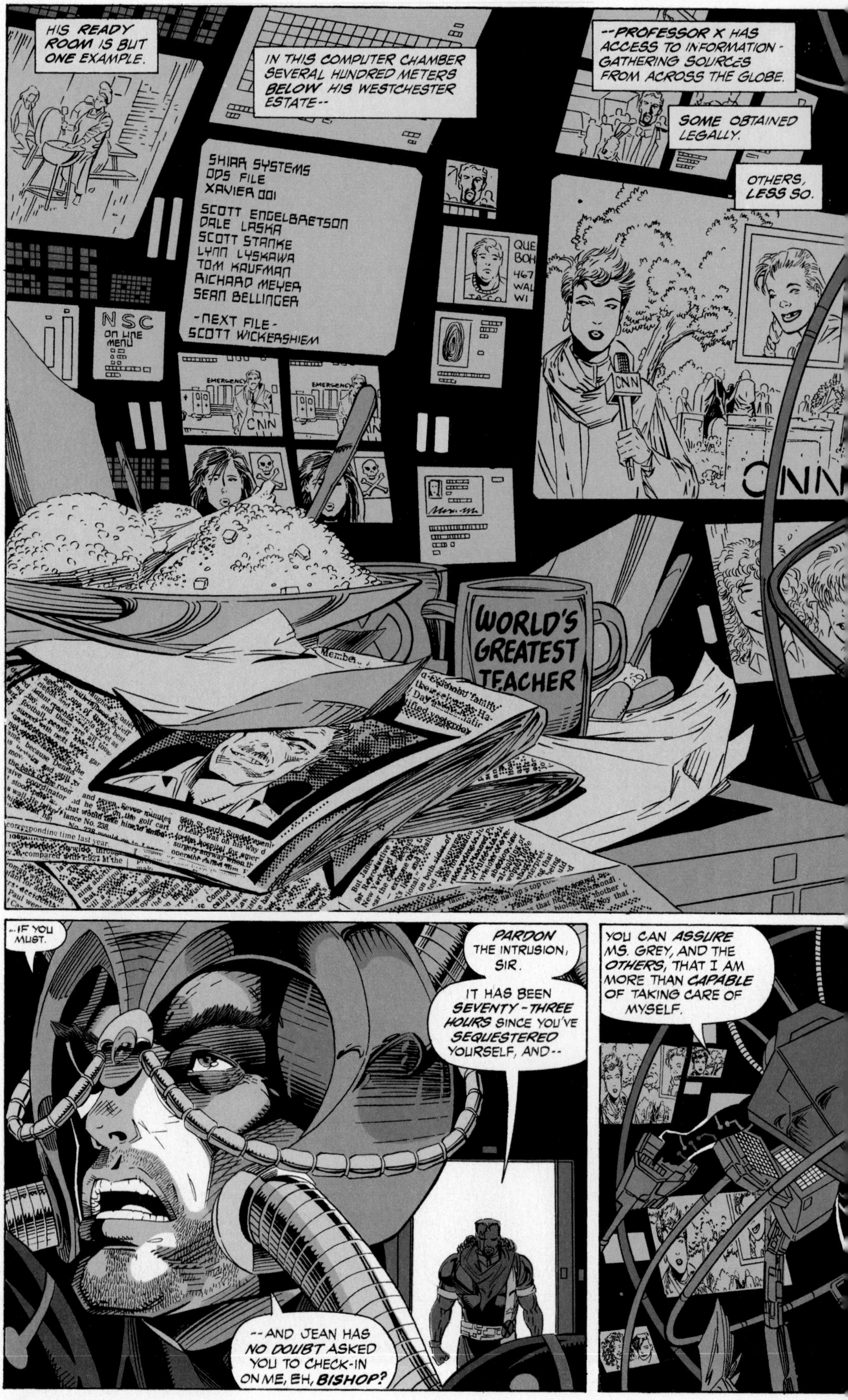

HIS READY ROOM IS BUT ONE EXAMPLE.

IN THIS COMPUTER CHAMBER SEVERAL HUNDRED METERS BELOW HIS WESTCHESTER ESTATE--

--PROFESSOR X HAS ACCESS TO INFORMATION-GATHERING SOURCES FROM ACROSS THE GLOBE.

SOME OBTAINED LEGALLY.

OTHERS, LESS SO.

SHIAR SYSTEMS
ODS FILE
XAVIER 001
SCOTT ENGELBRETSON
DALE LASKA
SCOTT STANKE
LYNN LYSKAWA
TOM KAUFMAN
RICHARD MEYER
SEAN BELLINGER
-NEXT FILE-
SCOTT WICKERSHIEM

NSC
ON LINE
MENU

CNN

WORLD'S GREATEST TEACHER

SSESSED OF THE
ST POWERFUL
TANT MIND ON
PLANET--

--HIS BRAIN CAN ASSIMILATE AND PROCESS IMPOSSIBLY HUGE AMOUNTS OF RAW DATA IN AN ASTONISHINGLY SHORT AMOUNT OF TIME.

ALL OF WHICH PLACES CHARLES XAVIER IN THE UNENVIABLE ROLE OF LONE WITNESS, TO WHAT MAY VERY WELL BE THE FIRST DAY...

...OF THE END OF THE WORLD.

BWENT

ENTER.

BWENT

I SAID ENTER...!

STAN LEE
ESENTS AN ADVENTURE
THE UNCANNY X-MEN
IN...

"...FOR THE CHILDREN!"

S. LOBDELL, WRITER
B. PETERSON, PENCILER
A. MILGROM, INKER
C. ELIOPOULOS, LETTERER
M. JAVINS, COLORIST
B. HARRAS, EDITOR
T. DeFALCO, EDITOR IN CHIEF

I DON'T
OUBT THAT, SIR.
NONE OF US DOES.
ACTUALLY, I WAS HOPING TO DISCUSS A MATTER OF A MORE PERSONAL NATURE.

OF COURSE.
HOW EGO-CENTRIC OF ME.
CONTINUE.

WHILE IT SHAMES ME TO ADMIT THIS...
...IT IS OBVIOUS TO ALL PARTIES CONCERNED THAT ADMITTING ME INTO THE X-MEN WAS--
--PREMATURE--
--AT BEST.
IN THE FUTURE WHERE I WAS RAISED, MY "DIRECT APPROACH" WAS MORE THAN ACCEPTABLE--
--INDEED, IT WAS ABSOLUTELY NECESSARY.
CLEARLY, THAT IS NOT THE CASE IN THE HERE AND NOW.
RATHER THAN CONTINUE AS A DISRUPTIVE INFLUENCE...
...I REGRETFULLY TENDER MY RESIGNATION.
AT THE RISK OF SOUNDING INSENSITIVE--
--RUBBISH!
THOUGH IT OFTTIMES SEEMS THE CONTRARY, ATTENDING XAVIER'S MEANS MORE THAN FIGHTING FOR A WORLD THAT BOTH FEARS AND HATES US.
THIS SCHOOL IS ALSO ABOUT LEARNING.
IF YOU FAIL, THEN I FAIL.
THAT'S NOT GOING TO HAPPEN, BISHOP, YOU NEVER STRUCK ME AS ONE TO GIVE UP EASILY, THEREFORE...
...YOUR RESIGNATION IS NOT ACCEPTED.
DO I MAKE MYSELF CLEAR?
CRYSTAL, SIR.
FINE.
PLEASE ASK ORORO TO BRING THE VAN AROUND OUT FRONT IN FIVE MINUTES.
DONE. AND PROFESSOR...
...THANK YOU.
HMMRP

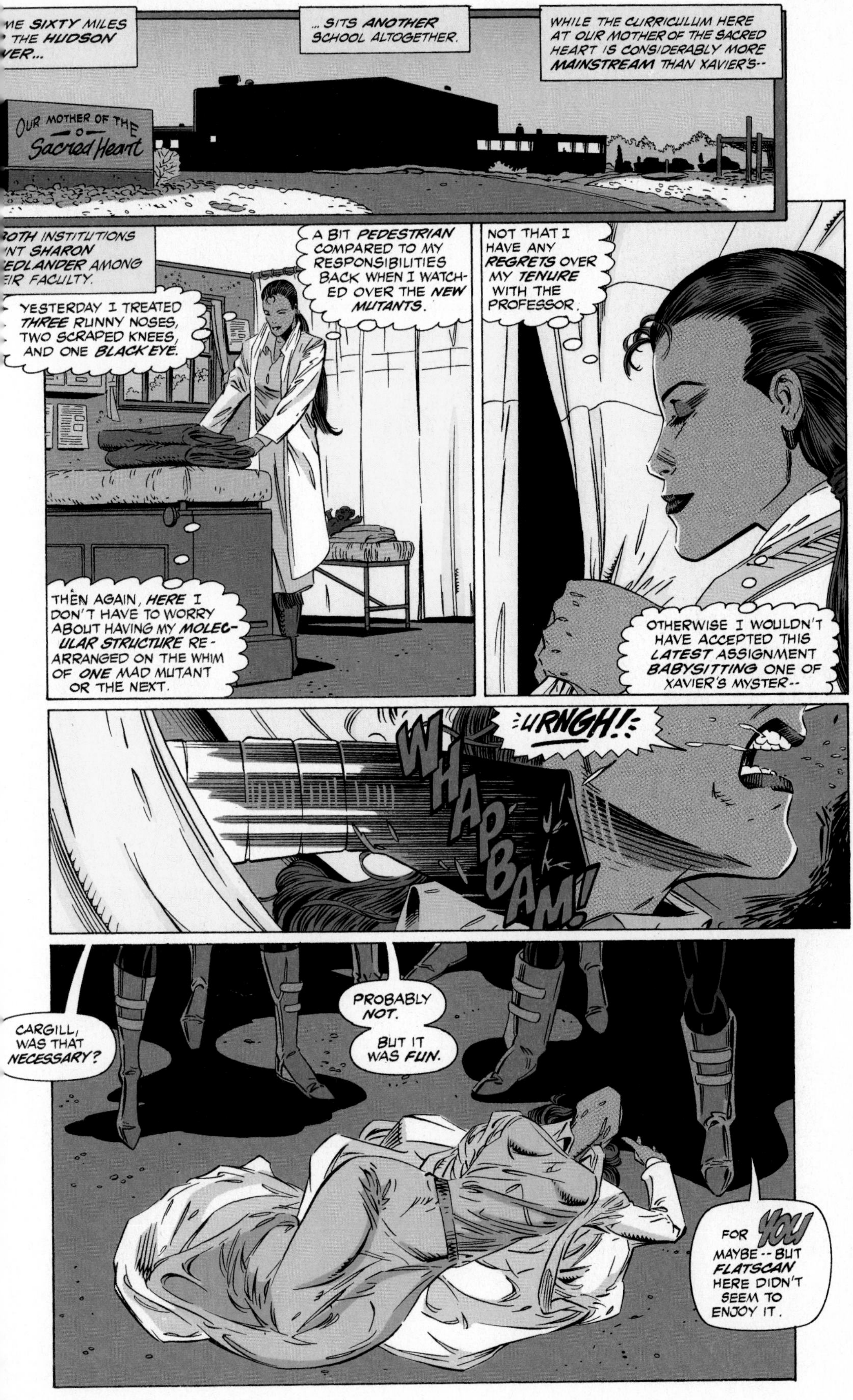

ME SIXTY MILES
THE HUDSON
VER...

...SITS ANOTHER SCHOOL ALTOGETHER.

WHILE THE CURRICULUM HERE AT OUR MOTHER OF THE SACRED HEART IS CONSIDERABLY MORE MAINSTREAM THAN XAVIER'S--

OUR MOTHER OF THE Sacred Heart

BOTH INSTITUTIONS
NT SHARON
EDLANDER AMONG
EIR FACULTY.

YESTERDAY I TREATED THREE RUNNY NOSES, TWO SCRAPED KNEES, AND ONE BLACK EYE.

A BIT PEDESTRIAN COMPARED TO MY RESPONSIBILITIES BACK WHEN I WATCHED OVER THE NEW MUTANTS.

NOT THAT I HAVE ANY REGRETS OVER MY TENURE WITH THE PROFESSOR.

THEN AGAIN, HERE I DON'T HAVE TO WORRY ABOUT HAVING MY MOLECULAR STRUCTURE REARRANGED ON THE WHIM OF ONE MAD MUTANT OR THE NEXT.

OTHERWISE I WOULDN'T HAVE ACCEPTED THIS LATEST ASSIGNMENT BABYSITTING ONE OF XAVIER'S MYSTER--

URNGH!
WHAPBAM!

CARGILL, WAS THAT NECESSARY?
PROBABLY NOT.
BUT IT WAS FUN.
FOR YOU MAYBE -- BUT FLATSCAN HERE DIDN'T SEEM TO ENJOY IT.

XAVIER'S...
GOOD MORNING, CLASS.
WELCOME TO DANGER ROOM 101.
AS YOU KNOW FROM YOUR SYLLABUS, THE OBJECT OF THIS COURSE IS TO KEEP YOU ALIVE--
--USING YOUR MUTANT POWERS WHEN YOU CAN...
...SURVIVING WITHOUT THEM WHEN YOU CAN'T.
WITH STORM AND CYCLOPS BOTH OFF CAMPUS--YOU'RE REALLY GETTING INTO THIS SUBSTITUTE INSTRUCTOR ROLE, JEAN.
YES, WARREN-- I AM.
NOW, SHUSH.
BISHOP AND GAMBIT--IF YOU'LL PLEASE LOSE YOUR WEAPONS...?
IT'S ALWAYS BEEN MY BELIEF THAT A SOLDIER SHOULD NEVER DIVEST HIM-SELF OF THE SECURITY OF HIS ARMAMENTS.
MON DIEU! DOES THE MAN SLEEP WITH A TEDDY BEAR AS WELL?
I HEARD THAT, GAMBIT.
TO KEEP THINGS FAIR, BISHOP-- I'LL REFRAIN FROM USING MY TELE-KINETIC POWERS DURING THIS EXERCISE.
YOUR ASSIGNMENT IS TO CROSS THE ROOM WITHOUT USE OF YOUR MUTANT POWERS... AND TOUCH ME.
ALL YOU GOT T'DO IS ASK.
DON'T NEED NO DANGER ROOM FOR DAT, CHERE.
SO, WHAT'S THE CATCH?

THAT'D BE ME, GAMBIT.
BUT NOT TO WORRY ABOUT THE ODDS!
COURTESY OF THE SHI'AR HOLOGRAM TECHNOLOGY...
...YOU WON'T KNOW WHICH ME IS ME--
--AND WHICH IS NOT!
YOU REALIZE, MON AMI-- THIS IS A THINLY VEILED 'TEMPT AT FORCING YOU'N ME TO MAKE NICE?
ARE YOU CASTING ASPERSIONS UPON MY PROFESSIONALISM, LEBEAU?
DE NAME IS GAMBIT, HOMMES.
AND YES.
I MAY NOT LIKE YOU ANY MORE THAN I CAN TRUST YOU --
-- BUT YOU ARE NONETHELESS AN X-MAN.
AS SUCH, I WILL DEFEND YOU AS IF YOU'RE NOT THE HOMICIDAL TRAITOR TO THE CAUSE THAT I SUSPECT YOU ARE.
AIN'T DAT AS COMF'TING AS ALL GET OUT?
ANNNNND--
--BEGIN!
FOR A BODY WHOSE REFERENCES AN' PRIOR WORK HISTORY IS SOME HUNDRED YEARS IN THE FUTURE --
--YOU'RE A FINE ONE TO QUESTION ANOTHER BODY'S LOYALTY!
TRUE, "MON AMI".
TOO TRUE, INDEED.

CENTRAL PARK.
NEW YORK CITY.
"DETECTIVE CHARLOTTE JONES."
HUNH
I'VE BEEN WORKING OUT OF MANHATTAN HOMICIDE FOR TWO MONTHS--
--SO WHY DOES IT STILL SOUND SO UNREAL?
NOT AS THOUGH I DIDN'T WORK HARD--AS IF I DIDN'T EARN IT.
RAISING TIM DURING THE DAY, WORKING NIGHTS... STUDYING FOR THE EXAMS EVERY FREE MINUTE IN BETWEEN.
NO, THE BIG QUESTION IS WHY I'M WILLING TO RISK EVERYTHING I'VE STRIVED FOR--
--TO HELP A GROUP OF MUTANT OUTLAWS?
THANK YOU FOR MEETING US ON SUCH SHORT NOTICE CHARLOTTE.
I TRUST YOU BROUGHT THE INFORMATION I REQUESTED.
THE CORONER'S REPORT IS RIGHT HERE, PROFESSOR.
IT'S YOURS--QUID PRO QUO.
TELL ME, HOW DO I KNOW I'M DOING THIS OF MY OWN FREE WILL?
HOW CAN I BE SURE THAT YOU'RE NOT USING YOUR MENTAL POWERS ON ME?
CHARLOTTE?! THAT IS--
--A PERFECTLY RESONABLE QUESTION, STORM.
PROPERTY OF NYC CORONERS OFFICE
HONESTLY, DETECTIVE..?
... THERE IS NO WAY FOR YOU TO TRULY KNOW.
IN THIS MAT I'M AFRAID YO GOING TO HAV TO TRUST
THAT WAS HONEST. NOT OVERLY REASSURING, BUT HON--
SHARON?!
BY THE BRIGHT LADY, CHARLES-- WHAT IS IT?
A PSIONIC CALL FOR HELP, ORORO!
PRIMAL... UNFOCUSED
...A FINAL, FATAL ACT OF DESPERATION

EANWHILE...
UH... WARREN?
I'M TRYING, JEANNIE--
I'M TRYING.
TOO LITTLE TOO LATE, IT WOULD SEEM.
DON'T DO NOBODY NO GOOD TO BRAG BEFORE THE FACT, BISHOP. ONE NEVER KNOWS WHAT WILL HAP--
UICKLY, MY X-MEN-- YOU ARE NEEDED!
WHA--?!
NOT 'LESS A HOLOGRAM CAN GO SHOUTIN' INSIDE A PERSON'S HEAD!
ANOTHER HOLOGRAM...?!
IT IS THE PROFESSOR'S PSIONIC PROJECTION -- BUT I'VE NEVER FELT ONE THIS INTENSE BEFORE.
NO TIME TO APOLOGIZE OR TO EXPLAIN! EVERYONE REPORT TO THE HANGAR DECK, IMMEDIATELY!
SIXTY-FIVE MILES, DUE NORTH! I WILL ELABORATE EN ROUTE!
THERE IS NOT A MOMENT TO LOSE, FOR INNOCENT HUMAN LIVES HAVE ALREADY BEEN LOST...
...AND DOZENS MORE, I FEAR HANG IN THE BALANCE!

OUR MOTHER OF THE SACRED HEART.
..ROUND AND ROUND!
THE WHEELS ON THE BUS GO ROUND AND ROUND...
..ALL THROUGH THE TOWN!
SCHOOL BUS
HMMMP?
THAT'S ODD.
THE HORN ON THE BUS GOES BEEP, BEEP, BE--
EXIT
WHY ISN'T SISTER IGNAZIO OUT FRONT, WAITING FOR THE KIDS?
CLASS STARTS AS SOON AS I LET THESE STUDENTS OFF AT THE STOOP. SO WHY DOES THE SCHOOL...
...LOOK LIKE A MORGUE?

--ALL THROUGH..THE TOWN!
HE'S STOPPING.

HEY, MR. CORSI-- YOU LETTING US OFF HERE?
NO, TEDDY...
...I'M NOT.

IF I'M WRONG ABOUT THIS, SHARON CAN HELP CONCOCT A COVER STORY.
KC-SHNK
IF I'M RIGHT-
--IF WE'R BEING SET-UP..

...LET'S PRAY I'M NOT TOO LATE.
OUR MOTHER OF THE Sacred Heart
DON'T WANT THE KIDS TO CATCH ON...
...SO LET'S BACK THIS BABY--
--SLOWLY.

HE NEEDN'T HAVE WORRIED.
BSK KABOOOM!!
I TRUST WE GOT THEIR ATTENTION.
AND I TRUST THAT YOU ARE AN IDIOT, KLEINSTOCK!
IF YOU AND YOUR BROTHERS HAVE JEOPARDIZED THE GIFTED WITH YOUR RECKLESS BEHAVIOR--
--YOU WILL ANSWER TO NO LESS THAN CORTEZ HIMSELF!
SECURING THE UNIDENTIFIED MUTANT IS ONLY PART OF THE INQUEST, UNUSCIONE.
THERE IS ALSO THE CLEANSING OF YOUNG HUMANS FROM THE GENE POOL.
SUCH IS OUR RIGHT, OUR RESPONSIBILITY, AS ACOLYTES--
--AS MAGNETO'S CHOSEN.

THERE IS NOTHING IN MAGNUS'S READINGS THAT SAY WE CANNOT ENJOY OUR VICTORIES!
FOR DECADES, MUTANTS HAVE BEEN HUNTED, EN-SLAVED... ALL TOO OFTEN EXECUTED!
I AM ONLY TOO HAPPY TO RETURN THE FAVOR.
STAND DOWN, ERIC
WAIT UNTIL THE AR
HAS BEEN SECURE
YOU ARE BEING OVERLY CAUTIOUS, CARMELLA.
WE KNOW THE HOMO SUPERIOR ON THE BUS IS STILL IN THE LATENCY PHASE.
CERTAINLY, YOU ARE NOT FRIGHTENED BY THESE FILTHY FLATSCAAARRNNGH?!
BRFRAMM!
WATCH THE MOUTH, PAL!

TH THE SCHOOL TRASHED IT IS, I'M WHAT IS LEGALLY WN AS THE "LOCO PARENTE."
WHICH MEANS I'M RESPONSIBLE FOR KEEPING ALL RACIST AND DEROGATORY LANGUAGE TO A MINIMUM.
NATURALLY, ANY MENTION O' GENETIC CLEANSING IS OUT OF THE QUESTION!
SMASHK!
NICE TO KNOW TEN YEARS AS A COP WASN'T A TOTAL WASTE.
YOU ARE ONE OF XAVIER'S MINIONS, NO DOUBT?
I PREFER THE TERM "OPERATIVE."
URN "VOLUNTEER" IF YOU MUST.
MINION IS SO... DEMEANING.
RUST THAT WILL DO MORE THAN EMEAN YOU, HUMAN!
YOU HAVE SLAIN A FELLOW ACOLYTE-- AND THAT WILL COST YOU YOUR LIFE!
YOU COULDN'T HAVE MENTIONED THAT EARLIER?
I WOULD HAVE SETTLED FOR GIVING HIM A FLESH WOUND.
AS SOMEONE ABOUT TO BE CRUSHED BY MY PSIONIC EXO-SKELETON--
--YOU ARE SURPRISINGLY CALM.

MIGHT BE 'CAUSE DE MAN KNOWS HE'S GOT FRIENDS HE CAN COUNT ON!
KRSM
BRMR
WE HOPED THE ACOLYTES DISBANDED AFTER MAGNETO'S DEATH. *
OBVIOUSLY, THAT WASN'T THE CASE.
* X-MEN #3.--B.H.
BISHOP--Y'KNOW HOW STORM'S ALWAYS SAYIN' DERE ARE TIMES YOU SHOULD MELLOW OUT...
... REIN YOURSELF IN?
WHAT ABOUT IT?
THIS IS NOT ONE OF THOSE TIMES.

HUMAN LOVERS!
IS THAT... FRENZY?
OUGN
URNGH
CHARLES WONDERED WHERE THE ACOLYTES WERE RECRUITING NEW MEM--
EEYAGHH!
IF YOU WERE TRUE MUTANTS, YOU WOULD FOLLOW THE TEACHINGS OF MAGNUS!
YOU WOULD FIGHT AT OUR SIDE TO PURGE THE WORLD OF THE GENETICALLY IMPURE!
CARGILL IS RIGHT. WE SHOULD ALL BE WORKING TOGETHER!
ARE YOU READY, BROTHER?
MORE THAN.
TWINS, EH?
TRIPLETS TILL JUST RECENTLY.
YOU'LL PARDON US IF WE TAKE A MOMENT TO VENT OUR GRIEF?
FWOOSH
JEAN GREY HAS KNOWN WARREN WORTHINGTON III SINCE THE DAY SHE JOINED THE X-MEN.
SHE IS LESS FAMILIAR WITH ARCHANGEL--
-- THE MAN HE BECAME AFTER APOCALYPSE'S GENETIC EXPERIMENT.

SHE WONDERS IF HIS BODY CAN WITHSTAND THE FLAMES.
SPLOOSH
WARREN?!
YOU SEE HOW EASILY YOUR COMRADE HAS FALLEN, GREY.
THERE IS STILL A CHANCE TO SAVE YOURSELF-- TO CHANGE YOUR ALLIANCE.
IF YOU ARE NOT WITH US, YOU ARE AGAINST US.
MAKE NO MISTAKE, ACOLYTES--
--I AM MOST DEFINITELY AGAINST YOU!
YEARGH!
SVEN, HARLAN-- SHE'S DISCORPORATED MY PSIONIC-SKELETON!
THE MAGNETO I KNEW MAY HAVE BEEN DETERMINED, EVEN BRUTAL...
...BUT HE WOULD NEVER STRIKE OUT AT INNOCENT CHILDREN!
SLAM!

ASPHEMER!
MAGNUS WAS A *GREAT MAN*-- ONE WHO DIDN'T WAS NOT *AFRAID* TO MAKE *DIFFICULT* DECISIONS!
NOT *DARE* TO LLYSHAME HIS ME BY PAINTING A *COWARD*!
GOOD LORD! YOU'RE... MERGING?!
HE *DIED FOR* OUR SINCRIMES--
--SO THAT *MUTANTS* WILLMUST INHERIT *THE EARTH*!

GENTLEMEN, I'VE *SEEN* THE FUTURE...
...AND YOU'RE *NOT IT*!
BISHOP--CAN YOUR ABSORBING POWER *HANDLE* THEIR PLASMA BLAST?
LET'S FIND OUT.

HAVE T'KEEP DIS FIGHT AWAY FROM DE CHILDREN.
THIS IS WHAT YOU'VE LEARNED AS AN X-MAN, REMY--TO *RUN AWAY*?

PEOPLE CHANGE, JOANNA.
NEVER TOOK YOU AS DE MINDLESS SHEEP TYPE.
TIME DIS JUS' RIGHT.
PUT DE OBJECT IN MOTION...

MUTANTS NEED NOT LIVE IN FEAR OF HUMANS!
I HAVE HEARD MAGNUS'S WORDS!

I HAVE SEEN THE LIIIIGHHT!
SO I SEE, CHERE.

THE X-MEN ARE FAR MORE WORTHY OPPONENTS THAN CORTEZ LED US TO BELIEVE!
RRENT!
ALL THE MORE REASON WE NEED TO INCREASE OUR NUMBERS FOR THE SACRED WAR TO COME.
MY PSIONIC POWERS CAN DIVINE THE CHOSEN -- SO THEY MIGHT BE RAISED AMONG THEIR OWN PEOPLE...
... INSTEAD OF WALLOWING AMIDST THIS HUMAN STY!
L-LADY, PUT ME DOWN!
I DIDN'T DO NOTHING!
WHAT IS THIS--?!
XAVIER HAS PLAYED US ALL FOR FOOLS...
... THIS CHILD IS OBVIOUSLY FLAWED-- EVEN BY HUMAN STANDARDS!
THERE IS NO PLACE FOR IMPERFECTION IN OUR NEW ORDER!
AND THIS IS HOW YOU HONOR THE MEMORY OF MAGNETO?!
HIS ENTIRE FAMILY WAS WIPED OUT BY PEOPLE WHO FELT LIKE YOU DO.
SUPREMACISTS WHO BELIEVED THEY HAD A RIGHT TO DECIDE WHO LIVED AND DIED!

--WITH AS MUCH RIGHT TO LIVE IN ANYONE'S ORDER AS YOU.
THE CHILD HAS DOWN'S SYNDROME ACOLYTE--
NOTHING "NEW" ABOUT IGNORANCE...
...INTOLERANCE--
--HATING WHAT YOU DON'T UNDERSTAND.
SO LONG AS THERE ARE PEOPLE LIKE YOU, THERE'LL BE--
-- PEOPLE LIKE US...
... WHO'LL BE THERE TO STOP YOU.
NONSENSE-- THIS CHILD IS AS USELESS TO XAVIER...
...AS HE IS TO THE ACOLYTES!
HE BELONGS WITH THE REST OF THIS HUMAN KINDLING!
KLEINSTOCK-- "PURIFY" THEM!
ABOUT TIME!
DO YOU BELIEVETHINK WE'VE ANYTHING TO FEAR FROM YOU AND YOUR GENETIC TURN-COATS?!
NO!
WAM
DO THAT, ACOLYTE--AND I SWEAR BY ALL THAT'S HOLY I WILL HUNT YOU DOWN--AND MAKE YOU PAY IN KIND A THOUSANDFOLD!
FWAZZWAT!

THE SHOT GOES WIDE.
WHICH ONLY MEANS THE INTENDED VICTIMS WILL DIE--
BWRBOOOM!
--THAT MUCH SLOWER.
C'MON, REMY-- KEEP DE CARDS COMIN'!
HEY, MISTER-- YOU'RE AN ANGEL!
DID WE DIE IN THE 'SPLOSION?
LEAVE THE GUY ALONE DWAYNE-- CAN'TCHA SE HE'S TRYIN' SAVE US?
JERK.
CREATE A WALL OF ENERGY 'TWEEN DE FLAMES AND DE CHILDREN!
I'M NOT A JERK-- YOU ARE!
'LEAST I KNOW IF I'M DEAD OR NOT!
BISHOP, I SMELL GAS! IF THE FIRE REACHES THE TANK BEFORE--
IT WON'T, JEAN.
KEEP MOVING, LITTLE ONES-- AWAY FROM THE BUS!

KRA-KA-KA-BOOM!
E SOUND THAT FILLS E AIR IS NOT THE PLOSION OF THE BUS EY'D ALL EXPECTED--
--RATHER A CLAP OF THUNDER THAT SIGNALS THE ARRIVAL OF STORM...
... AND THE FIRE-DAMPENING RAINS THAT ARE HERS TO COMMAND!
BY THE BRIGHT LADY!
WHAT MONSTERS ARE THESE THAT WOULD THREATEN THE LIVES OF CHILDREN--
--NO MATTER WHAT THE CAUSE?!
ONSTERS, D SEEM-- AT'VE CAPED.
FORT'NATELY, WE SAVED DE CHILDREN.
DID WE, GAMBIT?
OR DID WE SENTENCE THEM-- TO A WORLD WHERE NO MAN IS SAFE..
...FROM HIS BROTHER?
IF WE WERE FIGHTIN' DE FIGHT ON OUR OWN...?
DEF'NITELY.
BUT DAT AIN'T DE CASE, STORMY.
NOT BY HALF...

LATER THAT NIGHT...
--AN ESTIMATED FOURTEEN SCHOOL EMPLOYEES IN THE BUILDING WHEN IT EXPLODED. AUTHORITIES ARE WITHOLDING NAMES UNTIL FAMILIES HAVE BEEN NOTIFIED.
WHILE NO ONE IS WILLING TO OFFICIALLY EXONERATE THE X-MEN--WITNESSES CONFIRM THEY WERE DEFENDING THE STUDENTS OF OUR MOTHER OF THE SACRED HEART...
... FROM A FANATICAL BAND OF GENETIC SUPREMACISTS KNOWN AS THE ACOLYTES.

SENATOR ROBERT KELLY, CHAIRMAN OF THE COMMITTEE ON MUTANT AFFAIRS, TOURED THE DEVASTATED AREA.
I WISH I COULD SAY THAT I'M SHOCKED BY WHAT I'VE SEEN HERE TODAY. THE TRUTH IS--I HAVE SPENT THE PAST TEN YEARS OF MY LIFE PREDICTING JUST SUCH AN INCIDENT.
THERE ARE PEOPLE IN THE GOVERNMENT AND THE LIBERAL MEDIA, WHO --
--FOR WHATEVER REASON--
--WOULD LIKE YOU TO BELIEVE WE HAVE NOTHING TO FEAR FROM THE MUTANT POPULACE.
I URGE THE AMERICAN PUBLIC TO WAKE UP AND SEE THE "MUTANT MENACE." FOR WHAT IT IS, IF FOR NO OTHER REASON THAN...
... FOR THE CHILDREN.

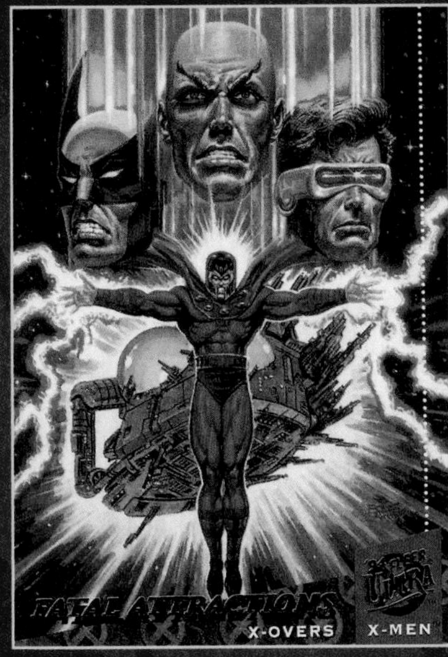

Fleer Ultra X-Men '94 trading-card art by Bob Larkin

Fleer Ultra X-Men '95 trading-card art by Greg & Tim Hildebrandt

Fleer Ultra X-Men '95 trading-card art by Ray Lago & Dan Lawlis

Ultra X-Men '95 Chromium trading-card art by Andy Kubert & Jung Choi

Fleer Ultra X-Men '96 trading-card art by Joe Jusko

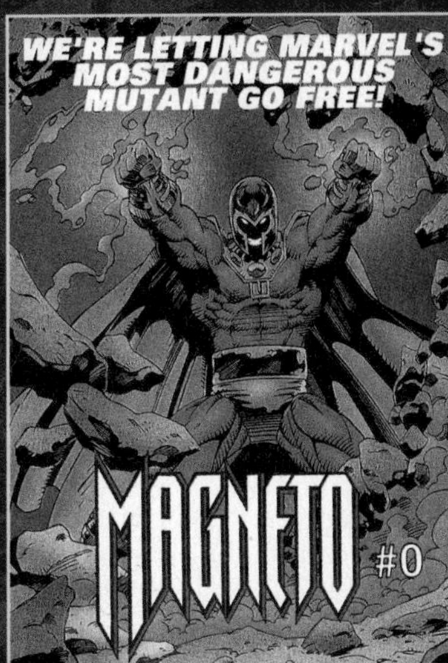

1993 promotional trading card advertising *Magneto #0*; art by Greg Capullo & Kevin Conrad

MARVEL COMICS
THE UNCANNY
X-MEN
$1.25 US
$1.60 CAN/UK 70p
299
APR
02461
APPROVED BY THE COMICS CODE AUTHORITY
PLAYERS AND PAWNS

SO WHAT DO YOU THINK?
THAT DEPENDS.
YOU WANT ME TO BE HONEST...
...OR REASSURING?

KUWAIT.
I WANT THE TRUTH, FORGE.
NO. I DON'T THINK YOU DO.
WE ALREADY KNOW THE TRUTH, HENRY--
--YOU WANT ME TO TELL YOU THAT WE'RE WRONG?
HUMOR ME. MAKE IT OFFICIAL.
*X-MEN #3.--B.H.
CONSIDERING THE FACT THAT HALF THE MARGINALLY CIVILIZED NATIONS OF THE WORLD ARE FRIGHTENED ENOUGH TO AGREE TO THIS MULTI-NATIONAL STRIKE FORCE--
--OUR LIST OF SUSPECTS IS UNDERSTANDABLY SHORT.
WHAT ABOUT THE ACOLYTES?
NONE OF HIS FOLLOWERS I'VE MET HAVE THAT KIND OF POWER.
CERTAINLY NOT ANY OF THOSE INVOLVED IN YESTERDAY'S SLAUGHTER IN NEW YORK.*
*LAST ISSUE.
I AGREE.
BUT WE HAVE NO WAY OF KNOWING HOW MANY MUTANTS BELONG TO THIS SECT OF--

OFFICIALLY, WHAT WE AVE HERE--IN ALL IKELIHOOD--ARE THE MAINS OF ASTEROID M.
PROBLEM BEING... IT'S ROUGHLY TWO THOUSAND TIMES TOO BIG FOR A LAND MASS THAT--
--EVEN AFTER THE EXPLOSION THAT TOOK OUT SEVENTY-FIVE PERCENT OF THE COMPLEX--
--SHOULD HAVE BEEN REDUCED TO A CINDER UPON RE-ENTRY INTO EARTH'S ORBIT.*
STAN LEE PRESENTS THE UNCANNY X-MEN IN
NIGHTLINES
SCOTT LOBDELL WRITER
BRANDON PETERSON PENCILER
DAN PANOSIAN INKER
CHRIS ELIOPOULOS LETTERER
MARIE JAVINS COLORIST
BOB HARRAS EDITOR
TOM DEFALCO EDITOR IN CHIEF
THE ONLY WAY IT COULD POSSIBLY STILL BE INTACT--
--IS IF SOMETHING--
--OR SOMEONE--
--GUIDED THESE REMAINS THROUGH THE PLANET'S ATMOSPHERE.
TRAPSING THROUGH MAGNETO'S STRONGHOLD-- FORMER OR OTHERWISE--IS NOT A PARTICULARLY WISE IDEA.
SAVE IT, FORGE. IN AMERICA, I'M A HIGH MUCK-A-MUCK IN THE NATIONAL SECURITY COUNCIL...
... AND YOU'RE THE FREELANCE EXPERT ON ADVANCED AND OBSCURE TECHNOLOGY. BUT HERE IN THE MID-EAST, WE'RE BARELY TOLERATED OBSERVERS.
IF IT IS OF ANY COMFORT-- THIS COMPLEX IS TOTALLY WITHOUT POWER...
AGENT GYRICH, COME QUICKLY! WE HAVE FOUND SOMETHING!

IF NOT FOR WHAT YOU SEE BEFORE YOU, I WOULD GO SO FAR AS TO SAY THIS PLACE IS ALL BUT LIFE-LESS.
YOU'VE FOUND SURVIVORS?
WE ARE NOT SURE...
...WE WERE HOPING YOU COULD TELL US.
THE MAN CALLED FORGE WAS IN THIS ROOM ONCE BEFORE...
...MOMENTS BEFORE ASTEROID M EXPLODED FAR ABOVE THE GREEN-WASHED PLANET EARTH, AND ALL ON BOARD WERE PRESUMED KILLED.
THE "STATUES" GENU-FLECTING TO THE EMPTY THRONE ARE EASILY RECOGNIZABLE AS THE ACOLYTES KNOWN ONLY AS ANNE MARIE AND DELGADO.
JUST AS THE EMPTY HUSK IN THE CENTER OF THE ROOM COULD ONLY HAVE --
--UNTIL RECENTLY--
--HOUSED THE BODY OF THE MOST DANGEROUS MUTANT ON EARTH...
...MAGNETO-- THE MASTER OF MAGNETISM!

NEW YORK CITY.
ABC NEWS STUDIOS.
I DON'T KNOW WHAT HAS ME MORE SURPRISED-- THE FACT YOU AGREED TO THIS TELEVISED DEBATE ON MUTANT RIGHTS...
...OR THAT YOU TOOK FIVE MINUTES TO EAT AND SHAVE FOR THE FIRST TIME IN TWO WEEKS.
WITH THE CURRENT STATE OF MUTANT AND HUMAN RELATIONS IN A RAPID STATE OF DECAY, JEAN--
--I'M AFRAID SUCH PERSONAL LUXURIES AS PRIVACY AND PHYSICAL APPEARANCE ARE NOT PARAMOUNT ON MY LIST OF PRIORITIES.
WE ALL APPRECIATE YOUR DEDICATION, PROFESSOR-- BUT YOU'RE STILL RE-COVERING FROM STRYFE'S ASSASSI-NATION ATTEMPT ON YOUR LIFE.* YOU'VE GOT TO TAKE IT EASY.
YES, THE VERY INCIDENT WHICH PROPELLED ME RELUCTANTLY, INTO THE NATIONAL SPOTLIGHT.
ALTHOUGH I WOULD MUCH PREFER TO CONDUCT MY AFFAIRS IN PRIVATE--PRIMARILY MY ROLE AS FOUNDER OF THE X-MEN--
--MY BRUSH WITH MARTYRDOM HAS ALTERED MY PUBLIC PERSONA FROM A WORLD-RENOWNED EXPERT ON GENE-TICS...
...TO WHAT THE MEDIA LIKES TO CALL A "MUTANT RIGHTS ACTIVIST."
OUR DETRACTORS HAVE BEEN USING THE PRESS TO THEIR ADVANTAGE FOR YEARS...
"...MAYBE IT'S TIME WE HAD SOMEONE TO COUNTER THE SENATOR KELLYS OF THE WORLD."
*U.XM #294. --BOB

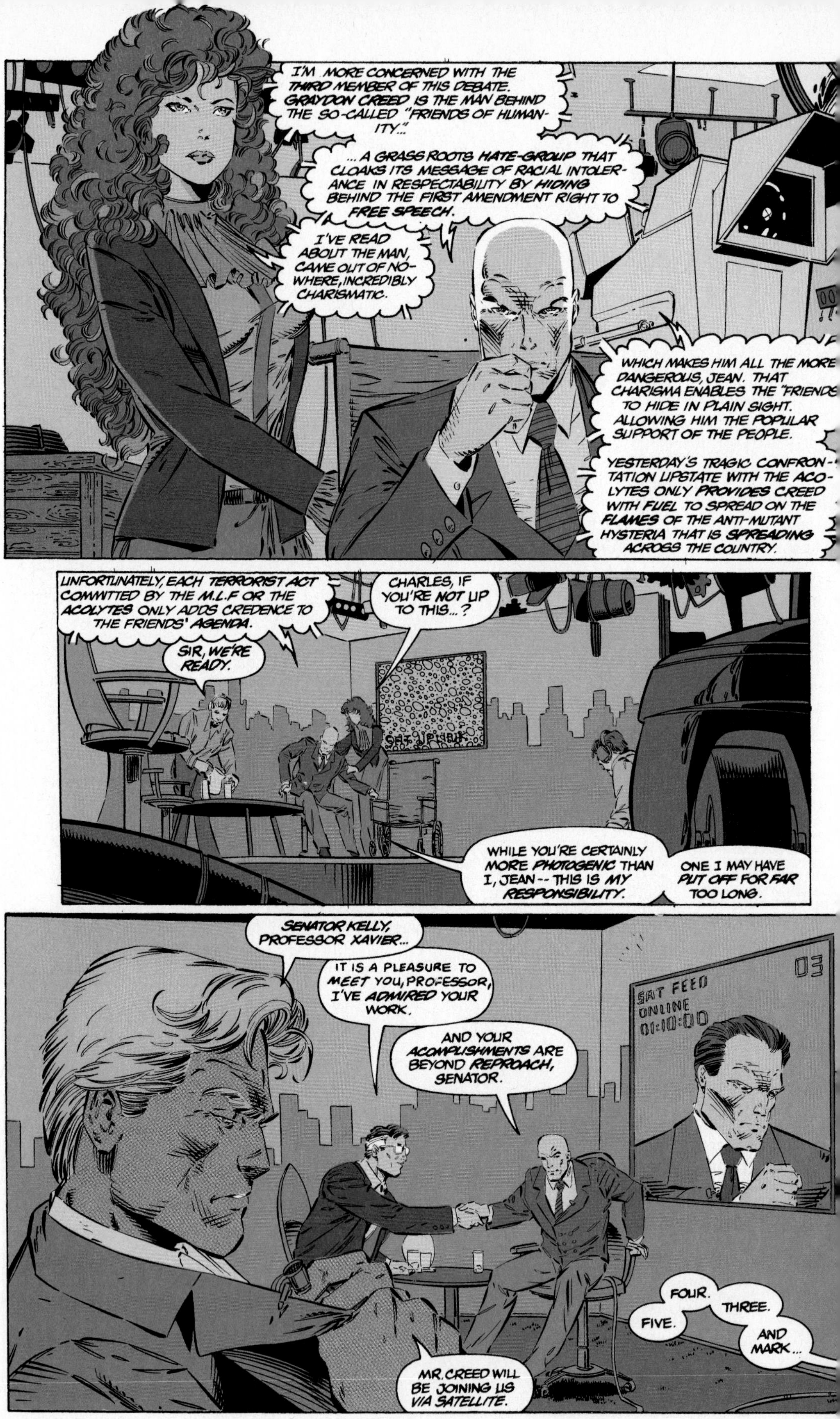

I'M MORE CONCERNED WITH THE THIRD MEMBER OF THIS DEBATE. GRAYDON CREED IS THE MAN BEHIND THE SO-CALLED "FRIENDS OF HUMANITY."

...A GRASS ROOTS HATE-GROUP THAT CLOAKS ITS MESSAGE OF RACIAL INTOLERANCE IN RESPECTABILITY BY HIDING BEHIND THE FIRST AMENDMENT RIGHT TO FREE SPEECH.

I'VE READ ABOUT THE MAN, CAME OUT OF NOWHERE, INCREDIBLY CHARISMATIC.

WHICH MAKES HIM ALL THE MORE DANGEROUS, JEAN. THAT CHARISMA ENABLES THE "FRIENDS" TO HIDE IN PLAIN SIGHT. ALLOWING HIM THE POPULAR SUPPORT OF THE PEOPLE.

YESTERDAY'S TRAGIC CONFRONTATION UPSTATE WITH THE ACOLYTES ONLY PROVIDES CREED WITH FUEL TO SPREAD ON THE FLAMES OF THE ANTI-MUTANT HYSTERIA THAT IS SPREADING ACROSS THE COUNTRY.

UNFORTUNATELY, EACH TERRORIST ACT COMMITTED BY THE M.L.F OR THE ACOLYTES ONLY ADDS CREDENCE TO THE FRIENDS' AGENDA.

CHARLES, IF YOU'RE NOT UP TO THIS...?

SIR, WE'RE READY.

WHILE YOU'RE CERTAINLY MORE PHOTOGENIC THAN I, JEAN-- THIS IS MY RESPONSIBILITY.

ONE I MAY HAVE PUT OFF FOR FAR TOO LONG.

SENATOR KELLY, PROFESSOR XAVIER...
IT IS A PLEASURE TO MEET YOU, PROFESSOR, I'VE ADMIRED YOUR WORK.
AND YOUR ACOMPLISHMENTS ARE BEYOND REPROACH, SENATOR.
03
SAT FEED ONLINE 01:10:00
FIVE.
FOUR.
THREE.
AND MARK...
MR. CREED WILL BE JOINING US VIA SATELLITE.

St. Mary's Boys Home

TONIGHT, ON A SPECIAL EDITION OF NIGHTLINE...

... "MUTANTS-- THE GENETIC TIMEBOMB?"

SITTING IN FOR TED KOPPEL, IS ELTON CAYER.

UNTIL YESTERDAY, PEOPLE ACROSS AMERICA HAD INDULGED IN A FALSE SENSE OF SECURITY--

--THAT THE EVER-GROWING MUTANT PROPULACE...

MUTANTS

GENETIC TIME BOMB

...AND THE RESULTING TENSIONS BETWEEN HUMANS AND THESE GENETIC ANOMALIES...

...WERE STRICTLY THE CONCERNS OF THOSE UNFORTUNATE ENOUGH TO LIVE AMIDST THE BATTLE GROUNDS OF THE NATION'S BIG CITIES.

IN THE SMALL TOWN OF MIDDLEBOROUGH, NEW YORK, FOURTEEN CORPSES HAVE SHATTERED THOSE ILLUSIONS... FOREVER.

THE CITIZENS OF THIS UPSTATE HAMLET WERE VICTIMS OF A SAVAGE "GENETIC-CLEANSING" AT THE HANDS OF A MUTANT TERRORIST GROUP KNOWN AS THE ACOLYTES...

WELL, TED-- WE'VE ESTABLISHED YOUR MUTANT POWER...

...IS DEFINITELY NOT THE ABILITY TO STAY UP PAST BEDTIME TO WATCH THE NEWS.

IT SEEMS THE ACOLYTES DIDN'T KNOW WHAT TEDDY MATSON'S LATENT ABILITIES WERE WHEN THEY ATTEMPTED TO KIDNAP HIM--

--NO MORE THAN THEY KNEW HE HAD DOWN'S SYNDROME.

IN UNUSCIONE'S WORDS, THAT MADE HIM "UNFIT" TO TAKE PART IN THEIR NEW WORLD ORDER.

FUNNY, AS MUTANTS THEY, MORE THAN ANYBODY, SHOULD KNOW DIVERSITY IS SOMETHING TO BE CELEBRATED-- NOT ASHAMED OF...

YOU ARE THE ONE THEY CALL "THE ARCHANGEL?"

YES, MOTHER SUPERIOR. DON'T BOTHER CALLING THE POLICE--

--I'LL BE GONE BY THE TIME THEY ARRIVE.

SON, NOT EVERYONE BELIEVES THAT ALL MUTANTS ARE TO BE FEARED AND HATED.
THERE ARE THOSE OF US WHO ARE GRATEFUL TO THE X-MEN FOR RISKING THEIR LIVES ON OUR BEHALF.
FAITH IS IMPORTANT--

--BUT IT'S COMFORTING TO KNOW WITH CERTAINTY THAT ANGELS TRULY DO WALK AMONG US.
I APPRECIATE THE SENTIMENT, MOTHER--BUT AFTER EVERYTHING I'VE DONE IN MY LIFE...
...SOMETIMES I THINK I'M BEYOND REDEMPTION.

THERE IS NO SUCH THING.

YOU COULD HAVE TOLD THE AUTHORITIES TEDDY WAS A MUTANT. YET YOU SPARED HIM THE SCORN AND SCRUTINY OF "PUBLIC SERVANTS" LIKE THE SO-CALLED "HONORABLE" SENATOR KELLY.
IF THERE IS ANYTHING I CAN DO FOR YOU OR YOUR COMPANIONS...?

IF THE GOVERNMENT WON'T DEFEND THE COMMON MAN THEN IT'S TIME WE DEFENDED OURSELVES.
YOU CAN PRAY, MOTHER.

PRAY FOR EVERY ONE OF US.
CLK

NO SANE MAN WILL ARGUE THAT MUTANTS--BY THEIR NATURE--ARE, IN SOME CASES, INFINITELY MORE POWERFUL THAN HUMAN BEINGS.
ALL MY ORGANIZATION, THE FRIENDS OF HUMANITY, IS ADVOCATING IS AN ORGANIZATION THAT LOOKS OUT FOR THE RIGHTS OF US HUMANS!
SOUNDS REASONABLE TO ME.
THE UNITED STATES GOVERNMENT IS AWARE OF ITS RESPONSIBILITIES TO ALL ITS CITIZENS, MR. CREED.
THIS'S ONE REASON I'M PROUD I SERVE AS THE CHAIRMAN OF THE COMMITTEE ON MUTANT AFFAIRS... IT'S WHY THE MUTANT GROUP X-FACTOR OPERATES UNDER FEDERAL AUSPICES.
THE CONCERN I SHARE WITH SENATOR KELLY REGARDING MR. CREED'S ORGANIZATION...
...IS THE FRIENDS OF HUMANITY'S WILLINGNESS--IN SOME CASES EAGERNESS--TO VIOLATE THE CIVIL RIGHTS OF ANYONE WHO DOES NOT FIT THEIR RATHER LIMITED DEFINITION OF "HUMAN."
COULD IT BE, PROFESSOR, THAT THEIR ADMITTEDLY QUESTIONABLE ACTIONS ARE A JUSTIFIABLE RESPONSE TO THE EVER-GROWING NUMBER OF ANTI-HUMAN FACTIONS AMONG THE HOMO-SUPERIOR POPULATION?
THESE ACOLYTES, THE BROTHERHOOD OF EVIL MUTANTS, THE MUTANT LIBERATION FRONT ARE BUT A FEW--
--ARE BUT A FEW OF THE HIGH PROFILE MUTANTS WHO, REGRETTABLY, GET THE LION'S SHARE OF MEDIA ATTENTION.
PERHAPS IF THE PRESS WERE MORE INCLINED TO FOCUS ON THE EXPLOITS OF OTHER MUTANTS SUCH AS THE X-MEN, WHO HAVE SERVED THE WORLD ON MORE THAN ONE OCCASION...
...OR REMEMBERED THERE ARE MANY, MANY MUTANTS WHO LIVE QUIET PEACEFUL LIVES, WHO GO TO WORK EVERYDAY. WHO CARE FOR THEIR FAMILIES...
...AND YET LIVE IN FEAR THAT PEOPLE LIKE MR. CREED'S ASSOCIATES WILL RIP EVERY INALIENABLE RIGHT FROM THEM, SIMPLY BECAUSE OF WHO THEY ARE!

THE PROFESSOR IS BEING DISGENUOUS, WHICH IS IN KEEPING WITH HIS REPUTATION AS AN APOLOGIST FOR MUTANTS. I THINK WE'D BE CURIOUS TO HEAR SENATOR KELLY'S FEELINGS ABOUT THE X-MEN--
--THE OUTLAWS RESPONSIBLE FOR THE DEATH OF HIS WIFE!
THAT'S NOT TRUE--B HOW DO I COUNTER HIS DISINFORMATION WITHOUT REVEALING THE CONNECTION TO MY STUDENTS?!

MR. CREED, I MUST SAY I RESENT THAT YOU'VE USED MY PERSONAL TRAGEDY FOR A CLEVER SENSATIONAL SOUND BITE.

YES, MY WIFE WAS KILLED IN THE MIDST OF A MUTANT INCIDENT, THAT INCLUDED, AMONG OTHERS, SEVERAL X-MEN... BUT THERE IS NO CONCLUSIVE EVIDENCE THAT ANY X-MEN IN PARTICULAR WERE RESPONSIBLE.

IT WOULD BE EASY... COMFORTABLE... TO PAINT ME AS A BITTER, REVENGE-CRAZED MAN BENT ON PUNISHING ALL MUTANTS FOR THE ACTIONS OF A HANDFUL.

I HAVE NOT--AND NEVER WILL--ADVOCATE THE BLANKET EXTERMINATION OF ANY RACE, MUTANT OR OTHERWISE.

GENOCIDE AS A POLITICAL AGENDA IS AS WRONG TODAY IN COUNTRIES LIKE BOSNIA AND SOMALIA, AS IT WAS IN GERMANY OVER FIFTY YEARS AGO.

WHILE I AM ALL FOR FINDING A WAY TO CONTROL THE MORE SCURRILOUS GENETICALLY CHALLENGED--AND I BELIEVE IN THAT WITHOUT EQUIVOCATION, WITHOUT HESITATION--

IT IS VITAL WE DO SO WITHOUT TRAMPLING ON THEIR RIGHTS AS AMERICAN CITIZENS.

WELL SPOKEN, SENATOR.
THE FACT THAT THE LEADERS OF THIS COUNTRY DECLINED TO IMPLEMENT THE MUTANT REGISTRATION ACT--
--ONLY ILLUSTRATES THE NEED FOR THE FRIENDS OF HUMANITY, PROFESSOR! SPECIAL INTEREST GROUPS ARE DESTROYING THIS NATION... THREATENING HUMANITY!

SOMEPLACE ELSE.
...AND WE'RE PUTTING OUR ELECTED OFFICIALS ON NOTICE AS OF NOW!
YOU'RE PART OF THE PROBLEM--
--WHEN YOU SHOULD BE PART OF THE SOLUTION!
I WILL SAY THIS ABOUT OUR MOST RECENT COMPETITOR...
THE MAN IS AN AMATEUR!
WORSE YET, HE'S...HUMAN!
HOW CAN WE EVEN CONSIDER CREED A MEMBER OF THE UPSTARTS?!
HE'S DONE NOTHING TO PROVE HIMSELF WORTHY, WHILE I HAVE--
--MURDERED MAGNETO.
YES.
WE KNOW.
JUST AS I DIS-PATCHED MOST OF THE HELLIONS--AND SHINOBI SCORED MAJOR POINTS WITH THE DEATH OF HIS FATHER, THE LATE SEBASTIAN SHAW.
IT SHOULD BE CLEAR BY NOW, EVEN TO ONE NOT PRIVY TO THE FUTURE, THAT LEADER-SHIP OF THE UP-STARTS IS NOTHING...
...IF NOT TRANSITORY.

FITZROY! I FOR ONE AM GETTING EXTREMELY TIRED OF YOUR CONSTANT REFERENCES TO "SHADES OF THINGS TO COME!"
IF YOU REALLY KNEW WHAT WAS GOING TO HAPPEN--YOU'D BE IN FIRST PLACE INSTEAD OF LAST!
OOO. THAT HURT.
WHAT'S WRONG, FABIAN--HAVE YOU SPENT SO MUCH TIME WITH YOUR FLOCK OF ACOLYTE "SHEEP," YOU CAN'T BEAR EVEN THE SLIGHTEST CHALLENGE TO YOUR AUTHOR--
BOYS, BOYS... PLEASE. A LITTLE DECORUM.
NEED I REMIND YOU WE FORMED THIS COMPETITION BECAUSE WE THOUGHT IT WOULD BE FUN?
--A BRIEF RESPITE FROM THE SHEER TEDIUM INHERENT IN MASSIVE WEALTH AND POWER.
THE UPSTARTS WERE FOUNDED AS ESCAPIST FARE OF THE HIGHEST ORDER--
I, FOR ONE, SAY THAT IF WE'RE NOT GOING TO ENJOY OUR PERPETUAL GAME OF ONEUP-MANSHIP--
--THEN WHY BOTHER?
I AGREE WITH SHINOBI.
THANK YOU, GAMESMASTER.
WHEN FIRST AP-PROACHED TO AR-BITRATE YOUR FRIENDLY RIVALRY, I WAS GIVEN THE IM-PRESSION YOU WOULD ALL BEHAVE IN A MANNER APPROPRIATE TO THE NEXT GENERATION OF LEADERS--
--INSTEAD OF THE SPOILED CHILDREN YOU ARE--
--PERHAPS YOU ALL NEED TO FOCUS MORE CLOSELY ON THE PRIZE AT HAND.
WHOEVER WINS THE MANTLE OF LEADERSHIP... ALSO INHERITS THE RESOURCES AND SERVITUDE OF ALL FOUR OF HIS FELLOW UPSTARTS.
IT'S THE CLOSEST ANY OF YOU ARE LIKELY TO COME TO OMNIP-OTENCE.
THEN STOP TRYING TO DIVIDE OUR ATTENTION WITH NEW CANDIDATES!
IF YOU INSIST.
THE MUTANT FITZROY HAS BEEN MOLDING FOR MEMBE SHIP WILL BE THE FINAL MEMBER OF THE UPSTARTS.
WHAT? I'VE TOLD NO ONE ABOUT HER! HOW...
THERE IS NOTHING I DON'T KNOW, TREVOR...
...IT'S PART OF MY CHARM.

HIS WAS THE CENE *LAST MONTH* CENTRAL PARK.

ESS THAN A WEEK RIOR, A YOUNG MUTANT AS NEARLY BEATEN TO EATH ON THE VERY POT THAT WOULD ATTRACT EVERAL *HUNDRED HOUSAND* FANS TO A ONE ORLD UNITY CONCERT.

"DURING AN *IMPROMPTU* PLEA FOR GENETIC HARMONY AND NONVIOLENCE, CHARLES XAVIER WAS STRUCK DOWN BY AN *UNIDENTIFIED AS-SAILANT*.

"WHILE THE *MAYOR* HAS BEEN *RELUCTANT* TO LABEL THIS A *BIAS CRIME*--

"--ALLEGEDLY BECAUSE AUTHORITIES COULD NOT *CONFIRM* OR *DENY* THE SUS-PECT *WAS* A MUTANT--

"--*THIS* MUCH IS *CLEAR*...

"...THE PROFESSOR WAS SHOT FOR TAKING A POLITICALLY ***IN***CORRECT PUBLIC STANCE...

"...THAT *MUTANTS* ARE *HUMANS* TOO."

I'M SURE I ECHO THE SENTIMENTS OF CIVILIZED PEOPLE EVERYWHERE, PROFESSOR, WHEN I SAY WE'RE GRATEFUL YOU'VE MADE A FULL RECOVERY.
BUT YOU MUST BE AWARE THERE ARE OTHERS WHO ARE ASKING "HASN'T HE LEARNED HIS LESSON?"
YOU'VE DONE YOUR PART... YOU SAID WHAT YOU FELT HAD TO BE SAID AND IT ALMOST COST YOU YOUR LIFE.
ARE YOU NOT GOING TO BE SATIS-FIED UNTIL YOU BECOME A MARTYR FOR A CAUSE THAT ISN'T EVEN YOURS?
THE ONLY THING MORE FRIGHTENING THAN DYING, ELTON--
--IS LIVING IN A WORLD WHERE ONE MAN IS TOO FRIGHTENED TO HELP ANOTHER.

I MUST ALSO OBJECT TO YOUR CONTENTION THAT THIS "CAUSE" IS NOT MY OWN.
A PERSON DOES NOT NEED TO BE BLACK TO UNDERSTAND APARTHEID IS WRONG. PEOPLE OF ALL RELIGIONS ARE RIGHT-FULLY HORRIFIED AND REPULSED BY THE CRIMES PERPETRATED AGAINST THE JEWS DURING THE HOLOCAUST.
SIMILARLY, ONE NEED NOT BE A VICTIM OF AIDS IN ORDER TO HAVE COMPASSION FOR THE HUNDREDS OF THOUSANDS OF PEOPLE...
... THOSE WHO HAVE SUFFERED...
... AND THOSE WHO HAVE DIED FROM THIS DISEASE.
WHEN THE TIME COMES THAT PEOPLE ARE RESTRICTED TO "HELPING THEIR OWN"--
--IS THE DAY, I BELIEVE, THERE WILL BE NO HOPE FOR ANY OF US.
I
ACHEM
FIND MYSELF AGREEING WITH MUCH OF WHAT PROFESSOR XAVIER HAS SAID.
AND I THINK YOU'RE BOTH HOPELESSLY MIS-GUIDED DREAMERS WHO BELIEVE IN A WORLD THAT DOES NOT AND CANNOT EXIST.
LOOK OUT YOUR WINDOW, GENTLEMAN, IT'S AN UGLY, DANGER-OUS PLACE OUT THERE.
ALL THE MORE REASON THAT WE BURY OUR DIF-FERENCES... BEFORE WE BURY OURSELVES.
WHEN WE RETURN, WE'LL INTRODUCE--VIA SATELLITE, ONE OF THE WORLD'S MOST HIGH PROFILE --
-- AND AT LEAST MARGINALLY SOCIALLY ACCEPTABLE --
--MUTANTS... A FORMER FULL-TIME AVENGER AND WORLD RENOWNED BIO-CHEMIST.

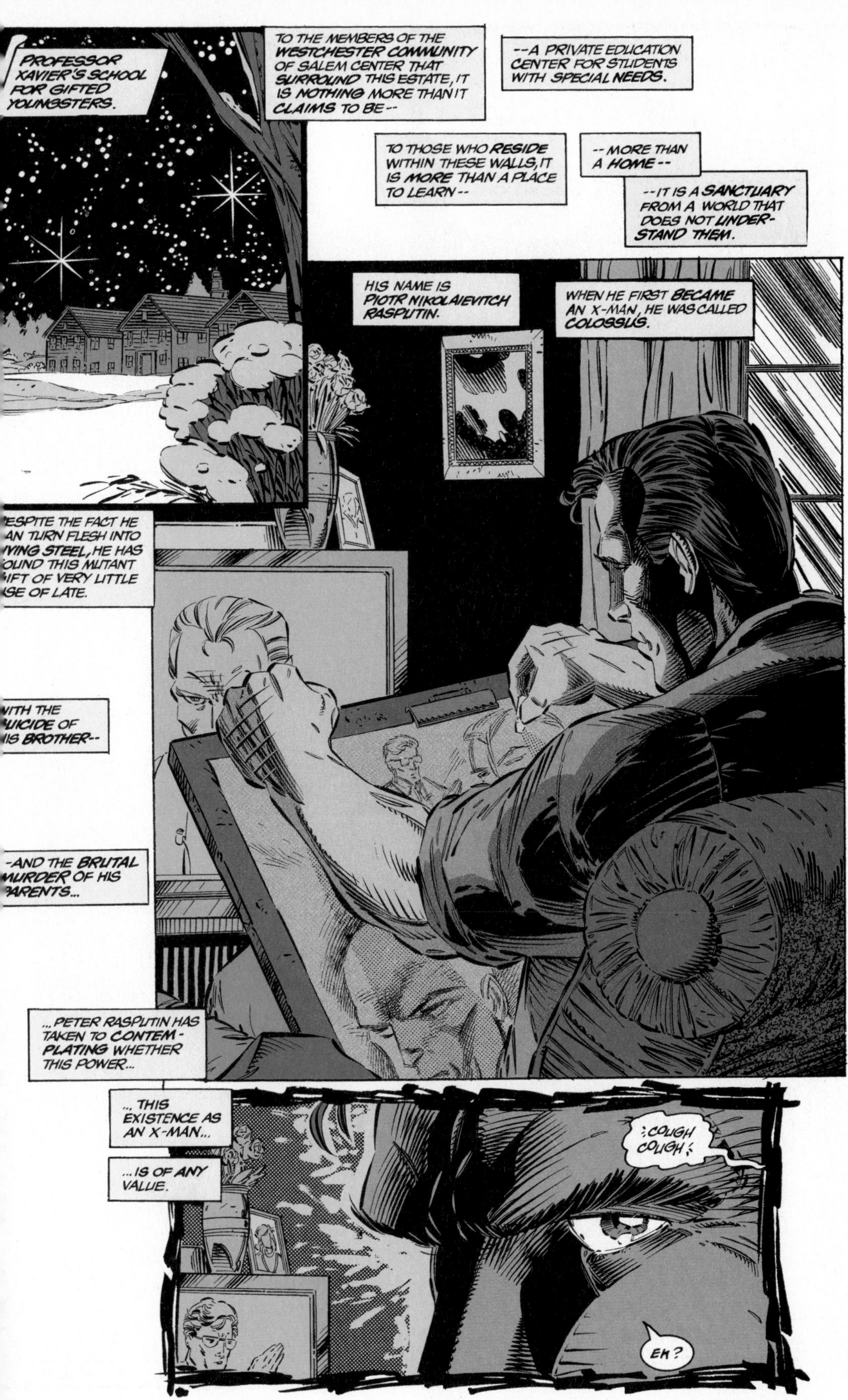
PROFESSOR XAVIER'S SCHOOL FOR GIFTED YOUNGSTERS.
TO THE MEMBERS OF THE WESTCHESTER COMMUNITY OF SALEM CENTER THAT SURROUND THIS ESTATE, IT IS NOTHING MORE THAN IT CLAIMS TO BE--
--A PRIVATE EDUCATION CENTER FOR STUDENTS WITH SPECIAL NEEDS.
TO THOSE WHO RESIDE WITHIN THESE WALLS, IT IS MORE THAN A PLACE TO LEARN--
--MORE THAN A HOME--
--IT IS A SANCTUARY FROM A WORLD THAT DOES NOT UNDERSTAND THEM.
HIS NAME IS PIOTR NIKOLAIEVITCH RASPUTIN.
WHEN HE FIRST BECAME AN X-MAN, HE WAS CALLED COLOSSUS.
ESPITE THE FACT HE AN TURN FLESH INTO IVING STEEL, HE HAS OUND THIS MUTANT IFT OF VERY LITTLE SE OF LATE.
WITH THE UICIDE OF IS BROTHER--
-AND THE BRUTAL MURDER OF HIS ARENTS...
...PETER RASPUTIN HAS TAKEN TO CONTEMPLATING WHETHER THIS POWER...
...THIS EXISTENCE AS AN X-MAN...
...IS OF ANY VALUE.
COUGH COUGH
EH?

‹SNOWFLAKE, WHAT ARE YOU DOING UP AT THIS HOUR? IT IS LATE... AND I TUCKED YOU IN HOURS AGO.› *
‹I WAS ASLEEP, PIOTR... HONEST.›
‹BUT I HAD A DREAM... THAT I NEEDED YOU, AND YOU WERE NOT THERE!›
‹YOU HAD-- LEFT-- WITH MOMMA, POPPA AND MIKHAIL.›
‹THAT WILL NOT HAPPEN, ILLYANA. FOR WHAT'S THE USE OF HAVING A BIG BROTHER--›
‹--IF I'M NOT HERE TO ALWAYS PROTECT YOU?›
‹I KNOW I AM BEING--WHAT DID JUBILEE CALL IT--A "CHOWDER HEAD"...›
‹YOU'RE STILL FEVERISH. YO SHOULD BE IN BED.›
‹BUT... I WANTED TO BE T FIRST TO GIVE YOU TH PRESENT I MADE.›
‹MY ENGLISH IS NO SO GOOD. I HOPE I SPELLED IT RIGHT.›
I LOVE PETER
‹YOU SPELLED IT EXACTLY RIGHT.›
‹NOW REST EASY, SISTER... KNOWING THAT NO MATTER WHAT, I WILL ALWAYS BE THERE FOR YOU.›
‹WE WILL BE THERE FOR EACH OTHER, PIOTR...›
‹... ALWAYS.›
* TRANSLATED FROM THE RUSSIAN. -- BOB

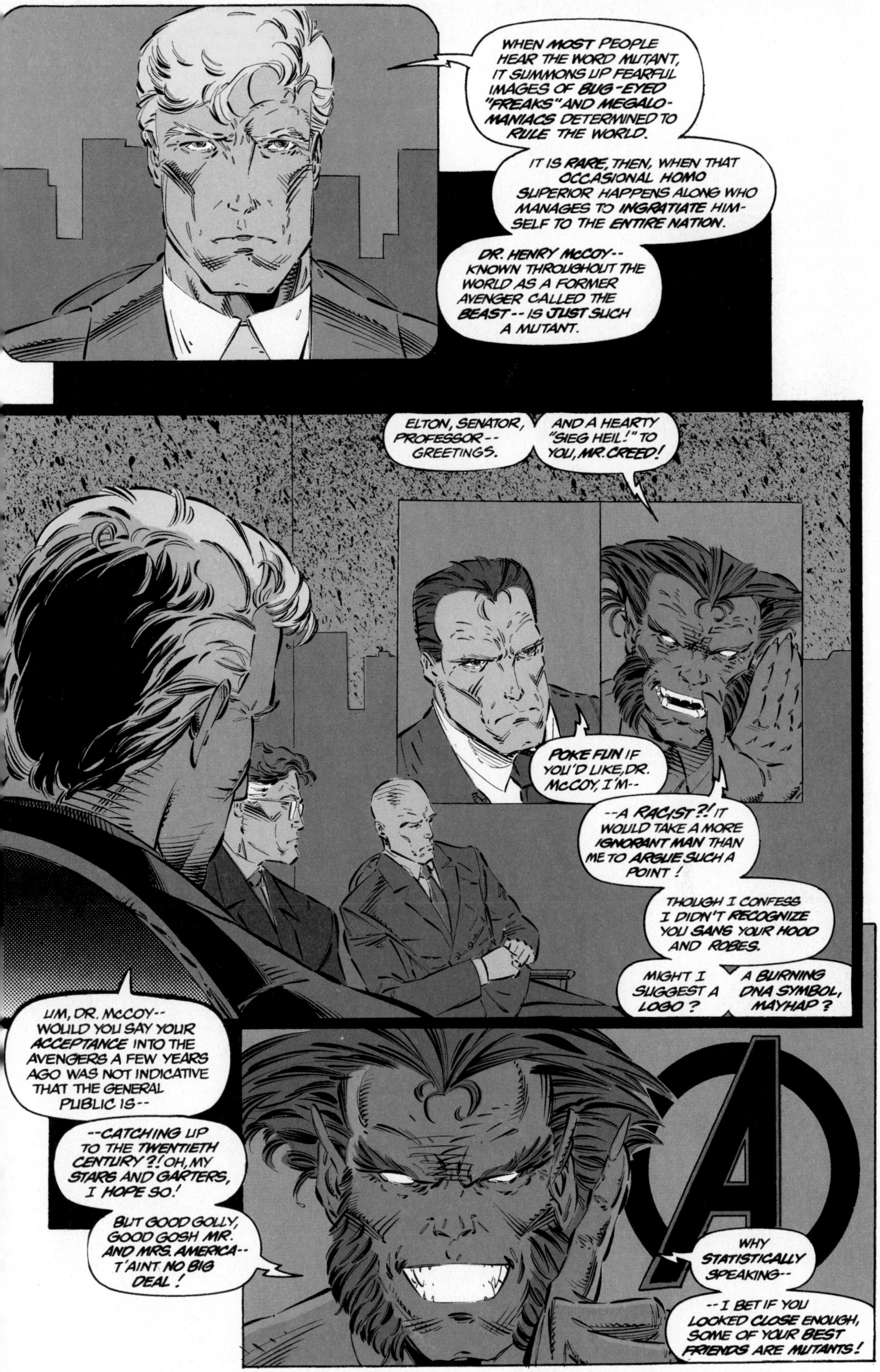

ELTON, SENATOR, PROFESSOR-- GREETINGS.
AND A HEARTY "SIEG HEIL!" TO YOU, MR. CREED!
POKE FUN IF YOU'D LIKE, DR. McCOY, I'M--
--A RACIST?! IT WOULD TAKE A MORE IGNORANT MAN THAN ME TO ARGUE SUCH A POINT!
THOUGH I CONFESS I DIDN'T RECOGNIZE YOU SANS YOUR HOOD AND ROBES.
MIGHT I SUGGEST A LOGO?
A BURNING DNA SYMBOL, MAYHAP?

UM, DR. McCOY-- WOULD YOU SAY YOUR ACCEPTANCE INTO THE AVENGERS A FEW YEARS AGO WAS NOT INDICATIVE THAT THE GENERAL PUBLIC IS--
--CATCHING UP TO THE TWENTIETH CENTURY?! OH, MY STARS AND GARTERS, I HOPE SO!
BUT GOOD GOLLY, GOOD GOSH MR. AND MRS. AMERICA-- T'AINT NO BIG DEAL!
WHY STATISTICALLY SPEAKING--
--I BET IF YOU LOOKED CLOSE ENOUGH, SOME OF YOUR BEST FRIENDS ARE MUTANTS!

THAT'S EXACTLY MY POINT! MUTANTS ARE TRYING TO HIDE AMONG THE REST OF HUMANITY--
--DOING WHO KNOWS WHAT AMOUNT OF DAMAGE TO OUR GENE POOL?!
WOW.
I NEVER THOUGHT OF IT THAT WAY.
HEAVEN FORBID WE ALL KEEP USING THE SAME WATER FOUNTAINS!
HERE'S AN IDEA-- WHY DON'T ALL US MUTANTS START WEARING SCARLET "M's" ON OUR CLOTHES?!
WAIT--I GOT IT...
...TATTOOS!
YOU CAN STENCIL TATTOOS ON OUR FOREARMS!
I REFUSE TO SIT HERE AND BE INSULTED BY THIS--THIS FREAK!
IF YOU'RE LEAVING ANYWAY, FORGIVE ME FOR FAST FOWARDING TO MY FINAL REBUTTAL AS I SAY--
--ON BEHALF OF MUTANTS EVERYWHERE...
PTHHHPHTH!
THANK YOU, ER... BEAST.
IT IS THIS FLAGRANT DISREGARD FO--
WE'LL CONCLUDE AFTER THESE MESSAGES...
Sigh

MEANWHILE AT HARRY'S HIDEAWAY...
HEE HA HA HO HOO HEH HEH
Harry's Hideaway
HA HA HA HO HO HO hee hee heh HO HA
ORORO, I'M NOT SURE I UNDERSTAND THE HUMOR BEHIND WHAT JUST OCCURRED.
JUDGING FROM THE EXPRESSION ON CHARLES' FACE--
--YOU ARE NOT ALONE.
EXACTLY WHAT IS THE SOCIAL SIGNIFICANCE OF A "RASPBERRY"?
THERE IS NONE, BISHOP!
NONE HA HOO haah WHATSOEVER!
BOBBY'S RIGHT. IT'S HANK'S WAY OF UNDERMINING THE VALUE OF CREED'S SENTIMENT THROUGH RIDICULE.
WARREN, I'M NOT SURE ANTAGONIZING THE ENEMY IS SUCH A GOOD IDEA--
--ESPECIALLY ON NATIONAL TELEVISION.
I AM INCLINED TO AGREE WITH DETECTIVE JONES. TO UNDERESTIMATE AN...
...AN...
...ENEMY?
THIS... WHAT DID THE OTHERS CALL HER... WAITRESS--
--THERE IS SOMETHING... FAMILIAR ABOUT HER.
CAN I GET YOU ANYTHING ELSE, SIR?
ANOTHER DR. PEPPER?
YES. THANK YOU.

BUT I WON'T BE BORN IN THIS TIME-LINE FOR ANOTHER SEVENTY YEARS.
I CAN'T POSSIBLY KNOW HER. CAN I?
A TOAST THEN, TO PROFESSOR XAVIER'S NEW CAREER AS THE MONTEL WILLIAMS OF MUTANTDOM--
--AND THE BEAST'S ATTEMPT TO SINGLE-HANDEDLY SET THE MUTANT MOVEMENT BACK THIRTY YEARS!
ORORO...?
BOBBY, I DON'T MEAN TO PUT A DAMPER ON THE FESTIVITIES...
...BUT SOMEHOW I THINK IT IS FITTING WE RAISE A GLASS IN HONOR...
...TO ALL THOSE WHO HAVE GONE BEFORE US.
WHETHER THEY HAVE FOUGHT AT OUR SIDE-- SUCH AS MIMIC, THUNDERBIRD, CYPHER, CABLE OR WARLOCK TO NAME BUT A FEW--
--OR SUPPORTED US, AS DID MARIKO YASHIDA OR SHARON FRIEDLANDER.
TO OUR ADVERSARIES. MAGNETO, THE HELLIONS, THE MARAUDERS--FOR MISSED OPPORTUNITIES AND FOR THE GOOD THEY COULD HAVE DONE.
FINALLY, HERE ALSO TO THE TIMES YET TO COME.
TO THE FUTURE.
INDEED.
TO THE FUTURE.

O WE'RE
WAY!
SOMEONE GET ME THAT FURRY BLUE MUTIE ON THE PHONE!
I SUPPOSE I SHOULD BE GRATEFUL HE WAITED TO MOON CREED UNTIL WE WERE AWAY AT COMMERCIAL!
IT WOULD APPEAR, PROFESSOR -- YOU AND I HAVE MORE IN COMMON THAN WE WOULD HAVE REALIZED?
I HAVE ALWAYS BELIEVED THAT UNDERNEATH EVERYONE'S SURFACE DIFFERENCES, WE ARE ALL FUNDAMENTALLY THE SAME.
I DON'T DOUBT EVEN MR. CREED IS ACTING IN THE BEST OF FAITH -- TWISTED THOUGH IT MAY BE.
THEN YOU'RE A BETTER MAN THAN I.
OFF THE RECORD, XAVIER. DO YOU HONESTLY FEEL THERE IS NOTHING TO FEAR FROM MUTANTS?
I ONLY WISH I WERE THAT NAIVE AGAIN, ROBERT.
OFF THE RECORD, I BELIEVE THAT MUTANTS -- AS A RACE -- WANT NOTHING MORE THAN TO PEACEFULLY COEXIST WITH HUMANS.
IT IS THE DETRIMENTAL AMBITIONS OF THE INDIVIDUAL --
-- MUTANT AND HUMAN --
-- WE MUST ALL GUARD AGAINST.
REST ASSURED -- I'M TAKING MEASURES TO PREVENT JUST SUCH THREATS.
AN WE GET TOGETHER OR DINNER WHILE I'M N TOWN? TOMORROW, PERHAPS?
ANOTHER TIME, I'M AFRAID. I'M OFF TO FRANCE AT FIRST LIGHT.
A FIELD TRIP WITH MY STUDENTS.
I NEVER THOUGHT I'D SEE THE DAY THESE TWO WOULD SIT DOWN AND TALK.
WELCOME TO THE NINETIES.

ACTUALLY, MS. GREY--
--THE SENATOR ISN'T THE MONSTER EVERYONE THINKS HE IS.
NOT ONCE YOU GET TO KNOW HIM.
A TELEPATHIC VOICE--INTRUDING IN MY HEAD?!
BUT WHO...?
IS KELLY'S AIDE SMILING TO BE POLITE--
--OR BECAUSE HE KNOWS SOMETHING HE SHOULDN'T?
AND IS A MUTANT IN THE SENATOR'S ENTOURAGE A GOOD THING--
--OR A DISASTER WAITING TO HAPPEN?
PROFESSOR, YOU MENTIONED FRANCE.
YES. THE CULMINATION OF THE MATTER THA HAS MONOPOLIZ MY ATTENTION THESE PAST FEW WEEKS.
I WAS IN PSIONIC CONTACT WITH SCOTT THROUGHOUT THE TEL CAST. WE ARE NOW READY TO MAKE OUR MOVE.
THE BLACKBIRD IS PRIMED AND FUELED, SIR.
I'VE JUST ALERTED THE GOLD TEAM--AND WOLVERINE INSISTED ON JOINING US--
--AND DR. MACTAGGERT WILL BE FLYING IN FROM GENOSHA TO MEET YOU AT HER COUNTRY ESTATE OUTSIDE OF PARIS.
EXCELLENT, CYCLOPS.
WE SHOULD BE IN THE AIR WITHIN THE HOUR.
WHAT DID I MISS? WHY ARE WE GOING TO FRANCE?
BECAUSE ALL THE EVIDENCE INDICATES IT'S THE BASE OF OPERATIONS OF THE ACOLYTES.
WE'RE TAKING THE BATTLE TO THEM.

MARVEL COMICS
THE UNCANNY
X-MEN
AN X-MEN ANNIVERSARY SPECTACULAR!
$3.95 US
$4.95 CAN
300
MAY
UK £2.60
APPROVED BY THE COMICS CODE AUTHORITY
30 YEARS
X-MEN
1963-1993
JR JR + DG

THE CALL WAS PLACED DIRECTLY TO THE CENTER OF HIS BRAIN.
"NIGHTCRAWLER! ALONE! NOW!"...
...FOLLOWED BY A SET OF COORDI-NATES.
I SUPPOSE I SHOULD BE ANNOYED AT THE PROFESSOR'S ASSUMPTION I WOULD DROP EVERY-THING--
--AS THOUGH I DO NOT HAVE MY OWN RESPONSIBILITIES AS LEADER OF EXCALIBUR.
AH, KURT WAGNER-- SIGH --YOU ARE KIDDING YOURSELF.
ONCE AN X-MAN...
...ALWAYS AN X-MAN!

WHATEVER DIRE EMERGENCY AWAITS, AT LEAST I WILL FACE IT IN...
... THE COMPANY OF...
...GOOD...
... FRIENDS?
SAVE US BOTH THE EFFORT...
... AND HOLD THAT POSE UNTIL I'VE COMPLETED THESE FINAL CONFIGURA-TIONS.
WAS?!
CAUTION IS ADMIRABLE, FORGE--
--BUT REST ASSURED IT IS ME, NIGHTCRAWLER!
EASILY SAID.
FNAM!
NOT QUITE AS EASILY PROVEN.

THE MUTANT CALLED FORGE WAS BORN A CREATOR, BLESSED WITH AN INVENTIVE ABILITY THAT GOES FAR, FAR BEYOND THAT OF GENIUS.
IN THIS CASE, HE HAS CREATED A CONTAINMENT GUN CAPABLE OF ENVELOPING A TARGET IN A RESTRAINT COCOON.
FORTUNATELY, FOR NIGHTCRAWLER--
--HE IS NOT WITHOUT HIS OWN GENETIC ATTRIBUTES.
THE CRACKLE OF FLAME, A BURST OF BRIMSTONE--
BAMF!
--A SUDDEN IMPLOSION OF AIR RUSHING IN TO FILL THE VOID...
... ARE ALL MANIFESTATIONS OF HIS ABILITY TO TELEPORT FROM ONE PLACE--

ANOTHER.
IT ME,
EIN
REUND--
LISTEN CLOSELY, NIGHTCRAWLER.
I ONLY HAVE TIME TO GO OVER THIS ONCE.
OR HAVE
U ALWAYS
EN THIS
TENSE...
. AND I
MPLY NEVER
OTICED?

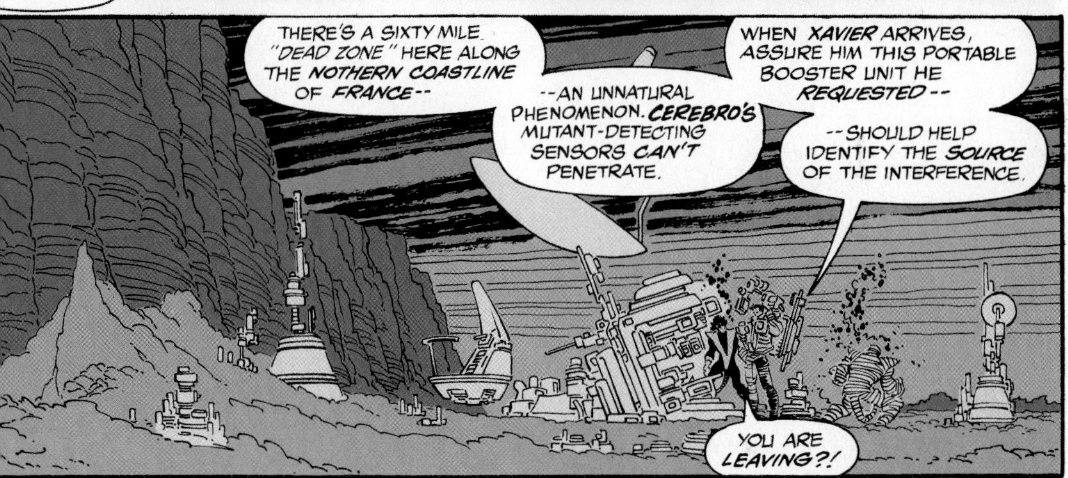

THERE'S A SIXTY MILE "DEAD ZONE" HERE ALONG THE NOTHERN COASTLINE OF FRANCE--
--AN UNNATURAL PHENOMENON. CEREBRO'S MUTANT-DETECTING SENSORS CAN'T PENETRATE.
WHEN XAVIER ARRIVES, ASSURE HIM THIS PORTABLE BOOSTER UNIT HE REQUESTED--
--SHOULD HELP IDENTIFY THE SOURCE OF THE INTERFERENCE.
YOU ARE LEAVING?!

Y TECHNOLOGY CAPABLE OF
DING MUTANTS IS PROBABLY
S ADEPT AT LOCATING
THEM.
THE FEWER MUTANTS IN THE IMMEDIATE AREA--

--THE LESS CHANCE YOU'LL BE DETECTED.
AND WHAT OF IT? THIS WOULD NOT BE THE FIRST TIME YOU AND I HAVE FACED--

I'M NOT AN X-MAN, KURT -- NOT ANY-MORE.
I CAME HERE TONIGHT STRICTLY AS A FAVOR TO XAVIER.
YOU WANT TO FIGHT THE "GOOD FIGHT..."?
ENJOY YOURSELF.
I PREFER TO LIVE IN THE REAL WORLD.
YOU ARE SUGGESTING THE REST OF US ARE LIVING A FANTASY?
A GROUP OF MUTANTS--
--RISKING THE
LIVES TO CREAT
A WORLD WHER
EVERYONE IS
TREATED EQUA
IT'S THE STUFF OF DREAMS, KURT--
--AND DREAMS ARE FOR PEOPLE THAT SLEEP.
I PREFER TO THINK OF THEM AS WINDOWS, MEIN FRUEND--
--GLIMPSES OF THE WORLD AS IT CAN BE TOMORROW...
...INSTEAD OF THE WAY IT IS TODAY.
WHICH DOES NOT MEAN WE DO NOT MAKE ALLOWANCES FOR REALITY.
IF WE DID NOT, THE X-MEN WOULD NEVER HAVE BEGAT EXCALIBUR...
...THE NEW MUTANTS--FOR BETTER OR FOR WORSE--NEVER WOULD HAVE EVOLVED INTO X-FORCE...
...AND X-FACTOR WOULD NOT HAVE ASSUMED THE GOV ERNMENT RESPON SIBILITIES THAT ONC BELONGED TO FREEDOM FORCE.
ONE MIGHT ARGUE THE WOR "MUTANT" IS SYNONOMOUS WITH "CHANGE."
BAMF

"CAN YOU HELP ME BE NORMAL?"
IT WAS ONE OF THE FIRST QUESTIONS I ASKED CHARLES XAVIER.
HE HAD THE DECENCY NOT TO LAUGH IN MY FACE.
EVEN THOUGH HE, MORE SO THAN ANY OTHER MAN, KNEW THE FOLLY INHERENT IN THE QUESTION.
FOR IN A WORLD WHERE EVERY HUMAN LIFE IS AS UNIQUE AS A DROP OF WATER IN THE OCEAN--
--THERE IS NO SUCH CREATURE... AS NORMAL.
SPEAK ME, EBRO...
...POINT ME IN THE DIRECTION OF THE NEWEST MUTANT.
TELL ME HE OR SHE MAY BE THE ONE THAT WILL BRIDGE THE GAP BETWEEN HUMANS AND MUTANTS.
EVEN IF IT IS NOT THE TRUTH, TELL ME THERE IS STILL A REASON...
...TO HOPE.
SIXTEEN MILES SOUTH--
...A REUNION OF ANOTHER KIND WAS TO TAKE PLACE.
--ON A COUNTRY ESTATE ONCE OWNED BY THE CLAN MacTAGGERT...

TRAGEDY ARRIVED IN ITS STEAD.
IT'S CLEAR WE HAVE WASTED OUR TIME--DOCTOR MacTAGGERT IS NOWHERE TO BE FOUND!
DOESN'T MEAN WE SHOULDN'T HAVE BOTHERED, PETEY.
COLOSSUS--A YOUNG RUSSIAN WITH THE GOLDEN HEART OF A POET AND THE ARMORED BODY OF A WARRIOR.
WOLVERINE--THE CANADIAN POSSESSED OF AN ADAMANTIU SKELETON, DEADLY CLAWS AND A MUTANT HEALING FACTOR THA IS AS MUCH A CURSE AS IT IS A BLESSING.

STAN LEE PROUDLY PRESENTS... THE UNCANNY X-MEN'S 300TH ISSUE!
Legacies
SCOTT LOBDELL - WRITER
JOHN ROMITA, JR. - PENCILER
DAN GREEN - INKER
CHRIS ELIOPOULOS - LETTERER
STEVE BUCCELLATO - COLORIST
BOB HARRAS - EDITOR
TOM DeFALCO - EDITOR IN CHIEF
INDEED. AT THE VERY LEAST, OUR RECON CONFIRMED THERE'RE NO BODIES AMIDST THE WRECKAGE.
BISHOP-- FROM THE STREETS OF ARMAGEDDON SOME ONE HUNDRED YEARS IN THE FUTURE...
... THIS PEACE KEEPING OFFICER IS TRAPPED IN A PAST THAT MIGHT NOT BE HIS OWN.

GETHER WITH F TELEPATHIC N GREY--
--THE RAZOR-WINGED ARCH-ANGEL--
--STORM, MISTRESS OF THE WEATHER--
--AND THE INDOMITABLE ICEMAN...
...THEY MAKE UP THE X-MEN'S GOLD TEAM.
ORORO, IT'S IMPORTANT WE DON'T ALLOW THE FIRE TO SPEAD TO THE SURROUND-ING AREA.
RTAINLY, OFESSOR VIER.
ERE IS A REASON ORM IS THE LEADER OF THIS FACTION OF E X-MEN.
NOT THE LEAST OF WHICH HAS TO DO...
...WITH HER MUTANT COMMAND OF THE ELEMENTS.
TAKES SOME-G LESS THAN ONSCIOUS UGHT...
...AND A SELF-CONTAINED HURRICANE HOWLS FORTH FROM NOWHERE...
...AND VANISHES--
--JUST AS QUICKLY.

NOW FOR THE GOOD NEWS, PEOPLE:-
MOIRA WAS NEVER IN THE FIRE. THE SMELL OF BURNT FLESH IS DIS-TINCTIVE THAT WAY.
NONETHE-LESS, SOME-ONE WANTED US TO THINK SHE'S DEAD.
ALL THE MORE REASON TO--
P-TING
<MUTANT SWINE!>
<WE SHOULD HAVE SUSPECTED AS MUCH.>
YE OLDE ANGRY TOWNSPEOPLE HAVE ARRIVED.
MY CUE TO ERECT AN ICE SHIELD BETWEEN--
A MOMENT, ROBERT.
<CLEARLY IT WAS THEY WHO SET THE FIRE!> *
*TRANSLATED FROM THE FRENCH.--BH
LET THEM VOICE THEIR CONCERNS.
YOUR KIND ARE NOT WELCOME HERE, X-MEN!
WE ARE ACTING IN YOUR BEST INTERESTS!
NOW DISPERSE THIS ASSEMBLAGE IMMEDIATELY, OR--
THERE IS NO NEED TO EXACER-BATE THIS CONFRONTATION, BISHOP.
OR DID YOU THINK WE'D FORGOTTEN THE DAMAGE YOU DID LAST TIME YOU CAME TO FRANCE IN YOUR SO-CALLED "TRIAL" FOR MAGNETO?
*UNCANNY X-MEN #200. --BOB
THEY HAVE EVERY RIGHT TO DEFEND THEIR HOMES FROM-- WHAT THEY PERCEIVE TO BE-- A THREAT.

WE APOLOGIZE FOR ANY INCON-VENIENCE, GOOD PEOPLE.
WE WILL BE ON OUR WAY.
‹ WHA-- HAPPENED? THEY ARE GONE! ›
‹ AND NOT A MOMENT TOO SOON! ›
‹ BUT TO WHERE...?! ›
‹ WHAT DOES IT MATTER--THEY ARE GONE AND WE ARE SAFE! ›
DID I MISS SOME-THING? WHY ARE THEY ACTING LIKE... WE'VE LEFT?
BECAUSE IN THEIR MINDS, WE DEPART-ED AS THEY REQUESTED.
MIND CONTROL, CHUCK?
DON'T SEEM LIKE YOUR STYLE.
DESPERATE TIMES, DESPERATE MEASURES.
I WOULD IMAGINE YOU, WOLVERINE--MORE THAN ANY OF THE OTHERS--WOULD UNDERSTAND THAT.
DIDN'T SAY I DON'T UNDER-STAND IT.
JUST DON'T LIKE IT MUCH.
IS OF COMFORT, SAN...
... I LIKE IT EVEN LESS.

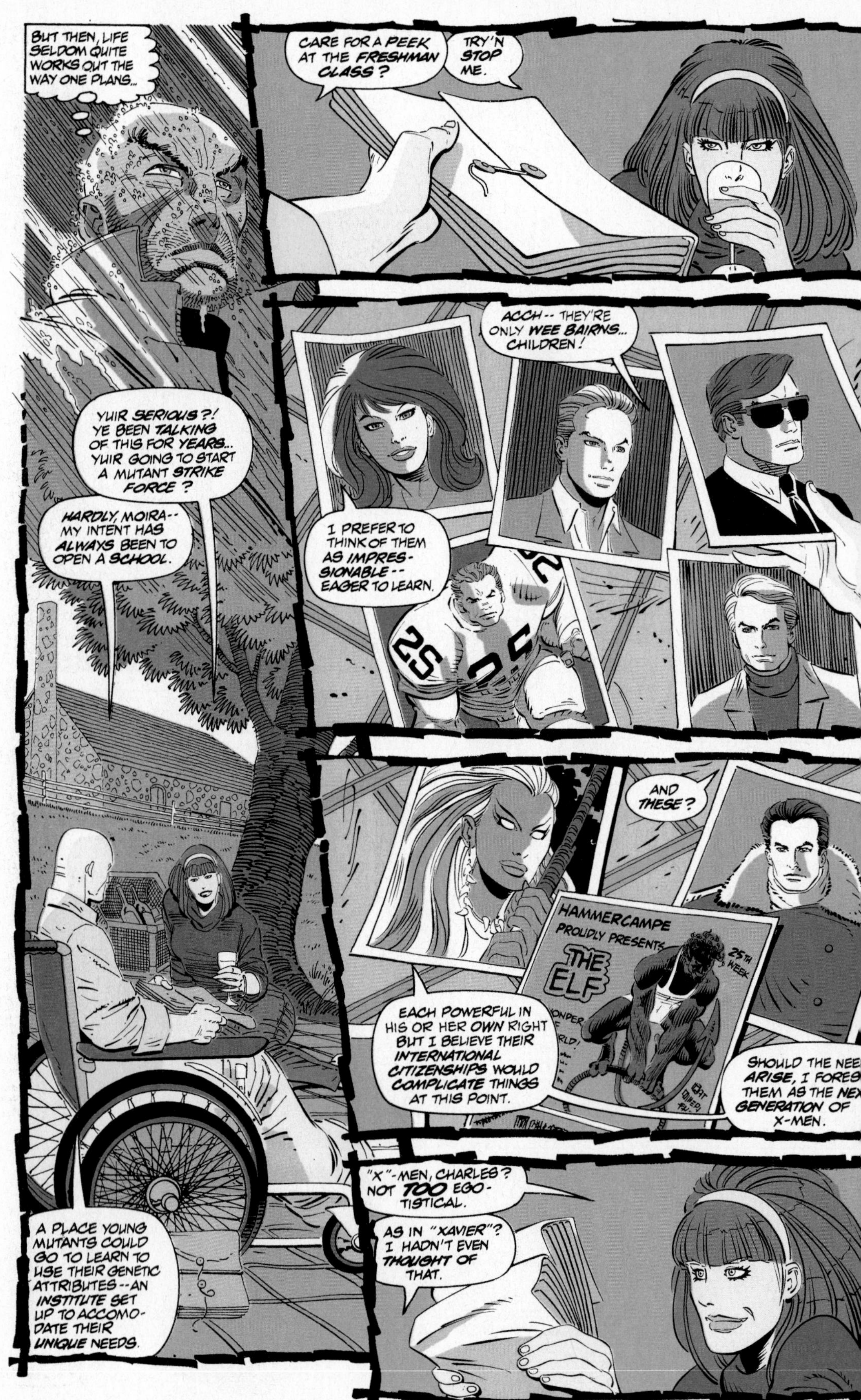
BUT THEN, LIFE SELDOM QUITE WORKS OUT THE WAY ONE PLANS...
CARE FOR A PEEK AT THE FRESHMAN CLASS?
TRY'N STOP ME.
YUIR SERIOUS?! YE BEEN TALKING OF THIS FOR YEARS... YUIR GOING TO START A MUTANT STRIKE FORCE?
HARDLY, MOIRA-- MY INTENT HAS ALWAYS BEEN TO OPEN A SCHOOL.
ACCH -- THEY'RE ONLY WEE BAIRNS... CHILDREN!
I PREFER TO THINK OF THEM AS IMPRES-SIONABLE-- EAGER TO LEARN.
AND THESE?
HAMMERCAMPE PROUDLY PRESENTS
THE ELF
25TH WEEK
EACH POWERFUL IN HIS OR HER OWN RIGHT BUT I BELIEVE THEIR INTERNATIONAL CITIZENSHIPS WOULD COMPLICATE THINGS AT THIS POINT.
SHOULD THE NEE ARISE, I FORES THEM AS THE NEX GENERATION OF X-MEN.
A PLACE YOUNG MUTANTS COULD GO TO LEARN TO USE THEIR GENETIC ATTRIBUTES -- AN INSTITUTE SET UP TO ACCOMO-DATE THEIR UNIQUE NEEDS.
"X"-MEN, CHARLES? NOT TOO EGO-TISTICAL.
AS IN "XAVIER"? I HADN'T EVEN THOUGHT OF THAT.

STANDS FOR SOMETHING 'TRA IN THEIR GENES, THE FACTOR WHICH SEPARATES UMANS FROM MUTANTS.
THEN LET'S BE PRAYING THESE CHILDREN HAVE THAT SOMETHING EXTRA--
--'CAUSE IF INTER-POL IS TO BE BELIEVED, THEY'RE GOING TO BE NEEDING IT SOONER THAN LATER.
THIS CAME OVER THE WIRE AN HOUR AGO.
HE'S... BACK?
WORSE'N BACK. HE'S PLOTTING SOMETHING AS WELL.
HE WAS AFTER THE SECURITY PARAMETER FOR CAPE CITADEL.
CAN YE IMAGINE, THE WORLD'S NUCLEAR ARSENAL IN THE HANDS OF--
--MAGNUS.
MAGNUS!!!
MAG
MAG
MAG
MAG
MAG
MAG
I AM SORRY, LORD CORTEZ...
...I AM LOSING THE TRANSMISSION.

YOU'VE DONE NOTHING WRONG, MILAN. THE TASK YOU SET FOR YOURSELF WAS MONUMENTAL...
...USING YOUR MUTANT ABILITY TO PSIONICALLY TRANFER MENTAL IMPULSES INTO ELECTROMAGNETIC VIDEO IMAGES IS DIFFICULT TO APPLY UNDER THE BEST OF CIRCUMSTANCES.
HAVING TO FIGHT THIS HUMAN'S FORMIDABLE WILL MAKES IT NEARLY IMPOSSIBLE.
I AM CONFIDENT THAT WHEREVER MAGNUS IS-- OUR TRUE LORD AND MASTER HAS BLESSED YOU FOR YOUR EFFORTS.
THE HOME OF THE ACOLYTES.
FOR DR. MOIRA MacTAGGERT-- THE PLACE IS A LIVING PURGATORY BETWEEN PAIN AND SUFFERING.
YOU HAVE SQUANDERED YOUR GIFT ENOUGH FOR ONE DAY, MILAN.
REST AND START FRESH ON THE MORROW-- IF YOU MUST.

C-CLATTER
KLIKT
I FEEL AS IF I'VE FAILED MY BRETHREN.

IF ONLY WE KNEW EXACTLY WHAT THIS FLATSCAN KNEW OF MAGNETO, WE COULD--
YOU HEARD WHAT VOGHT SAID.

SECRETS--
--LIKE GOOD FOOD...
...ARE BEST WHEN SAVORED.

NOT IN THIS CASE, CORTEZ! AFTER THE SINS SHE COMMITTED AGAINST THE LORD--
-- THE VERY LEAST WE SHOULD BE DOING IS CHEWING ON HER ENTRAILS INSTEAD OF TRODDING ABOUT HER BRAIN CELLS!

DO NOT QUESTION ME, VOGHT!
EVER.
FOR THE MOMENT, DR. MACTAGGERT LIVES.

DO NOT MAKE THE MISTAKE OF DISMISSING THIS WOMAN, SIMPLY BECAUSE SHE IS GENETICALLY INFERIOR.
SHE IS NOT SOMEONE TO UNDERESTIMATE.
THIS SAME GENE-TRASH WAS RE-SPONSIBLE FOR REARRANGING MAGNETO'S DNA STRUCTURE!
YES, SIR... I'LL START FRESH IN THE MORNING.
MAKING US ALL BEHOLDEN TO A HUMAN, CORTEZ? IF MAGNETO HADN'T ALREADY DIED, THIS WOULD CERTAINLY HAVE KILLED HIM!
AS THEIR ARGUMENT RAGES--
--THE YOUNG MAN IS IGNORED BY THE HIGHER MEMBERS OF HIS ORDER.
WERE HE ALLOWED TO SPEAK-- THE YOUNG NEOPHYTE MIGHT QUESTION THEIR ACTIONS.
THE MAN HE HAS CHOSEN TO FOLLOW, OF HIS OWN FREE WILL, HAD NO GREAT LOVE OF HUMANS... TRUE.
BUT MAGNUS UNDERSTOOD WHAT IT MEANT TO EXTEND KINDNESS --NOT EX-CLUDING ONE'S ENEMIES.
HE ONCE WROTE--
"EVEN THE FLY SHOULD FEEL AT HOME IN THE WEB."
EVEN IF THAT HOME--

--IS A CASTLE.
OR IN THIS CASE, THE ABANDONED MONASTERY THAT IS THE MONT SAINT FRANCIS.
CURRENTLY? WE'RE THIRTY MILES AWAY FROM OUR RENDEZVOUS WITH NIGHT-CRAWLER.
BUT I DIDN'T CALL TO GIVE YOU A PROGRESS REPORT--
RATHER, RECEIVE ONE.
HOW IS MY SISTER FEELING?
ILLYANA IS RESTING AS COMFORTABLY AS POSSIBLE, PETER... HER COUGH SEEMS TO BE BREAKING UP.
AND THE FEVER, STEVIE?
CLIMBING, I'M AFRAID.
I'LL KEEP YOU POSTED.
SEE THAT YOU DO, MS. HUNTER.
RELAX, COLOSSUS, I KNOW JUST HOW IT FEELS WHEN YOU'RE WAIT--
I DOUBT THAT YOU DO, ROBERT.
PARDON?
I CAME FROM A CLOSE, LOVING HOUSEHOLD--ONLY TO HAVE LOST EACH MEMBER OF MY FAMILY TO ONE TRAGEDY AFTER ANOTHER.
ILLYANA IS THE MOST IMPORTANT PERSON IN MY LIFE.
WITHOUT HER, I HAVE NOTHING.
DON'T DEMEAN MY FEELINGS BY CLAIMING YOU "UNDERSTAND."
FOR YOU MOST CER-TAINLY DO NOT.
EXCUSE ME FOR CARING!
TIN HEAD!

ACCORDING TO THE RECORDS WE "APPROPRIATED" FROM THE F.A.A. COMPUTERS-- AN UNIDENTIFIED AIRCRAFT WAS SPOTTED IN THE AIRSPACE OVER MIDDLEBOROUGH TWO DAYS AGO.
IT IS SAFE TO ASSUME IT WAS THE ACOLYTES, ESCAPING AFTER THEIR ATTEMPTED "GENETIC CLEANSING."*
CEREBRO PROJECTED A FLIGHT PLAN, COMBINED WITH THE INFORMATION THE PROFESSOR GATHERED OVER THE PAST TWENTY-FOUR HOURS--
--INDICATES THE ACOLYTE BASE IS SOMEWHERE IN THE NORTH OF FRANCE.
* IN UNCANNY X-MEN #298.--Bob

EXCEPT FOR BOBBY'S MUTTERED RAMBLINGS, THE CABIN FALLS SILENT AT THE MENTION OF FORGE'S NAME.
FOR THOUGH NO ONE WOULD DARE TO MENTION IT UNLESS SHE BROUGHT IT UP FIRST--
--THERE IS UNFINISHED BUSINESS BETWEEN "THE MAKER" AND THE "WIND RIDER" NAMED STORM.

A SHORT WHILE AGO, HE'D ASKED HER TO MARRY HIM--
--TO LEAVE THE TEAM THAT HAD BECOME HER FAMILY.
HER DECISION WAS TAKEN OUT OF HER HANDS WHEN HE RETRACTED THE PROPOSAL--

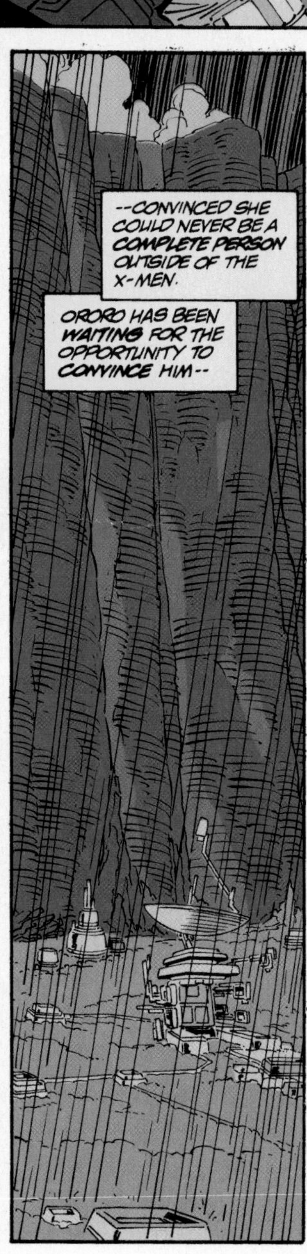
--CONVINCED SHE COULD NEVER BE A COMPLETE PERSON OUTSIDE OF THE X-MEN.
ORORO HAS BEEN WAITING FOR THE OPPORTUNITY TO CONVINCE HIM--

BUT UNLESS FORGE'S AUGMENTATION CONSOLE CAN PUNCTURE THEIR CLOAKING DEVICE--
--THIS COULD MEAN WEEKS OF SEARCHING FOR THE PROVERBIAL NEEDLE.
LIKE THERE'S SOMETHING WRONG WITH BEING AN ONLY CHILD.
"ALMOST NONEXISTENT."
HIS ALUMINUM-FOIL HEAD IS GONNA' BE NON-EXISTENT WHEN I LOB THIS MEGA SNOW-BALL UPSIDE HIS FACE!

D PERHAPS SELF AS L...
...THAT HE WAS WRONG.
KURT, YOU ARE... ALONE?
I AM AS SURPRISED AS YOU ARE.
I ASSUMED FORGE WOULD STAY AT LEAST UNTIL THE REST OF YOU ARRIVED--
--YET HE BOLTED OUT OF HERE AS IF...
...THE SENTINELS WERE...

HULDIGUNG.
DID I JUST STICK MY TAIL IN MY MOUTH?
HA!
NOT AT ALL, MY FRIEND.
TELL ME, HAVE YOU BEEN TAKING CARE OF MY KITTEN?

THIRTY MILES UP THE COAST-LINE...
SHE WILL LIVE... UP UNTIL THE MOMENT SHE IS OF NO USE TO US!

EMEMBER, I WAS
ERE WHEN SHE USED
R TECHNOLOGY TO
RN THE X-MEN AGAINST
EACH OTHER!
WHILE THEY EVENTUALLY PROVED TOO STRONG-WILLED FOR THE PROCESS TO LAST...
...THINK HOW MANY NEW RECRUITS WE COULD ENLIST TO OUR GLORIOUS CRUSADE!
OUR RANKS HAVE GROWN STRICTLY FROM MUTANTS WHO HAVE SEEN THE WISDOM OF MAGNETO'S WAY--
--WHY SULLY THE MOVEMENT WITH RELUCTANT CONVERTS?
BECAUSE THE ENTIRE WORLD IS NOT AS BRIGHT AS YOU AND I, VOGHT.

BECAUSE MOST PEOPLE ARE LIKE LAMBS WHO WILL GO SILENTLY TO SLAUGHTER AT THE HANDS OF THE HUMANS--
--IF WE DO NOT PROTECT THEM IN MAGNUS'S NAME.

AND MOST IMPORTANTLY, BECAUSE I SAID SOOOOOOWW!
WOULDN'T WANT TO ARGUE
WITH YOU :COG: EH, FABIAN?
NOT YOU... THE MAN WHO MURDERED--

SHUT UP, WOMAN!
THEY'LL KILL US BOTH!
NO ONE IS INTERESTED IN YOUR LIES!

IT'S THE TRUTH, CORTEZ.
REMEMBER...?
... I WAS THERE, TOO -- WHEN YOU

ENOUGH, HUMAN SOW!
YOU'VE ABUSED EVEN THE MODICUM OF COURTESY I'VE EXTENDED!

OUR BELIEFS MAY SEEM FOOLISH TO YOU, BUT MAGNETO IS OUR RELIGION...
...THIS PLACE IS OUR TEMPLE.
WE WILL NOT HAVE IT TAINTED BY THE BLASPHEMOUS RANTINGS OF A CONDEMNED WOMAN!
BOTH KNOW...
...TRU
SUMMON MILAN, IMMEDIATELY!
YOU WERE RIGHT, VOGHT-- SHE WAS UNDESERVING OF OUR COMPASSION!
SUCH AS IT WAS.
TAKE THE REMAINDER OF HER MEMORIES AT ONCE--
--AND DO WHAT YOU'D LIKE WITH THE MINDLESS HUSK THAT REMAINS.
GLADLY.
AGAIN, THEY IGNORE THE YOUNG NEOPHYTE.
TO THEIR EYES, HE IS AS MUCH A PART OF THE MONASTERY WALLS--
--AS THE STONE AND MORTAR.
THEIR MISTAKE.
AS A PERSON, HE HAS HIS OWN FEARS...
...HIS OWN FRUSTRATIONS.
HIS OWN... DOUBTS.
PLEASE...
...HELP ME.
I--I AM NOT ALLOWED TO SPEAK TO YOU.
WHY IS THAT?
COULD IT BE THEY'RE AFRAID
OF A MER HUMAN?

SEE
E WAY
FF: YOU
LOOK AT HIM WHEN
YOU THINK NO ONE'S
WATCHING.

IN YOUR *GOUGH* H-HEART
YOU KNOW HE'S LYING.

"LORD CORTEZ WAS WITH OUR SAVIOR AT THE MOMENT OF HIS DEATH. MAGNUS ENTRUSTED HIM WITH THE--"
DIDN'T ANYONE ASK--
...DIDN'T YOU WONDER..

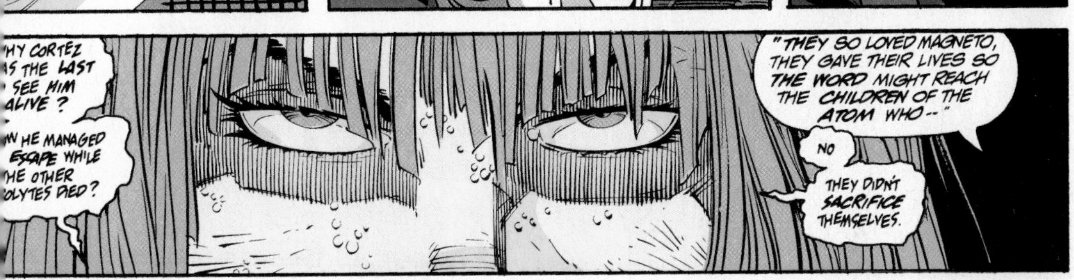
HY CORTEZ
AS THE LAST
SEE HIM
ALIVE?
W HE MANAGED
ESCAPE WHILE
THE OTHER
OLYTES DIED?
"THEY SO LOVED MAGNETO, THEY GAVE THEIR LIVES SO THE WORD MIGHT REACH THE CHILDREN OF THE ATOM WHO--"
NO
THEY DIDN'T SACRIFICE THEMSELVES.

CORTEZ LEFT THEM TO DIE--
--AFTER HE USED HIS POWER TO KILL MAGNETO!
NEIN!
WILL NOT
ISTEN TO
OUR LIES
NOTHER
OMENT!

HE'LL ABANDON YOU AS SURELY AS HE DID HIS "BRETHREN" ON ASTEROID M.
HE'S USING YOU--USING ALL THE ACOLYTES...

...WHEN HE'S DONE
HE'LL SLAY YOU ALL--AS EASILY AS HE KILLED MAGNETO!

TEN MILES AWAY...
ONE MILE ABOVE...
I HAVE TO TELL YOU, BISHOP-- I WAS NOT OVERLY THRILLED WHEN THE PROFESSOR INVITED YOU TO JOIN THE X-MEN.
INDEED?
HERE I THOUGHT YOU WERE COLD, RUDE AND DISMISSIVE TO EVERYONE.
I AM. BUT THAT'S ANOTHER STORY.
I JUST WANTED YO TO KNOW THAT YO DOUBLE-BARRELLE TAKE NO PRISONER DIRECT APPROAC IS--
--TOTALLY INAPPROPRIATE FOR THIS ERA.
SO I'VE BEEN TOLD ON MORE THAN ONE OCCASION.
WHAT I WAS GOING TO SAY IS THAT IT'S "--HAVING AN EFFECT ON THE PROFESSOR."
--WE'RE ACTUALLY TAKING THE INITIATIVE AGAIN.
WE'RE NOT WAITING AROUND THE MANSION FOR ONE EVIL MUTANT OR THE OTHER TO ATTACK--
EVERYONE FROM THUNDERBIRD TO WOLVERINE TO CABLE WAS UNABLE TO INSPIRE HIM TO ALTER HIS METHOD OF OPERATIONS.
I THINK CHARLES MIGHT TAKE YOUR PRESENCE IN OUR CENTURY AS A SIGN THAT IF YOU'RE THE FUTURE... HE MIGHT BEST GET STARTED FORGING IT NOW.
I AM HONORED IF I HAVE HAD AN EFFECT AT ALL O SUCH A REVERED MAN.
NOW PUT ME DOWN

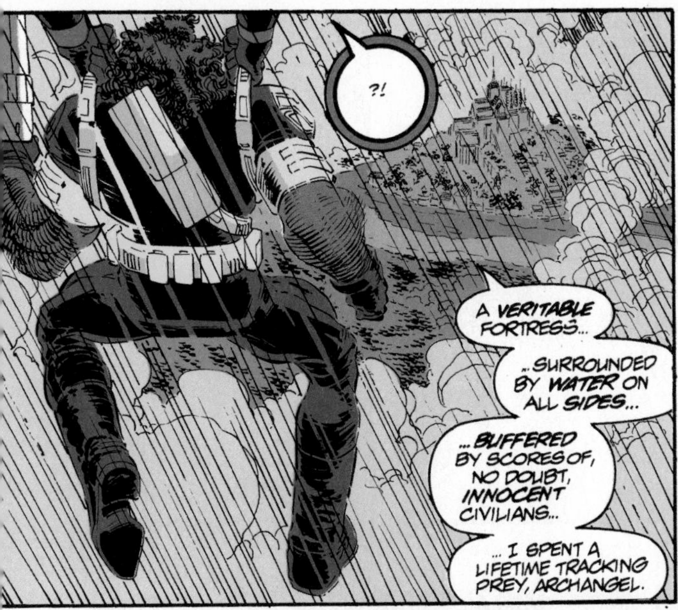

?!
A **VERITABLE** FORTRESS...
...SURROUNDED BY **WATER** ON ALL **SIDES**...
...**BUFFERED** BY SCORES OF, NO DOUBT, **INNOCENT** CIVILIANS...
...I SPENT A LIFETIME TRACKING PREY, ARCHANGEL.

TRUST ME.
WE'VE **FOUND** THE ENEMY.

GAMESMASTER!

I **DEMAND** AN AUDIENCE!

YOU CLAIM TO BE AN **OMNIPATH**--YOUR MIND IN **ALL** PLACES AT ALL **TIMES**.

AS **LEADER** OF THE **UPSTARTS**, I DEMAND YOU TO CONTACT **SHAW**, **FITZROY** AND **CREED**!

IT APPEARS I MAY HAVE **NEED** OF THEIR RESOURCES.

AS **USUAL**, CORTEZ--YOUR REACH FAR EX-**CEEDS** YOUR **GRASP**.

WHILE IT IS TRUE, YOU'VE **ACCRUED** THE MAJORITY OF POINTS IN THE UPSTART COMPETITION **TO DATE**--

--IT SEEMS I NEED REMIND YOU THAT DOMINION OVER THE OTHER UPSTARTS ONLY COMES UPON COMPLETION OF THE GAME.
TRZZT

FOR THE MOMENT, I'M AFRAID...
... YOU WILL HAVE TO MAKE DUE WITH THE HERD OF MINDLESS SHEEP YOU'VE TAKEN SUCH CARE TO TEND

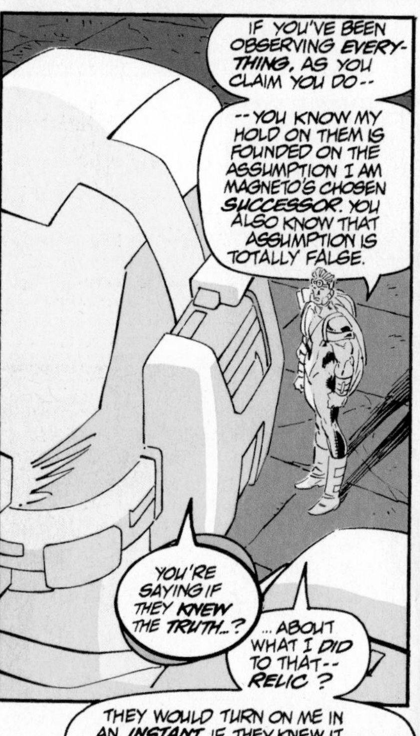
IF YOU'VE BEEN OBSERVING EVERY-THING, AS YOU CLAIM YOU DO--
--YOU KNOW MY HOLD ON THEM IS FOUNDED ON THE ASSUMPTION I AM MAGNETO'S CHOSEN SUCCESSOR. YOU ALSO KNOW THAT ASSUMPTION IS TOTALLY FALSE.
YOU'RE SAYING IF THEY KNEW THE TRUTH...?
... ABOUT WHAT I DID TO THAT--RELIC ?
THEY WOULD TURN ON ME IN AN INSTANT IF THEY KNEW IT WAS I WHO KILLED THEIR PRECIOUS MAGNUS. THAT'S WHY I MAY NEED THE PROTECT--

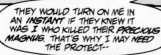

NO!
EH ?

I CAME TO HEAR YOU DENY HER LIES !
INSTEAD I LEARN THEY'RE ALL TRUE !
WHAT ?!
NEOPHYTE, STAND WHERE YOU ARE !
TOO LATE, HE'S "MORPHING" THROUGH THE WALL !
TRZZT
TRZZT

YOU KNEW HE WAS THERE, DIDN'T YOU ?!
YOU SET ME UP ! WHY?!
THE ANSWER SHOULD BE OBVIOUS, CORTEZ. ANYTHING TO KEEP THE GAME INTERESTING.
OTHER-WISE...
... WHY BOTHER ?

ORTEZ HAS
E MUTANT
BILITY--
I HAVE DARED MUCH--
--SACRIFICED EVERYTHING...
... ONLY TO SEE MY PLANS FRUSTRATED BY A CHILD!
TO ENHANCE
NOTHER
UTANT'S
OWER TO
E FURTHEST
EGREE.

--THE NEOPHYTE IS CAPABLE OF TRAVERSING GREAT DISTANCES THROUGH MASS...
...WITH CORTEZ'S UN-EXPECTED--UNWANTED "ASSISTANCE"...

THAT
OURNEY...

...COULD PROVE FATAL.
SPLOOSH

AFTER EVERYTHING HE HAS HEARD THIS DAY--
...HIS TRUST, BETRAYED--
--HIS ILLUSIONS, SHATTERED.
--HE WOULD JUST AS SOON SURRENDER HIMSELF TO THIS DEADLY EMBRACE OF MUD AND WATER.

WHAT--YOU'RE THROWING A PARTY AND FORGOT TO INVITE THE ACOLYTES, BUB?

NOT QUITE, WOLVERINE. BISHOP HERE IS CONVINCED THIS IS WHERE THEY'RE HOLDING UP.

WE OPTED TO WAIT FOR THE REST OF YOU--TO MOVE IN AS A UNIT.

WE CAN'T INVADE THIS MONASTERY WITHOUT SOME KIND OF CONFIRMATION THAT MOIRA IS BEING HELD HERE!

CYCLOPS, MUST I REMIND YOU I AM RESPONSIBLE FOR THE GOLD TEAM? BISHOP'S INSTINCTS HAVE PROVEN--
--CORRECT, IT WOULD SEEM.
CEREBRO HAS LOCATED AN UNIDENTIFIED MUTANT...

ON THE CONTRARY... WE'RE NOT GOING ANYWHERE AT ALL!

"...JUST THIS MOMENT REGAINING CONSCIOUSNESS."

NJOUR.
URNNM?
<AT LEAST YOU'RE ALIVE. THAT'S A GOOD SIGN.>

VAS!
YOU--YOU'RE A HUMAN, AREN'T YOU?!
I DON'T THINK ANYONE HAS EVER PHRASED IT THAT WAY, BUT...YES, I'M HUMAN.
GUILTY AS CHARGED.

I KNOW YOU'RE NOT VERY BRIGHT FOR CATCHING A NAP IN THE GROTTO FIVE MINUTES BEFORE THE TIDE COMES IN.
OTHER THAN THAT, YOU'RE A PERSON IN TROUBLE.

WHAT MORE DO I NEED TO KNOW?

SHE'S DEAD BEFORE A SOUND CAN ESCAPE FROM WHAT WERE--
--UNTIL ONLY MOMENTS AGO--
--HER LUNGS.

I--
--I DON'T EVEN KNOW
YOUR NAME.
AS YOU SAID, NEOPHYTE SHE WAS A HUMAN...

...PROOF ENOUGH THAT CORTEZ WAS TELLING THE TRUTH.
HE SAID YE WERE CAVORTING WITH THE ENEMY
WE WERE SENT TO "ESCORT" YE HOME.
LORD CORTEZ'S PRIVATE GUARD!
WHY DID YOU HAVE TO KILL HER?!
SHE DID NOTHING TO YOU-- SHE WAS NO THREAT TO THOSE OF US WITH MUTANT ABILITIES!
"BY THEIR VERY EXISTENC HOMO SAPIENS POSE A TH TO MUTANTS EVERYWHER THE ONE MUST REJECT OTHER!"
ACK!
PARALYZED BY... SANYAKA'S PSIONIC... WHIP.
HAVE YOU BEEN AWAY SO LONG, CHILD, YOU'VE ALREADY FORGOTTEN MAGNETO'S LESSONS?
AND HERE'S ADVICE TO YOU, FLATSCAN!
BE MORE CAUTIO OF THE STRAYS YO CHOOSE TO ADOPT YOUR NEXT LIFE...
...YOU NEVER KNOW WHAT COMPANY HE'LL BRING WITH HIM.
NO, BUB...
...YA NEVER DO.
YEEAAIRRGH
SLICE!

...OPS.
GUESS SEVERIN' YOUR PSIONIC WHIP CAUSED ENOUGH FEEDBACK TO TEMORARILY FRY YOUR BRAIN.
HOW EMBARRASSING.
YE LOUSY TRAITOR! SANYAKA WAS A DEVOTED FOLLOWER OF THE CAUSE--
--YE HAVE NO RIGHT T'BE MOCKIN' THE MAN WHILE HE'S DOWN.
OLE 'SPOOR WILL HAVE YE REGRETTIN' WHAT FOR YE DID T'ME FRIEND!
AS YA'CAN PROBABLY TELL BY THE TON OF ICE...
...COURTESY OF THE ICEMAN...
...I GOT A FEW FRIENDS OF MY OWN.
BUB.
SWAM!
HERE I WAS HOPING FOR A "SPLAT"!
C-CAN IT BE, KATH? ARE THESE... THE MIS-GUIDED?
DON'T FEIGN IGNORANCE, NEOPHYTE! IT'S CLEAR YOU LURED US HERE--
--OUTSIDE THE SHIELDING OF THE MONASTERY WALLS...
...ALERTING THESE HEATHENS TO OUR WHEREABOUTS!
BUT NO MATTER--
--I WILL WARN THE OTHERS OF THE X-MEN'S ARRIVAL!
ZAKT!
OUHN
ON BEHALF OF US "HEATHENS"--
--WE'D JUST AS SOON TELL THEM OURSELVES.
THANK YOU.

I DON'T UNDERSTAND.
SHE WAS NO THREAT TO THEM, YET..
... THEY... KILLED HER
ONLY BECAUSE
SHE WAS HUMAN?

I READ OF THE DEATH CAMPS IN WHICH MAGNUS WAS RAISED.
I CAN NOT--
WILL NOT--
BELIEVE THE ONLY THING HE LEFT TO US, HIS "CHILDREN"...
...WAS MORE OF THE SAME UNREASONING HATRED THAT CAUSED THE SLAUGHTER OF HIS FAMILY.
I'VE DEDICATED MY LIFE TO THE MAN.
HIS LIFE MUST BE... MORE.. THAN THIS.

THERE IS ANOTHER WAY, SON.
A PATH WHICH EVEN MAGNETO WALKED FOR A BRIEF TIME.
THERE ARE THOSE OF US WHO BELIEVE THE WORLD IS LARGE ENOUGH TO ACCOMMODATE BOTH MUTANTS AND HUMANS.
WE FIGHT--IT SEEMS, EVERY WAKING MOMENT OF OUR LIVES--TO BRING TO FRUITION A BETTER WORLD.

WE WANT TO INSURE THE HORROR WHICH SO SCARRE YOUR CHOSEN AVATAR NEVER COME TO PASS AGAIN.
TELL ME, NEOPHYTE--A YOU STRONG ENOUGH TO LI THE DREAM
WILL YO HELP US

ST OUTSIDE THE
NASTERY WALLS...?!
W COULD THEY'VE
TTEN THIS CLOSE
ITHOUT US
KNOWING?!

MY SCANNING ABILITY WAS MUFFLED BY THE CLOAKING DEVICE WHICH SHIELDS THIS SACRED PLACE!

THEY ARE SO NEAR, I CAN SENSE THEIR PRESENCE... NINE IN ALL!

THEN THE TIME HAS COME MY BRETHREN... THE FINAL BATTLE IN OUR HOLY WAR TO CLAIM THIS WORLD IN MAGNUS' NAME!

BUT LET THE ACOLYTES DRAW FIRST BLOOD. BRING ME THE WOMAN, JAYITZ!

IF THE NEOPHYTE REVEALS MY SECRET-- BETRAYS ME--WORD OF MY ACTIONS WILL SURELY TURN MY FOLLOWERS AGAINST ME!

MY ONLY HOPE--TO PREVENT THE X-MEN FROM CONVINCING THE ACOLYTES OF MY HAND IN MAGNETO'S DEATH-- IS TO RAISE THE STAKES.

SPEAKING FOR MYSELF-- I ENJOY THE SUSPENSE!
A VARIATION ON THEME, EH-- MEIN FRUEND?
THIS TIME I HIT THEM HIGH
AND YOU HIT THEM LOW!
BUT COLOSSUS DOES NOT REPLY--
--AT LEAST, NOT IN WORDS.
FOR THOUGH HE STANDS AND FIGHTS THIS DAY, HIS HEART IS NOT IN THE WINNING OR THE LOSING.
IT IS INVESTED IN THE HOPES AND DREAMS OF A LITTLE GIRL SOME THREE THOUSAND MILES AWAY, ACROSS THE SEA...
I DON'T BELIEVE ANYONE EVER ACCUSED THE X-MEN OF TURNING DOWN A HAND.

GKAK!
THERE'S NO WAY THEY COULD HAVE GOTTEN SO FAR-- SO QUICKLY-- WITHOUT HELP!
AH, THE KLEINSTOCK BROTHERS, IN YOUR NATIVE SWISS...
...GUTEN MORGEN.
CONSIDERING WHAT HAPPENED LAST TIME MS. GREY SLAMMED THE TWO OF YOU TOGETHER--*
--YOU'LL UNDERSTAND IF I OPT TO TAKE YOU OUT IN A SINGLE BLAST.
*UNCANNY #298.--Bob

LISTEN TO YOU, BISHOP-- YOU FINALLY GET TO DRAW ON YOUR PAST EXPERIENCES IN THE TWENTIETH CENTURY--
--AND SUDDENLY YOU'RE AN EXPERT ON ALL THINGS ACOLYTAL.
"ACOLYTAL", SNOWBALL?
HANK ASSURED ME IT WAS A WORD.
HANK LIED!
GUYS-- PLEASE!
JEAN IS CORRECT. TOTAL CONCENTRATION IS PARAMOUNT.
WE HAVE NEVER FACED A GROUP THIS FOCUSED-- THIS FANATIC.
THEY SEEM MORE THAN WILLING TO DIE FOR THEIR CAUSE.
WORKS OUT FINE-- I'M MORE THAN WILLIN' TO ACCOMODATE 'EM!
THE CHILD--?!
HE'S DONE HIS PART-- LET HIM GO!
BAMF

WHILE THE OTHERS ARE DISTRACTED, I CAN FULFILL ME SACRED RESPON-SIBILITY...
...TO SIPHON THE MEMORIES OF WHAT YOU DID TO OUR LORD AND MAAAAAAHH!
THE DOCTOR HAS BEEN THROUGH ENOUGH...
...LEAVE HER ALONE.
BUT MILAN CANNOT HEAR WARREN'S WORDS OVER THE SOUNDS OF HIS OWN SCREAM!
SIMILARLY, THE SOUND OF SHATTER-ING GLASS--
-- JOINS THE CACAPHONY WHICH ROCKS THIS ANCIENT BUILDING TO ITS CORE!
AS THE BANK OF MONITORS EXPLODES, THE INFORMATION THE MUTANT GATHERED--
--THE LIFE AND TIMES OF MOIRA MacTAGGERT...
... IS LOST TO THE ACOLYTES, FOREVER!
CORTEZ IS EAGER TO EXTRICATE HIMSELF FROM HIS FOLLOWERS, WITHOUT SO MUCH AS A BY YOUR LEAVE.
HARDLY THE LEADERSHIP QUALITIES I ADMIRE MOST IN A PERSON.
COULD IT BE HIS AGENDA FAR EXCEEDS HIS ASPIRATIONS AS AN ACOLYTE?

LESS THAN A WEEK SINCE WE NEARLY KILLED YOU, ARCHANGEL...
... AND YOU'RE FOOLISH ENOUGH TO AGAIN OPPOSE OUR WILL?
TOOK IT AS... LUCKY OMEN
WHAP
WARREN, I AM HERE--
--RELAX! GO LIMP!
NO PROB THERE, ELF.
FEEL LIKE UNUSICONE'S
PSIONIC EXO-SKEL
CLOSED DOWN MY NERVE SYNAPSES.
PLEASE... ENOUGH...
HARDLY ENOUGH, ACOLYTE!
YOU AND YOUR BRETHREN HAVE BEGUN A REIGN OF TERROR THAT-- ¿uhh?!
--THAT WILL CONTINUE LONG AFTER I'VE CRUSHED YOUR METAL FRAME IN MY PSYCHIC GRIP

M AFRAID YOU
RE AS *SHORT*
ON *POWER*--

--AS YOU ARE
ON *COMPASSION,*
UNUSCIONE.

AARGH!

PERHAPS I SHOULD SHOW *YOU* THE SAME MERCY YOU PREPARED TO SHOWER UPON THE *CHILDREN* OF MIDDLEBOROUGH...?

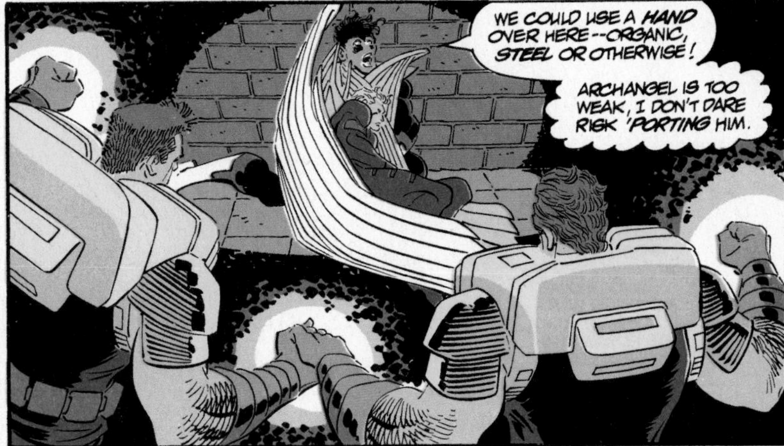

WE COULD USE A *HAND* OVER HERE--*ORGANIC, STEEL* OR OTHERWISE!
ARCHANGEL IS TOO WEAK, I DON'T DARE RISK *'PORTING* HIM.

I'M ON MY WAY, KURT...
COMPROMISING MY DESIRES IN PLACE OF MY RESPONSIBILITY.
AGAIN.

PATHETIC!
YOU'RE AS MUCH A WASTE OF A MUTANT-GENE AS YOU WERE WHEN YOU FOUNDED X-FACTOR.
WOMP!
THOSE WERE THE DAYS, HUH?

I, ON THE OTHER HAND, AM STRONGER!
I FOUND ACCEPTANCE...

...WHAT?
WW--
WHA--?
WHAT ARE YOU DOING?

ADAPTING.
FWOMMP!
Y'SEE, THE LAST TIME I WAS BEATEN THIS SEVERELY WAS BY MIKHAIL RASPUTIN--*
--WHO SHOWED ME THERE WAS A LOT MORE TO MY ICE POWER THAN I REALIZED.
*UNCANNY #291.--Bob

I HAVEN'T HAD THE OPPORTUNITY-- OR THE REASON-- TO BE AGGRESSIVELY CREATIVE.
SO, WHO'S NEXT?

THE MIGHTY CYCLOPS AND HIS X-MEN--SUPPRESSING ANY MUTANT WHO DIDN'T EMBRACE THE MAINSTREAM!
YOU WERE SO EAGER TO MAINTAIN THE STATUS QUO.
URMMPF
THERE ARE THOSE OF US WHO WILL NO LONGER BE OPPRESSED BY HUMANS...
...EVEN IF IT MEANS KILLING FELLOW MUT--
WHU-?!
WHA-?!
COULD BARELY HEAR UNDERNEATH ALL THOSE FINGERS, FRIEND--BUT I GET THE GIST OF YOUR ARGUMENT.

ZAKT!
AND YOU'RE WRONG.
THE X-MEN FIGHT TO PROTECT THE RIGHTS OF ALL LIVING HUMAN BEINGS--
--REGARDLESS OF WHETHER THEY'RE HUMANS, MUTANTS--
--FRIEND OR FOE.
YOU'RE WELCOME TO LIVE ANY LIFE YOU WANT...
...UP UNTIL THE MOMENT YOU THREATEN SOME-ONE ELSE'S!

MOIRA?!
PLEASE PLEASE PLEASE BE ALIVE!

YE HAD TO WAIT...
...FOR THE FINAL REEL?
YOU KNOW CHARLE HE THRIVES ON THE LAST MINUTE RESCUES.

NOW HOLD TIGHT, MOIRA, I'LL HAVE YOOOOW!
SRRRIP
HEIGHT O' RUDENESS--
--HEIGHT O'!
FIRST YOU CRASH THE PARTY--
--CRASHED IT!
THEN YOU TRY TO SCOOTER OFF WITH THE HOST O'HONOR?

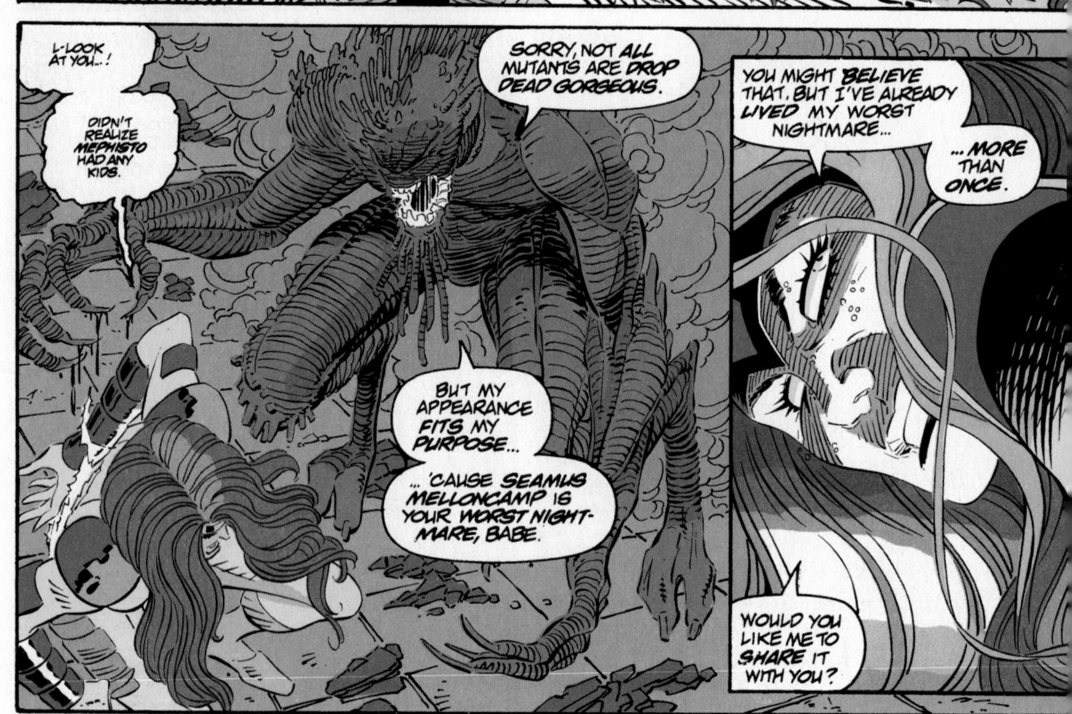
L-LOOK AT YOU...!
DIDN'T REALIZE MEPHISTO HAD ANY KIDS.
SORRY, NOT ALL MUTANTS ARE DROP DEAD GORGEOUS.
BUT MY APPEARANCE FITS MY PURPOSE...
...'CAUSE SEAMUS MELLONCAMP IS YOUR WORST NIGHT-MARE, BABE.
YOU MIGHT BELIEVE THAT. BUT I'VE ALREADY LIVED MY WORST NIGHTMARE...
...MORE THAN ONCE.
WOULD YOU LIKE ME TO SHARE IT WITH YOU?

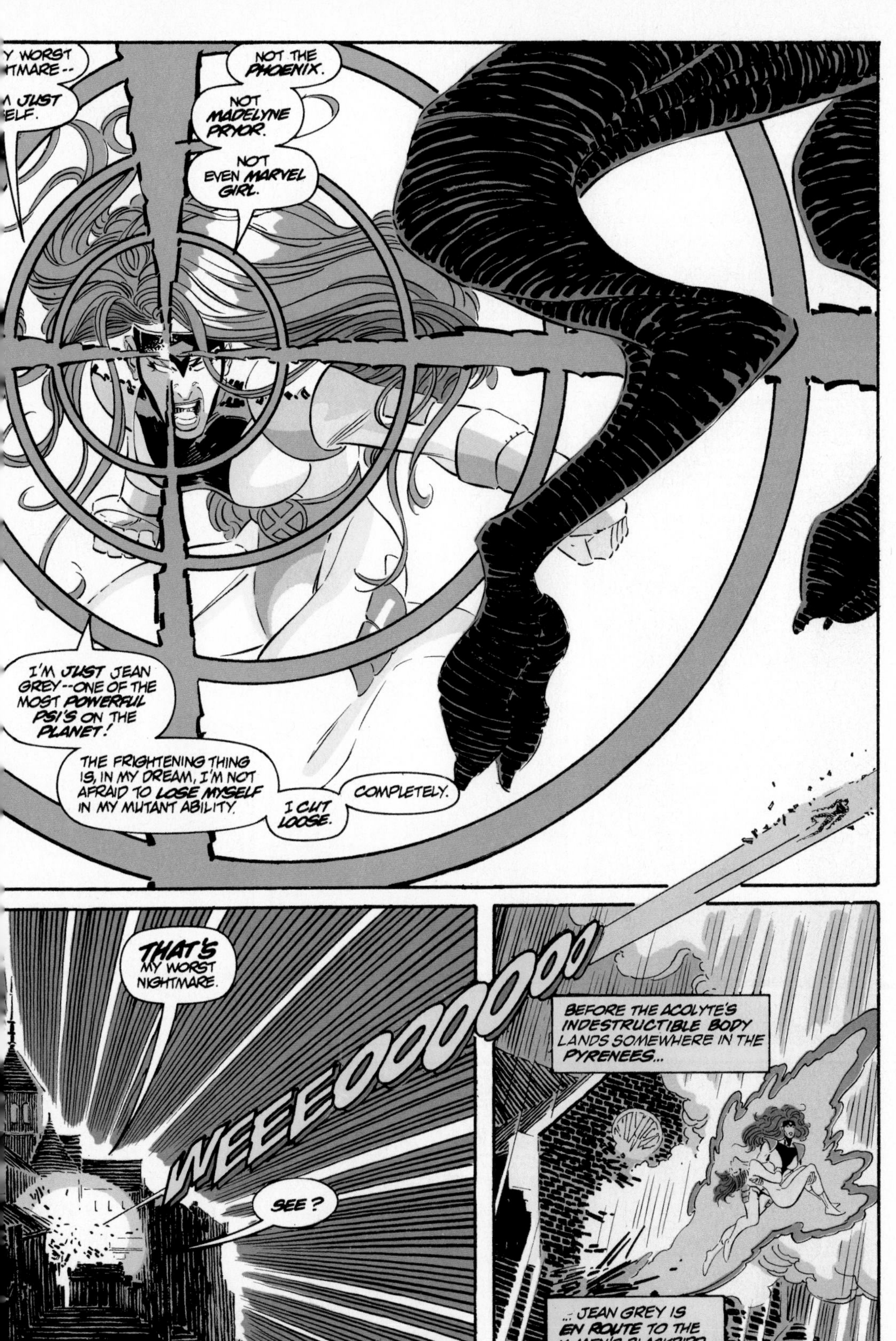

Y WORST
TMARE--
M JUST
ELF.
NOT THE PHOENIX.
NOT MADELYNE PRYOR.
NOT EVEN MARVEL GIRL.
I'M JUST JEAN GREY--ONE OF THE MOST POWERFUL PSI'S ON THE PLANET!
THE FRIGHTENING THING IS, IN MY DREAM, I'M NOT AFRAID TO LOSE MYSELF IN MY MUTANT ABILITY.
I CUT LOOSE.
COMPLETELY.
THAT'S MY WORST NIGHTMARE.
WEEEOOOOOOO
SEE?
BEFORE THE ACOLYTE'S INDESTRUCTIBLE BODY LANDS SOMEWHERE IN THE PYRENEES...
...JEAN GREY IS EN ROUTE TO THE X-MEN'S BLACKBIRD...
...AND THE MEDICAL FACILITIES WITHIN.

WHILE ONE BATTLE CONCLUDES--
--THE X-MEN HAVE NO ILLUSIONS THAT THEY'VE WON THE WAR.
THE ACOLYTES ARE DOWN, BUT PROFESSOR X AND BISHOP ARE AMONG THE MISSING!
I AM IN NO DANGER, CYCLOPS.
BUT BISHOP MAY NEED YOUR ASSISTANCE ON THE MONASTERY'S TURRETS.

OH, MASTER OF THE ENERGY THAT BLANKETS MOTHER EARTH--
--PLEASE DELIVER US FROM YOUR ENEMIES...
...SO THAT WE, YOUR CHILDREN, MAY CONTINUE TO SEEK OUR RIGHTFUL DOMINION OVER EARTH...

--NOW AND FOREVER.
AMEN.
I KNEW IT WAS YOU, AMELIA.
YOUR PSI-PATTERNS ARE UNMISTAKABLE.

ARE THEY, SIR?
AFTER ALL THESE YEARS?
--BECAUSE YOU'D CONVINCED ME YOU WANTED NO PART IN MY CLASS OF ORIGINAL STUDENTS.
YOU CLAIMED YOU HAD NO DESIRE TO TAKE SIDES IN--

THAT WAS WHEN I STILL HAD A FAMILY... PEOPLE WHO CARED FOR ME!
BEFORE I LOST EVERYONE I LOVE--LOST THEM TO THE FLATSCANS!

?!

...HIS WAY!
HOW DID YOU GET THIS, CHILD?
WHERE DID IT COME FROM?

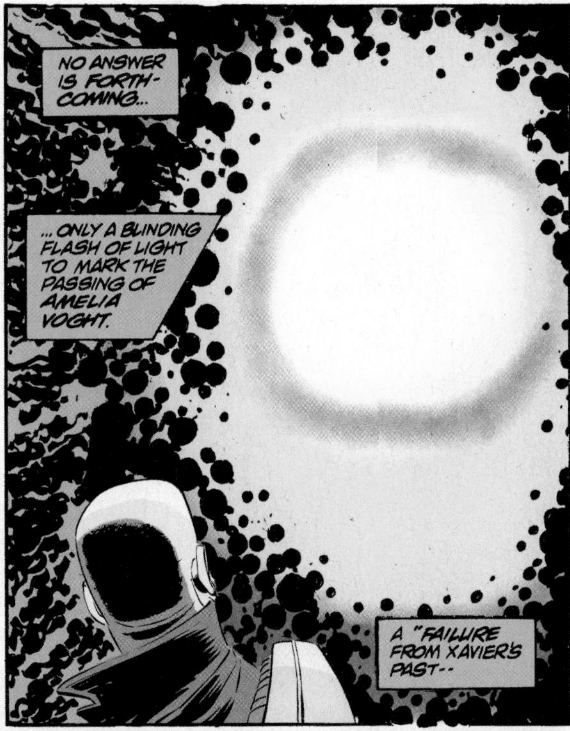
NO ANSWER IS FORTHCOMING...
...ONLY A BLINDING FLASH OF LIGHT TO MARK THE PASSING OF AMELIA VOGHT.
A "FAILURE FROM XAVIER'S PAST--

-SOMEHOW TIED TO THE STRUGGLE ET TO COME.
THE FIRE NEXT TIME.

GH ABOVE THE MONT AINT FRANCIS...
CURSE THIS STORM! IT INTERFERES WITH THE SATELLITE CAPABLE OF TRANSPORTING ME OUT OF THIS FIASCO!
C'MON, WOMAN, LOCK ON.
LOCK ON...
ANOTHER THIRTY-SECONDS, CORTEZ WOULD HAVE BEEN GONE.
UNFORTUNATELY FOR HIM --
SKRUCHK
BISHOP IS UNWILLING TO WAIT THAT LONG.

UNHAND ME YOU--
--TEMPORAL ABERRATION!
MAYBE.
EVENTUALLY.
BUT FIRST, EXPLAIN SOMETHING TO ME.
YOU'VE GOT ALL THE TRAPPINGS OF A MAJOR PLAYER, BUT --GET THIS-- IN THE FUTURE WHERE I WAS RAISED...
...NO ONE HAS EVER HEARD OF YOU.
THAT EITHER MEAN YOU SCRATCHED SOMEWHERE ALON THE LINE...
...OR MAYBE YOU DIED IN THE HER AND NOW!
BISHOP, NO!
CLOSER, 'RORO-HE CAN'T HEAR YA' OVER THE WIND!

IF YOU DON'T KNOW WHO I AM--
--THEN I'LL ASSUME YOU'RE IGNORANT AS TO HOW MY POWERS WORK.
ALLOW ME TO DEMON-STRATE.
THEY'RE BASED ON ENERGY--AND MY ABILITY TO AMPLIFY IT TO ANY DEGREE I SO CHOOSE.
YOU SEE, I MAKE IT A POINT TO BE INTIMATELY AWARE OF EVERY ASPECT OF MY ENEMIES--POTENIAL OR OTHERWISE.
THEIR STRENGTH WEAKNESSES...

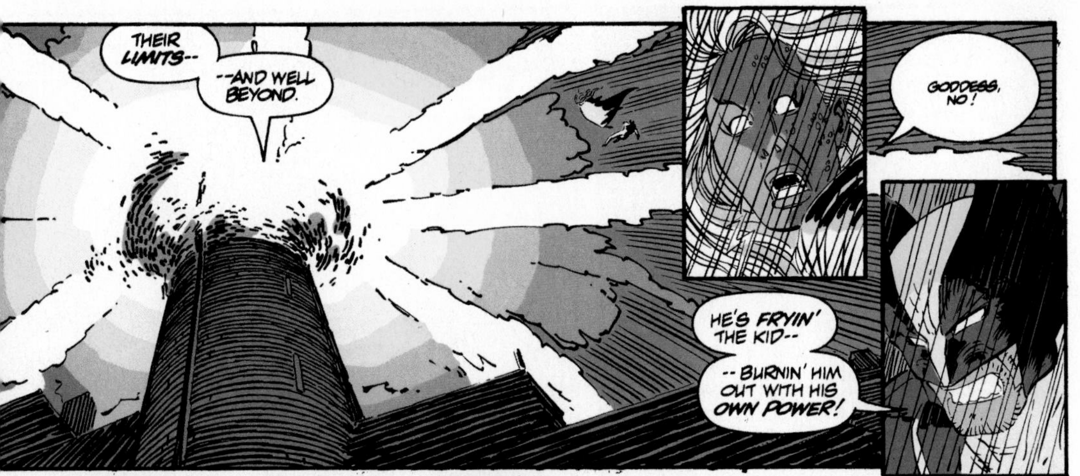
THEIR LIMITS--
--AND WELL BEYOND.
GODDESS, NO!
HE'S FRYIN' THE KID--
-- BURNIN' HIM OUT WITH HIS OWN POWER!

I KNOW THAT YOU-- FOR ALL INTENTS AND PURPOSES--ARE A WALKING POWER CELL...
...ONLY AS STRONG OR WEAK AT THE AMOUNT OF APPROPRIATED ENERGY IN YOUR BODY AT ANY GIVEN TIME.
TELL ME, BISHOP-- HAVE YOU EVER DARED EXHAUST ALL THAT ENERGY...

... EXPEND IT FROM EVERY PART OF YOUR BODY IN A SINGLE BLAST?

I'LL TAKE YOUR SILENCE AS A "NO".
NOW, AS MUCH AS I'VE ENJOYED THIS DIVERSION-- I MUST BE GOING.
YOU'LL FORGIVE ME, OF COURSE, IF I KILL YOU BEFORE I LEAVE?

GUIDE MY HAND, MAGNUS...
...THAT YOUR WILL BE DONE.
CORTEZ!
I WON'T STAN BY AND LET YO TAKE THE LIF OF ANOTHER MUTANT--
-- THE WAY YOU TURNED MAGNETO FROM SAVIOR TO A MARTYR!
WHAT I DID TO THAT FOSSIL, BOY--
--IS NOTHING COMPARED TO THE FATE THAT AWAITS YOU.
A SINGLE BLAST WILL REDUCE YOU TO SO
SNIKT
I...
...I'M STILL
BREATHING?
LUCKY YOU.

ORORO?
REST EASY, BISHOP--ROBERT IS BRINGING THE BLACK-BIRD.
I SUPPOSE YOU WILL INTERROGATE ME--SUBVERT MY WILL AND ENLIST ME IN YOUR CAUSE?
DESPITE WHAT YOU MAY HAVE BEEN TAUGHT--THE X-MEN DON'T WORK THAT WAY.
IF THE DAY COMES YOU CHOSE TO STAND WITH US--
--IT MUST BE YOUR OWN DECISION.
THAT DAY THAT I TRUST
...YOU WILL HEAR FROM ME.
UNTIL THEN, I AM AFRAID I MUST FIND MY OWN WAY IN THE WORLD.
FOR YOU AND MAGNETO ARE BOTH GREAT MEN, PROFESSOR XAVIER--
--AND YOUR DREAMS MIGHT BE MORE SIMILAR...
...THAN EITHER OF YOU REALIZE.
End.

FABIAN CORTEZ ALWAYS BELIEVED HIMSELF TO BE ABOVE PETTY SENSATIONS SUCH AS PAIN.
WRITHING ABOUT IN AGONY WAS FOR LESSER BEINGS... FOR HUMANS.
THAT WAS BEFORE WOLVERINE.
BEFORE COLD, HARD ADAMANTIUM PIERCED HIS CHEST-- PUNCTURING THE HEATED CAVITY WHICH HOUSED HIS FRAGILE LUNGS.
CERTAINLY, IT WAS BEFORE HE FOUND HIMSELF IN THE GRIP OF VOGHT'S TRANSUBSTANTIATION PROCESS.
EPILOG
SCOTT LOBDELL -- SCRIPT
BRANDON PETERSON -- PENCILS
DAN PANOSIAN -- INKS: PAGES 1-4
AL MILGROM -- INKS: PAGES 5-8
RICHARD STARKINGS -- LETTERS
GLYNIS OLIVER -- COLORS
IT WILL HURT LESS IF YOU CEASE YOUR STRUGGLES.
YOU ARE ALMOST HERE M'LORD.

WHTCH!
I WAS IN THE HOSPITAL FOR A WEEK!
WHY'D YOU WAIT S'LONG TO LIBERATE ME..?
AS YOU CAN, NO DOUBT, ATTEST--
--MY MUTANT MODE OF TRANSPORT IS NOWHERE NEAR AS ENJOYABLE AS, SAY, NIGHT-CRAWLER'S.
I HAD TO INSURE YOUR WOUNDS WERE SUFFICIENTLY HEALED...
...THE LAST THING I NEED TO BE ACCUSED OF IS TRYING TO KILL OUR ANOINTED LEADER.
AND IT IS HARDLY THE WAY TO ADDRESS HE WHO SPEAKS IN THE VOICE OF MAGNETO.
SARCASM ISN'T YOUR STRONG SUIT, WOMAN...
NO, FABIAN.
IT IS NOT.

WHAT'S THE MATTER, CORTEZ -- TROUBLE IN PARADISE?
GAMES-MASTER?

EXCELLENT! NO DOUBT YOU'VE COME TO AWARD ME POINTS FOR THE DEATH OF THE X-MAN, BISHOP -- HE MUST HAVE DIED WHILE I WAS RECOVERING IN FRANCE.
MY LEADERSHIP OF THE UPSTARTS WILL BE UNDISPUTED!
ON THE CONTRARY CORTEZ ...
...ON BOTH COUNTS.
IT SEEMS THE YOUNG MAN IS MORE RESILIENT THAN ANYONE GAVE HIM CREDIT FOR -- THE EXCEPTION BEING FITZROY.
AS TO YOUR ROLE AS CZAR OF THE UPSTARTS...
...LET'S JUST SAY YOU SHOULD HOLD OFF CHANGING THE TITLE ON YOUR STATIONERY ANY TIME SOON...

I'M SORRY TO INFORM YOU, RECENT COMPLICATIONS HAVE ARISEN --
-- WHICH NECESSITATE THAT I TAKE AWAY ALL THE POINTS YOU'VE ACQUIRED TO DATE.

NO! I WILL NOT ALLOW THIS TO HAPPEN!
MAGNETO'S DEATH WAS A DIRECT RESULT OF MY ACTIONS!
WHAT POSSIBLE "COMPLICATIONS" COULD CHANGE THAT?!

FIGURE IT OUT FOR YOURSELF...
DON'T FADE AWAY ON ME WHILE I'M SPEAKING TO YOU!
I'M NOT LIKE THE REST OF THE UPSTARTS!
I WAS BORN ROYALTY -- AND I WILL NOT BE DISMISSED LIKE A BOTHERSOME CHILD!
CURSE HIM!
WITH MY HOLD OVER THE ACOLYTES GROWING MORE TENUOUS BY THE MOMENT--
--MY DOMINION OVER THE UPSTARTS IS NO LONGER AN AMUSING DIVERSION...
...IT IS NOW A MATTER OF SALVATION!
HOW COULD I POSSIBLY LOSE THE POINTS FOR MAGNUS'S DEATH, UNLESS..?
...
NOOO!
SKRASH!

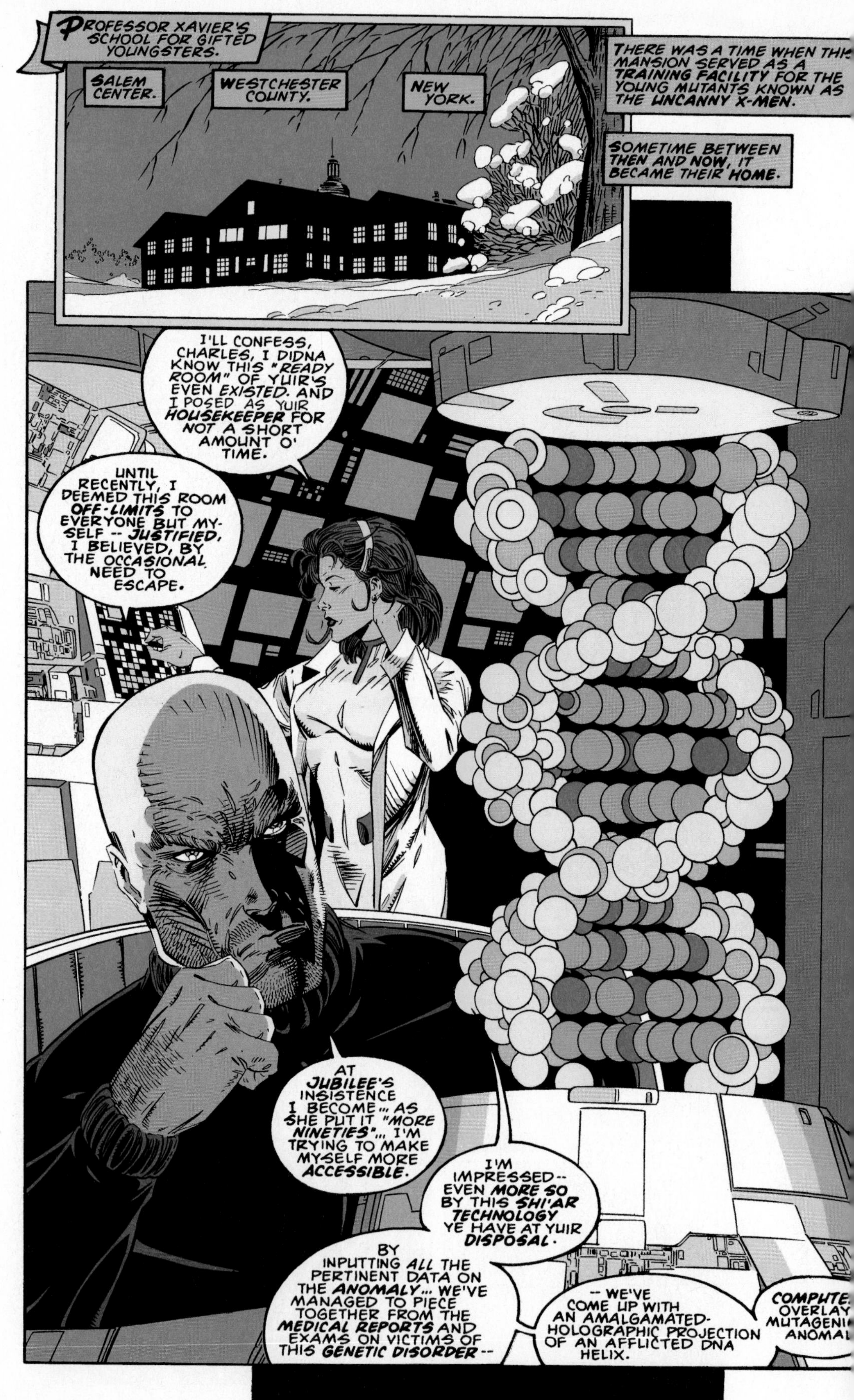
PROFESSOR XAVIER'S SCHOOL FOR GIFTED YOUNGSTERS.
SALEM CENTER.
WESTCHESTER COUNTY.
NEW YORK.
THERE WAS A TIME WHEN THIS MANSION SERVED AS A TRAINING FACILITY FOR THE YOUNG MUTANTS KNOWN AS THE UNCANNY X-MEN.
SOMETIME BETWEEN THEN AND NOW, IT BECAME THEIR HOME.
I'LL CONFESS, CHARLES, I DIDNA KNOW THIS "READY ROOM" OF YUIR'S EVEN EXISTED. AND I POSED AS YUIR HOUSEKEEPER FOR NOT A SHORT AMOUNT O' TIME.
UNTIL RECENTLY, I DEEMED THIS ROOM OFF-LIMITS TO EVERYONE BUT MY-SELF -- JUSTIFIED, I BELIEVED, BY THE OCCASIONAL NEED TO ESCAPE.
AT JUBILEE'S INSISTENCE I BECOME... AS SHE PUT IT "MORE NINETIES"... I'M TRYING TO MAKE MYSELF MORE ACCESSIBLE.
I'M IMPRESSED-- EVEN MORE SO BY THIS SHI'AR TECHNOLOGY YE HAVE AT YUIR DISPOSAL.
BY INPUTTING ALL THE PERTINENT DATA ON THE ANOMALY... WE'VE MANAGED TO PIECE TOGETHER FROM THE MEDICAL REPORTS AND EXAMS ON VICTIMS OF THIS GENETIC DISORDER--
-- WE'VE COME UP WITH AN AMALGAMATED-HOLOGRAPHIC PROJECTION OF AN AFFLICTED DNA HELIX.

Overlay:Complete
Acch, CHARLES-- HAVE YE EVER SEEN SUCH A VILE SIGHT? THE WORST PART IS, AS NEAR AS WE CAN TELL, THE ANOMALY HAS EFFECTED EACH VICTIM'S GENES DIFFERENTLY.
AS IF THIS WEE INTRUDER IS MUTATING ITSELF WITH EACH NEW VICTIM.
NO MATTER HOW REPULSIVE THE THOUGHT, MOIRA--
--I'M AFRAID THAT YOU AND I MUST ACCEPT THE REALITY THAT SOMETHING... OR SOMEONE... HAS RELEASED A VIRUS UPON THE UNSUSPECTING MUTANT POPULACE.
WHILE I WAS IN GENOSHA, TENDING TO THE HANDFUL OF SICK AND DYING...*
...I WAS HOPING AGAINST HOPE THAT IT WAS STRICTLY A MUTATE PROBLEM CAUSED BY THEIR ACCELERATED BIOLOGIES.
* X-FACTOR #90 --B.H.
SIMILARLY, THE INFORMATION I HAVE BEEN GATHERING OVER THE LAST SEVERAL WEEKS* HAS PROVED INCONCLUSIVE UNTIL THIS MOMENT.
WE CAN NO LONGER IGNORE THE OBVIOUS.
* SINCE #298 --B.H.
I CANNAE BELIEVE THE FATES CAN BE THIS CRUEL.
IS PAIN AND SUFFERING--
DEATH AND DYING--
ALWAYS GOING TO BE THE LEGACY OF BEING BORN A MUTANT.
LEGACY.

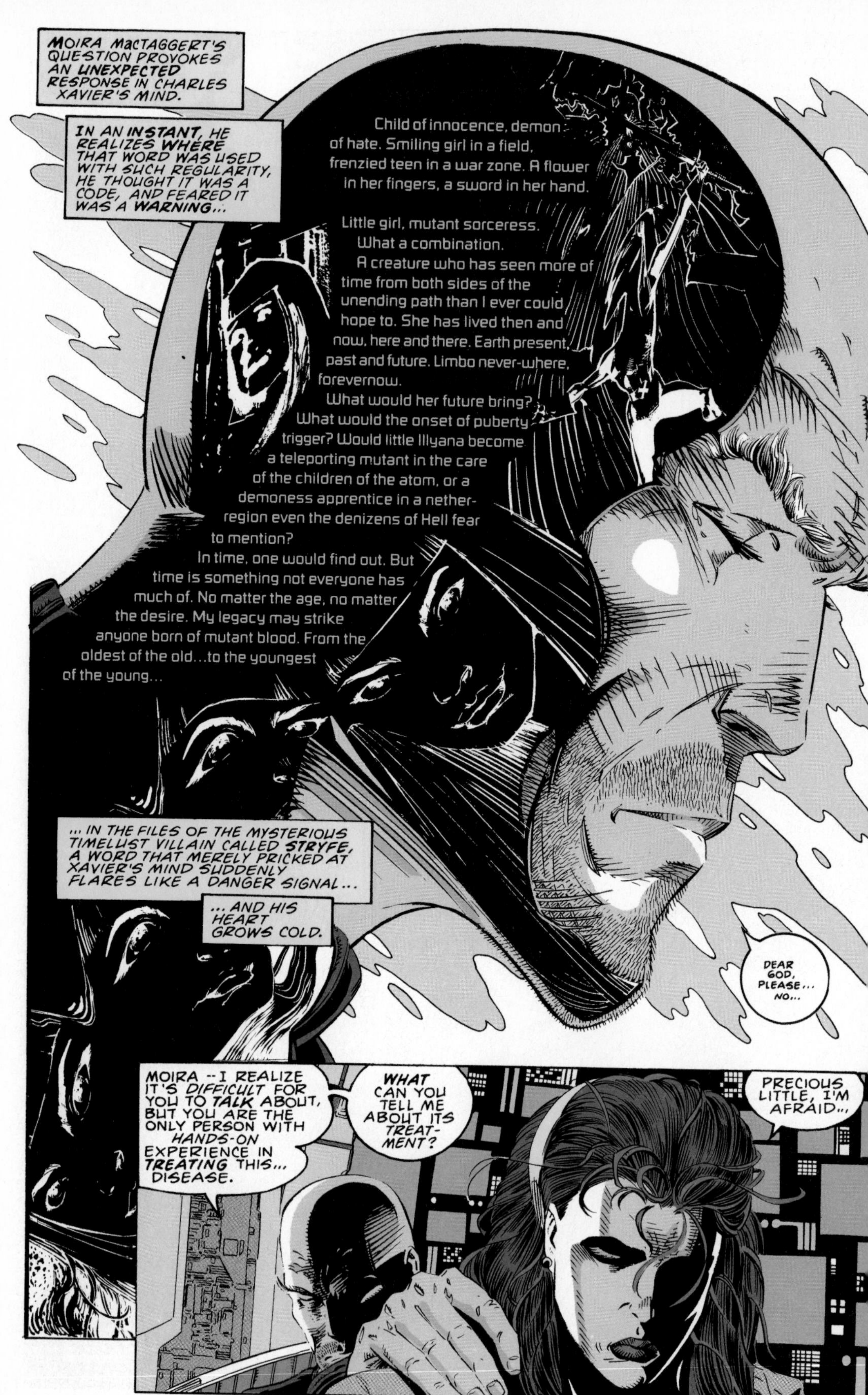
MOIRA MacTAGGERT'S QUESTION PROVOKES AN UNEXPECTED RESPONSE IN CHARLES XAVIER'S MIND.
IN AN INSTANT, HE REALIZES WHERE THAT WORD WAS USED WITH SUCH REGULARITY, HE THOUGHT IT WAS A CODE, AND FEARED IT WAS A WARNING...
Child of innocence, demon of hate. Smiling girl in a field, frenzied teen in a war zone. A flower in her fingers, a sword in her hand.
Little girl, mutant sorceress. What a combination. A creature who has seen more of time from both sides of the unending path than I ever could hope to. She has lived then and now, here and there. Earth present, past and future. Limbo never-where, forevernow. What would her future bring? What would the onset of puberty trigger? Would little Illyana become a teleporting mutant in the care of the children of the atom, or a demoness apprentice in a nether-region even the denizens of Hell fear to mention? In time, one would find out. But time is something not everyone has much of. No matter the age, no matter the desire. My legacy may strike anyone born of mutant blood. From the oldest of the old...to the youngest of the young...
...IN THE FILES OF THE MYSTERIOUS TIMELUST VILLAIN CALLED STRYFE, A WORD THAT MERELY PRICKED AT XAVIER'S MIND SUDDENLY FLARES LIKE A DANGER SIGNAL...
...AND HIS HEART GROWS COLD.
DEAR GOD, PLEASE... NO...
MOIRA --I REALIZE IT'S DIFFICULT FOR YOU TO TALK ABOUT, BUT YOU ARE THE ONLY PERSON WITH HANDS-ON EXPERIENCE IN TREATING THIS... DISEASE.
WHAT CAN YOU TELL ME ABOUT ITS TREATMENT?
PRECIOUS LITTLE, I'M AFRAID...

"... IN EVERY ONE OF THE CASES I'VE BEEN *IN-VOLVED* IN--
"--THE RESULTS ARE ALL *EXACTLY* THE *SAME*.
"WHAT I'M TRYING TO TELL YE, IS THERE *IS NO TREATMENT*.
"*ONCE* CONTRACTED--
"--THIS VIRUS IS *TERMINAL*."
CLICK

Marvel Universe 1994 "Fatal Attractions" trading-card art by Kerry Gammill, Greg Adams & Paul Mounts

The government-sponsored mutant team X-Factor encountered a group of refugees who had fled Genosha, an island nation whose government transformed mutants into mutate slaves. After rescuing these refugee "X-Patriots" from the mutant mercenary Random, X-Factor convinced them to return home, explaining that Genosha's anti-mutant regime had recently fallen and the new government was working to free the mutates.

However, when X-Factor and the X-Patriots arrived in Genosha, they discovered that most of the mutates were dying of a mysterious and incurable disease, which Genoshan doctors were helpless to treat or understand. One mutate escaped the hospital's quarantine, and X-Factor — concerned that he might infect others — volunteered to track him down. Multiple Man found the mutate dying and unable to breathe. After a moment's hesitation, he gave the mutate CPR, even though it meant exposing himself to the virus.

Meanwhile, X-Factor's government liaison Val Cooper was secretly abducted by strange wormlike creatures. Although she was returned unharmed, her behavior became sinister and manipulative — and she seemed to be in league with a mysterious group that was manipulating Quicksilver, trying to increase his feelings of alienation by subtlely driving a wedge between him and his estranged wife Crystal.

Later, the X-Men were called to Muir Island by their old foe Mastermind, who was also dying of a mysterious disease. Colossus, still very upset by his parents' recent deaths and worried about Illyana's failing health, became increasingly resentful at being constantly separated from his family by X-Men business.

The villainous X-Cutioner attacked the island hoping to kill Mastermind, and the X-Men drove him off — but Colossus received a massive injury during the battle, a large dent in his metallic head that made it impossible for him to return to human form. Despite the X-Men's and the doctors' efforts, Mastermind died.

Later, after the X-Men's jet was downed in Antarctica by a member of the Upstarts, Professor X's life was saved by a mysterious cloaked figure who resided in an electro-magnetically shielded Antarctic citadel.

The Upstarts' next target was Forge, and the X-Men raced to Texas to protect him. The X-Men defeated the attacking Trevor Fitzroy — but Colossus, absolutely fed up with the X-Men's priorities once again stopping him from being by Illyana's side, beat Fitzroy nearly to death before the X-Men restrained him.

Back at the X-Mansion, Professor X and Moira MacTaggert noted the worrying similarity between Illyana's symptoms and those of Mastermind and the Genoshan mutates. And as Shadowcat arrived from England to be

MARVEL COMICS
THE UNCANNY
X-MEN
$1.25 US
$1.60 CAN/UK 85p
303
AUG
APPROVED BY THE COMICS CODE AUTHORITY
02461
IF YOU READ ONLY ONE X-TITLE THIS MONTH-- THIS ISSUE MUST BE IT!

JUBILEE...
... ARE YOU IN HERE?
THOUGH VOICED IN GENUINE CONCERN, JEAN GREY'S QUESTION RINGS AS HOLLOW AS THE SOUND OF HER FOOT-STEPS UPON THE COLD METAL FLOOR.
FOR THE TRUTH IS, SHE KNOWS EXACTLY WHERE JUBILEE IS..
... HOW LONG SHE'S BEEN HERE...
... WHY THE GIRL CHOSE THE PRO-FESSOR'S READY ROOM...
... AND EXACTLY WHAT HER YOUNGEST TEAMMATE IS THINKING.
SHE KNOWS THESE THINGS BECAUSE SHE IS A MUTANT--
-- BORN WITH THE POWER TO READ MINDS, AND TELE-KINETICALLY MOVE OBJECTS WITH MERE THOUGHT-WAVES.
THERE HAVE BEEN MANY TIMES IN HER LIFE -- FIRST AS MARVEL GIRL...
... LATER AS A GENETIC TEMPLATE TO THE COSMIC ENTITY CALLED THE PHOENIX...
... THAT JEAN HAS FELT BLESSED BY THE ABILITY TO REACH OUT AND TOUCH ANOTHER'S MIND.
TO SHARE THEIR PAIN, THEIR JOY--
-- THEIR FEELINGS OF HOPELESSNESS, OF HAPPINESS.
THIS IS NOT ONE OF THOSE TIMES.

I KNOW, I KNOW--
"THIS AREA IS OFF-LIMITS! ALL OF PROFESSOR XAVIER'S MOST IMPORTANT INFORMATION IS STORED HERE!
"IF YOU WANT SOMEPLACE TO SULK--TRY THE DANGER ROOM!"
YOU'RE LIKE, NOT THE ONLY PERSON WHO READS MINDS, YA' KNOW.
NOT AT ALL. BUT I'M APPARENTLY MUCH BETTER AT IT THAN YOU ARE.
THE ONLY REASON I'M HERE IS TO MAKE SURE YOU'RE OKAY AFTER...
TZZZT
...AFTER EVERYTHING THAT HAPPENED.
IF YOU'RE WAITING FOR ME TO WILT AND START BLUBBERIN', FORGET IT.
I DON'T DO THAT CRYIN' THING.
BUT--
--IF YO TO KNOW I'M THIN CAN SUM IN TWO W

STAN LEE PRESENTS THE
UNCANNY X-MEN
GOING THROUGH THE MOTIONS
SCOTT LOBDELL WRITER
CHRIS ELIOPOULOS LETTERER
JOE ROSAS COLORIST
BOB HARRAS EDITOR
TOM DeFALCO EDITOR IN CHIEF
RICHARD BENNETT SPECIAL GUEST ARTIST
DAN GREEN INKS PGS. 8, 14-18
YES. SOMETIMES IT DOES.
WOULD YOU LIKE TO TALK ABOUT IT?
WHY?
PKOP
PRIP
TKOT
IS TALKING ABOUT IT GOING TO CHANGE ANYTHING?

NOT EVEN A LITTLE, JUBILEE.
THE ONLY THING THAT MIGHT CHANG IS THE WAY YOU FE ABOUT WHAT YOU--
--WHAT ALL OF US--
--HAVE JUST GONE THROUGH.
FINE!
THEN YOU START-- MS. SALLY JEANGREY RAPHAEL -- TELL ME WHAT YOU'RE FEELING!
FAIR ENOUGH.
I'M SAD. HURT. ANGRY.
FRUSTRATED.
BUT MOSTLY... CONCERNED.
ABOUT ME?
YES. ABOUT YOU.
I...
...I DON'T KNOW WHY I SHOULDDA BEEN SURPRISED BY EVERYTHING THAT WENT DOWN--

--IT'S NOT LIKE WE DIDN'T SEE IT COMING A MILE AWAY.
BUT IT'S DIFFERENT WHEN IT ACTUALLY HAPPENS.
NO MATTER WHAT YOU DO TO PSYCH YOURSELF UP...
JUBILEE
"...NO MATTER HOW MUCH YOU SAY TO YOURSELF, 'I CAN HANDLE THIS,' YA' REALLY CAN'T.
"IT'S, LIKE, MAKING ALL YER STOMACH MUSCLES TIGHT 'CAUSE YOU'RE EXPECTING A PUNCH TO THE GUT--
"--THEN AT THE LAST SECOND, LIFE DECIDES T'KICK YA' IN THE TEETH INSTEAD.
"I MEAN, IT WAS JUST--WHAT, SIX HOURS AGO--
"--PRACTICALLY EVERY-BODY WAS EITHER STILL CLEANING UP IN TEXAS...
"--OR HANGING OUT IN JAPAN WITH THE HEAD TWINS.
"THE WHOLE MANSION WAS AS QUIET AS A--
"--IT WAS REAL QUIET.

"'CEPT IN THE MED-LAB.
"THAT'S WHERE EVERY-BODY WAS HANGIN' ON ACCOUNT OF THE PIM-UH...
"...ON ACCOUNT OF ILLYANA BEIN' SICK AND ALL.
"ME AND HER WERE IN THE SICK BED PART, WHILE DOC MacTAGGERT AND THE PROF WERE BUTTIN' HEADS OVER WHAT TO DO FOR PETER'S SISTER."
I DINNAE MEAN T'BE SO NEGATIVE, CHARLES--BUT THIS IS GETTING US NOWHERE.
WE NEED A FRESH PERSPECTIVE ON THIS INFORMATION WE HAVE CONCERNING THE CHILD'S GENETIC DETERIORATION. AND BARRING THAT--
--WE NEED A MIRACLE.
ONCE THE GOLD TEAM RETURNS FROM DALLAS WITH FORGE, I AM CERTAIN WE CAN--AT THE VERY LEAST--FIND SOME TREATMENT TO ARREST THE PROGRESS OF THIS... DISORDER.
"CERTAIN," ARE YE?
WHERE THERE'S LIFE, MOIRA...
UMMM, AUF WIEDERSEHEN...
ACCH, GESUNDHEIT.
SAUERKRAUT.
"HERE I WAS SCORIN' MAJOR POINTS WITH MY BI-LINGUALISM--
"--BUT THE BIGGEST SMILE OF THE NIGHT WASN'T EVEN MINE..."
KATYA!
"KATYA, WHAT?

E WAS FERRING ME, BILEE.
KATYA IS RUSSIAN FOR "KITTY."
DUH WITH A CAPITAL "H".
LIKE I'M NEW TO THIS PLANET OR SOMETHING?
"MMMAYBE I COULD HAVE SHOWN LESS 'TUDE, BUT THERE WAS SOMETHING ABOUT KITTY PRYDE THAT JUST TOTALLY TORKED ME OFF.
"SHE HADN'T BEEN AN X-MAN IN, LIKE, A ZILLION YEARS...
"...THEN FIVE MINUTES BACK IN THE MANSION, AND SHE'S ACTING LIKE THIS IS HER CRIB."
THANK YOU FOR KEEPING AN EYE ON HER WHILE I GOT SOME FRESH LINEN.
NO BIGGIE.
NOT LIKE I HAVEN'T BEEN KEEPIN' AN EYE ON HER FOR THE PAST FEW WEEKS.
‹KATYA--YOU'VE RETURNED! ANY WORD FROM BROTHER?!› *
‹YES, ILLYANA. HE WILL BE HOME BY DAWN, AND HE ASKED THAT YOU PROMISE TO GET PLENTY OF REST BEFORE HE COMES BACK.›
* TRANSLATED FROM THE RUSSIAN.--BOBSKI
"I DIDN'T HAVE CLUE ONE WHAT THEY WERE TALKIN' ABOUT--
"--BUT IT WAS CLEAR KITTY JUST BEIN' THERE PAINTED ILLYANA FIVE SHADES OF HAPPY.
"WHICH IS THE PART THAT I DON'T GET..."

...KITTY'S OLD, LIKE -- WHAT-- SIXTEEN, SEVENTEEN?
ILLYANA IS BARELY SEVEN, YET THE TWO OF 'EM ACT LIKE THEY'RE THE BESTEST BUDS IN THE WORLD.
FOUR ON THE FLOOR. FRONT-WHEEL DRIVE. TOTALLY ALIGNED.
THEY GO BACK A LONG WAY.
THERE WAS A TIME, WHEN ILLYANA WAS OLDER THAN SHE IS NOW...
...WHEN SHE AND KITTY WERE CLOSER IN AGE.
YER LOSIN' ME, RED.
NOT SURPRISING. HERE--
-- IT'D BE EASIER IF I SHOWED YOU.
I REALIZE YOU'RE NOT A BIG FAN OF STUDYING, BUT ALL THE INFORMATION ABOUT THE X-MEN'S PAST-- IN ALL ITS INCARNATIONS-- IS IN THE ARCHIVES.
FROM THE FIRST GRADUATING CLASS HERE AT XAVIER'S SCHOOL FOR GIFTED YOUNGSTERS--
--THROUGH THE SECOND GENERATION X-MEN, TO X-FACTOR, AND THE--
-- THE PRE-X-FORCE DUDES, THE NEW MUTANTS... I'M NOT A TOTAL SHIRK.
SO WHO'S THE HOT-LOOKING BLONDE?

MAYBE I SHOULD START AT THE BEGINNING..
... WHEN ILLYANA WAS FIRST BROUGHT TO THE STATES AS THE LUNATIC ASSASSIN *ARCADE'S* HOSTAGE, WE--
HER, I RECOGNIZE!
DO YOU WANT TO *HEAR* THIS, OR NOT?
SHEESH. 'SCUSE ME FOR BREATHIN'.
AFTER AN UNFORTUNATE ENCOUNTER WITH AN INTER-DIMENSIONAL WARLORD CALLED *BELASCO*, ILLYANA *EMERGED* FROM "LIMBO--"
--SEVEN YEARS OLDER, HER MUTANT ABILITY TO CREATE TELEPORTATION DISCS FULLY DEVELOPED...
... BUT HER CHILDHOOD *SHATTERED*.
POLAROID
ALTHOUGH SHE JOINED AND WORKED *WELL* WITH THE OTHER MEMBERS OF THE PROFESSOR'S *NEW MUTANTS*--
--SHE'D ALWAYS FELT AS IF SHE, AS SHE PUT IT, WAS "AN *OUTSIDER AMONG OUTSIDERS*."
MAYBE IT WAS THEIR *AGE*--
--MAYBE THEIR MUTUAL FEELINGS ABOUT *NOT* QUITE FITTING IN...
... BUT SHE AND KITTY BECAME THE BEST OF FRIENDS.
INSEPARABLE.
EVEN AFTER ILLYANA *REVERTED* BACK TO HER ORIGINAL AGE...
... AFTER SHE WAS RETURNED TO HER *PARENTS* IN RUSSIA...
ENGLAND
... KITTY MADE IT A POINT TO STAY IN TOUCH THROUGH *CARDS* AND LETTERS.
EVEN THOUGH THE KID HAD *NO MEMORIES* ABOUT THEM BEIN' FRIENDS?
EVEN THOUGH.
HUNH.
COOL.

LOOK, IF YOU WANT TO GO CHECK ON PETER OR -- LIKE SOMEONE IMPORTANT...
I'M ALREADY DOING THAT, JUBILEE.
NOW YOU WERE SAYING? KITTY HAD ARRIVED AND WAS WATCHING OVER ILLYANA --

"RIGHT. OKAY, SO I'M FEELIN' AS USEFUL AS A SEAT BELT ON A PAIR O' ROLLER BLADES --

"-- AND THINKIN' AT LEAST THE PROFESSOR WOULD HAVE SOME KIND OF ENCOURAGIN' WORDS.."

WHAT'S THE PROG, DOC? HOW MUCH LONGER IS SHE GONNA' BE HACKIN' AND WHEEZIN' HERSELF TO SLEEP...

...EVERY...

...NIGHT?

"HE WASN'T BEIN' RUDE OR NOTHIN', I COULD TELL.

"HE JUST DIDN'T SAY ANYTHING...

"... IT WAS LIKE HE COULDN'T BRING HIM-SELF T'CHOKE OUT THE WORDS.

"NOT THAT HE HAD TO.
"IT WAS ALL RIGHT THERE ON HIS FACE.

"NO MATTER WHAT THEY DID, THEY WEREN'T GONNA' PULL IT OFF...
"...'CAUSE ILLYANA WAS DYIN'.
"THERE WAS NOTHIN' ANY-ONE COULD DO ABOUT IT."

LOOK... PROFESSOR... IT'S NOT YOUR FAULT.

I HONESTLY DON'T KNOW HOW TO ANSWER THAT.

WHATEVER ILLYANA HAS CONTRACTED--

--HOWEVER SHE CONTRACTED IT--

--BEGAN BY ATTACKING HER BODY ON A MOLECULAR LEVEL...CENTERING IN ON HER NUCLEIC ACIDS...

...THE PURINE AND PYRIMIDINE BASES OF HER RECOMBINANT DNA ARE DETERIORATING AT AN INCREDIBLY ACCELERATED PACE. POLYMEASE PRODUCTION HAS PRACTICALLY CEASED.

AT THIS POINT, WE CAN'T EVEN STOP THE PROGRESS OF THIS VIRUS...

...LET ALONE HEAL THE DAMAGE ALREADY DONE.

"I FELT MAJORLY BUMMED FOR THE GUY.
"IT'S ONE THING IF AN X-MAN BUYS IT IN THE SLUGFEST DU JOUR...
"...BUT SHE'S JUST A KID.
"SNOW WHITE.
"LIKE, SHE WAS JUST BEIN' PUNISHED FOR BEIN' A MUTANT...
"...AND HE'S THE FATHER OF ALL MUTANTS.

"I WANTED TO, I DON'T KNOW... HUG HIM.
"TELL HIM NOT TO BLAME HIMSELF.
"THAT EVERYTHING WAS GONNA BE OKAY."

"INSTEAD, I LEFT..."

SEEIN' AS NOBODY NEEDS ME FOR NOTHIN', I'M GONNA GO TO BED.
RIGHT NOW.
IN MY ROOM.
BY MYSELF.
WITH NOBODY ELSE.
'CEPT ME.

JUBILEE, WAIT A MOMENT.
WHA'SUP? IF YER LOOKING FOR SOME-BODY T'MAKE A BEN & JERRY'S RUN, YOU'RE OUTTA LUCK.
HARDLY.
ILLYANA WANTED YOU TO KNOW HOW MUCH SHE APPRECIATES YOU LOOKING AFTER HER.
SHE WAS HOPING YOU COULD STAY AWHILE -- GET TO KNOW EACH OTHER.
WITH YOU PROVIDING THE SUB-TITLES?
HA! SOME-THING LIKE THAT.

UMMM, YEAH. SURE.
I GOTTA FEW MINUTES TO SPARE.
<BAMF THANKS YOU FOR HELPING HIM TALK.>
SHE SAID...
"IT WAS THEN THAT I GUESS MAYBE I KINDA REALIZED THAT KITTY MIGHT NOT BE HALF THE DWEEB I ALWAYS THOUGHT SHE WAS.
"'COURSE, NO SELF-RESPECTING TEEN I KNOW WOULD CALL HERSELF 'KITTY'..."

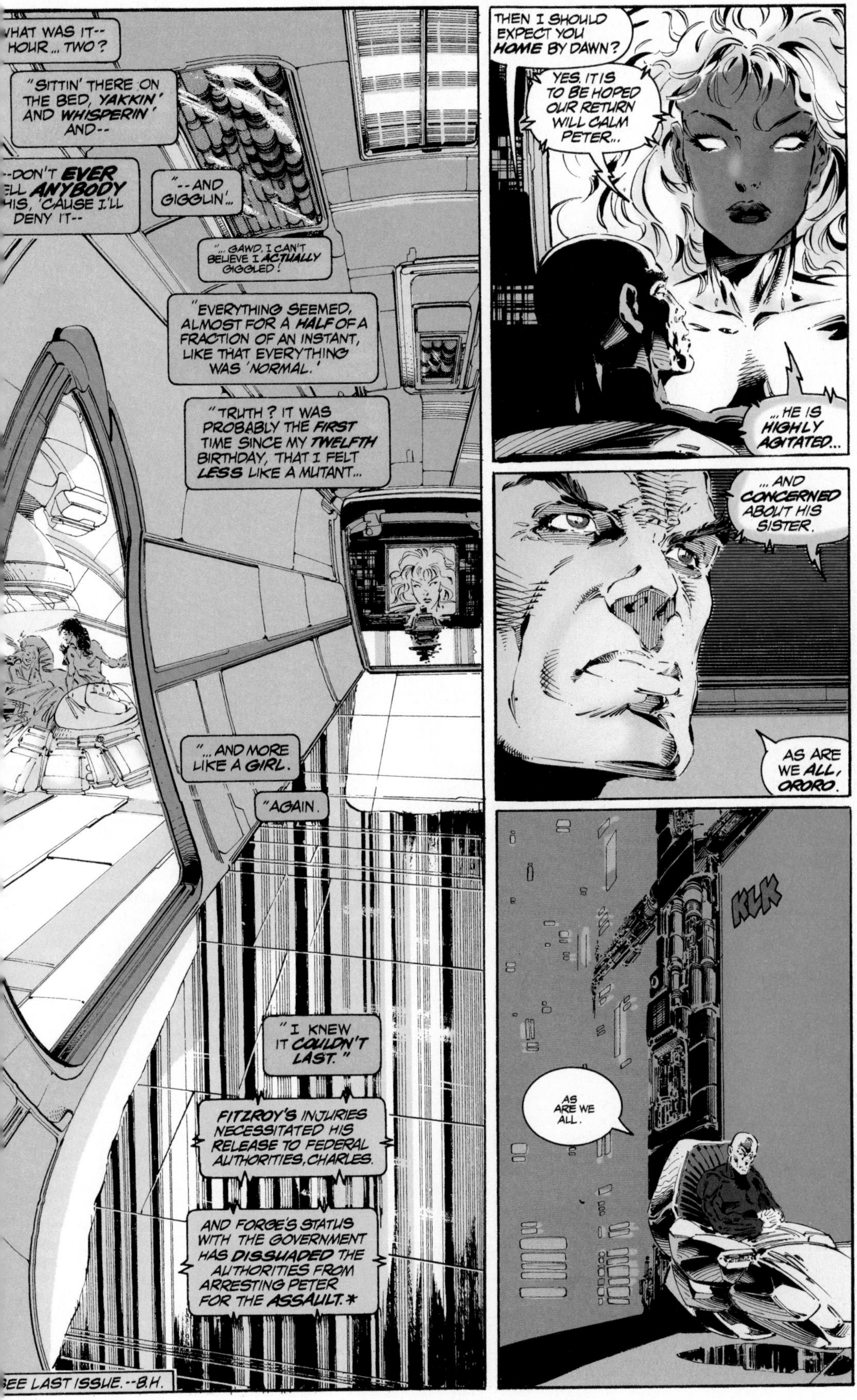

VHAT WAS IT--
HOUR... TWO?

"SITTIN' THERE ON THE BED, **YAKKIN'** AND **WHISPERIN'** AND--

--DON'T **EVER**
ELL **ANYBODY**
HIS, 'CAUSE I'LL
DENY IT--

"--AND GIGGLIN'...

"...GAWD, I CAN'T BELIEVE I **ACTUALLY** GIGGLED!

"EVERYTHING SEEMED, ALMOST FOR A **HALF** OF A FRACTION OF AN INSTANT, LIKE THAT EVERYTHING WAS 'NORMAL.'

"TRUTH? IT WAS PROBABLY THE **FIRST** TIME SINCE MY **TWELFTH** BIRTHDAY, THAT I FELT **LESS** LIKE A MUTANT...

"...AND MORE LIKE A **GIRL**.

"AGAIN.

"I KNEW IT **COULDN'T LAST**."

FITZROY'S INJURIES NECESSITATED HIS RELEASE TO FEDERAL AUTHORITIES, CHARLES.

AND FORGE'S STATUS WITH THE GOVERNMENT HAS **DISSUADED** THE AUTHORITIES FROM ARRESTING PETER FOR THE **ASSAULT**.*

*EE LAST ISSUE.--B.H.

THEN I SHOULD EXPECT YOU **HOME** BY DAWN?
YES. IT IS TO BE HOPED OUR RETURN WILL CALM PETER...
...HE IS **HIGHLY AGITATED**...

...AND **CONCERNED** ABOUT HIS SISTER.
AS ARE WE **ALL**, **ORORO**.

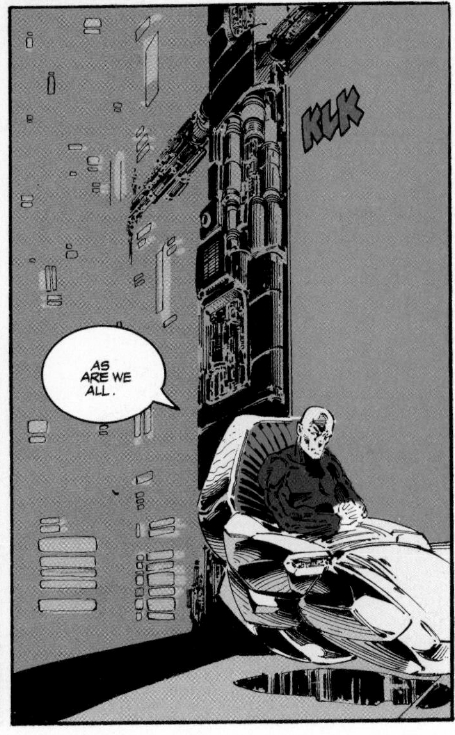

KLK
AS ARE WE ALL.

"BEFORE ANYBODY KNEW WHAT HAPPENED--
"--EVERYTHING JUST CURDLED."
UH, PROF-- WE COULD USE A HAND HERE.
WHECCH! CA CHUHH PR BRU
GKACCH!
SHE'S GONE INTO COMPLETE RESPIRATORY ARREST! HER LUNGS HAVE SHUT DOWN!
HURRY, MO SHE CAN' BREATH
ONE CC OF NOREPENEPHRINE, MOIRA--IMMEDIATELY!
GIVE DR. MACTAGGERT ROOM TO WORK, KATHERINE!
P... COUH HOUKKT PIOTR...?
‹HE'LL BE HERE SHORTLY, SNOWFLAKE.›
‹HOLD ON... PLEASE... JUST HOLD ON.›
I DON'T UNDERSTAND THIS! I THOUGHT THIS VIRUS ONLY AFFECTED HER MUTANT POWERS-- LATENT OR OTHERWISE.
SO DID WE, AT FIRST!
APPARENTLY IT WASN'T CONTENT WITH FEASTING ON HER MUTANT GENES.
THERE, CHILD--REST EASY.
TSSST

"--CRYIN' OVER HER BESTEST FRIEND...
"... I GUESS I WAS EMBARRASSED FOR BEIN' JEALOUS IN THE FIRST PLACE.
"THAT LOOK IN HER EYES WAS LIKE SOMEBODY WATCHIN' THEMSELF DIE."
FORGIVE ME, ILLYANA.
FORGIVE ME FOR WHAT I'M ABOUT TO DO...
TH-THAT DEVICE, PROFESSOR... WHAT IS IT?!
IT IS OF SHI'AR ORIGIN... I CONFESS TO NOT FULLY UNDER-STANDING HOW IT WORKS.
SUFFICE IT TO SAY, IT MAY BE ILLYANA'S LAST HOPE.
YE KNOW FULL WELL THIS MOLECULAR COHESION UNIT WILL DO NOTHING MORE THAN MAINTAIN HER GENETIC INTEGRITY AT ITS CURRENT STATE!
I REFUSE TO LET YE DOOM THIS CHILD TO A LIFE IN A COMA!
AND I, MOIRA--I REFUSE TO SIT BACK AND DO NOTHING!
INSTEAD...

INSTEAD YOU'RE GOING TO SENTENCE HER TO--TO "THIS"?
TO LIVE A LIFE WITHOUT THE ABILITY TO THINK?
WITHOUT THE CAPABILITY TO SMILE...
... WITHOUT THE CAPACITY FOR LOVE?
SIR, ILLYANA WAS MY BEST FRIEND IN THE ENTIRE WORLD.
I... I'D DO ANYTHING FOR HER AND SHE--
--SHE'D DO THE SAME.
AND THAT "ANYTHING" INCLUDES KNOWING WHEN TO HOLD ON...
WHEN TO...
...LET GO.
"ABOUT THEN, JUST KIND OF PHASED OUT
"DEATH AND DYIN WAS NEVER A B DINNER TOPIC I SOUTHERN C
"WHILE THE THRE OF THEM TALKED IT OUT AMONGS THEMSELVES, I
"... I DID SOMETHING KIND OF...
"... I GUESS THE WORD IS, 'STRANGE'?"

ERE THEY ARE...
"... DEBATIN' OVER WHETHER THEY SHOULD HELP HER LIVE OR...
...OR NOT...
"... AND THE ONLY THING I CAN THINK OF IS HELPIN' HER WITH HER STUPID OLE' DOLL.
" I MEAN, IF I OULDN'T DO ANY-HING TO MAKE HER BETTER...
"... I GUESS I WAS WILLIN' TO SETTLE FOR MAKIN' HER HAPPY.
"LIKE I SAID...
"... STRANGE.
"FOR ME.

"BEIN' SELFLESS ALWAYS TAKES A LOT OUT OF ME...
"...SO I FOUND THINGS TO DO IN THE KITCHEN TO KEEP BUSY TILL THE HEAVY STUFF WAS OVER.
"BY THE TIME I GOT BACK, I GUESS I MISSED MOST OF THE EXCITING STUFF.
"THE DOCTORS GRIMM WERE KNEE-DEEP IN LAST MINUTE SCENARIOS, AND--
"--KITTY AND ILLYANA WERE BOTH IN LALA LAND.
"I GUESS I COULDDA JUST LEFT 'EM TO SLEEP--
"--BUT I FELT THAT SHE SHOULDN'T BE ALONE WHEN...
"I JUST FELT SHE SHOULDN'T BE ALONE JUST THEN.

"I START READING WHERE KITTY DOZED OFF.
"YEAH, SO IT WAS IN ENGLISH, BIG DUP.
"IT WAS THE THOUGHT."
"TAKING THE LITTLE GIRL IN HER ARMS SHE FLEW UP WITH HER IN BRIGHTNESS AND JOY, HIGH, SO HIGH--
"--AND THERE WAS NO COLD, OR HUNGER, OR SORROW--
"--FOR SHE WAS WITH GOD."*
*FROM "THE LITTLE MATCHGIRL" BY HANS CHRISTIAN ANDERSEN
I WANNA TELL YA THINGS'RE GONNA BE OKAY...
... BUT, ALL I CAN DO IS BE HERE FOR YA.
OPE...
...THAT'S ENOUGH.
"I GUESS YOU KNOW WHAT HAPPENED THEN."

"... WHEN HE SNAGGED A CLUE.
"PETER ?
"I DON'T TH
HE EVEN SA
COMIN'."
WHILE EVERYONE IS GATHERED HERE-- WHO IS LOOKING AFTER MY SISTER?
IF I CAN'T TRUST ANY OF YOU TO ATTEND TO HER NEEDS IN MY ABSENCE, THEN PERHAPS I SHOULD NOT LEAVE HER IN YOUR CARE?

HTEN UP,
OPLES!
HAVEN'T
EEN SO MANY
NG FACES
INCE THE
HAMPIONS
SBANDED.

"DRAKE WAS READY TO MAKE WITH HIS LAME-O 'HUMOR'...

PETER?
SON...

...I'M SORRY.
WE... DID EVERYTHING WE COULD.

"THE BIG GUY DIDN'T MAKE A SOUND.
"NO REACTION AT ALL.
"DIDN'T SOB.
"DIDN'T PUNCH ANYBODY.
"DIDN'T EVEN TURN AROUND...

"SINCE I BEEN HANGING WITH YOU GUYS--"
--I GOT TO MIX IT UP WITH BROOD-THINGS, SENTINELS, ACOLYTES AND EVERYTHING.
SO HOW IS IT YA CAN SAVE THE WORLD EVERY MORNING, PRE-WHEATIES...
...BUT WHEN IT COMES TO SAVIN' ONE LITTLE GIRL...
...ZIP?!
YOU ASKED ME WHAT I'M FEELIN', RED?!
I FEEL LIKE I JUST WANT TO BE LEFT ALONE!
C'MERE.
JUBILEE, WE COME INTO THIS WORLD ALONE--
--AND WE LEAVE THE SAME WAY...

THE TIME WE SPEND IN BETWEEN...
...TIME SPENT ALIVE, SHARING, LEARNING...
...TOGETHER...
...IS ALL THAT MAKES LIFE WORTH LIVING.
END.

RVEL
MICS
ERSARY
SUE
X-FACTOR
APPROVED BY THE COMICS CODE AUTHORITY
FATAL ATTRACTIONS
OUT OF THE LIGHT AND INTO THY FATHER'S SHADOW

Havok hologram statue by Dario Grangroth, based on Quesada's artwork

X-Factor #92 hologram original art by Joe Quesada, Al Milgrom & Tom Smith

MARVEL COMICS
X-MEN ANNIVERSARY ISSUE
X-FACTOR
$3.50 US
$4.40 CAN
92
JUL
UK £2.60
APPROVED BY THE COMICS CODE AUTHORITY
FATAL ATTRACTIONS
OUT OF THE LIGHT AND INTO THY FATHER'S SHADOW

WAUNTAUGH, VIRGINIA.
"YOU HAVE TO UNDERSTAND... THIS IS A HOSPICE. WE DON'T WORK HERE FOR THE PAY. BELIEVE ME, IT ISN'T MUCH. WE WORK HERE...
GOOD AFTERNOON, NURSE. WE ARE THE ACOLYTES--
--AND WE'RE HERE TO SLAUGHTER FLATSCANS!
"...BECAUSE WE CARE.
"PEOPLE COME TO US AT THEIR WEAKEST, THEIR MOST VULNERABLE. AND WE HELP THEM TO FACE DEATH WITH A LITTLE DIGNITY... AND A LITTLE LOVE."
"NURSE MURRAY... LESLIE... IF THIS IS TOO DIFFICULT... YOU DON'T HAVE TO --"
"NO, DOCTOR COOPER. I NEED TO TALK ABOUT IT. I THINK IT'S THE ONLY WAY...

"... I'LL BE ABLE TO UNDERSTAND."
MUST YOU KLEINSTOCKS ALWAYS BE SO MELO-DRAMATIC?
AH, JAVITZ -- YOU SIMPLY HAVE NO... FLAIR!
WHAT GOOD IS THE KILL IF IT'S NOT EXE-CUTED WITH A LITTLE PANACHE? SOME VERBAL FEINTING BEFORE PLUNGING IN THE SWORD?
WE'RE NOT HERE FOR AMUSEMENT! WE'RE HERE T' DELIVER RETRIBUTION --
-- IN MAGNETO'S NAME!
AGREED, SPOOR --
"UNDERSTAND? THERE'S NO UNDERSTANDING THESE -- "
"QUIET, PIETRO -- LET HER TALK."

SO LET'S DO IT!
"I WANTED TO GET UP... SAY SOMETHING... DO SOMETHING! BUT I WAS SO SCARED... ROOTED TO THE SPOT.
RACHET
"ALL I COULD DO WAS WATCH...
"...LIKE A HELPLESS, SCARED LITTLE CHILD...
"...AS THE MASSACRE BEGAN.
"THERE WAS NOTHING YOU COULD HAVE DONE! THOSE MEN ARE BRUTAL! VICIOUS BEYOND --"
"YOU DON'T HAVE TO EXPLAIN IT TO ME, MISTER SUMMERS. I EXPERIENCED IT.
SCHOOK
"FIRSTHAND."

DOCTOR'S HERE--
WHOOM
"I'VE WORKED WITH THE DYING FOR OVER SIX YEARS. SOUNDS DEPRESSING... BUT IT'S NOT.
"WHEN PEOPLE FACE DEATH, THEY CHANGE. IT'S LIKE ALL THE WALLS BETWEEN US ARE JUST BROKEN DOWN. THE SOUL... SHINES THROUGH.
--TIME FOR YOUR FIVE O'CLOCK SHOT!
"I'VE WATCHED PEOPLE DIE. HELD THEM WHILE THEY LET GO. I KNOW IT'S HARD TO BELIEVE... BUT THEY RADIATED SUCH JOY...
"...SUCH -- SANCTITY..."
WHAT ARE YOU DOING--?!
CALL IT AN ACT OF DIVINE VENGEANCE.
OR CALL IT COLD-BLOODED MURDER.
MAKES NO DIFFERENCE TO ME.
"THE WORST THING THOSE ANIMALS DID, DOCTOR COOPER -- WAS TO ROB THOSE SOULS OF THEIR RADIANCE.
WHY?! WHAT

DESERVE IT?
WHAT IN GOD'S NAME DID I... DID ANY OF US DO --
-- TO DESERVE TO BE TREATED LIKE THAT?!
THE WAY THE ACOLYTES LOOK AT IT, LESLIE -- YOUR BIGGEST MISTAKE WAS BEING BORN --
-- HUMAN.
THEN... THEN WHAT THEY SAY IS TRUE? THE MUTANTS -- THEY HATE US --
-- JUST FOR BEING... NORMAL?
"NORMAL" IS A RELATIVE CONCEPT, NURSE MURRAY.
BUT I DIDN'T MEAN --
I KNOW YOU DIDN'T.
AND I WANT YOU TO KNOW THAT THE FOLLOWERS OF MAGNETO ARE NO MORE TYPICAL EXAMPLES OF MUTANTKIND THAN HITLER'S WERE TYPICAL EXAMPLES OF HUMANKIND.
C'MON, ALEX... PIETRO, LESLIE NEEDS HER REST.
-- I CAN'T THINK OF A WORD LOATHSOME ENOUGH --
WAIT...
Hmm?
WHAT KIND OF MAN CAN THIS MAGNETO BE...
... TO INSPIRE SUCH INSANITY ?

THAT'S A QUESTION I'VE ASKED MYSELF--
--TOO MANY TIMES--
--OVER TOO MANY --
BOOP
BOOP
--YEARS..?
OOP BOOP OOP OOP
BOOOOOOOOOOOOP
WHAT IS IT? WHAT'S WRONG?
OUTTA HERE! NOW!
WE'RE LOSING HER!
DR. JOHNSON

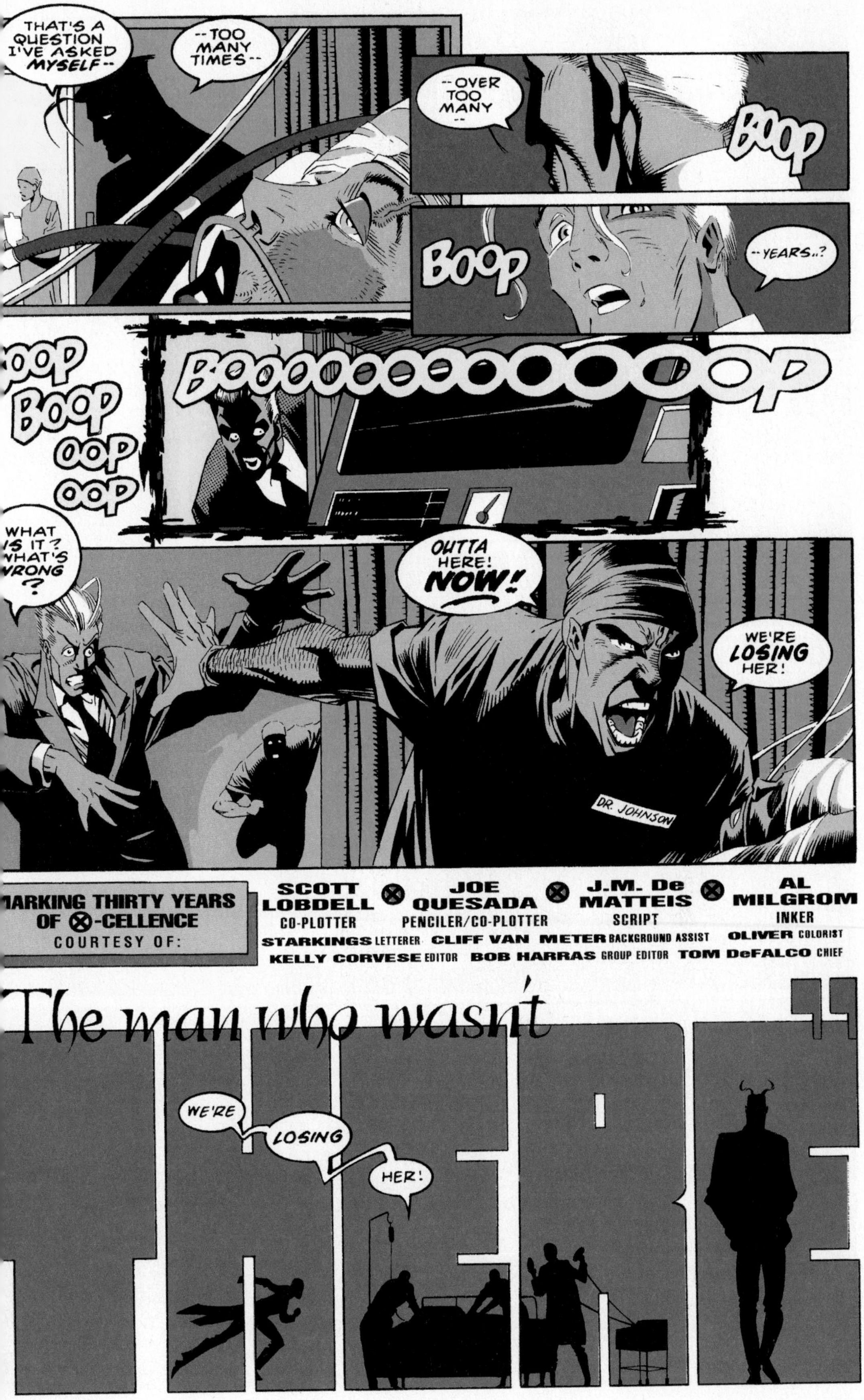

MARKING THIRTY YEARS OF X-CELLENCE COURTESY OF:

SCOTT LOBDELL CO-PLOTTER · JOE QUESADA PENCILER/CO-PLOTTER · J.M. DeMATTEIS SCRIPT · AL MILGROM INKER

STARKINGS LETTERER · CLIFF VAN METER BACKGROUND ASSIST · OLIVER COLORIST

KELLY CORVESE EDITOR · BOB HARRAS GROUP EDITOR · TOM DeFALCO CHIEF

The man who wasn't THERE

WE'RE
LOSING
HER!

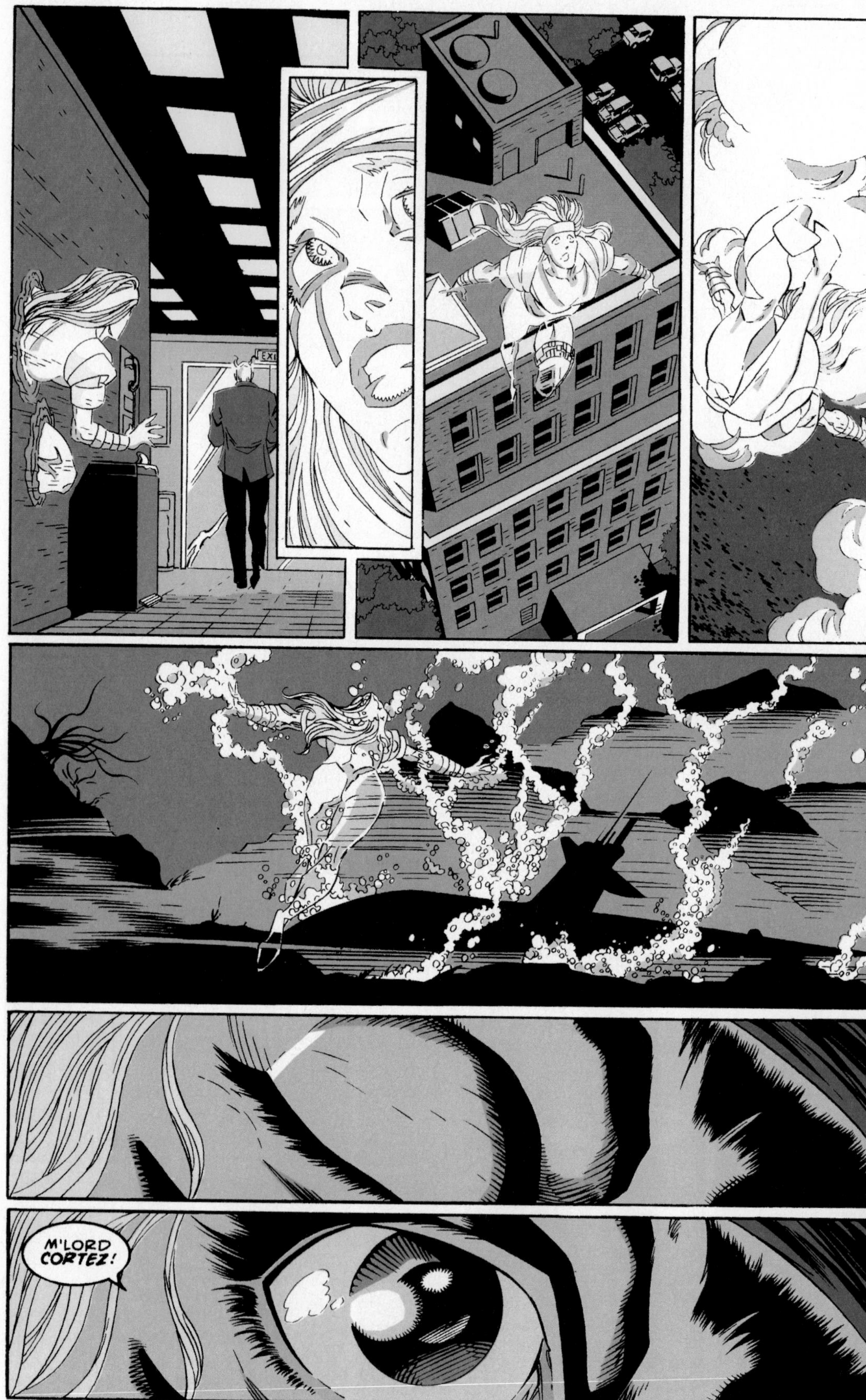
EXIT
M'LORD CORTEZ!

THE REMAINS OF THE RUSSIAN SUBMARINE LENINGRAD -- SOMEWHERE IN THE ATLANTIC.
I HAVE RETURNED, M'LORD.
OBVIOUSLY.
I...I'M READY TO MAKE MY REPORT AT YOUR ORDER.
STOP GROVELING, SCANNER -- AND SPIT IT OUT!
WE'VE DEALT THE HUMANS A HORRIBLE BLOW. BUT... I... AH... I STILL WONDER, M'LORD --
YES?
THOSE PEOPLE WERE NO THREAT TO US. TO ANY MUTANTS. WHY --
WERE THEY HUMAN?
YES.
AND... CORRECT ME IF I'M WRONG... HASN'T THE BOOT HEEL OF HUMANITY ALWAYS TRAMPLED OUR KIND?
Y-YES. YES, M'LORD.
THEN THEY WERE A THREAT.
AH, SCANNER, DON'T YOU SEE? THEY'RE GENETICALLY LINKED: ONE MIND, ONE HEART, ONE SOUL. TWISTED. EVIL. FULL OF HATRED FOR ALL THAT'S DIFFERENT.
YOUR NAIVETÉ TOUCHES ME.
BUT YOU HAVE TO LEARN... AND LEARN QUICKLY... THAT COMPASSION FOR HUMANS -- EVEN THE WEAKEST ONES -- IS EXTREMELY DANGEROUS.
OUR TRUE LORD AND MASTER... THE GREAT MAGNETO... WOULD WANT YOU TO UNDERSTAND THIS.
BUT... BUT, THE MASTER'S SON! HE SEEMED SO UPSET BY WHAT WE'D DONE! HE --
-- IS MY CONCERN!
AAAH!
REST ASSURED... QUICKSILVER WILL BE MINE --
-- OURS --
-- BY NIGHTFALL!

"I HAVE CERTAIN... OPERATIVES IN PLACE THAT... EVEN NOW...
...C'MON, ALEX -- LET'S GET DOWN TO THE HOLDING CELL --
"ARE SEEING TO IT!"
-- AND CHECK UP ON OUR PRIZE PACKAGE.
THE PENTAGON.
WELL, SPOOR -- WHAT HAVE YOU GOT TO SAY FOR YOURSELF?
HARD T'TALK BEHIND THIS MUZZLE, HAVOK, M'LAD. SO WHY DON'T YE CUT ME LOOSE --
-- AND I'LL GIVE YE A MOUTHFUL.
YOU SEEM TO THINK THIS IS FUNNY.
-- AND, CONSIDERING THAT YOUR BUDDIES GOT AWAY CLEAN --
-- THE FULL WEIGHT OF THE LAW'S COMING DOWN ON YOUR UGLY HEAD.
FLATSCAN LAW, POLARIS. DON'T MEAN A BLOODY THING T' ME!
MAYBE WE'LL JUST SKIP THE LAW, THEN! MAYBE WE'LL JUST TAKE YOU OUT HERE AND NOW!
THAT'LL BE ENOUGH, GUIDO!
BUT --!
WE DO THINGS BY THE BOOK HERE --
-- UNDERSTOOD?

YOU'VE
GOT
NOTHING!
FAR AS I'M CONCERNED, YOU GAVE UP YOUR RIGHTS THE MOMENT YOU ENGAGED IN THE MURDER--
--EXCUSE ME... "GENETIC CLEANSING" --
--OF INNOCENT HUMAN BEINGS!
FWZAAM
NOW YOU'LL COOPERATE WITH US -- OR I SWEAR I'LL --
THE ONLY THING YOU'RE GOING TO SWEAR, SUMMERS-- IS TO BACK OFF!
YOU BACK OFF, VAL! I'M HANDLING THIS MY--
YOU DO WHAT I SAY-- NOW --OR I'LL HAVE YOU OUT OF HERE... AND OFF THIS TEAM SO FAST --
--EVEN QUICKSILVER'S HEAD'LL SPIN!
SOMEBODY MENTION MY NAME?
THE --
--SON?

WHY ARE YOU WASTING TIME QUESTIONING THIS ANIMAL? WE SHOULD JUST DIG A VERY DEEP HOLE -- THROW HIM IN --
-- AND TOSS SEVERAL TONS OF DIRT IN AFTER HIM.
NO DOUBT HE'LL FEEL RIGHT AT HOME.
WHAT IS IT WITH YOU PEOPLE? HAS EVERYONE BEEN TAKING ATTITUDE LESSONS FROM THE PUNISHER?!
NEXT TO THIS AFFRONT TO DECENCY, VALERIE, THE PUNISHER SEEMS AS PURE AS CAPTAIN AMERIC-
THE SON!
Huh?!
DID I MISS SOMETHING? I MEAN--
-- DID THE POPE JUST WALK IN THE ROOM--
UNBE-LIEVABLE.
'TIS SACRILEGE!
I BOW BEFORE YE -- IN SUR-RENDER AND SUBMISSION --
ONLY BEGOTTEN SON --
-- OF THE MIGHTY, WRATHFUL LORD.
LOOKS LIKE, AFTER ALL THESE YEARS OF WANTING TO BE GOD --
-- PIETRO FINALLY GOT HIS WISH!

ONE HOUR LATER.
WAIT A MINUTE--!
HEY! I SAID WAIT A MINUTE!
SO YOU DID.
BUT WE DON'T HAVE A MINUTE!
ADY-- HAT S YOUR ROB-EM?
AT THE MOMENT-- YOU ARE.
YOU HINK YOU CAN JUST AKE PIETRO AND O OFF TO KENTUCKY NVESTIGATING POOR'S CONFESSION... ND LEAVE THE REST OF US HERE?!
AS A MATTER OF FACT... I DO.
THE ONLY REASON SPOOR TOLD US ANYTHING IS BECAUSE HE THINKS QUICK-SILVER IS THE SECOND COMING!
IF HIS INFORMATION IS CORRECT... IF THE ACOLYTES ARE PLANNING TO HIT OUR MILITARY INSTALLATION AT CAPE HAYDEN--
--THEN THE LAST THING WE NEED IS ALL OF YOU THERE FLEXING YOUR MUSCLES AND MAKING MATTERS WORSE!
I'M BETTING PIETRO WILL HAVE THE SAME EFFECT ON THE OTHERS THAT HE HAD ON SPOOR... AND HELP US AVOID A BLOODBATH--
AND IF HE CAN'T?
THEN I BROUGHT ALONG SOME INSURANCE--
HEY, BUD -- HOW'S IT HANGIN'?
RANDOM?!
YOU'RE LEAVING US BEHIND-- AND TAKING THAT MUTANT BOUNTY-HUNTER WITH YOU?
ARE YOU OUT OF YOUR MIND !?!
WHAT I AM, SUMMERS --IS IN CHARGE!
BUT--
NOW SHUT YOUR MOUTH AND GET AWAY FROM THE HELICOPTER--
--WE'RE IN A HURRY!
YOU ON THEM LORNA?
BEST I CAN--
GOOD. LET'S GET THAT NEW TRANSPORT FORGE WHIPPED UP FOR US AIR-BORNE!
THERE'S SOMETHING OUT-OF-WHACK HERE --
-- AND I'M BLOODY WELL GONNA FIND OUT WHAT!

... LORNA -- IF YOU DON'T START STEERING THIS THING STRAIGHT -- MY STOMACH'S GOING TO COME UP OUT MY NOSE!
PLEASE, GUIDO -- NO JOKES! I'M TRYING TO CONCEN-TRATE!
WHO'S JOKING?! ANYBODY GOT AN ALKA-SELTZER?
ALEX! MAKE HIM STOP!
KNOCK IT OFF, GUIDO -- LORNA'S USING HER MAGNETIC POWER TO PRO-PEL THIS BABY AND KEEP TABS ON THE 'COPTER --
-- IF YOU KEEP DISTRACTING HER WITH YOUR IDIOTIC BANTER --
-- WE'RE NEVER GONNA MAKE IT TO CAPE HAYDEN!

LORNA-- ARE YE SURE YE'RE UP TO THIS?!
PIECE
OF
CAKE!
PLEASE DON'T TALK ABOUT FOOD!
THIS IS PECULIAR. I'VE CALLED UP ALL THE FILES ON CAPE HAYDEN-- AND IT'S AS LOW PRIORITY AS A MILITARY BASE CAN GET.
ANOTHER CASUALTY OF THE BUDGET CUTS. SCHEDULED TO BE SHUT DOWN NEXT YEAR--
--NOW WHAT WOULD THE ACOLYTES WANT WITH A PLACE LIKE THAT?!
OBVIOUSLY... TARGETING AREAS RANDOMLY. THEY DON'T CARE WHO... OR WHERE--
--LONG AS THEY'RE KILLING "FLATSCANS!"
JAMIE-- ARE YE ALL RIGHT? Y' LOOK AWFUL!
NOTHING TO WORRY ABOUT, KIDDO! I'M JUST--
LORNA-- WHAT'D YOU DO?! WHY'D YOU HIT THE BRAKES?!
IT WASN'T ME, ALEX, SOMETHING GRABBED US! FROM OUTSIDE!
URKK!
NICE, GUIDO. VERY NICE. NOW HOW ABOUT CLEANING IT UP?

YEAH, SURE -- BUT FIRST--
-- COULD SOMEBODY PLEASE TELL ME WHO THAT IS?
NEVER SEEN HIM BEFORE!
JUST WHAT WE NEED A NEW COSTUMED LUNA TIC OUT TO
NO... TAKE A GOOD LOOK AT HIM...
"... HE DOESN'T APPEAR HOSTILE. IN FACT --
"--HE LOOKS LIKE HE'S... WAITING. PONDERING.
"AS IF THERE'S SOMETHING HE WANTS TO SAY TO US --"

"--BUT HE'S NOT SURE IF THIS IS THE RIGHT TIME."
WHOOSH
GUESS IT WASN'T.
SHOULD WE FOLLOW HIM?
UH-UH. WE FILE HIM UNDER "M" FOR MYSTERY -- AND COME BACK TO HIM LATER.
RIGHT NOW WE NEED YOU TO GET US MOVING AGAIN--
WITH PLEASURE, LOVER -- BUT NOT UNTIL GUIDO--
I'LL CLEAN IT UP! I'LL CLEAN IT UP!

CAPE HAYDEN.
...ISN'T IT TIME YOU STOPPED... PRETENDING, VALERIE?
PRETENDING? I -- I DON'T KNOW WHAT YOU'RE --
I DON'T BELIEVE A WORD OF WHAT YOU TOLD US ABOUT THIS PLACE.
THE ACOLYTES MAY BE BLOODTHIRSTY... BUT THEY'RE NOT STUPID. IF THEY'RE WILLING TO RISK TAKING ON THE U.S ARMY --
--THERE'S GOT TO BE SOMETHING HERE THEY'RE HUNGRY FOR.
I'M TELLING YOU PIETRO-- THERE'S NOTHING! THIS IS PROBABLY THE SLEEPIEST LITTLE ARMY BASE THIS SIDE OF --
OKAY MUTIES --
WHA--?
--"BEETLE BAILEY--"
--FREEZE! RIGHT WHERE YOU ARE!
"BEETLE BAILEY," Huh?
THEN HOWCUM I'M NOT LAUGHING?
QUIET -- AND STEP AWAY FROM THE HUMAN... NICE AN' SLOW.
YOU'VE GOT FIVE SECONDS FREAKS
--OR YOU'RE BOTH DEAD.
FIVE
FOUR.

THREE..?!
-- TWO... ONE... ZERO. OKAY. GO AHEAD: SHOOT.
Oh -- BUT YOU DON'T HAVE YOUR GUNS, DO YOU?
TH- THAT'S IMPOSSIBLE!
MIRACULOUS. ISN'T IT -- WHAT WE "MUTIE FREAKS" CAN DO WHEN WE PUT OUR MINDS TO IT?
YOU'RE THE ONE WITH THE BLOODLINE FOR RACISM, MISTER MAXIMOFF--
--OR NEED I REMIND YOU OF THE WAR YOUR FAMILY HAS BEEN WAGING AGAINST HUMANKIND FOR FAR TOO MANY YEARS?
Oh... BUT WHAT AM I SAYING? YOU WORK FOR OUR SIDE NOW --
-- DON'T YOU?
YOUR "SLEEPY" LITTLE ARMY BASE IS GETTING MORE AND MORE INTERESTING, VALERIE.
WHAT IN THE WORLD WERE YOU THINKING, MS. COOPER -- BRINGING THESE TWO HERE? YOU DON'T HAVE CLEARANCE FOR --
WHAT I THINK IS NONE OF YOUR BUSINESS, SENATOR! AS FOR CLEARANCE, MY POSITION AS MUTANT LIAISON GIVES ME SECURITY CLEARANCE FAR BEYOND YOURS!
SO GET OUT OF MY FACE--
-- AND GET OUT OF MY WAY!

...I SEEM TO DETECT A -- CHANGE IN YOU, VALERIE.
FOR THE BETTER, I HOPE.
I HAVEN'T DECIDED, YET. ALTHOUGH... IF YOU'RE LOOKING FOR APPROVAL... A BIT OF HONESTY WILL HELP IMMEASURABLY.
T'PUT IT IN LAYMAN'S TERMS, LADY--
--WHAT THE IS GOIN' ON HERE?
I WAS GOING TO TELL YOU.
WHEN?
WHEN I THOUGHT THE TIME WAS RIGHT.
VALERIE... THE TIME IS RIGHT.
WHAT IS IT THE ACOLYTES WANT HERE?
SEVERAL MONTHS AGO, THE SENATE HELD A CLOSED DOOR MEETING OF SEVERAL SECRET COMMITTEES CONCERNED WITH... YOU'LL EXCUSE THE EXPRESSION --
-- THE MUTANT PROBLEM.
THEY AUTHORIZED THE USE OF... AND THESE ARE THEIR WORDS, NOT MINE -- "PRUDENT AND NECESSARY FORCE WITH WHICH TO CONTAIN POTENTIAL MUTANT ABERRATIONS." THAT WHEN "PROJECT: WIDE-AWAKE" WAS FUNDE
"WIDEAWAKE?" WHAT'S IT DO?
SET OFF A REALLY BIG ALARM CLOCK IN KELLY'S BEDROOM WHENEVER ANOTHER GEE-CEE HITS PUBERTY?
KLIK
NOT--
--EXACT

SENTINELS !?!
PROTOTYPES -- COMBINING THE FINEST FEATURES OF THE CLASSIC MODELS --
-- WITH THE EVOLVING -- AND FAR SUPERIOR -- NIMROD TYPE.

THE SENATE DECIDED THAT THE PRIVATE SECTOR HAS HAD CONTROL OF THE SENTINELS FOR TOO LONG, SO --
SO THEY DECIDED TO GO INTO THE MUTANT-SLAUGHTERING BUSINESS FOR THEMSELVES.
AND YOU KNEW ABOUT THIS?!
HAVOK? I SPECIFICALLY ORDERED YOU TO --
I DON'T WANT TO HEAR ANOTHER LECTURE ABOUT FOLLOWING ORDERS, MEIN FÜHRER --
-- JUST ANSWER THE QUESTION: HAVE YOU KNOWN ABOUT THIS ALL ALONG?!
GENTLEMEN... LADIES -- THE FIRST RESPONSIBILITY OF A DEMOCRACY IS TO THE MAJORITY.
THE SAD TRUTH IS -- THE MAJORITY OF AMERICANS FEARS MUTANTKIND -- AND, FRANKLY, AS LONG AS THERE ARE MANIACS LIKE THE ACOLYTES OUT THERE --
-- THEIR FEARS ARE WHOLLY JUSTIFIED.
Y'WANT REASON T'FEAR US? THEN JUST WAIT'LL YE SEE WHAT WE DO T'YOUR PRECIOUS PROTOTYPES!
I DINNA THINK YOU'LL--
RAHNE
--NO.
WHAT?! PIETRO -- YE CANNA BE --

I CAN'T BE SERIOUS?
YOU SHOULD KNOW BY NOW -- THAT I'M THE MOST SERIOUS MAN ALIVE.
AND WITH GOOD REASON.
I UNDER-TAND THE PSYCHES F THE ACOLYTES ND THEIR KIND FAR ETTER THAN YOU... R VAL... OR SENATOR KELLY EVER COULD...
"... BECAUSE THE BLOOD OF THEIR 'SAVIOR' RUNS IN MY VEINS. HE MAY NOT HAVE RAISED ME -- BUT MAKE NO MISTAKE --
" -- I AM MAGNETO'S SON --
"-- AND MY INHERITANCE... HAS BEEN A GRISLY ONE.
"I KNOW THE BROKEN HEART THAT CURSES HOMO SAPIENS WITH EVERY ANGRY BEAT.
"I KNOW THE TWISTED MIND THAT ACTUALLY TAKES PRIDE IN BEING CALLED... AN 'EVIL MUTANT.'"
I'M NOT GOING TO EXPLAIN OR DEBATE THE FORCES THAT CREATE SUCH MEN... THAT DROVE ME TO SUCH DESPERATE ENDS --
-- BECAUSE THE ONLY PERTINENT QUESTION IS: DO THESE MEN EXIST?
AND, IF THEY DO, DO HUMANS HAVE A RIGHT TO PROTECT THEMSELVES FROM THEM --
-- IN WHAT EVER WAY THEY CAN?
ARE YE SAYING -- THAT THEY DO?

MY FATHER MAY BE DEAD-- BUT HIS PRESENCE LIVES ON.
THE MAN WHO ISN'T THERE--
KKRAAAK
--SOWING THE SEEDS OF HATRED IN FRIGHTENED, EMBITTERED MUTANTS.
I BELIEVE... TO THE BOTTOM OF MY SOUL... THAT HUMANKIND NOT ONLY HAS A RIGHT TO PROTECT ITSELF FROM MAGNETO'S LEGACY--
IT MUST PROTECT ITSELF!
BLOWING THROUGH THE SIDE OF A MOUNTAIN --NOW THAT'S AN ENTRANCE WITH STYLE!
SPARE US YOUR POSTURING, JAVITZ, AND ATTEND TO THE TASK AT HAND--
I WANT THIS BASE THROWN INTO ABSOLUTE CHAOS--
AND I WANT THE SON OF MAGNUS!

YOU WANT HIM -- YOU'VE GOT HIM
-- COURTESY OF SENYAKA!
YOU'RE ALL STARTING TO SOUND LIKE THE KLEIN-STOCKS!
THIS ISN'T A GAME! WE'RE NOT HERE TO PUMP UP OUR EGOS! THE CAUSE IS ABOUT WORKING TOGETHER... SELF-SACRIFICE --
-- IN THE NAME OF OUR LORD!
TELL YOU WHAT, FRENZY, YOU FOLLOW YOUR PATH TO SALVATION --
-- AND LET ME FOLLOW MINE!
AAOOOGA AAOOOGA
DID WE JUST WIN SOMETHING?
I DOUBT IT --
-- UNLESS YOU CONSIDER THE ACOLYTES A PRIZE!
GUESS SPOOR WAS TELLING THE TRUTH!
HOW UTTERLY UNLIKE HIM.
SKIP THE CHARACTER ANALYSIS, SUMMERS -- AND GET THIS TEAM MOVING!
I DON'T WANT TO SEE A REPEAT OF WHAT HAPPENED IN VIRGINIA!
AND YOU WON'T! BUT JUST REMEMBER, VAL... WHEN THIS IS OVER --
-- WE'VE GOT A LOT TO TALK ABOUT!

THEY MUST BE HERE TO TAKE OUT THE SENTINELS!
OR CAPTURE THEM.
THINK OF THE DAMAGE HOSE ANIMALS COULD DO WITH SUCH POWER IN THEIR HANDS!
FRANKLY, I DON'T GIVE A FLAMIN' WHAT THEY WANT--
--LONG AS I GET MY FEE WHEN THE SMOKE CLEARS!
YOUR GENEROSITY OF SPIRIT IS HUMBLING, RANDOM!
HEY, I DON'T SEE YOU NOT CASHIN' YOUR CHECK ON PAYDAY!
LISTEN TO YOU... HAGGLING OVER A HANDFUL OF SILVER! JUDASES -- ONE AND ALL --
-- BOUGHT AND PAID FOR BY YOUR FLATSCAN MASTERS!
I HAVE SOME MILD ADMIRATION FOR XAVIER'S OTHER MISGUIDED FOLLOWERS --
-- BUT YOU BOOT-LICKING SLIME SIMPLY... TURN MY STOMACH.
I THINK I'VE GOT SOME ALKA-SELTZER LEFT!
GUIDO... PLEASE!
YOU WORSHIP A DEAD MEGALO-MANIAC... I WORSHIP THE ALMIGHTY DOLLAR --
GUESS WHICH ONE OF US IS GONNA RETIRE TO THE FIVE-BEDROOM HOUSE ON MAUI?
ZZACHOOM
RANDOM... WAIT! WE NEED A --
-- PLAN OF ATTACK --
SECURITY?
YES, SENATOR?

"THIS IS TURNING... UGLY.
SENYAKA --
-- DOWN!
FWASH
"THE BASE IS EXPENDABLE
THANKS FOR TAKING OUT THE INCOMING, BROTHERS --
-- BUT I'LL FINISH HIM OFF!
"AND SO IS X-FACTOR.
WELL, WELL -- SENYAKA, THE NURSE KILLER. THIS WHIP OF YOURS HAS REALLY DONE SOME SERIOUS DAMAGE.
I MEAN... GRABBIN' IT LIKE THIS SHOULD BE CAUSING ME NO END OF EXCRUCIATING PAIN.
"BUT THE SENTINELS MUST BE PROTECTED AT ALL COSTS!
AN' DON'T GET ME WRONG, LITTLE MAN. IT IS.
I MEAN, I'M REALLY HURTING.
"PREPARE TO INITIATE OPERATION VANISH...
OUCH.
BLOOOM
"... ON MY COMMAND."
WHY, POLARIS?
BEFORE I CRUSH THE LIFE OUT OF YOU WITH MY PSIONIC SKELETON -- JUST TELL ME --
-- WHY DENIGRATE YOURSELF -- AND YOUR RA BY PLAYING MONKEY TO THESE FLATSCAN ORGAN GRINDERS?!

TAKE MY WORD FOR IT, UNUS-IONE --
LORNA DANE IS NOBODY'S MONKEY!
DO WHAT DO BECAUSE LOVE MY IND -- AND ECAUSE I'M ICK TO DEATH F HATE-ONGERS LIKE YOU AND SENATOR KELLY --
-- WHO ARE SO AFRAID OF UNIQUENESS AND DIVERSITY --
-- THAT YOU REDUCE ALL PEOPLE... HUMAN AND MUTANT... TO CONVENIENT STEREOTYPES AND LABELS!
THE LADY MAKES NICE SPEECHES.
MAYBE YOU'VE GOT A NICE SPEECH TO MAKE --
-- BEFORE I SNAP YOUR NECK?
SPEECH? ME? UH-UH!
I'M JUST A BIG --
KLUTZ
-- DUMB
WHOOPS!
KRREKK
SEE? I TOLD YOU -- WHAT A KLUTZ! KNOCKED THE BEAM RIGHT OUT!
AND HERE COMES THE ROOF!
ARE... YOU... CRAZY?
NOPE.
TOK
Y'SEE... I'M THE KINDA GUY... YOU DROP A BUILDING ON 'IM -- HE JUST ABSORBS THE ENERGY!
WHICH MEANS I GET BIGGER AND STRONGER AND --
-- NOW I KNOW THIS IS HARD TO BE-LIEVE --
-- EVEN MORE HAND-SOME!
HEY! YOU'RE NOT LISTENING!
SKTAM
THAT'S THE PROBLEM WITH KIDS TODAY -- ALL THAT SESAME STREET AND MTV --
-- THEY'VE SIMPLY GOT NO ATTENTION-SPAN!

TWO AGAINST ONE? GUYS, GUYS... THIS JUST ISN'T RIGHT!
DIDN'T YOUR FATHERS TEACH YOU HOW TO FIGHT FAIR?
POK
POK
POK
POK
POK
POK
NOW ME --
-- I ALWAYS FOUGHT FAIR.
BUT, OF COURSE -- I HAD TO.
Y'SEE, I WAS A PRETTY SOLITARY KID --
--AN' THE ONLY ONE I EVER HAD TO FIGHT WITH --
--WAS MYSELF!
YOU'VE BEEN WORKING ALONGSIDE FLATSCANS SO LONG, HAVOK -- THAT YOU'VE BECOME JUST LIKE THEM:
SOFT...
WEAK...
INFERIOR!
OUT TO DESTROY THE "INFERIOR" RACE -- IN MAGNETO'S NAME?
DON'T YOU KNOW WHAT AN INSULT THAT IS TO THE MEMORY OF THE VERY MAN YOU CLAIM TO WORSHIP?
FIFTY YEARS AGO, MAGNUS BARELY SURVIVED A HOLOCAUST THAT DESTROYED ALMOST ALL OF HIS PEOPLE!
ALL BECAUSE SOME LUNATIC TOOK IT UPON HIMSELF TO DECIDE WHO DESERVED TO LIVE -- AND WHO DIDN'T!
WHERE'S THE SENSE IN RESURRECTING THAT KIND OF EVIL -- IN THE NAME OF ONE OF ITS VICTIMS ...?!
YOU'VE SEEN THIS PLACE, HAVO YOU'VE SEEN THE SENTINEL YOU TELL ME --
-- WHERE'S THE SENSE IN LETTING THE FLATSCANS DO TO MUTANTS WHAT HITLER DID TO THE JEW DOESN'T IT MAKE MORE SENSE TO STRIKE FIRST -- AND DESTROY THEM ALL --
-- BEFO THE NEX HOLOCA ?

NO
IT
DOESN'T!
PATHETIC, ISN'T IT? BROTHER AGAINST BROTHER.
WHILE THE HUMANS PREPARE THEIR WEAPONS OF GENOCIDE.
YOU COULD END THIS, YOU KNOW. INSTANTLY.
YES, SON OF MAGNUS--
--I'M TALKING TO YOU.
THEN TALK. BUT BE QUICK ABOUT IT --
--I'M NOT A VERY PATIENT MAN.

I CUT A PATH THROUGH YOUR DOPPELGANGERS, MADROX -- AND NOW I'M GOING TO CUT A PATH THROUGH YOUR HEART!
BUT BEFORE I SLICE YOU OPEN LIKE A PIECE OF RIPE FRUIT --
--I THINK I'LL TAKE OUT YOUR EYES.
AFTER ALL, YOU'VE BEEN BLIND TO MAGNETO'S TRUTH FOR SO LONG--
--THAT IT SEEMS ONLY FITTING!
STOP IT... STOP!
Oh... DEAR GOD... PLEASE--
--IT HURTS!
STOP BEGGING IT'S EMBARRASSING.
NOW BE STILL... AND FACE YOUR DEATH WITH SOME DIGNI--
--TURRK!
I'M SORRY, MELLANCAMP--
--I TRULY AM.
SLAM
POK
KAPLOOSH
SPAK
OOOSH
BUT YOU DIDN'T LEAVE ME ANY CHOICE.
EASY
KAFF KAFF
--FOR YOU TO SAY...

AC
MMAND
CEIVED.
ITIATE.

SENATOR KELLY, I PRESUME?
FRENZY, ISN'T IT?
Oh, RIGHT. YOU'RE THE MUTANT EXPERT. KNOW MORE ABOUT ME THAN I KNOW ABOUT MYSELF.

PROBABLY GOT A BIG FAT FILE MARKED: "EXTERMINATE. TOO DANGEROUS TO LIVE."
I'M NOT AFRAID OF YOU. ANY OF YOU. THERE'S A SECURITY TEAM HEADED HERE RIGHT NOW AND --
--AND BY THE TIME THEY ARRIVE... YOU'LL BE DEAD.
KILL ME--AND YOU'LL BE THE GREATEST ALLY I'VE EVER HAD!
"GEE-CEE MURDERS UNITED STATES SENATOR." EVEN THE ACLU WILL BE SCREAMING FOR MUTANT BLOOD.
THERE'LL BE A "PROJECT WIDEAWAKE" IN EVERY STATE IN THE UNION. THEY'LL BE POPPING UP ALL OVER THE FREE WORLD.

A MARTYR TO THE CAUSE, KELLY. DOESN'T SEEM LIKE YOUR STYLE.
BUT I'LL DO WHAT I CAN TO OBLIGE...
...YOU!
IN CASE YE DINNAE NOTICE, SENATOR, I JUST SAVED YUIR LIFE. A LOT OF PEOPLE WOULD THINK THAT WAS A MISTAKE. THEY'D SAY YUI'RE AS BAD IN YUIR WAY AS MAGNETO WAS IN HIS.
BUT I'M STILL NAIVE ENOUGH T'BELIEVE THAT EVEN THE HARDEST HEART CAN BE CHANGED BY AN ACT OF SIMPLE KINDNESS.
PROVE ME WRONG, SENATOR--
--AN' I JUST MIGHT BE BACK--
--T'FINISH WHAT FRENZY STARTED.

THIS HAS ALL BEEN STAGED FOR YOUR BENEFIT, YOU KNOW.
MINE?
DON'T FEIGN SURPRISE, PIETRO. I SAW YOU DOWN THERE... STANDING APART FROM THE OTHERS. OBSERVING. PONDERING. YOU TOWER ABOVE US ALL, SON OF MAGNUS.
TO YOUR DULL EYES, I APPEARED TO BE STANDING STILL, CORTEZ. BUT IN THE TIME IT TOOK YOU TO BLINK -- I WAS ACROSS THIS COMPLEX SEVERAL TIMES --
--SAVING THE LIVES OF THE FL--
--THE HUMANS YOU'RE SO DESPERATE TO DESTROY.
YOU ALMOST SAID "FLAT-SCANS," DIDN'T YOU?
AN ABHORRENT TERM.
AN APT ONE... AS YOU WELL KNOW.
IF THERE'S A POINT TO THIS-- I'D ADVISE YOU TO MAKE IT. NOW. YOU'RE GETTING ON MY NERVES.
YOUR FATHER WAS A VISIONARY--
MY FATHER WAS A --
--AND YOU SHARE THAT VISION --
--NO MATTER HOW HARD YOU MAY TRY TO DENY IT... REPRESS IT...
AGREE TO LEAD THE ACOLYTES, PIETR GUIDE THEM TO THE PROMISED LAND YOUR FATH DREAMED OF --
--AND I'LL CALL AN END TO THIS MINDLESS BLOODLETTING THIS VERY INSTANT!

GUIDE YOUR BAND OF DEMENTED LITTLE BROWN SHIRTS IN A BLOODY CRUSADE AGAINST EVERYONE THEY HATE AND FEAR?
DO YOU REALLY EXPECT ME TO JUMP FOR JOY AND AGREE TO SUCH AN ABSURD SUGGESTION?
AGREE? NO. Ah... BUT I DO EXPECT YOU TO PONDER IT.
YOU CAN'T DENY THE URGINGS OF FATE, SON OF MAGNUS. YOU HAVE BEEN CHOSEN TO --
MY FATE IS MY OWN, CORTEZ!
I CHOOSE WHAT I WANT TO DO... WHERE I WANT TO GO --
GO AHEAD... KILL ME. IT WON'T CHANGE ANYTHING.
THE TRUTH I BRING IS ONE YOU ALREADY KNOW. YOU ARE MAGNETO'S SON --
-- MAGNETO'S HEIR.
AND NO MATTER HOW FAST YOU RUN -- YOUR HERITAGE WILL OVERTAKE YOU --

--IN THE END. NOW, VOIGHT! TRANSPORT US OUT OF HERE!
NO!
I'LL SEE YOU AGAIN, PIETRO--
--VERY SOON, I THINK.
HEY! I THOUGHT THIS WAS A "NO SMOKING" ZONE!
THEY'RE TAKING OFF!
BUT... WHY? THEY DIDN'T TAKE OUT THE SENTINELS--OR DO ANY MAJOR DAMAGE TO THE BASE--!
PERHAPS OUR AIMS WEREN'T AS OBVIOUS AS ALL THAT, HAVOK!
PERHAPS OUR MAIN GOAL TODAY WAS TO PLANT A SEED--
--WHICH, IN TIME, WILL GROW INTO AN OAK SO TALL, SO STRONG--
--THAT EVEN THE LORD MAGNUS HIMSELF--

-- WOULD LOOK UPON IT WITH AWE...
THE SENTINELS! WHAT IF I WAS WRONG? WHAT IF THEY'VE MANAGED TO TELEPORT THEM OUT, TOO?!
ALEX... LOOK -- HEY'RE ONE!
NO... IT WAS KELLY. HE HAD A BACK-UP PLAN... TO MOVE THE SENTINELS OUT BEFORE --
HAKK --
VAL..?
-- BE-FAKKK!
VAL... WHAT-- WHAT'S WRONG?
I --
HAAKKK!
I DON'T--
VAL?! ACH! WHAT IS THAT HORROR!
HEY, VAL... IT'S NOTHING TO BE EMBARRASSED ABOUT. I DID THE SAME THING BACK ON THE SHIP AND --
ZIP IT, GUIDO!
I REMEMBER!
WHAT WAS IT? TELL US!
THEY... TOOK ME! * THE ACOLYTES! IMPLANTED THAT... THAT DISGUSTING THING IN ME!
CONTROLLED MY MIND! THEY MADE ME --
-- THEY MADE ME --
* SEE X-FACTOR #87 --KELLY C.

Oh, PLEASE -- YOU'VE GOT TO FORGIVE ME!
I... I DIDN'T MEAN TO BRING YOU HERE!
-- TO BETRAY YOU LIKE THIS!
I WAS PROGRAMMED! I HAD TO --
AND WAS LYING ABOUT "PROJECT: WIDEAWAKE" PART OF THE PROGRAMMING?
N-NO, BUT --
I DON'T WANT TO HEAR YOUR LAME EXCUSES --
ALEX, YE DINNAE HAVE THE RIGHT TO --
I HAVE EVERY RIGHT!!
VAL... I'M TRULY SORRY FOR WHAT THE ACOLYTES DID TO YOU... BUT, IN SOME WAYS, IT'S NO DIFFERENT THAN WHAT YOU'VE BEEN DOING TO US --
ALL ALONG!
YOU DON'T UNDER-STAND --
-- "PROJECT WIDEAWAKE" IS ONLY IN PLACE AS A FAIL-SAFE --
-- IN CASE X-FACTOR... DOESN'T WORK.
PIETRO -- YOU UNDERSTAND... I DID WHAT I HAD TO DO -- FOR NATIONAL SECURITY!
I... I WAS JUST FOLLOWING ORDERS!

AN UNFORTUNATE CHOICE OF PHRASE, VALERIE.
ONE THAT ECHOED AGAIN AND AGAIN AT NUREMBERG-- WHEN THE MURDERERS OF MY FATHER'S PEOPLE--
--OF MY PEOPLE--
--SOUGHT EXPIATION OF THEIR SINS.
BUT-- YOU CAN'T POSSIBLY COMPARE THIS TO--!
YOU... ALL OF YOU... YOU'RE NOT JUST SOME HIRED UNDERLINGS-- YOU'RE MY FRIENDS!
YOU'RE MY FRIENDS!
"SOME OF MY BEST FRIENDS ARE MUTANTS"?
AH, VALERIE-- HOW VERY TYPICAL--
--OF A FLAT-SCAN.
THE END

BEHOLD...
THE SON OF MAGNETO!
30TH ANNIVERSARY
BONUS PIN-UP

X-Force #25 hologram original pencils by Greg Capullo, and inks by Kevin Conrad

Full cover art without hologram

1993

MARVEL COMICS

X-MEN

NIVERSAR

SSU

X-FORCE

50 US
40 CAN
25
UG
£2.60

APPROVED BY THE COMICS CODE AUTHORITY

FATAL ATTRACTIONS

HOME IS THE WARRIOR

BEHOLD NOW THE EXODUS

PROLOGUE
SOMEWHERE IN HEAVEN, A SHEPHERD SITS ALONE... WONDERING WHICH OF HIS MANY SHEEP WILL MAKE FOR THE EASIEST FLEECING.
AND HE CHIDES HIMSELF FOR HAVING THE THOUGHT, FOR HE FULLY REALIZES THAT IF HE IS TO RULE IN PARADISE--
-- HE MUST SHELTER THE FLOCK, PROTECT IT... NOT LEAD IT TO THE SLAUGHTER.
SHALL THE CHILDREN BE FIRST?
YES.
SINCE MY OWN CHILDREN SEEM UNATTAINABLE, LET US THEN INVITE HIS.
IF THE CHILDREN OF THE ATOM ARE WILLING TO ACCEPT THE TRUTH--
--THAT THE DREAM IS DEAD, THE DREAMER A FOOL--
--THEN PERHAPS THEIR KIN WILL AWAKEN...
...AND FINALLY-- FINALLY-- CHARLES XAVIER'S FOOLISH QUEST FOR A HOLY GRAIL--
-- WILL BE OVER!
CANNONBALL
BOOMER
FERAL
WARPATH
RICTOR
SHATTERSTAR
SIRYN
SUNSPOT
FATAL ATTRACTIONS
A CELEBRATION MARKING THIRTY YEARS OF X-CELLENCE
Featuring
X-FORCE

CAMP VERDE HAD BEEN A SMALL, ISO-LATED RESERVATION HERE IN THE ARIZONA VASTES UNTIL ITS EOPLE WERE KILLED AN UNSOLVED, UN-ECIPITATED SLAUGHTER.
AS SOLE SURVIVING MEMBER OF HIS TRIBE, JAMES PROUDSTAR NOW CONTROLS THE LAND.
HE HAS TURNED HIS FORMER HOME INTO THE HIDEOUT AND HEADQUARTERS FOR THE MILITANT MUTANT OUTLAWS KNOWN AS X-FORCE.
AH, JUST SMELL THAT DUSTY AIR!
SNIFF SNIFF
MORE'N DUST, BOOMER-BABE.
WHAT IS IT, FERAL?
BUT AS THIS BAND RETURNS FROM A TENSE MISSION IN WHICH TWO FORMER FRIENDS, THE MUTANT PYROMORPH RUSTY COLLINS AND THE MUTANT GIRL KNOWN ONLY AS SKIDS--
PEOPLE BEEN HERE. SOMEONE'S STILL HERE, TOO!
YOU SURE?
HSSS
O' COURSE, SHE'S SURE, RIC.
WERE FREED ROM A RADICAL NTI-MUTANT RGANIZATION, ALLED THE RIENDS OF UMANITY--
-THE X-FORCE EMBERS EMERGING ROM THE INTER-ERSONNEL ASSAULT ARRIER'S CARGO AY DOORS HAVE TO WONDER--
-WHY IS IT THAT HENEVER THEY ETURN HERE, IT EVER FEELS AS F THEY'RE COMING HOME?
HAT IS MISSING ROM THIS RAM-HACKLE COMPOUND HEY'VE TRIED SO ARD TO TURN INTO PROPER BASE OF OPERATIONS?
SIGH--HERE WE GO AGAIN.
LET'S FAN OUT AN' SCOPE OUT THE COMPLEX.
WHAT ABOUT RUSTY AND SKIDS, SAM?

WE'LL LEAVE 'EM IN THE IPAC FOR NOW, BOBBY.
THEY'RE STILL BRAIN-FRIED, SO THEY CAN'T HELP MUCH-- GEEZ, THEY'D TAKE US OUT SOON AS TAKE OUT AN INTRUDER, RIGHT?
SPLIT INTO FOUR-TWO'S. BOOMER WITH ME, WE GOT THE TARA SECTION.
BOBBY AN' RIC--TAKE THE LYD.
TERRY AN' JIMMY--HIT THE GARAGE.
'STAR AN' FERAL, YOU GOT THE WEAPONS DEPOT.
WE ALL MEET IN THE COMM-ROOM. STAY IN CLOSE CONTACT--AN' NO STUPID SOLO FIGHTIN'!
STAR--FERAL--YOU TWO UNDERSTAND THAT?
HSSSTT
WE HEAR YOU, CANNONBALL. WE HEAR YOU!
AND...
WELCOME TO TARA
LIVIN' QUARTERS LOOK CLEAR RIGHT NOW, BOOMER.
BUT SOMEONE WAS HERE.
SAM--? EVERYTHING OKAY?
HOW CAN YOU TELL?
AH BEEN SKETCHIN' OUT IDEAS FOR LINKIN' ALL THE BUNKER COMPOUNDS TOGETHER--
--AN' SOMEON FINISHED OFF ALL MY DESIGN FOR THE CAMP
--AN' THE DID A MUC BETTE JOB THAN WOULD'VE! AH WANT T KNOW WHO DID THIS A WHY!

SKREEEEEEEEEE
FIFTY METERS AWAY, IN THE ACCESS TUNNEL LEADING TO THE VEHICLE STORAGE AND MAINTENANCE BUNKER...
GOTTA REMEMBER TO WEAR EARPLUGS 'ROUND YOU AN' YOUR SONIC SCREAM, TERRY.
YOUR PRETTY BLUE EYES SEE ANYTHING YET?
FWOOKT
SKREEEEE
TERRY--?! WH--
?!
...
FWAPHOOM
PHWOOMPH

INSIDE THE MEDI-LABS, TWO HUNDRED METERS NORTHEAST OF THE VEHICLE STORAGE AREA...
YOU HEAR ANYTHING ANYMORE, BOBBY?
NO.
I THOUGHT IT WAS SIRYN'S SONIC SCREAM--
--BUT IT WAS CUT OFF RATHE ABRUPTLY AS I SHE WERE HIT WITH A SONIC DAMPENER.
LITTLE YELLOW DIFFERENT
WELL, LET'S HEAD OVER THERE AN' FIND OUT--
--'CAUSE IT'S PRETTY OBVIOUS THERE'S NO ONE HERE.
THE TWO OF YOU NEVER CEASE TO AMAZE ME WITH YOUR CARELESSNESS.
THAT'S THE FIRST RIGHT ANSWER YOU'VE HAD SINCE I'VE KNOWN YOU, DACOSTA.
GAS--?!
PHNUM TOOK
PHNUM TOOK
SSSSSTHSSSSS

THE WEAPONS DEPOT, IFTY FIVE METERS OUTHWEST OF THE ARAGE...
HAVE YOU PICKED UP A SCENT?
MTHIN'.
T I N' KNOW AT...
AS ANYONE TOLD OU HOW HEAVY OUR ACCENT ETS WHEN YOU RE EXCITED?
O, BUNS-- UT IF JOU UM A EW BARS...
SHALL WE GO FIND SOME-ONE TO USE THESE ON?
WHY NOT? WHOEVER WAS HERE, AIN'T HERE NOW.
WRONG!
DON'T WORRY--
--THEY WERE JUST MAGNESIUM BURSTS MEANT TO TEMPORARILY BLIND YOU--
--AFTER ALL, SINCE YOU WERE MY RECRUITS--
--YOU DON'T REALLY THINK I'D BE IDIOTIC ENOUGH TO ENGAGE THE TWO OF YOU IN COMBAT, DO YOU?

NOW TO FIND SAM AND--
THBRUMMM
WELL, TAKE THREE BIG GUESSES WHO-EVER YOU ARE, AS TO WHAT JUST HAPPENED--
--SAM FOUND YOU!!
TWAPOOM
SKRUNSH
OUCH-MAKER
NOW WHY DON'T YOU COME OUTTA THE SHADOWS, MISTER, SO WE CAN SEE WHO--
--OMILORD--
--YOU--?!

I HAVE TO SERIOUSLY QUESTION YOUR STRATEGY, SAM. YOU DID EXACTLY WHAT I WANTED...
... I MEAN, BLASTING ME, OF ALL PEOPLE-- INTO A WEAPON'S RACK?
THAT'S LIKE PUTTING THE WOLF IN CHARGE OF THE HEN-HOUSE.
BACK TO FRONT
FEATURING THE RETURN OF CABLE TO THE PAGES OF X-FORCE!!
BROUGHT TO YOU BY FABIAN NICIEZA GREG CAPULLO
WITH
WIACEK, GREEN, RYAN, PALMIOTTI, HANNA, CONRAD, MILGROM
INKERS
CHRIS ELIOPOULOS
LETTERER
GEORGE ROUSSOS
COLORIST
BOB HARRAS
PLATOON LEADER
TOM DeFALCO
BACK IS FRONT

CABLE!
IT CAN'T BE! BUT--
YOU'RE ALIVE!
UHM... I-UHM--
OBVIOUSLY, TABITHA--
I CAN'T BELIEVE IT! HOW DID YOU SURVIVE?
CABLE OL' PAL...
OUCH-MAKER
BOOM
EH--?
HOW'S THIS FOR STRATEGY? THE BEAUTIFUL BLONDE DIS-TRACTS YOU--
THAT'S REAL IMPRESSIVE, SAM. YOU'VE GOT THE ANGRY YOUNG MAN POSE DOWN PAT.
POSE?
I LIKE THE "BEAUTIFUL BLONDE" PART MYSELF.
LIKE YOU WOULD KNOW NUTHIN' 'BOUT BLONDE 'LESS IT CAME INNA BOTTLE!
HEY, BOSS, NICE T'SEE YOU BACK.
SNIFF
SNIFF
YOUR SCENT IS DIFF'RENT.
I AM DIFFERENT, MARIA.
EACH BATTLE SHOULD CHANGE A MAN.
IT IS AN HONOR, SIR, TO SEE A RESPECTED WARRIOR RETURN FROM A BATTLEFIELD WHERE HE WAS THOUGHT CANCELED.

SPEAK FOR YOURSELF, 'STAR!
OT ALL OF US RE THRILLED TO SEE IS MURDERER ALIVE AGAIN!
RICTOR, DACOSTA... I NEVER EXPECTED TO SEE THE TWO OF YOU WITH X-FORCE AGAIN.
BUT TRUTH TO TELL, I'M GLAD YOU'VE BOTH COME BACK
SHUMPH
WHAT ABOUT MY FATHER, CABLE? I SAW YOU KILL HIM WHEN I WAS A BOY.
WASN'T ME, KID. STRYFE MURDERED YOUR FATHER, RIC.
MY TWIN, WITH HIS HELMET OFF, SO IT LOOKED LIKE IT WAS ME. WHY, I DON'T KNOW--BUT STRYFE NEVER NEEDED A REASON TO KILL, DID HE?
YOU'RE--
--GLAD--?
AS FOR YOUR FATHER, ROBERTO, HE WAS KILLED BY THE EXTERNAL GIDEON!
WHAT--?!
I DON'T HAVE A FIGHT WITH EITHER OF YOU.
AND NEITHER OF YOU HAS ONE WITH ME.
WHEN DID YOU FIND ALL THIS OUT?
JUST RECENTLY. DURING THE TIME I SPENT--MISSING IN THE TIME STREAM--
--BETWEEN LIFE AND DEATH, HERE AND THERE--
--I LEARNED A LOT OF THINGS.

LIKE WHAT?
LIKE KNOWING HOW MUCH I NEED X-FORCE NOW--AND NOT JUST TO ACCOMPLISH MY GOALS--
--BUT BECAUSE, MUCH TO MY SURPRISE, ALL OF YOU MAKE A DIFFERENCE IN MY LIFE.
IT'S OBVIOUS YOU KIDS BELIEVED IN MY MORE FORCEFUL INTERPRETATION OF XAVIER'S DREAM TO ONE EXTENT OR ANOTHER.
YOU JUST HAVE TO LOOK AT HOW YOU'VE CHOSEN TO LIVE TO KNOW THAT.
'ZACTLY THE POINT--OUR CHOICE--
--YOU SAY YOU NEED US, CABLE, BUT MAYBE WE DON'T NEED YOU!
SAM, WHAT'S GOTTEN INTO YOU? YOU'RE ACTING BIZARRE!
"ACTING'S" A GOOD CHOICE OF WORDS.
SAM... YOU'VE BEEN WEIGHED DOWN BY THE BURDEN OF LEADERSHIP SINCE I LEFT--
--FORCED TO MAKE THE KINDS OF DECISIONS NO ONE YOUR AGE SHOULD HAVE TO MAKE.
YOU'VE WRESTLED WITH THE RESPONSIBILITY OF LIVES BALANCING ON YOUR EVERY WORD.
TELL ME THE TRUTH, SAM--TELL YOURSELF THE TRUTH--THAT IT ISN'T TOO MUCH FOR ANY ONE MAN OR WOMAN TO BEAR?
TELL ME YOU HAVEN'T FELT YOURSELF ALONE AND APART FROM EVERYONE AROUND YOU? IT'S THE ISOLATION OF LEADERSHIP--AND IT ISN'T PLEASANT, I KNOW.
SO--TELL ME THAT YOU HAVEN'T PURPOSELY DISTANCED YOURSELF EMOTIONALLY FOR FEAR OF BEING HURT OR HURTING OTHERS?
AH--HAVE--

M SORRY, SAM --
--FOR EVERYTHING I DID TO YOU--
I TRIED HARD TO BE A MILITARY LEADER THAT I FORGOT WHERE I CAME FROM--
-- AND FOR EVERYTHING I DIDN'T DO FOR YOU.
I FORGOT THAT SOLDIERS FIGHTING TOGETHER ARE MORE THAN PROGRAMMABLE MACHINES --
-- THEY'RE BROTHERS-IN-ARMS --
--THEY'RE A FAMILY--
--AND I WANT TO TRY TO DO RIGHT BY YOU, SON --
--BY ALL OF YOU.
HEY, YOU GAVE ME A REASON TO GO ON LIVING AFTER MY FAMILY WAS KILLED, CABLE...
AYE.
...AS FAR AS I'M CONCERNED YOU'VE DONE ALL RIGHT SO FAR.
WELL, THINGS ARE SURE GONNA BE DIFFERENT AROUND HERE WITH YOU BACK--
--THEY CAN NEVER BE THE SAME AGAIN--
--BUT THE ROAD REMAINS THE SAME--
--AND WE ALL RIDE IT TOGETHER.
THEN IT'S LUCKY FOR ME, I'M WEARING A BRAND NEW PAIR OF SHOCK ABSORBERS JUST IN CASE IT GETS BUMPY.

TWO HOURS!
HIJOS DE--
THEY BEEN TALKIN' FOR TWO HOURS NOW!
HOW MUCH LONGER THEY GONNA BE DOWN THERE?

YOU SAY SOMETHING, RIC?
SORRY. PORNO FOR PYROS. YOU KNOW HOW I ZONE OUT ON THEM.
I SAID, PROUDSTAR--

--I SHOULD BE A PART OF THEIR MEETING!

WHAT AN EGO YOU CARRY WARRIOR.
IT IS, I GUESS, HEAL IN SOME WAY
--BUT A GOOD SOLDI KNOWS WHE TO FIGHT--
--AND WHEN TO ALLOW HIS LEADE THE OPPOR-TUNITY TO CONDUCT STRATEGI BUSINESS

CERTAINLY NOT I.
NOW QUIET YOURSELF--
--OR I WILL DO SOME TEMPORARY DAMAGE TO YOUR LARYNX AND SPARE US ALL YOUR COM-PLAINING.
WELL, WHO CARES WHEN THEY'S DONE ANYWAYS?
ALL I KNOW IS WITH THE BIG KAHUNA BACK 'STEAD OF MILKSOP SAMMY, WE CAN START KICKIN' SOME SERIOUS BUTT!
YOU'RE JUST HAPPY 'CAUSE HAVING CABLE BACK PROTECTS YOU--
--FROM GETTING RUN OUT OF HERE BY US!
YEAH, RIGHT, GERONIMO--LIKE I'M JUS' SHOOR THAT'S WHAT I WAS RILLY, RILLY, RILLY WORRIED ABOUT!
I'M SHOOR...
WELL, WHO THE HECK EVER SAID I WAS A GOOD SOLDIER?!

INSIDE THE MEDICAL TRIAGE BUNKER...

THEY DON'T LOOK LIKE MAD TERRORISTS, NOW, DO THEY?

S'NOT FUNNY, CABLE. RUSTY AN' SKIDS AIN'T RESPONSIBLE FOR THEIR CONDITION...OR WHAT THEY DID.

I KNOW, SAM. STRYFE DIDN'T LOBOTOMIZE THEM, BUT HE JUST AS WELL MIGHT HAVE.

THEIR BRAINS HAVE HAD SPECIFIC NEURAL TISSUE IMPLANTS WHICH FORCE THEM TO BEHAVE THE WAY THEY DO.

ONCE... SEVERAL YEARS AGO FOR ME -- TWO THOUSAND YEARS IN THE FUTURE FOR YOU --

--STRYFE DID THE SAME THING TO MY SON, TYLER.

YOUR SON, TYLER? BUT YOU SAID HE WASN'T...

I LIED ABOUT TYLER TO KEEP MYSELF EMOTIONALLY DISTANT FROM YOU, SAM.

GUESS IT WORKED.

I'LL TRY TO FIND A NEW WAY.

WELL, UNTIL YOU DO-- WHAT CAN WE DO FOR RUSTY AND SKIDS? DO THEY STAY THIS WAY FOREVER...

... OR CAN THEY BE RETURNED TO NORMAL?

NOT WITH THE EQUIPMENT WE HAVE HERE, TABITHA.

MAYBE IF I COULD FIND A WAY TO CONTACT THE PROFESSOR. GET US UP TO GRAY-MALKIN...

WE CAN TAKE THE IPAC UNIT ORBITAL, CAN'T WE?
SURE. BUT NOT BEFORE WE'RE SURE WE KNOW WHAT WE'RE DOIN'.

STILL DON'T TRUST ME, DO YOU, SAM?
GIVE ME A GOOD ENOUGH REASON TO, SIR.

YOU WANT SOME CONCRETE ANSWERS FROM THE HORSE'S MOUTH, RIGHT, SAM?
FINE. YOU DESERVE IT. HERE GOES--
MY ORIGINAL NAME IS NATHAN DAYSPRING, DELIVERED TO THE FUTURE BY A WOMAN NAMED ASKANI--
--AND RAISED TO BE THE SAVIOR FOR THE REBELLION AGAINST THE CANAANITE RULE OF THE EXTERNAL HIGH-LORD, WHOM YOU KNOW IN THIS TIMELINE AS APOCALYPSE.
WE LOST THE WAR IN MY FUTURE, SAM.
SO I RETURNED TO THIS TIMELINE--WHICH HAPPENS TO BE A FOCAL POINT FOR ALL HISTORY WHICH MAY HAPPEN--
--TO ENSURE THAT MADMEN LIKE APOCALYPSE--
--WOULD NEVER HAVE THE OPPORTUNITY AGAIN TO CREATE THE KIND OF HELL THAT MY WORLD HAS BECOME.
AND YOU, SAM, WERE PART OF MY PLAN. THE HOPE I WAS GOING TO DE-VELOP A HIGH-LORD TAUGHT AND RAISED BY THE VIEWS OF BOTH XAVIER AND MAGNETO--
--THE ONE PERSON WHO, SOMEDAY IN THE FUTURE--CAN BECOME MANKIND--AND MUTANTKIND'S SAVIOR!
THEN A MONKEY WRENCH GOT THROWN INTO THE WORKS.
I NEVER KNEW UNTIL RECENTLY THAT THE CHAOS-BRINGER, A WORLDWIDE FOMENTOR OF ANARCHY FROM MY TIME KNOWN AS STRYFE, HAD COME BACK HERE AS WELL AND WAS, APPARENTLY, MY EXACT DUPLICATE.
I HAVE MY SUSPICIONS AS TO WHY THAT IS. BUT UNTIL I KNOW FOR SURE, I THINK I'LL KEEP THAT TO MYSELF.
I NEVER HAD THE CHANCE TO VERIFY WHAT I BELIEVE AFTER WE WERE BOTH SUCKED INTO THE TIMESTREAM. I ESCAPED, STRYFE DIDN'T.
WHICH BRINGS US TO THE HERE AND NOW. HOW'S THAT FOR STRAIGHT TALK?
PRETTY GOOD.

WELL, YOU DID ASK.
AND THERE ARE STILL SOME ANSWERS I CAN'T GIVE YOU, SAM.
BOTH BECAUSE I CAN'T REVEAL POTENTIAL FUTURES TO YOU--
-- BUT ALSO BECAUSE I HAVE BECOME A TRAVELER SO MIRED IN THE TIMESTREAM--
-- THAT I'M NOT SURE WHICH FUTURE BELONGS TO THIS PARTICULAR TIME-LINE ANYMORE!
DROGA! HOW ARE YOU EVER ABLE TO MAKE ANY DECISIONS THEN?
DO IT DAY BY DAY, DACOSTA. ANYWAY, I'VE LEARNED--
--THE FUTURE IS WHAT YOU MAKE IT.
AN' WHAT CAN YE MAKE OF THIS ONE THEN, CABLE?
TELL YOU WHAT, THERESA-- AND JUST TO PROVE MY POINT OF A SECOND AGO--
-- I CAN ONLY GO SO FAR AS TO PREDICT THAT IN OUR IMMEDIATE FUTURE--
--SOMEONE IS GOING TO SPIT TEETH ON THE DESERT SAND!!

MAYBE WE SHOULD WAIT... FOR ONCE.
FOR HIM TO ATTACK FIRST, PROUDSTAR?
--BUT AS AN EMISSARY. A FERRYMAN TO A BETTER PLACE!
JULIO ESTEBAN RICHTER, KNOWN AS RICTOR--
JAMES PROUDSTAR, FOR NOW, THE WARPATH--
SHATTERSTAR, YOU WHO ARE NOT TRULY OF OUR BLOOD--
MARIA CALLASANTOS--CALLED FERAL--
--I AM EXODUS!
FOR NOW, I HAVE COME SEEKING ONLY SAMUEL GUTHRIE AND ROBERTO DACOSTA.
FOR THEY ARE THE FIRST CHOSEN TO CONVENE WITH THE OVERLORD.
SHEESH! LOOKS LIKE NO ONE CARES ABOUT US TODAY, HUH?
WELL, PUT THAT VIBE-SHOCK YOU'RE BUILDING UP AWAY, RIC--
--'CAUSE THIS GUY LOOKS LIKE HE'LL JUST LAUGH IT OFF!
I BELIEVE WE CAN CANCEL HIM, IF NEED BE.
YOU WOULD.

YOUR INTENTIONS ARE OBVIOUS, FELLOW MUTANTS--
--AND ALTHOUGH IT PAINS ME TO ASSAULT YOU ALL FOR THE MISGIVINGS OF A FEW, I DO WHAT I MUST.
FAZZASHAKK
YOU STILL STA
PROUDSTA
I AM IMPRESSED.
WE FORCED YOU TO DO THIS--
'CAUSE WE
ABOUT PROTECTIN
OURSELVES ?!
NO. YOU THOUGHT ABOUT ATTACKING ME...
...AND DO YOU CHILDREN OF X-FORCE NOT PRIDE YOURSELVES SO MUCH ON TURNING THOUGHT INTO DEED ?
YUP-- WE DO!!
AN' WE ALWAYS WILL!
SKR

KEEP POUNDIN' 'IM, SIRYN!
BOBBY, BOOMER FOLLOW UP! KEEP HIM OFF BALANCE SO ME AN' CABLE CAN COME IN TIGHT--!
CABLE--?
IT'S A GOOD MANEUVER. DO IT--
ONE FOR SAMMY.
THIS IS GONNA TURN INTO A GUY-THING, AIN'T IT?
I HAVE NOT COME HERE TO DO BATTLE WITH YOU!
I HAVE COME ONLY TO MAKE AN OFFER TO THE PERPETUATORS OF THE DREAM!
I DO NOT WISH TO HURT ANY OF MY GENETIC BRETHREN!
FAZZA SHAKK RAKOOM
YOU GOT A FUNNY WAY A' SHOWIN' IT...

I COME FOR THE PRIMARY CHOSEN CHILDREN OF THE ATOM, ONLY.
I GRANT YOU AN ESCAPE FROM THIS ASYLUM CALLED EARTH.
THE HARBINGER OF THE MAGNETIC STORM WISHES TO CARRY YOU BOTH AWAY FROM HERE--
--AND LIFT YOU TO A BETTER PLACE.
AS THE SOLE REMAINING ACTIVE PARTICIPANTS FROM XAVIER'S SECOND GENERATION--
--I GRANT ONLY THE TWO OF YOU THIS BOON.
SECOND GEN--?
WHAT ABOUT XI'AN COY MANH--? WHAT ABOUT RAHNE SINCLAIRE?
THE FORMER HAS SPURNED HEAVEN, THE LATTER HAS NOT BEEN OFFICIALLY APPROACHED.
IT WAS HOPED YOUR PARTICIPATION WOULD LEAD TO OTHERS JOINING OUR CAUSE.
WHOSE CAUSE?

ALL WILL BE REVEALED WHEN THE GATES OF HEAVEN OPEN TO GREET YOU.
WELL, NO GATES'RE GONNA OPEN UNLESS THE OTHER NEW MUTANTS COME WITH US--

--AN' THAT MEANS BOOMER AN' RICTOR.

MASON-
ON -- IXNAY
THE
UDINGMEAY--
KAY?
HE HAS NOT REQUESTED THEIR AUDIENCE.
BUT AH HAVE.
... VERY WELL, I ACQUI-ESCE.
IN WHICH CASE, INCLUDE RUSTY AN' SKIDS ON THAT LIST, TOO.
THE TWO IN YOUR MEDICAL LABORATORY? THEY ARE TAINTED IN MIND, IF NOT IN BODY.
HEAVEN HAS TO ACCEPT ALL OF GOD'S CHILDREN WHO HAVEN'T SINNED O' THEIR OWN CHOICE--
--THE GOOD LORD DOESN'T THROW FISH BACK.
THIS IS A STUPID MOVE, SAM! STRATEGI-CALLY, IT'S--
YOU WERE RIGHT BEFORE, ABOUT ME BEIN' TIRED--
--MAYBE IT'S HIGH TIME WE WENT TO A BETTER PLACE THAN THIS--
--DID BETTER THINGS THAN THIS--
SO IT SHALL BE...
NOT ALL
US'RE BEIN'
KED, SAM--
R HAD YE
NVENIENTLY
SSED THAT
ACT?
SOMEONE HAS TO LEAD THE WAY, TERRY.
IF IT WORKS FOR US--MAYBE THE REST OF Y'ALL CAN FOLLOW...

HEAVEN AWAITS THOSE WHO PRAY!!

FAZZASHAKKAKROOM

NOOO--!!

FEKT! HOW COULD GUTHRIE BETRAY US LIKE THIS?!

SAM KNEW WHAT HE WAS DOING ALL ALONG, DIDN'T HE?

AND SO DID YOU, CABLE!

YEAH.

WHEN HE GRABBED MY SHOULDER, SA PLANTED HIS COMM-LINK TRACER, JUS LIKE I TRAINE HIM TO DO.

IT'S A DANGEROUS PLOY, BUT HOW BETTER TO FIND OUT WHO IS BEHIND ALL THIS?

I SEE! AND WHY GO ALO WHEN YOU CA TRICK YOUR OPPONENT INT ALLOWING A LARGER STRI FORCE TO COM ALSO?

I WOULD NOT HAVE GIVEN GUTHRIE CREDIT FOR THE FOOJKIES.

HUMPH. NEITHER WOULD I.

THEN NEITHER ONE OF YOU SEES WHAT SAM IS QUICKLY BECOMING.

AND WHAT THAT

THE BEST THAT ALL HIS TEACHERS HAD TO OFFER!

HAT COULD VERY WELL , THERESA. I JUST PE THIS TEACHER UGHT HIM THAT WHEN AYING A GAME OF HIDE AND SEEK--
"--IT'S A LOT MORE FUN IF YOU HIDE WHERE OU CAN BE FOUND!"

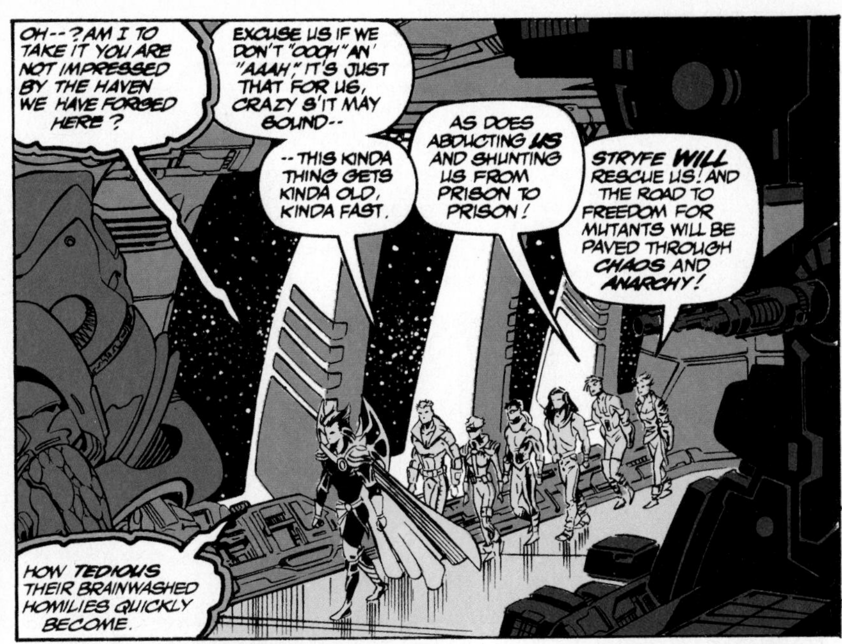

OH--? AM I TO TAKE IT YOU ARE NOT IMPRESSED BY THE HAVEN WE HAVE FORGED HERE?
EXCUSE US IF WE DON'T "OOOH" AN' "AAAH," IT'S JUST THAT FOR US, CRAZY S'IT MAY SOUND--
--THIS KINDA THING GETS KINDA OLD, KINDA FAST.
AS DOES ABDUCTING US AND SHUNTING US FROM PRISON TO PRISON!
STRYFE WILL RESCUE US! AND THE ROAD TO FREEDOM FOR MUTANTS WILL BE PAVED THROUGH CHAOS AND ANARCHY!
HOW TEDIOUS THEIR BRAINWASHED HOMILIES QUICKLY BECOME.

Y'KINDA GET USED T'THEM--LIKE MUZAK.
YOUR ALLUSION ESCAPES ME, GIRL.
BE WARNED, I DO NOT LIKE BEING MOCKED.

WELL, AH DON'T MUCH LIKE PEOPLE TRYIN' T'IMPRESS ME WITH FANCY THINGS AN' HOT AIR, EXODUS.

LIKE AH SAID A SECOND AGO, NOT T'SOUND JADED...

...BUT NICE SPACE STATION Y'GOT HERE AN' ALL, BUT WE BEEN THERE, AN' WE DONE THAT...

...SO WHEN DO YOU REALLY START IMPRESSIN' US?

YOU DO NOT SEEM TO UNDERSTAND, SAMUEL GUTHRIE...
... PERHAPS YOU HAVE BEEN ON ORBITAL STATIONS BEFORE...
... BUT YOU HAVE BEEN ON **THIS** PARTICULAR ONE **TWICE** NOW...
... FOR YOU ARE WALKING THROUGH THE FORMER HOME OF THE MUTANT **CABLE** -- THE PLACE YOU KNEW AS **GRAYMALKIN**...
... THE REFUGE WE HAVE CHRISTENED **AVALON!**

SAM, IS HE RIGHT? **HOW** COULD IT HAVE HAPPENED?
AH DON'T RIGHTLY KNOW, RIC. LOTS OF THE TECH-NOLOGY **LOOKS** KINDA THE SAME--
-- BUT DIFFERENT AS WELL, SAM, AS IF IT HAD BEEN BLENDED WITH THE WORKS OF *OTHER* RACES!
SHIP--? I MEAN, **PROFESSOR** -- ARE YOU STILL INSIDE THE SYSTEM?
INDEED! WE **HAVE** MADE SOME IM-PROVEMENTS.
IF YOU ARE REFERRING TO THE SENTIENT COM-PUTER PRESENCE PREVIOUSLY ABOARD THIS VESSEL--
-- I AM AFRAID YOU ARE WASTING YOUR BREATH.

ARE YOU SAYIN' YOU **KILLED** THE PROFESSOR, EXODUS. 'CAUSE IF YOU DID --
WE... **ALTERED**... ITS PRO-GRAMMING.
WHY?

FOR THE SAME REASON WE DO **EVERYTHING** HERE ON AVALON, SAM--

ALL OUR TIONS ARE RFORMED R THE EATER OD OF ANTKIND.
YOU-- SIR!
BOBBY--!
NO. IT CANNOT BE!
THESE TWO CAN BE CURED.
THE IRON CONTENT IN THEIR BLOOD BLOCKED...
...BY REROUTING THE CIRCULATORY FLOW...
...FROM THE BIOLOGICALLY AFFECTED PORTIONS OF THEIR BRAINS.
IN ESSENCE, DESTROYING THE BRAIN TISSUE WHICH WAS SURGICALLY AND TELEPATHICALLY ALTERED BY THE MADMAN STRYFE...
...THEREBY FREEING THEM TO THINK FOR THEMSELVES ONCE AGAIN!
W-WHAT-- WHAT HAPPENED TO US--?
SAM, BOOM-BOOM--GUYS-- WHERE ARE WE?
ALLOW ME TO OFFICIALLY WELCOME YOU TO AVALON, SON AND DAUGHTER OF THE ATOM...
...YOUR NEW HOME, A PLACE...
...ALL MUTANTS DEEMED WORTHY OF IT WILL SOON CALL...

"-HEAVEN!"
BACK IN SPACE AGAAAINN!
SILENCE YOUR HISSING, CAT.
I DON'T LIKE THIS.
I REALLY DON'T LIKE THIS.
IN FACT, I DON'T LIKE THIS ONE BIT.
WHAT? WHAT DO YOU SEE, CABLE?
WE'RE STILL LOCKED ONTO SAM'S SIGNAL, CABLE.
SUPER-IMPOSE THE TRACKING COORDINATES OVER THE GRID DISPLAY I'M FEEDING YOUR CONSOLE NOW.
LOOK AT THAT! I KNEW I REALLY DIDN'T LIKE THIS ONE BIT!
YOU DON'T MEAN TO TELL ME SAM AND THE OTHERS ARE ABOARD...?
DON'T PANIC YET, JAMES. OUR PROBES AREN'T GETTING THROUGH CLEANLY.
AS IF I WERE SPEAKING ENGLISH TO A JAPANESE OPERATOR.
I'M GOING TO SEND A HIGH-ENERGY PULSE OVERRIDE SIGNAL.
YOU KNOW, SUDDENLY I DON'T LIKE THIS ANY-MORE, TOO...

THE OVERRIDE PULSE SHOULD BE HITTING THE MAIN CLOAKING SCREENS RIGHT ABOUT-- NOW!
ZZXXXTHTTTTSHSHSHSHSH
I KNEW IT!!
GRAYMALKIN!
SOMEONE HAS TAKEN IT FROM IT!!
YE HAVE T'STAY STEADY, CABLE. WHOEVER DID THIS IS GOING T'BE VERY DIFFICULT T'DEAL WITH.
YOU DON'T UNDERSTAND, THERESA. GRAYMALKIN IS ALL I HAVE.
ALL THAT REMINDS ME OF WHERE I'VE BEEN--THE LIFE I LOST--AND WHERE I NEED TO GO!
YE HAVE US, NATHAN! WE HAVE EACH OTHER!
YOU MUST FORGET ABOUT WHAT YOU'VE LOST--YOUR PAST IS OUR FUTURE!
WHAT YOU HAD, WHAT YOU NO LONGER HAVE-- IT'S NOT AS IMPORTANT AS MAKIN' THE POSSIBILITIES HAPPEN!
YE'R THE ONE WHO PLANTED THESE SEEDS IN OUR TIME-- NOW IT'S TIME T'SEE IT GROW AND BE HARVESTED!
WELL NOW, D'WE SIT AN' STEW OR D'WE MOVE FORWARD?
WE MOVE FOWARD. WE FIND THE OTHERS, THEN WE ROLL RIGHT OVER THE PEOPLE WHO DID THIS--
--BECAUSE HEAVEN ALSO AWAITS THOSE WHO PREY!

I GIVE YOU CREDIT, SAM. YOU TOOK A GREAT RISK BLINDLY COMING HERE.

BLIND, IT SEEMS, BUT **NOT** UNPREPARED.

YOU HAVE GROWN **MUCH**. YOU HAVE LEARNED MUCH.

BELIEVE IT OR NOT, I **DO** OWE QUITE A BIT O' THAT TO **YOU**.

TO BELIEVE THAT WERE TRUE WOULD BE AN **HONOR**.

AND I WOULD RELISH THE OPPORTUNITY FOR YOU -- AND FOR **ME** -- TO LEARN **MORE** FROM EACH OTHER.

I WISH FOR YOU TO **STAY**, SAM. ALL OF YOU -- STAY.

AS YOU PONDER MY OFFER, ASK YOURSELVES, "THOUGH WE ARE FOREVER MARKED AS **CHILDREN OF THE ATOM** --

-- ARE WE STILL CHILDREN OF **CHARLES XAVIER'S** DREAM?"

AND, AS YOUR INDEPENDENCE WILL ATTEST, YOUR REPLY MUST BE **NO**, THEN FOLLOW THAT QUESTION WITH THIS...

... "IS THE PATH OF THIS -- MAN CALLED **CABLE** -- THE **RIGHT** ONE FOR MUTANTS TO FOLLOW?"

FOR I ASSURE Y X-FORC IT IS **NOT**

I OFFER THE **ONLY** WAY -- AS HAVE FRO THE BEGIN-NING.

WHAT'S THE PLAN, CABLE?
I'M GOING TO OVERRIDE THE BODYSLIDING TECHNOLOGY--
--FIND SAM'S UNIT AND TELEPORT THEM HERE.
THEN I'M GOING TO PROGRAM THIS ENTIRE STATION TO OBLITERATE IT-SELF!
YEAH, IT'S A REAL JOY TO BE SITTING ON A WEAPON THAT CAN DESTROY THE ENTIRE PLANET BELOW!
WHAT A HYPOCRITICAL RATIONAL, NATHAN DAYSPRING.
IF YOU CANNOT ATTAIN THE JOYS OF HEAVEN, THEN NO ONE ELSE SHOULD?
REAL INTERESTING DEFINITION OF HEAVEN, EXODUS.
HOW DARE YOU DEFILE THE HOLY SANCTITY OF AVALON WITH YOUR POISONED WORDS!!
DON'T TALK TO ME ABOUT SANCTITY, EXODUS. I'VE SPENT MY LIFE FIGHTING FANATICS LIKE YOU!
I'VE SEEN TOO MANY GOOD PEOPLE DIE BECAUSE OF ZEALOTRY AND BIGOTRY--AND I'VE HAD ENOUGH!
EEACHOW

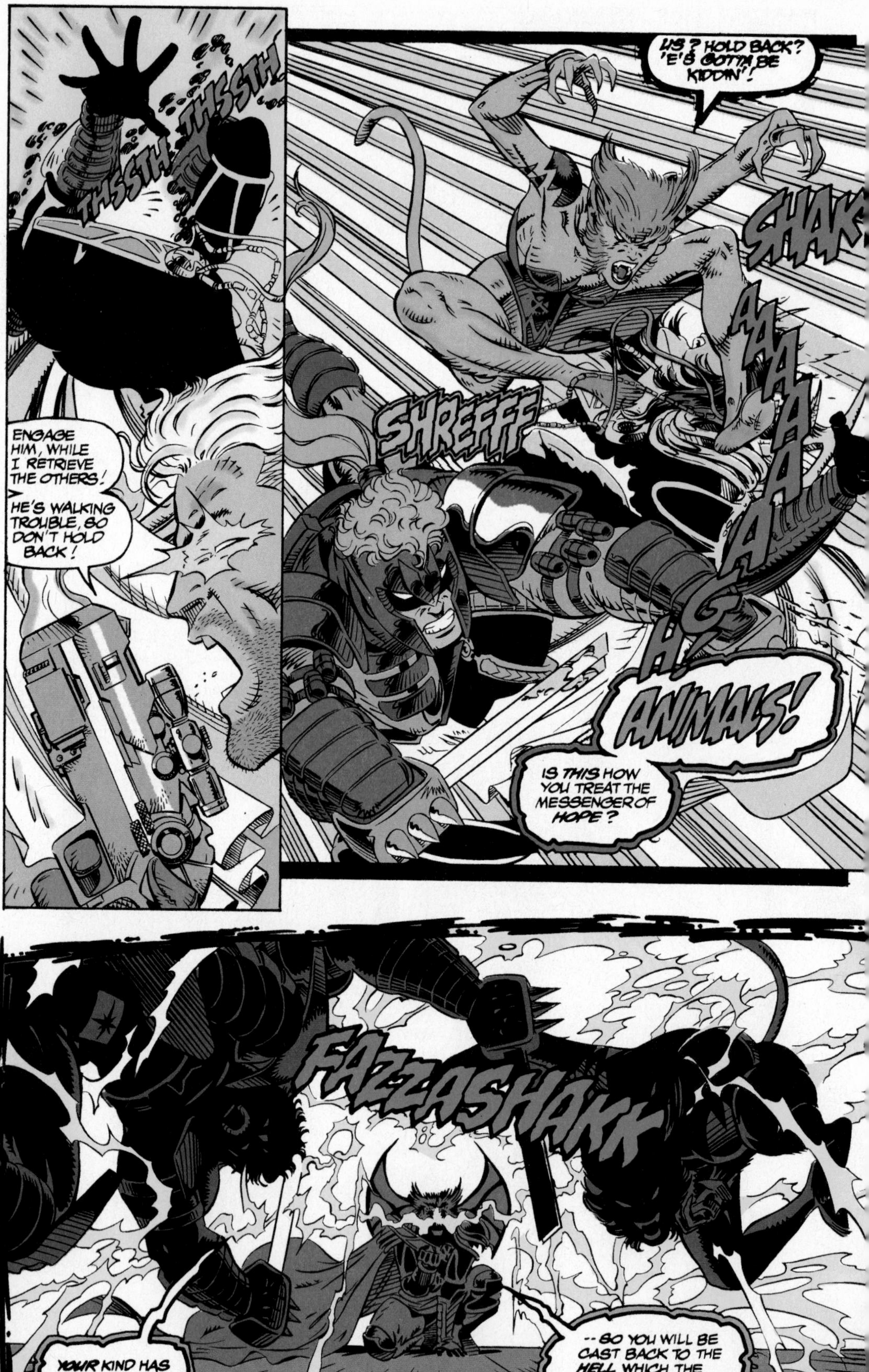

THSSTH THSSTH
ENGAGE HIM, WHILE I RETRIEVE THE OTHERS!
HE'S WALKING TROUBLE, SO DON'T HOLD BACK!
US? HOLD BACK? 'E'S GOTTA BE KIDDIN'!
SHAK
SHREFFF
AAAAAAAGH!
ANIMALS!
IS *THIS* HOW YOU TREAT THE MESSENGER OF *HOPE*?

MMY, FOLLOW
Y SONIC
REAM--
ST AN' TIGHT!
SKREEEEEEEEEE
GRUMMKRASH
THEN AGAIN, IF YOU'RE TRYING TO HURT MY FRIENDS--
--WHAT YOU ARE DOESN'T MATTER NEARLY AS MUCH AS WHAT YOU'RE DOING, DOES!
DID YOU GET ALL THAT THROUGH THE SOUND OF YOUR GLASS JAW SHATTERING?
GIRL NEVER CEASES TO AMAZE ME.
SHAME TO BE KNOCKING YOUR HEAD OFF, SINCE YOU LOOK INDIAN TO ME.
I'VE FOUND SAM AND PROGRAMMED AN OVER-RIDE LINK TO THE STATION'S TELEPORT SYSTEMS--
--X-FORCE-- WE'RE MOVING OUT!
VSHYMMMMMMMMMM
NO-- THEY MUST NOT SULLY THE OVERLORD... WITH THEIR VIOLENT WAYS--

MMMMMYSHWW
SAM, C'MON-- PACK IT UP! YOU'RE OUT OF HERE, NOW!
BUT WHAT ABOUT YOU?
I'M GOING TO TRY AND RETRIEVE THE PROFESSOR'S SENTIENT PROGRAMMING FROM THE SYSTEMS--
--AND THEN I'M GOING TO BLOW THIS PLACE TO PIECES!
NO.
NO? WHAT DO YOU MEAN, "NO"?!
GRAYMALKIN IS LOST TO ME.
IT'S BECOME COMPLETELY CO-OPTED BY THE ALIEN SYSTEMS INTRODUCED INTO ITS CENTRAL DATANET--
--AND YOU KNOW WHO'S RESPONSIBLE, SAM!
DO YOU HONESTLY WANT HIM HOVERING OVER THE PLANET LIKE SOME MAD GOD?!
MAGNUS SAYS THIS PLACE IS GOING TA BECOME A SAFE HOME FOR MUTANTS, IF THAT'S WHAT THEY WANT.
HE SAVED RUSTY AN' SKIDS -- AN' THEY'VE DECIDED TO STAY HERE.
THEY HAVE EVERY RIGHT TA MAKE THEIR OWN CHOICE -- JUST LIKE THE REST O' US DO.
WE CAN CONTINUE TA FIGHT BACK HOME ON EARTH FOR WHAT WE BELIEVE IN -- THAT DOESN'T MEAN EVERYONE HAS TO.
THE RIGHT TA MAKE OUR OWN CHOICES, THE RIGHT OF SELF-DETERMINATION--
--IS THE ARGUMENT WE USED AGAINST XAVIER TA GAIN OUR OWN FREEDOM--
--WHO ARE WE TA TELL OTHERS THEY DON'T HAVE THE SAME RIGHTS?

THINK, IT
S THE TWO
YOU THAT
T ME INTO
S MORAL
AGMIRE
BEGIN
TH.
I NEVER WANTED TO BECOME A TEACHER AGAIN --OR A FATHER.
NOW LOOK AT THE CHOICES MY STUDENTS-- MY CHILDREN--ARE FORCING ME TO MAKE.
COMPUTER: OVERRIDE ACCESS. BODYSLIDE BY EIGHT--IPAC BOUND.
DISENGAGE MOORING LOCKS--SET AUTO-PILOT FOR RETURN TO ORIGINATION CO-ORDINATES...
NO!! CABLE-- WE WON'T LEAVE WITHOUT YOU...
VSHYMMMMMMMMMMM
ARE THEY FLEEING?
NO. THE CHILDREN HAVE GONE, BUT I SENSE THE BUTCHER OF MY MASTER'S HOPE REMAINS ABOARD...
"...NEEDING STILL TO SEEK OUT A MECHANICAL SOUL--
"--WITH WHICH TO REPLACE THOSE PARTS LONG-LOST TO HIM."

GRAYMALKIN'S CENTRAL CORE.
IRONIC, HE THINKS, THAT HE'S WALKING INTO A SUICIDE MISSION IN ORDER TO SAVE A COMPUTER PROGRAM...
...SINCE YEARS AGO, THE SAME COMPUTER PROGRAM RISKED ITS "LIFE" TO SAVE HIM.
BUT THE IRONY ONLY SERVES TO DRIVE HIM HARDER--
--TO SAVE THE ONE THIN
CABLE HAS HAD HIS ENTI
LIFE WHICH EVEN REMOT
FELL UNDER THE DEFINITI
OF "FATHER."
Systems Data
Access:
FIND PROGRAMMING CORE FILE: PROFESSOR.
Processing:
COME ON...
...I'M A DEAD MAN...
...STANDING HERE, DEAD TO RIGHTS...
...ALL FOR A STUPID COMPUTER PROGRAM...
Why, Nathan, I am not certain if I should be thanking you for your tenacity —
— or chiding you for your insults:.
PROFESSOR! YOU'RE STILL ALIVE!!
Other than a mild case of indigestion due to this alien programming in my system, I am on-line:.
WELL, I'M GETTING YOU OUT OF THERE RIGHT NOW!
THEN I'M GOING TO TRY AND FIND A WAY TO ACTIVATE THE AUTO-DESTRUCT SEQUE--
I BELIEVE ALLOWING YOU TO RETRIEVE THIS SMALL PIECE OF YOUR PAST WAS MORE THAN GRACIOUS OF ME...

RELY YOU DO
EXPECT ME
LLOW YOU TO
TROY MY HOME--
--AS EASILY AS YOU DID MY HOPE OF BRINGING ALL OF THE CHILDREN UNDER MY FOLD?
FOR GIVEN TIME, CABLE, THEY WOULD HAVE SEEN THE LIGHT.
SO... IT IS YOU. IN FULL ARMOR, NO LESS.
TIME IS SOMETHING I'VE SEEN PLENTY OF, MAGNETO. AND IN ALL THAT TIME, I'VE ONLY SEEN YOU FAIL.
...TIME AND TIME AGAIN! YOUR WAY LEADS TO OPPRESSION AND BITTERNESS, MAGNETO. AND ENDS IN DEATH.
SAM AND THE OTHERS WOULD NEVER HAVE CHOSEN TO STAY WITH YOU!
AND YOU BELIEVE YOU OFFER A BETTER PATH?
YOU DON'T GET IT, DO YOU?
THEY HAVEN'T CHOSEN TO FOLLOW MY PATH ANYMORE--
--I'VE CHOSEN TO FOLLOW THEIRS!
AND THAT'S A ROAD WHICH YOU AND I ARE BARRELING DOWN FROM OPPOSITE DIRECTIONS--
--WHICH MEANS, WE'RE GEARING UP FOR A HEAD-ON COLLISSION!
9

YOU ARE A SMALL-MINDED FOOL, NATHAN DAYSPRING!
WE COULD HAVE SIMPLY PASSED EACH OTHER BY ON THE ROAD ACKNOWLEDGING OUR DIFFERENT WAYS, YET WISHING THE OTHER SAFE JOURNEY--
--SINCE OUR GOALS--THE SALVATION OF MUTANTKIND--REMAIN THE SAME--
--YET YOU HAVE CHOSEN TO TURN THIS INTO A BATTLE!
WHICH, SINCE HALF OF YOU IS MADE OF METAL--
--AND I AM THE OVER-LORD OF THE FATAL ATTRACTION--
--MAKES YOUR DECISION UTTERLY DEVOID OF REASON!
SAM AND THE OTHERS SHOULD HAVE BEEN MINE, MAN OF TOMORROW!
THEY COULD HAVE HELPED ME BUILD A GLORIOUS HOME FOR OU PEOPLE!
AND THEY WERE MINE ONCE. MINE TO MELD AND FORM... BUT THAT IS LOST--
BUT WHAT I FIND MOST GALLING OF ALL, CABLE--
--IS THAT IN YOUR ARROGANCE--
--YOUR EGO--
--AND IN YOUR OUTRIGHT STUPIDITY--
--YOU WOULD CHOOSE TO THROW AWAY ALL THAT THOSE CHILDREN HAVE TO OFFER YOU--

"--BY ALLOWING YOURSELF TO BE KILLED AT MY HANDS!!"
YEEAAAARRGH!
Y DOES YOUR N LACK OF TH CAUSE YOU MAKE THE ME MISTAKES ER AND OVER AGAIN?
ODD, THAT I SHOULD BE ASKING YOU THAT... LOOK AT THE VICIOUS CYCLE I HAVE PLACED MYSELF IN...
...BUT YOU--YOU CHOSE THE NAME CABLE FOR ALL IT IMPLIES-- A LINK--
--BETWEEN THEN AND NOW--BETWEEN THE DESIRE FOR A BETTER WORLD AND THE NEED TO FIGHT FOR IT...
--AND NOW LOOK AT YOU... LOST... ADRIFT...
...AND FINALLY, LITERALLY AND FIGURATIVELY-- A MAN OUT OF TIME...
PROF-- F'SS-- OR...
I am inside of you, Nathan. Barely:.

YOU STILL LIVE?
WHY WOULD A MAN, WHO IS SO MUCH ARTIFICE, DESPERATELY CLING TO LIFE?
BECAUSE... I'M NOT... A MACHINE...
...I...AM... A... MAN--!
A MAN... WHO JUST BEAT YOU--
--BECAUSE... X-FORCE...IS MINE, MAGNUS AND YOU'VE LOST THEM FOR GOOD.
...BODYSLIDE BY ONE--IPAC BOUND--
VSHYMMMMMMMMMMMM
"YOU RUN AWAY FO NOW, CABLE, AND FO THE SAKE OF SAM AND THE OTHERS, I WILL ALLOW IT.
"BUT THE DAY WILL COME, WHEN YOU WILL NOT BE ABLE TO HIDE FROM YOUR PAST--OR YOUR FUTURE--THE DAY WILL COME SOON...
OH, MY LORD!
IS HE-- IS HE-- ALIVE?
WE BETTER PREP THE MEDICAL LAB ON TOUCH-DOWN.
BUT I'M NOT SURE IT'S GOING TO MAKE A DIFFERENCE.
GRAYMALKIN-- DIDN'T DETONATE? HAS CABLE FAILED?
That would depend o your definition of failu Roberto.
PROFESSOR--? YOU'RE ALIVE! EXCELLENT!
Magnus retains the use the station, but Nathan successfully removed programming from the central core --
-- while still also manag to maintain the overrid on the station's inter-planetary teleportatio systems:.

a personal, and
selfish, stand-
I would call
an's endeavors an
uhelming success:
S'THAT... GOOD ENUFF... F'R YOU... DACOSTA--?
BETTER THAN THAT, CABLE...
...YOU CAME BACK WITH YOUR HEART AND SOUL AND LEFT YOUR MATERIAL POSSESSIONS BEHIND--
"--IF ANYTHING, YOU HAVE SHOWN ME THAT YOU HAVE CHANGED--
"--YOU HAVE CHOSEN LIFE OVER DEATH, BLOOD OVER METAL--
"--AND YOU HAVE RESTORED OUR HOPE IN A BATTERED, BUT UNBROKEN DREAM..."
HE WAS NOT NEARLY THE CHALLENGE WE EXPECTED, MY LORD.
REALLY, EXODUS? I THOUGHT HE WAS A FAR GREATER THREAT THAN I HAD ANTICIPATED.

THIS WAS NOT A PHYSICAL COMBAT, MY FRIENDS--
--BUT A PHILOSOPHICAL ONE.
AND ULTIMATELY, BY ROBBING ME OF THE CHANCE TO FORGE THE MINDS OF THE NEXT GENERATION OF MUTANTS--

--IT IS A BATTLE WHICH CABLE HAS WON.

R NOW, WE'D ST TURN OUR ENTIONS TOWARDS VIER'S BROOD, TER THEM HAVEN, D SEE HOW THEY LL RESPOND.
AS FOR CABLE AND HIS X-FORCE UNIT.. WELL, IRONICALLY ENOUGH, THERE IS ALWAYS TOMORROW, ISN'T THERE...?
FATAL ATTRACTIONS CONTINUES IN UNCANNY X-MEN #304!
neXt- HOW DOES CABLE FEEL ABOUT HIS BRUSH WITH DEATH AND THE CHANGES IN X-FORCE SINCE HE LEFT THEM?

JRJR
+
PANOSIAN

THE UNCANNY
X-MEN
APPROVED BY THE COMICS CODE AUTHORITY
FATAL ATTRACTIONS
AN OFFER OF SALVATION...
...A BETRAYAL MOST BITTER!

Uncanny X-Men #304 hologram original pencils by Greg Capullo, and inks & colors by Kevin Conrad & Carlos Lopez

MARVEL COMICS
THE UNCANNY
X-MEN
CELEBRATING 30 YEARS OF X-MEN
$3.95 US
$4.95 CAN
304
SEPT
UK £2.95
APPROVED BY THE COMICS CODE AUTHORITY
FATAL ATTRACTIONS
AN OFFER OF SALVATION...
...A BETRAYAL MOST BITTER!
JR JR + PANOSIAN

SOMETHING LESS THAN FIVE MINUTES AGO...
... THE ACOLYTES, FAITHFUL FOLLOWERS OF THE MUTANT MASTER OF MAGNETISM, MAGNETO-- LEARNED THE TRUTH ABOUT THE "DEATH" OF THEIR PERSONAL SAVIOR.
O THE UNFORTUNATE REGRET OF FABIAN ORTEZ-- THEY ALSO EARNED OF HIS PART N THE AFFAIR.
TH IS GOOD R HIM!
AGREE, OTHER-- SHOULD E THAT SUFFERS RST!
UNUSCIONE, CARSIL?! I ORDER YOU TO...!
SHUT-UP, CORTEZ-- YOU'RE IN NO POSITION TO DEMAND ANY-THING!
WE'RE NO LONGER YOUR MINDLESS FLOCK! SAVE YOUR BREATH--
--FOR THE SCREAMS I INTEND TO TEAR FROM YOUR LUNGS!
THEY DIDN'T TAKE IT WELL.

URGHN
ENOUGH!
WITH MY ABILITY TO EXTEND ANOTHER MUTANT'S POWER, IT'S A SIMPLE MATTER FOR ME TO EXTRICATE MYSELF FROM UNUSCIONE'S PSIONIC GRIP!
WERE THAT IT WERE ONLY AS SIMPLE TO DIVEST YOURSELF OF THE CRIMES YOU'VE COMMITTED AGAINST MAGNETO--OUR LORD AND SAVIOR.
THAT IS THE THIRD TIME IN AS MANY MINUTES YOU PEOPLE HAVE ECHOED SUCH ACCUSATIONS!
HAVE THE MONTHS WE SPENT TOGETHER--CONTINUING MAGNUS'S WORK ON BEHALF OF MUTANTKIND--MEANT NOTHING TO YOU PEOPLE?
AFTER EVERYTHING WE'VE BEEN THROUGH... WHY ARE YOU SO WILLING TO TAKE THE WORD OF A STRANGER OVER MINE?

RHAPS, CORTEZ, S BECAUSE THEY ISE WHAT YOU READY KNOW IN IR HEART. THAT M NOT A RANGER" AT ALL.
HER, I THE VOICE MAGNETO!
M EXODUS-- NAMED BY NUS HIM- SELF--
-- FOR I AM THE GUIDE BY WHICH MUTANTS WILL RISE FROM THE GENETIC QUAGMIRE THAT IS HUMANITY.
I OFFER A SOJOURN UNTO PARADISE FOR ALL THOSE WHO ARE FAITHFUL... IN THOUGHT AND DEED... TO MAGNETO'S CAUSE.
ILE IT WAS NOT INTENT TO N YOUR SUBTERFUGE, R SE -- I REGRET WAS NECESSARY ORDER THAT I GHT MAKE MY OWN ENTIONS CLEAR.
HE TOLD US YOU TRIED TO KILL MAGNETO-- LEAVING HIM TO DIE ON ASTEROID M! *
YOGHT...?
DISSIPATING THE AIR AROUND YOU IS THE LEAST OF THE HORRORS I SHOULD VISIT UPON YOU FOR HAVING BETRAYED OUR TRUST!
* X-MEN #3 --B.H.
PARDON, AMELIA BUT MAGNUS IS A FORGIVING MAN, CAPABLE OF GREAT KINDNESS.
HE BARES NO ILL WILL TOWARDS FABIAN FOR THE MAN'S AMBITION-- AND NEITHER SHALL WE.
NOW AS WE DISCUSSED, PREPARE YOUR- SELVES, CHILDREN OF MAGNUS.
PREPARE YOURSELVES FOR THE ASCENSION.

RELUCTANTLY--
--EAGER TO EXTRACT THEIR VENGEANCE--
--THEY TURN TO GO...
...TAKING CORTEZ'S DREAM OF THE LEADERSHIP OF THE ACOLYTES WITH THEM.
I SPENT MONTHS OF MY LIFE CULTIVATING THOSE--THOSE SHEEP--TO WORK ON MY BEHALF!
I GAVE THEM A PURPOSE--I GAVE THEM SOMETHING TO BELIEVE IN!
YOU HAVE NO RIGHT TO WALK IN HERE AND--
ON THE CONTRARY, I HAVE EVERY RIGHT.
IT IS CALLED DESTINY, CORTEZ.
IT IS CALLED... POWER.
JUST SO WE ARE CLEAR WHEN WE MEET AGAIN IN THE FUTURE, IF IT WERE UP TO ME--
--I WOULD HURL YOU INTO OBLIVION LIKE THE INSIGNIFICANT FLEA THAT YOU ARE.
AS IT IS, MAGNUS HAS DECIDED YOU SHOULD SUFFER...
...SLOWLY.
A VICTIM OF SOMEONE ELSE'S LEGACY.

HAS ONLY
APPENED
WICE BEFORE
HIS LIFE...
...THAT CHARLES XAVIER HAS NOT RECOGNIZED THE REFLECTION IN THE MIRROR.
THE FIRST WAS ON THE AFTERNOON HE REALIZED-- WITH STARTLING CER-TAINTY--HE WAS DIFFERENT FROM ANYONE ELSE HE'D EVER KNOWN.
LONG BEFORE HE'D EVER HEARD THE WORD MUTANT, IT WAS PAINFULLY CLEAR HIS INCREDIBLE MIND SET HIM APART FROM THOSE AROUND HIM.
ALONE IN THE CROWD.
THE SECOND TIME WAS WHEN HE WOKE ON A WINDSWEPT MORNING IN FAR-OFF TIBET...
...AND REALIZED HE WOULD NEVER WALK AGAIN.
HILE THE FACE WAS
HE SAME, HE FELT--
OR A TIME--THAT HE
AS SOMEHOW LESS
HAN A PERSON FOR
HIS HANDICAP.
FINALLY, ON THIS
ORNING, IT IS
ANOTHER EMOTION
THAT HAS TWISTED
AND CONTORTED
HIS FEATURES... BOTH
NSIDE AND OUT.
FOR ON THIS MORNING, HE HAS TO BURY ILLYANA RASPUTIN...
...AN INNOCENT CHILD WHO TRUSTED HIM.
ON THIS DAY, HIS IS A FACE MARRED BY FAILURE.

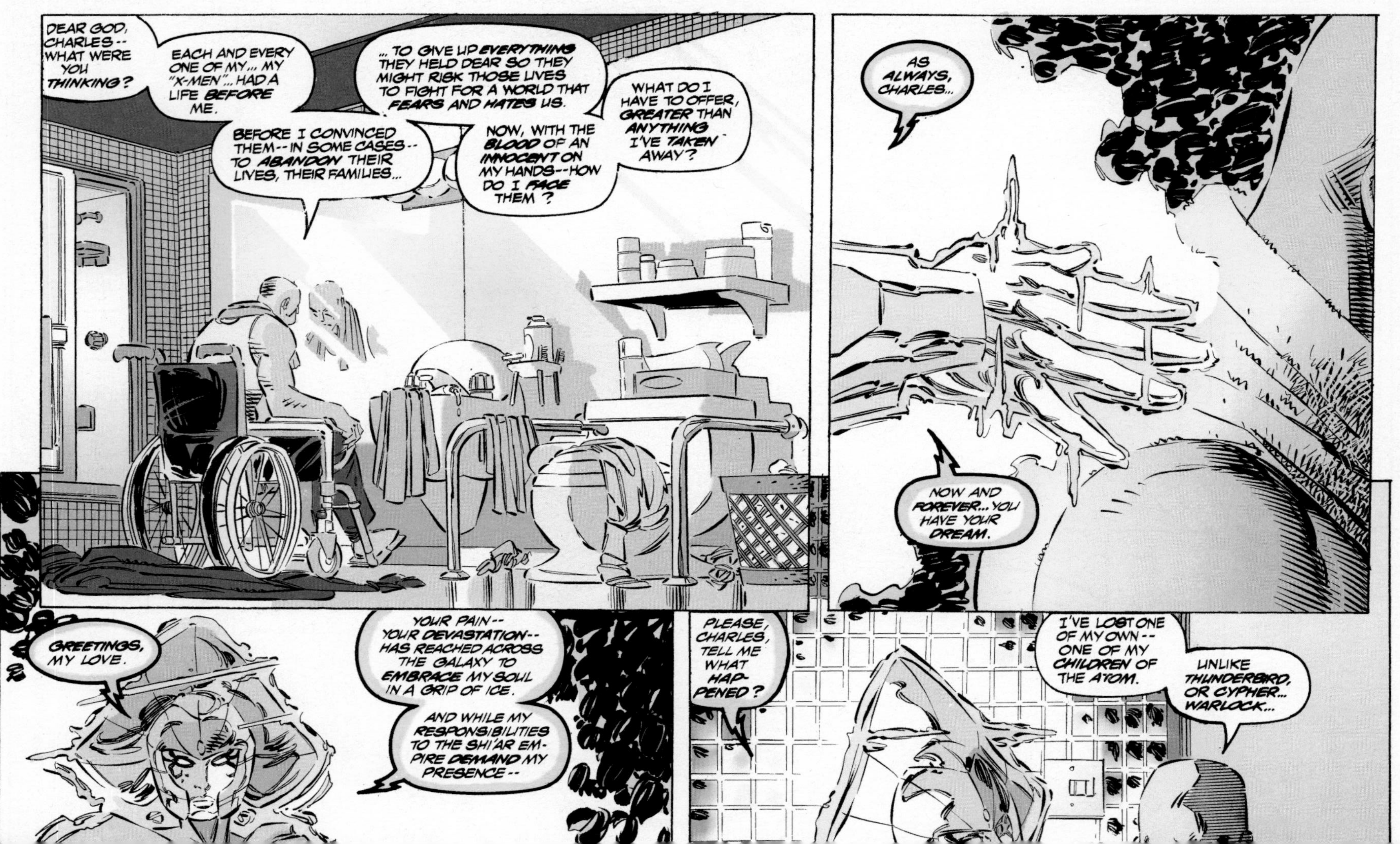
DEAR GOD, CHARLES-- WHAT WERE YOU THINKING?
EACH AND EVERY ONE OF MY... MY "X-MEN"... HAD A LIFE BEFORE ME.
BEFORE I CONVINCED THEM--IN SOME CASES--TO ABANDON THEIR LIVES, THEIR FAMILIES...
...TO GIVE UP EVERYTHING THEY HELD DEAR SO THEY MIGHT RISK THOSE LIVES TO FIGHT FOR A WORLD THAT FEARS AND HATES US.
NOW, WITH THE BLOOD OF AN INNOCENT ON MY HANDS--HOW DO I FACE THEM?
WHAT DO I HAVE TO OFFER, GREATER THAN ANYTHING I'VE TAKEN AWAY?
AS ALWAYS, CHARLES...
NOW AND FOREVER... YOU HAVE YOUR DREAM.
GREETINGS, MY LOVE.
YOUR PAIN-- YOUR DEVASTATION-- HAS REACHED ACROSS THE GALAXY TO EMBRACE MY SOUL IN A GRIP OF ICE.
AND WHILE MY RESPONSIBILITIES TO THE SHI'AR EMPIRE DEMAND MY PRESENCE--
PLEASE, CHARLES, TELL ME WHAT HAPPENED?
I'VE LOST ONE OF MY OWN-- ONE OF MY CHILDREN OF THE ATOM.
UNLIKE THUNDERBIRD, OR CYPHER... WARLOCK...

--PLEASE ALLOW THIS HOLOGRAPHIC IMAGE TO OFFER WHAT LITTLE SOLACE SPACE AND DISTANCE MIGHT ALLOW.
LILANDRA...
MAJESTRIX LILANDRA OF THE HOUSE OF NERAMANI...
...SOVEREIGN OF THE VAST SHI'AR EMPIRE... THE ONE TRUE LOVE OF CHARLES XAVIER'S LIFE.
I'M AFRAID I FALL FAR SHORT OF BEING WORTHY OF YOUR KINDNESS.

...ILLYANA WAS A CHILD WHO HAD EVERY RIGHT TO BELIEVE IN ME AND...
...I FAILED HER.

WHILE I DO NOT KNOW THE SPECIFICS, MY LOVE... I DO KNOW YOU COULD NOT POSSIBLY HAVE FAILED HER HERE...
...IN YOUR HEART.

I KNOW CHARLES FRANCIS XAVIER WELL ENOUGH TO KNOW THAT YOU DID EVERYTHING YOU COULD.
AND IN THE END, THAT IS ALL ANYONE OF US CAN EVER DO.

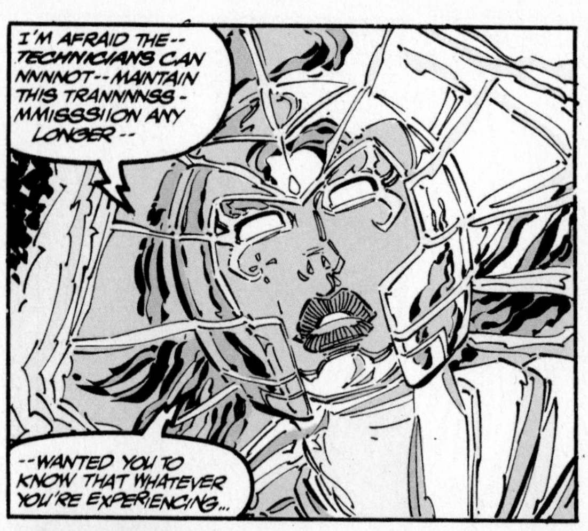

I'M AFRAID THE-- TECHNICIANS CAN NNNNOT--MAINTAIN THIS TRANNNNSS-MMISSSIION ANY LONGER--
--WANTED YOU TO KNOW THAT WHATEVER YOU'RE EXPERIENCING...

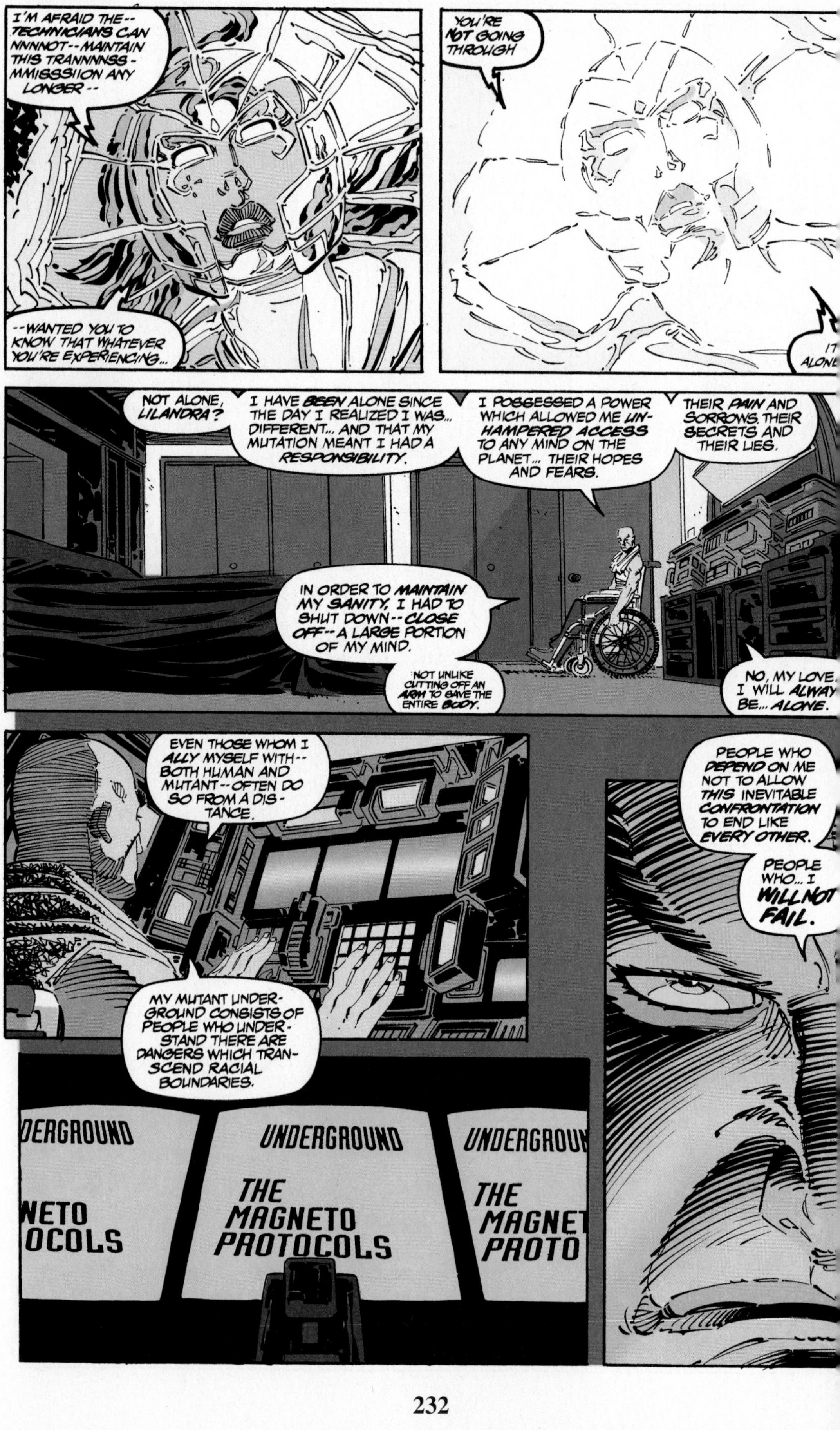

NOT ALONE, LILANDRA?
I HAVE BEEN ALONE SINCE THE DAY I REALIZED I WAS... DIFFERENT... AND THAT MY MUTATION MEANT I HAD A RESPONSIBILITY.
I POSSESSED A POWER WHICH ALLOWED ME UN-HAMPERED ACCESS TO ANY MIND ON THE PLANET... THEIR HOPES AND FEARS.
THEIR PAIN AND SORROWS. THEIR SECRETS AND THEIR LIES.
IN ORDER TO MAINTAIN MY SANITY, I HAD TO SHUT DOWN--CLOSE OFF--A LARGE PORTION OF MY MIND.
NOT UNLIKE CUTTING OFF AN ARM TO SAVE THE ENTIRE BODY.
NO, MY LOVE. I WILL ALWAY BE... ALONE.

EVEN THOSE WHOM I ALLY MYSELF WITH--BOTH HUMAN AND MUTANT--OFTEN DO SO FROM A DIS-TANCE.

MY MUTANT UNDER-GROUND CONSISTS OF PEOPLE WHO UNDER-STAND THERE ARE DANGERS WHICH TRAN-SCEND RACIAL BOUNDARIES.

PEOPLE WHO DEPEND ON ME NOT TO ALLOW THIS INEVITABLE CONFRONTATION TO END LIKE EVERY OTHER.

PEOPLE WHO... I WILL NOT FAIL.

DERGROUND
NETO
OCOLS

UNDERGROUND
THE MAGNETO PROTOCOLS

UNDERGROU
THE MAGNET
PROTO

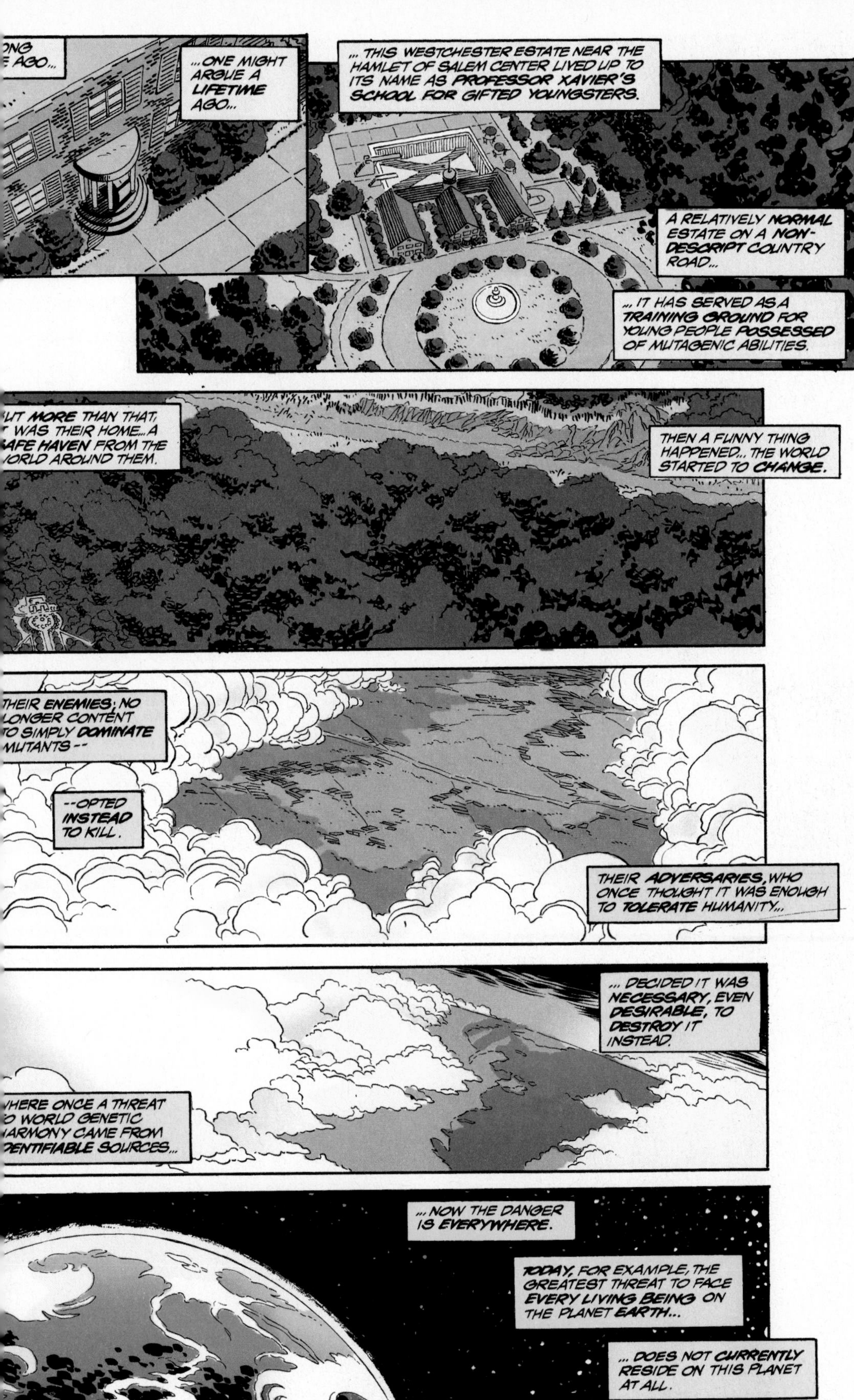

...ONE MIGHT ARGUE A LIFETIME AGO...
... THIS WESTCHESTER ESTATE NEAR THE HAMLET OF SALEM CENTER LIVED UP TO ITS NAME AS PROFESSOR XAVIER'S SCHOOL FOR GIFTED YOUNGSTERS.
A RELATIVELY NORMAL ESTATE ON A NON-DESCRIPT COUNTRY ROAD...
... IT HAS SERVED AS A TRAINING GROUND FOR YOUNG PEOPLE POSSESSED OF MUTAGENIC ABILITIES.
WAS THEIR HOME... A
THEN A FUNNY THING HAPPENED... THE WORLD STARTED TO CHANGE.
THEIR ENEMIES; NO LONGER CONTENT TO SIMPLY DOMINATE MUTANTS --
--OPTED INSTEAD TO KILL.
THEIR ADVERSARIES, WHO ONCE THOUGHT IT WAS ENOUGH TO TOLERATE HUMANITY...
... DECIDED IT WAS NECESSARY, EVEN DESIRABLE, TO DESTROY IT INSTEAD.
HERE ONCE A THREAT WORLD GENETIC ARMONY CAME FROM DENTIFIABLE SOURCES...
... NOW THE DANGER IS EVERYWHERE.
TODAY, FOR EXAMPLE, THE GREATEST THREAT TO FACE EVERY LIVING BEING ON THE PLANET EARTH...
... DOES NOT CURRENTLY RESIDE ON THIS PLANET AT ALL.

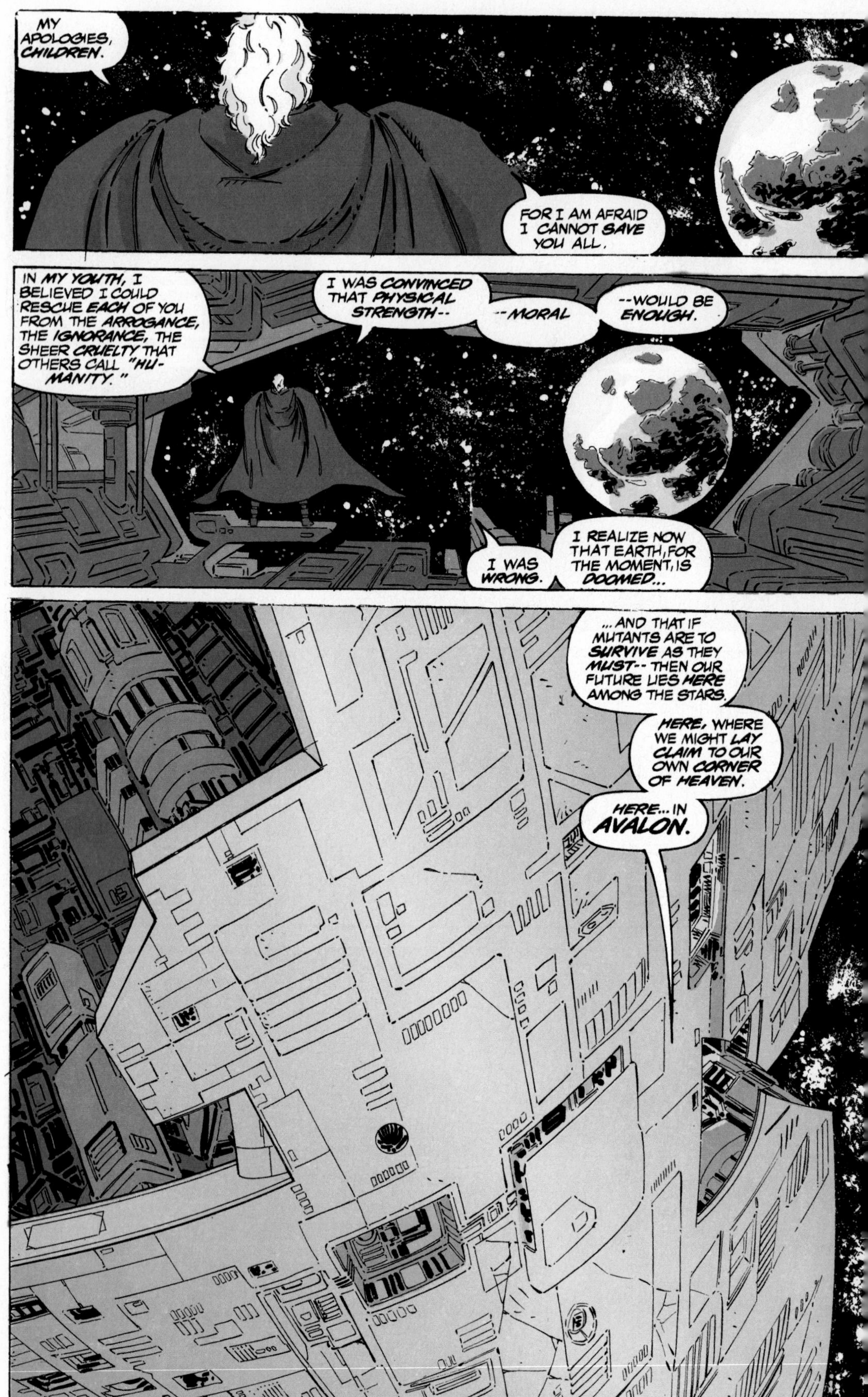

MY APOLOGIES, CHILDREN.
FOR I AM AFRAID I CANNOT SAVE YOU ALL.
IN MY YOUTH, I BELIEVED I COULD RESCUE EACH OF YOU FROM THE ARROGANCE, THE IGNORANCE, THE SHEER CRUELTY THAT OTHERS CALL "HU-MANITY."
I WAS CONVINCED THAT PHYSICAL STRENGTH--
--MORAL
--WOULD BE ENOUGH.
I WAS WRONG.
I REALIZE NOW THAT EARTH, FOR THE MOMENT, IS DOOMED...
...AND THAT IF MUTANTS ARE TO SURVIVE AS THEY MUST-- THEN OUR FUTURE LIES HERE AMONG THE STARS.
HERE, WHERE WE MIGHT LAY CLAIM TO OUR OWN CORNER OF HEAVEN.
HERE... IN AVALON.

HERE WAS A TIME WHEN HIS MAN WOULD HAVE SCOFFED AT THE HOUGHT OF TALKING O HIMSELF.

BUT THAT TOO HAS CHANGED.

IT MAY HAVE CHANGED ON THE NIGHT HE "DIED" ON A FLAMING ASTEROID AS IT PLUNGED INTO EARTH'S ATMOSPHERE...

... WHEN THE ACOLYTE CALLED CHROME TRANSMUTED THIS MAN'S CRITICALLY WOUNDED BODY INTO OMNIUM--

-- INSURING HE'D SURVIVE THE FIERY CRASH TO EARTH.

HIS BENEFACTOR DIED, SO THAT HE MAY LIVE.

BUT FAR MORE LIKELY IT ALL CHANGED ON THE NIGHT, DECADES EARLIER, WHEN HE LOST THE ONE GREAT LOVE OF HIS LIFE...

... THE ONLY THING HE EVER TRULY CREATED IN A LIFE THAT HAS SINCE, IT SEEMS, BEEN ABOUT NOTHING MORE THAN DEATH AND DESTRUCTION.

TRUE, IT IS DESTRUCTION IN THE SAME WAY A BLANK CANVAS IS SCARRED BY A SWATH OF PAINT...

... BUT IT IS DESTRUCTION NONETHELESS.

AT MUCH, AT LEAST... HIS NEED
DESTROY IN ORDER TO CREATE...

... FOR BETTER OR FOR WORSE...
... HAS NOT CHANGED.

"THERE WAS SO MUCH I HAD TO SHOW YOU, ANYA," HE WHISPERED TO THE EMPTY VESSEL HE CLUTCHED TO HIS CHEST--
--AS IF TRYING TO BREATHE LIFE INTO HER AGAIN THROUGH THE SHEER FORCE OF HIS INDOMITABLE WILL.
LONG BEFORE HE'D BECOME MAGNETO, MASTER OF MAGNETISM...
EVEN BEFORE HE CHOSE THE NAME MAGNUS...
... HE WAS ERIC LEHNSHERR. A MAN NOT UNLIKE ANY OTHER OF HIS TIME.
A YOUNG VICTIM OF THE CONCENTRATION CAMP WHICH CLAIMED HIS FAMILY--
-- A BOUT OF HEPATITIS DELAYED THE MANIFESTATION OF HIS MUTANT POWERS UNTIL WELL INTO ADULTHOOD.
POWERS WHICH SPRUNG SAVAGEL FROM HIS CHEST ON THE NIGHT A PANICKED CROWD PREVENTED HIM FROM RESCUING HIS FIRST-BORN DAUGHTER.
"AS I RETURN YOU TO THE EARTH," HE WHISPERED IN A VOICE RAVAGED BY LOSS, "SO DO I BURY MY HOPE--MY HEART. MY FUTURE.
"FOR HOW CAN I--HOW CAN ANYONE--FIND A PLACE IN A WORLD WHERE NOT EVEN THE INNOCENTS ARE SAFE?"
IN THAT MOMENT OF HIS DARKEST DESPAIR, DESTINY CONSPIRED TO SPARE THE WORLD OF FIRE NEXT TIME.
HIS DAUGHTER DEAD-- HIS WIFE HAVING ABANDONED HIM OUT OF FEAR--HE HAD NO REASON TO GO ON.
BLAM
UNTIL MAN, ONCE AGAIN, PROVIDED HIM WITH ONE.

E SOLDIERS HAD BEEN SEARCHING FOR HIM SINCE E PREVIOUS DAWN--
-- SHORTLY AFTER THEY'D COME ACROSS THE REMAINS OF A SMALL VILLAGE, SOME SIXTY KILOMETERS TO THE EAST...
A TOWN REDUCED TO MASS GRAVE BY THE INGLE MOURNFUL CRY F A MAN WHO WAS NCE A FATHER.
A MAN WHO WAS ONCE A MAN.
THEY WERE CONVINCED THEY COULD AMBUSH HIM.
BRING HIM DOWN.
BRING HIM TO JUSTICE.
THEIR JUSTICE.
HUMAN JUSTICE.
THEY WERE FOOLS.
"HOW
"DARE
"YOU...?!
"BY THE POWER INVESTED IN US BY THE AUTHORITY OF GOD AND MAN--" SAID THE SOLDIER...
"--WE'RE ARRESTING YOU FOR ATROCITIES AGAINST HUMANITY."
"DO NOT... SPEAK TO ME OF... 'AUTHORITY'..." HE CHOKED...
"... FOR I HAVE BEEN A VICTIM OF THE WHIMS-- THE CRUELTIES--
"--THE ATROCITIES OF 'MAN' SINCE THE MOMENT...
"...OF MY BIRTH.
"BUT NOW, I HAVE BEEN REBORN...
"... IN A BODY THAT IS NOTHING BUT POWER!
"I AM SERVING NOTICE ON YOUR PRECIOUS HUMANITY...
"... THAT I WILL NEVER YIELD
"NEVER
AGAIN!

THE FIRST TIME HE HAD USED HIS POWER--IT WAS UNTHINKING. AS MUCH A SHOCK TO HIM AS TO THE VICTIMS OF ITS INITIAL MANIFESTATION.
A PRIMAL CRY OF FRUSTRATION--OF MISDIRECTED AGGRESSION--AGAINST THE PEOPLE WHO HAD ALLOWED HIS DAUGHTER TO DIE.
THUS, HE MIGHT HAVE BEEN FORGIVEN HIS INITIAL CRIME OF PASSION.
BUT ON THIS EVENING, HIS ACTIONS WERE DELIBERATE.
THEY WERE THE ACTIONS OF A MAN WHO COULD NO MORE OF THE AFFRONTS TO HIS PERSONAL DIGNITY--
--TO EVERYTHING HE'D ONCE HAD AND LOST.
A MAN WHO FOUND IT WITHIN HIMSELF TO REACH INTO THE VERY HEART OF THE PLANET--
--AND USE WHAT HE FOUND THERE TO SMITE HIS ENEMIES.
"I SPENT MY CHILDHOOD UNDER THE OPPRESSION OF OTHERS!" HE RAGED--
--HIS VOICE NEARLY DROWNED BY THE PLAINTIVE WAIL OF THE EARTH MOLESTED BY HIS INTIMATE MANIPULATIONS.
"AS AN ADULT, I WILL NOT STAND BY AND LET OTHERS--
"--THOSE YOU HAVE ARBITRARILY DECIDED ARE SOMEHOW 'UNWORTHY,' 'UNDESERVING'--
"--SUFFER AS I HAVE SUFFERED BEFORE THEM!"

IN THAT MOMENT...
...THE MOMENT HE USED HIS POWER TO FORCE ONE SOLDIER TO SLAY HIS COMRADES--
--THE WORLD LOST ONE OF ITS MOST VALUABLE RE-SOURCES.
IT LOST THE HEART AND SOUL OF ERIC LEHNSHERR...
...AND FOUND IN ITS PLACE AN ENTITY KNOWN AS MAGNETO.
BDAM
IN THE SILENCE THAT FOLLOWED, ALL THAT WAS LEFT OF WHAT HAD GONE BEFORE WAS THE BLOOD OF STRANGERS...
...THE REMAINS OF A LITTLE GIRL...
...AND THE SHADOW OF A MAN...

I DON'T WANT TO DO THIS, CHARLES--
--RATHER, I HAVE TO.
I MUST BE STRONG, BECAUSE YOU AND YOUR X-MEN ARE TOO WEAK TO DO THAT WHICH MUST BE DONE!

FOR THIS REASON-- ABOVE ALL OTHERS-- HAVE I BEEN SPARED FROM THE SWEET SURRENDER THAT IS OBLIVION... THE COLD EMBRACE THAT IS DEATH... AGAIN AND TIME AGAIN.
FOR NO MATTER WHAT HAPPENS TO YOU AND ME, THE WELFARE OF THE CHILDREN IS PARAMOUNT.
WHETHER THEY BE THE INNOCENT, LIKE , DOUG AND ANYA BEFORE THEM--
-- THE LOST, SUCH AS MY ACOLYTES...
...OR THE MISGUIDED, LIKE THE FOOLS YOU COUNT AMONG THE X-MEN...
...THEY NEED TO BE PROTECTED! THEY NEED TO BE AWAKENED FROM THE DREAM IN WHICH YOU'VE LULLED THEM!
WHETHER YOU ADMIT IT OR NOT, THEY NEED...
MAGNETO!
THOUGH THE WORDS ECHO OFF THE EMPTY WALLS OF AVALON-- THE THOUGHTS THEY CONVEY, THE VERY EMOTIONS--CAN BE FELT AS FAR AWAY AS THE EARTH BELOW.
FOR WHILE NEITHER MAN WOULD ADMIT IT, PROFESSOR XAVIER AND MAGNETO ARE TWO SIDES TO THE SAME COIN...
... TWO MEN CONVINCED THEIR WAY IS MUTANT-KIND'S ONLY HOPE.

MEANWHILE...
SO... WHAT'S THE STORY, ORORO...?

DID THE PROFESSOR PUT EVERYONE ON A STRICT DIET?
NOT AT ALL, KITTEN.
WITH ALL THAT HAS HAPPENED IN RECENT DAYS, I AM AFRAID WE HAVE HAD LITTLE TIME TO ATTEND TO SHOPPING.
"SHOPPING"? HA!

WHAT AN UTTERLY NORMAL THING TO DO.
YOU USE THE WORD "NORMAL" AS IF IT WERE SOMETHING DESIRABLE. AN UNATTAINABLE GOAL YOU WISH TO ACHIEVE.
MAYBE.
JUST THINK IF WE LIVED NORMAL LIVES, I'D STILL BE IN DEARBORN, HOLDING MY PARENTS' MARRIAGE TOGETHER...

... YOU'D STILL BE IN KENYA...
...AND ILLYANA...?
...MY BEST FRIEND WOUL STILL BE ALIVE.

ADMIT IT, ORORO -- AREN'T THERE TIMES YOU WISH YOU WERE "NORMAL"?
HONESTLY...?
NO.
NOT FOR A MOMENT.
NOT ONCE.

WHILE THERE IS UNDENIABLY MUCH EACH OF US MUST SACRIFICE AS A RESULT OF OUR GENETIC BIRTHRIGHT...
FWOOSH

HOSE SAME MUTANT WERS EXPOSE US TO NDERS UNTOLD -- TEN FORCING US TO OK AT LIFE IN ALL ITS RIAD DIVERSITY WITH UR EYES WIDE OPEN....
...CHALLENGING US TO ENJOY EVERY DAY -- EVERY MOMENT OF OUR LIVES.
SUCH AS TAKING ADVANTAGE OF YOUR WEATHER MANIPU-LATING ABILITIES TO SNAG US SOME PERSONAL TIME ?
A GUILTY PLEASURE, I CONFESS.
EIRD, 'T IT?
UP HERE, TOGETHER -- JUST YOU AND ME, AGAIN -- IT'S AS IF NOTHING'S CHANGED SINCE I LEFT THE X-MEN.
UT HAS, TTEN.
ND THEREIN ES THE KEY OUR SUR-VAL. OUR RY SANITY.
FOR NATURE HAS A WONDROUS WAY OF CHANGING EVERY-THING ABOUT US. MOTHER EARTH HER-SELF IS IN A PERPETUAL STATE OF MOTION.
FOR EVERY ACTION WE TAKE, SUCH AS MY MANIPULATING THE WIND AND STORM --
-- THE BRIGHT LADY CAN BE TRUSTED TO ACT UPON IT, EXERTING HER OWN WILL ON OUR BEHALF. AND WE, IN THE END, MUST MARVEL AT HER WISDOM... AND HER GLORY.
A DRAMATIC RENDITION OF "EVERY CLOUD HAS A SILVER LINING..."?
TELL ME, ORORO... WHERE IS THE "GLORY" IN ILLYANA'S DEATH ? OR DOUG'S FOR THAT MATTER ?
OR JOHN PROUDSTAR'S ?
SOMETIMES A CLOUD IS JUST A CLOUD... AND WE SUFFER UNDER ITS SHADOW.

BUT THE SHADOW PASSES, KITTEN.
IT PASSES.
FOR A MOMENT, THERE ARE NO WORDS BETWEEN THEM...
...NO LOST YEARS.
FOR A MOMENT, THEY ARE AGAIN TWO FRIENDS BASKING IN THE SUNLIGHT--
--SEIZING THE DAY. FORGETTING THEIR MUTUAL SORROW.
THEN, REALITY INTRUDES...
...AGAIN.
WHA--?!
PETER-- NO!
WHAT ARE YOU DOING?!
I WOULD THINK, KATYA, THE ANSWER IS OBVIOUS.
I AM GETTING ON WITH MY LIFE.
RATHER...
...WHAT PASSES FOR A "LIFE" WITHOUT MY SISTER... MY BROTHER... MY PARENTS.

W?! BY PHYSICALLY
STROYING YOUR PAST?
TRYING TO ERASE
AT PART OF YOU THAT
N STILL CREATE--
AT CAN CAPTURE
ARTS AND SOULS
N A CANVAS?
DO YOU REALLY BELIEVE IT'S THAT EASY.

NO, KATYA. I DO NOT BELIEVE ANYTHING IS EASY ANY MORE.
BUT IF YOU FEEL THAT STRONGLY ABOUT THIS WORK...
...TAKE IT.

I FEEL
AT STRONGLY?!
HAT ABOUT
U, PETER?
U'VE BARELY
POKEN A WORD
NCE ILLYANA
DIED!
WHAT ARE YOU FEELING?!

NOTHING.

, PETER.
IF YOU NEED ME FOR... ANYTHING...

...I'LL BE...
...

THE XAVIER MANSION IS BUT ONE OF MANY TREASURES HIDDEN AMONG THE DENSE FORESTRY THAT MAKES UP WESTCHESTER'S HUDSON RIVER SHORELINE.
CONSIDER, FOR EXAMPLE, THE HOLLOWED REMAINS OF SALEM CENTER'S FIRST MISSION HOUSE OF WORSHIP --
-- LOCATED IN A CLEARING DIRECTLY ABUTTING THE X-MEN'S GROUNDS.
ONCE IT WAS A PLACE WHERE PILGRIMS, PRINCES AND PAUPERS CAME TO WORSHIP...
...AND TWO GOVERNORS CAME TO WED.
THOUGH LONG SINCE ABANDONED, IT IS HERE THAT THE CHILDREN OF THE ATOM HAVE COME TO BURY THEIR FALLEN...
I'M A LITTLE VAGUE ON THIS ENTIRE "MEMORIAL SERVICE," BANSHEE.
THE GIRL IS DEAD... WHAT MORE IS THERE THAN THAT?
ACHHH, QUITE THE SENTIMENTAL LAD YE ARE.
ARE YOU BEING SARCASTIC?
AYE. AREN'T YE?
OR ARE YE GOING TO TELL ME THAT IN YUIR FUTURE, LIFE JUST GOES STEAM-ROLLING ON AHEAD...
...THAT NOBODY TAKES THE TIME TO MOURN THE PASSING OF A FRIEND?
YE MAKE IT ALL SO TEMPTING-- SUCH A WARM AND TENDER PLACE--IT'S A WONDER YE MADE THE BACKWARDS TREK IN THE FIRST PLACE.
YOU SOUND AS IF YOU DO NOT BELIEVE I AM FROM YOUR FUTURE, SEAN.

RHAPS I SHOULD
L YOU WHAT
TLE I KNOW OF
UR FATE?
W IT WAS LONG
MORED AMONGST
E HALLS OF THE
E THAT YOU WERE
E LAST HOPE, THE
STODIAN, OF THE
XT GENERA--
AND PERHAPS I SHOULD GO LEAP IN FRONT OF A BUS, BISHOP.
THEN ALL YUIR LITTLE STORIES FROM THE FUTURE-- YUIR BEST LAID PLANS--WILLNAE MEAN MUCH OF ANY-THING, EH?
MAKE NO MISTAKE, BISHOP, I BELIEVE YE ARE FROM THE FUTURE--
--I JUST DON'T THINK YE ARE FROM MINE.
YE SAY YUIR FROM A DARK PLACE, A TOMORROW WHERE NO ONE KNOWS HOW TO DREAM--OR STRIVE FOR A BETTER WAY.
WHERE YE DON'T EVEN KNOW WHAT IT IS TO MOURN THE PASSIN' OF A PRECIOUS LIFE.
IF I BELIEVED THAT THAT WAS THE FACE OF TOMORROW--
--THE REST O'US AND ME, WOULD BE FOOLS TO GO'ON.
AND THOUGH THE X-MEN ARE A GOODLY NUMBER OF THINGS, SON...
...WE ARE NAE FOOLS.

ONE HOUR LATER, AS THE NOON SUN SHINES HIGH OVER-HEAD--
TO BELIEVE THAT ILLYANA IS LOOKING DOWN UPON THIS ASSEMBLAGE OF HER FRIENDS AND FAMILY--
--AND IS ELATED TO SEE YOU ALL HERE, DRAPED IN THE COLORS WORN IN TH DEFENSE OF A DREAM IN WHICH SHE WAS ENGAGED FOR ALMOST HALF HER LIFE.
AND BLAZE IT DID, MY FELLOW X-MEN, FOR ILLYANA TRIUMPHED AGAINST THE DARK... AND INNOCENCE RE-TURNED HOWEVER BRIEFLY.
SO, TOO, MUST WE LEARN FROM HER EXAMPLE, MY FRIENDS.
AND WITH THOSE FINAL WORDS, THEY'D LIKE TO BELIEVE THE SERVICES HAVE CON-CLUDED.
THAT THE HEALING CAN BEGIN.

A LIFE THAT, WHILE TRAGICALLY SHORT, WAS FILLED TO OVER-FLOWING WITH ENOUGH CONTRADICTIONS TO FILL SEVERAL LIVES.
A LIFE IN CONSTANT STATE OF TURMOIL.
BURDENED BY DEMONS NOT OF HER OWN MAKING-- SHE REMAINED AN ANGEL AT HER CORE.
FRIGHTENED BY THE DARKNESS WHICH HAD, FOR A TIME, GRIPPED HER SOUL-- SHE WAS BRAVE ENOUGH TO STOKE THE EMBERS OF LIGHT THAT SMOLDERED IN HER HEART...AWAITING AGAINST GREAT ODDS TO BLAZE BRIGHT ONCE MORE.
SHE TAUGHT US TO CLING TO LIFE WITH BOTH HANDS, TO WREST WHAT HAPPINESS WE CAN FROM EACH AND EVERY MOMENT OF OUR LIVES.
IF WE CAN TAKE HER LESSONS TO HEART, ILLYANA WILL NEVER TRULY DIE.
SHE WILL HAVE WON HER BATTLE.
SHE WILL LIVE WITHIN EVERY ONE OF US UNTIL WE BREATHE OUR LAST.
AMEN.
UNAWARE THAT HIGH ABOVE--
--AND CLOSING FAST--
--THE END IS UPON THEM.

OH, SAM...
AH KNOW, KITTY.
WE'VE BEEN THROUGH THIS BEFORE -- BUT IT DON'T GET ANY EASIER, DOES IT ?
I DO NOT UNDERSTAND WHY WE INDULGE IN THIS MASOCHISTIC "MOURNING PROCESS" -- WHEN WE SHOULD BE ADDRESSING THE RECENT ASSAULT ON CABLE.*
DON'T LOOK AT ME, SHATTERSTAR...
MAYBE SAMMY DOESN'T THINK IT'S ANY OF THE X-MEN'S BUSINESS.

* SEE X-FORCE #25. --BOB

OR MAYBE HE'S BEEN DISTRACTED, FERAL.

LOSING A FRIEND CAN DO THAT TO YOU. NOW, TELL ME...

...WHO -- EXACTLY -- WAS RESPONSIBLE FOR THIS ATTACK ON X-FORCE'S LEADER ?

AND WHY DO I GET THE FEELING I'M NOT GOING TO LIKE THE ANSWER ?

PETER ?

A MOMENT, SON.

I JUST WANT YOU TO KNOW HOW TERRIBLY SORRY I AM.

ARE YOU,... SIR ?

WHY DO I DOUBT THAT ?

IT BECAUSE HAVE TROUBLE LIEVING ANY- ING YOU SAY?
WHEN YOU ASKED ME TO LEAVE THE UST-ORDYNSK! COLLECTIVE-- *
--YOU SAID--AND I REMEMBER THE WORDS AS IF YOU SAID THEM ONLY YESTERDAY--"POWER SUCH AS YOURS BELONGS TO THE WORLD, PETER--TO BE USED FOR THE GOOD OF ALL."
ORORO...
...I THINK SOMETHING'S BREWING.
* GIANT-SIZE X-MEN #1.--BOB
NOTHING MORE THAN YOUR WORD, I FT MY FAMILY--MY LIFE--AND DIDN'T OK BACK. I THRILLED TO THOSE WORDS, OFESSOR. THEY MADE ME PART OF A LARGER WHOLE.
NEVER ONCE DID I FALTER--DID I QUESTION--THE VALIDITY--THE COST--OF YOUR DREAM!
NO, GODSPOTIN XAVIER--I DID NOT FAIL YOU.
YOU--YOU AND YOUR DREAM--FAILED ME!
WORSE, IT FAILED ILLYANA.
AND FOR THAT--I WILL NEVER FORGIVE YOU.
PETER! HOLD ON. YOU'RE--
--ABSOLUTELY RIGHT, SON.
HOW FORTUITOUS FOR EVERY-ONE...

...THAT I HAVE CHOSEN THIS MOMENT TO RETURN!
FOR IT IS OBVIOUS THAT AT LEAST SOME OF YOU NOW UNDER-STAND WHAT I HAVE KNOWN FOR YEARS!
IF MUTANTS--AS A RACE--ARE TO SURVIVE, WE MUST STOP CONCERNING OURSELVES WITH THE AC-CEPTANCE OF HUMANS...
...AND INSTEAD CONCENTRATE ON THE THREATS FACING HOMO SUPERIORS!
MAGNETO?!
THEN WHAT WE FEARED WAS TRUE--
--YOU'RE ALIVE!!

HOW OBSERVANT, CYCLOPS.
NO. I OBVIOUSLY DID NOT "DIE" DURING THE FALL OF ASTEROID M.
THANKS TO YOU, X-MEN, I WAS CRITICALLY WOUNDED-- AND WOULD SURELY HAVE GONE THE WAY OF ALL FLESH IF NOT FOR ONE OF MY ACO-LYTES, WHO SACRIFICED HIMSELF FOR ME.
I SPENT MONTHS TENDING TO MY WOUNDS, CONTENT, TO SIT BACK AND WATCH AS THE GENETIC FACTIONS OF THE PLANET TORE EACH OTHER APART.
STRYFE. APOCALYPSE. MR. SINISTER. THE UPSTARTS. THE DARK RIDERS. THE MOST RECENT INCAR-NATION OF THE BROTHER-HOOD OF EVIL MUTANTS...
... AND YOU X-MEN, X-FORCE, X-FACTOR RESPONDING IN EVER-MORE DESPERATE KIND. HOW FRACTURED YOUR DREAM HAS BECOME, CHARLES.
IT PROVIDED ME WITH HOURS OF AMUSEMENT AS I AWAITED THE MOMENT OF MY RETURN--INTENT, AS I WAS, TO WADE THROUGH THE BODIES OF THE MUTANT CIVIL WAR AND TAKE MY PLACE AS LEADER OF THE SURVIVORS.
AS IT IS, UNEXPECTED DEVELOPMENTS NECESSITATED I TAKE A MORE ACTIVE ROLE AS SAVIOR TO MY GENETIC BRETHREN.

CRASHING FUNERAL MAGSTER?
TRES TRACKY.
ROBERT IS RIGHT-- HAVE YOU BECOME SO INTIMATE WITH THE CONCEPT OF DEATH THAT YOU NO LONGER RESPECT THE PASSING OF OTHERS?
ON THE CONTRARY, STORM.
I AM HERE BECAUSE OF MY RESPECT FOR THOSE WHO HAVE GONE BEFORE ME-- AND TO PREVENT OTHERS FROM SHARING THEIR FATE.
I AM HERE TO OFFER EACH OF YOU SANCTUARY FROM THE COMING FIRE-STORM OF DEATH THAT WILL SOON RAGE ACROSS THIS PLANET.
I'VE RETURNED TO OFFER YOU AN ALTERNATIVE TO THE GENOCIDE OF OUR PEOPLE.
I'M HERE TO OFFER YOU...
...SALVATION.

BELIEVE HIM, SCION OF XAVIER-- JUST AS WE, WHO HAVE COME TOGETHER FROM THE FOUR CORNERS OF THE WORLD, HAVE ACCEPTED THAT MAGNUS IS OUR ONLY HOPE.
HE LIVES! MAGNETO LIVES, JUST AS EXODUS CLAIMED!
PRAISE BE TO MAGNETO-- HIS WORD IS OUR LAW.
THE ACOLYTES?! JEAN, HOW DID THEY--
--POSSIBLY GET THIS CLOSE?! MAGNETO MUST SOMEHOW BE USING HIS ELECTRO-MAGNETIC POWERS TO JAM MY PSIONIC POWERS.
IT IS BUT ONE OF THE ARSENAL OF POWERS THAT ARE MY FATHER'S TO COMMAND, CYCLOPS!
BUT NEVER BEFORE TO THIS DEGREE, PIETRO...
WELL, DON'T GO GETTIN' TOO EXCITED, KIDS-- HE AIN'T GONNA BE STAYING FOR LONG.
STAY CALM, WOLVERINE. UNTIL WE KNOW WHAT WE'RE UP AGAINST...
...YOU'RE THE DROP-DEAD-LAST PERSON I WANT SLUGGING IT OUT WITH MAGNETO!

YOU WOULD DO WELL TO HEED SCOTT'S ADVICE, LOGAN.
MY NEAR DIS-CORPORATION WITHIN EARTH'S E.M. FIELD HAS LEFT ME MORE POWERFUL THAN EVEN I IMAGINED.
ARGHH!
FORCED MY... CLAWS TO... RETRACT ?!
MAGNETO -- !
ERIC, PLEASE... THERE'S NO NEED FOR THIS !
I AM NEEDED, XAVIER -- TO LEAD OUR PEOPLE TO A BETTER WORLD !
THEY -- WE -- NEED TO TRAVEL FROM THIS PLACE OF DEATH AND DECAY...
... AND CAN NO LONGER BE HAMPERED BY THE CONVENTIONS OF MAN.
ANY MORE THAN I CAN ALLOW YOU AND YOUR PATHETIC KINDRED SPIRITS TO HANDICAP MY EFFORTS TO SAVE YOU DESPITE YOURSELVES !
STORM, MA'AM -- AH CAIN'T MOVE !
HE IS MAGNETICALLY GRIPPING THE IRON FIBERS IN OUR BLOOD, SAMUEL.
WHILE WE ARE STILL POSSESSED OF OUR ABILITIES, WE HAVE NO WAY OF CONSCIOUSLY ACCESSING THEM.
AND IF THOSE POWERS ARE IN-VOLUNTARY...?
THERE IS NO NEED FOR YOU TO ATTACK, X-MEN... FOR I DID NOT COME TO ENGAGE YOU IN BATTLE.
RATHER, I HAVE COME TO HELP YOU... TO HELP ALL MUTANTS.

BUT IN ORDER TO DO THIS--I MUST DEMAND TOTAL LOYALTY FROM THOSE WHO COUNT THEMSELVES AMONG MY FOLLOWERS.
SENYAKA--ISN'T IT?
YOU DID MUCH MORE THAN "SERVE," ACOLYTE--YOU ENGAGED IN THE GENETIC CLEANSING OF DOZENS OF INNOCENT PEOPLE!*
SICK AND DYING HUMANS WHO WERE OF NO THREAT TO ANYONE!
AND THESE ACTS WERE COMMITTED IN YOUR NAME, FATHER--YOU ARE ULTIMATELY RESPONSIBLE FOR THE HEINOUS CRIMES!
YES, M'LORD. WORDS CANNOT EXPRESS THE JOY WHICH SWELLS MY HEART TO OVERFLOWING SEEING YOU STILL WALK IN OUR MIDSTS.
I ONLY HOPE YOU WILL CONTINUE TO ALLOW ME TO SERVE YOU AS I HAVE IN YOUR ABSENCE.
* X-FACTOR #92.--Bo
"CRIMES," MY SON--IS IT A CRIME TO PUT AN ANIMAL OUT OF ITS MISERY?
WHAT YOU WITNESSED WAS THE TOSSING OF THE GAU LET--THE FIRST SIGN OF MUTANTS TAKING THE INITIATIVE TO FREE THEMSELV FROM THE HUMAN'S OPPRESSION AT LAST!
HAD I NOT BEEN IN THE ANTARCTIC, GATHERING MY STRENGTH, RENEWING MYSELF IN BODY AND SOUL--I WOULD HAVE GIVEN MY ACOLYTES MY BLESSING.
BUT I DID NOT.
AND WHILE YOUR ZEAL IS ADMIRABLE, SENYAKA, ORDER MUST EVER BE MAINTAINED.
WHEN THE RIVERS OF THIS PLANET ROAR WITH THE BLOOD OF HUMANS--
--WHEN THE EARTH OPENS TO SWALLOW WHOLE ALL THOSE WHO OPPOSE ME--
--ALL THIS WILL BE DONE ON MY WORD AND MINE ALONE...
...THE WORD OF MAGNETO!

ER GOTT! MAGNETO
S BOUGHT INTO HIS
E AS "SAVIOR."
THE PARLANCE
THE LAND, HE
S BEEN READING
S OWN PRESS
RELEASES.
THIS IS A MAN WHO DEATH CANNOT STOP, KURT.
IS IT ANY WONDER HE BELIEVES HE IS THE GOD HIS FOLLOWERS PROFESS HIM TO BE?
HE, LIKE, PULPED THE GUY WITH HIS OWN COILS...
WE'RE TALKING FOUR-STAR GROSSNESS!
DO NOT WEEP FOR THIS PATHETIC MAN, FOR I HAVE NOT SLAIN HIM...
...RATHER HE HAS BEEN LIBERATED FROM THE ENSLAVEMENT THAT WAS HIS LIFE.
TRUST ONE WHO HAS DIED AND RISEN AGAIN--
--DEATH HAS A WAY OF PUTTING EVERYTHING INTO PERSPECTIVE.
ALLOW ME TO SHARE WHAT I HAVE LEARNED. KNOW YOU ALL, THE TIME FOR GAMES--
...FOR CHOOSING SIDES...
...FOR DEBATING THE ALLEGED MORALITY OF OUR ACTIONS...
...FOR QUESTIONING MY ULTIMATE AUTHORITY...
...HAS PASSED!
FROM THIS DAY FORWARD, ALL THOSE WHO DO NOT STAND WITH ME--WHETHER MUTANT OR NOT--CAN BE COUNTED AMONG MY ENEMIES!
THOSE WHO ARE NOT WILLING--WHO CANNOT FIND THE STEEL IN THEIR SOULS TO JOIN ME IN THE SANCTUARY I CONSTRUCTED HIGH ABOVE THE EARTH...
...SENTENCE THEMSELVES TO WALLOW IN THE MASS GRAVE THAT IS THE DESTINY OF THIS PLANET!
BEHOLD NOW--SALVATION! BEHOLD NOW--AVALON!

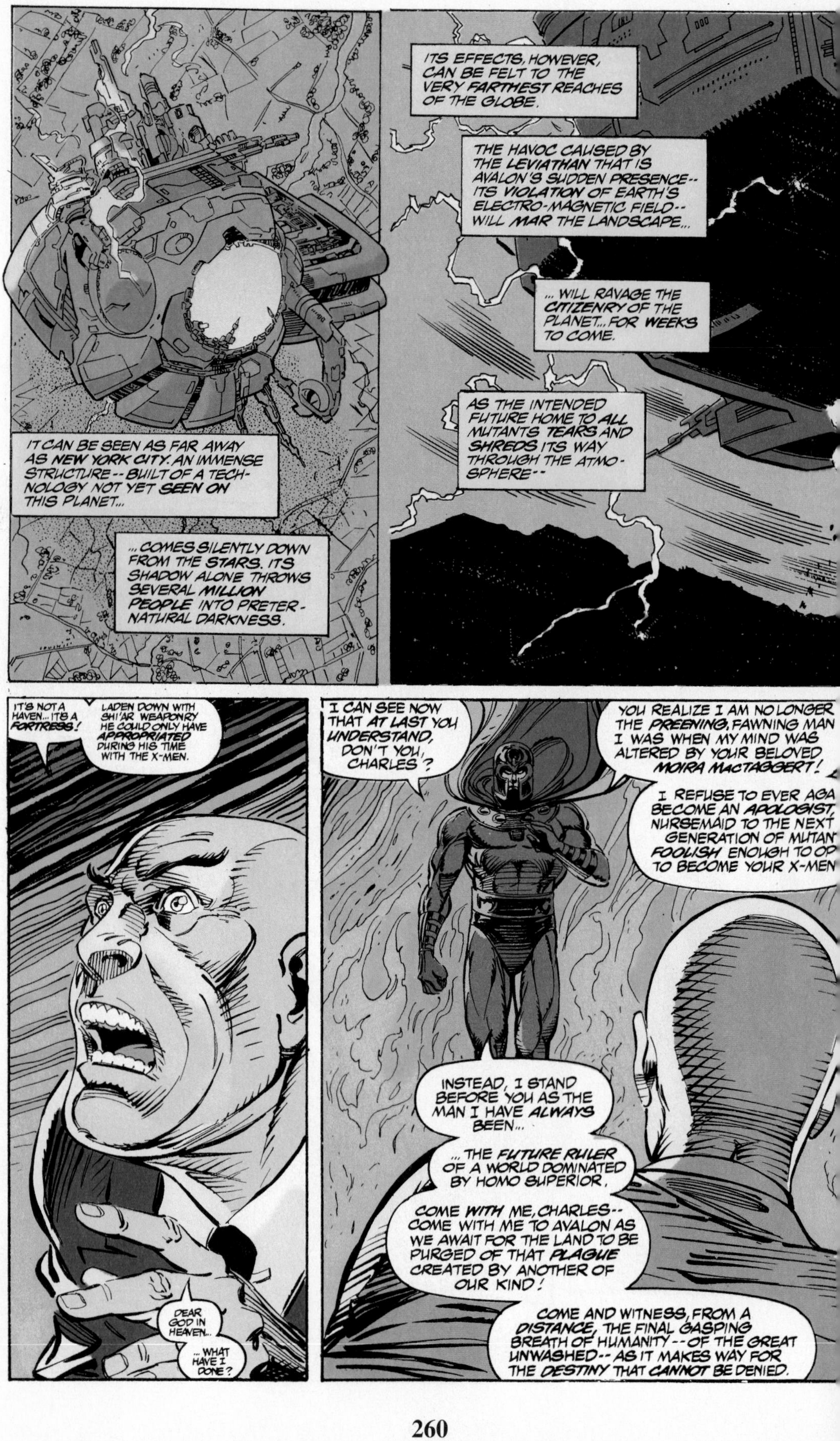

IT CAN BE SEEN AS FAR AWAY AS *NEW YORK CITY*. AN IMMENSE STRUCTURE -- BUILT OF A TECHNOLOGY NOT YET *SEEN ON* THIS PLANET...

...COMES SILENTLY DOWN FROM THE *STARS*. ITS SHADOW ALONE THROWS SEVERAL *MILLION PEOPLE* INTO PRETER-NATURAL DARKNESS.

ITS EFFECTS, HOWEVER, CAN BE FELT TO THE VERY *FARTHEST* REACHES OF THE GLOBE.

THE HAVOC CAUSED BY THE *LEVIATHAN* THAT IS AVALON'S SUDDEN PRESENCE -- ITS *VIOLATION* OF EARTH'S ELECTRO-MAGNETIC FIELD -- WILL *MAR* THE LANDSCAPE...

... WILL RAVAGE THE *CITIZENRY* OF THE PLANET... FOR *WEEKS* TO COME.

AS THE INTENDED FUTURE HOME TO *ALL* MUTANTS *TEARS* AND *SHREDS* ITS WAY THROUGH THE ATMO-SPHERE --

IT'S NOT A HAVEN... IT'S A *FORTRESS!*

LADEN DOWN WITH SHI'AR WEAPONRY HE COULD ONLY HAVE *APPROPRIATED* DURING HIS TIME WITH THE X-MEN.

DEAR GOD IN HEAVEN...

... WHAT HAVE I DONE?

I CAN SEE NOW THAT *AT LAST* YOU *UNDERSTAND*, DON'T YOU, CHARLES?

YOU REALIZE I AM NO LONGER THE *PREENING*, FAWNING MAN I WAS WHEN MY MIND WAS ALTERED BY YOUR BELOVED *MOIRA MacTAGGERT!*

I REFUSE TO EVER AGA BECOME AN *APOLOGIST*, NURSEMAID TO THE NEXT GENERATION OF MUTAN *FOOLISH* ENOUGH TO OP TO BECOME YOUR X-MEN

INSTEAD, I STAND BEFORE YOU AS THE MAN I HAVE *ALWAYS* BEEN...

... THE *FUTURE RULER* OF A WORLD DOMINATED BY HOMO SUPERIOR.

COME *WITH* ME, CHARLES -- COME WITH ME TO AVALON AS WE AWAIT FOR THE LAND TO BE PURGED OF THAT *PLAGUE* CREATED BY ANOTHER OF OUR KIND!

COME AND WITNESS, FROM A *DISTANCE*, THE FINAL GASPING BREATH OF HUMANITY -- OF THE GREAT *UNWASHED* -- AS IT MAKES WAY FOR THE *DESTINY* THAT *CANNOT* BE DENIED.

--SAVAGE WHIPPING WINDS SHRIEK ACROSS THE EASTERN SEABOARD...

... TIDES LASH AT THE COASTLINE WITH THE FURY OF A RAMPAGING HURRICANE.

BUT FAR WORSE THAN THE PHYSICAL DAMAGE -- IS THE HORROR INFLICTED UPON AN INNOCENT POPULACE.

FOR AT THIS MOMENT, WHAT HAS LONG BEEN SUSPECTED CAN NO LONGER BE DENIED.

MAGNETO HAS RETURNED.

AND NO HUMAN BEING WILL TRULY FEEL SAFE AGAIN.

EXODUS, BEGIN NOW THE ASCENSION.
OBSERVE, CHARLES, AS I TAKE THESE FROM YOU...
... AN ALMOST DOZEN MUTANTS, FREE FROM THE BONDS OF THE PERVERSE ALTRUISM IN WHICH YOU'D SEEK TO ENTOMB THEM.

NOT LONG AGO, XAVIER-- I TRIED YOUR PATH...
... NOW I ASK YOU, MY OLDEST FRIEND, DO YOU HAVE THE COURAGE TO DO WHAT I HAD DONE?
ARE YOU WILLING TO WALK DOWN MY PATH FOR A TIME?

DO YOU TRULY BELIEVE YOU ARE ATTEMPTING ANY-THING ORIGINAL, MAGUS?
DON'T YOU REALIZE THERE IS LITTLE DIFFERENCE BETWEEN YOU-- AND THE SAME MONSTER RESPONSIBLE FOR THE DEATH OF YOUR PARENTS AND SISTER?
CAN'T YOU SEE YOU'VE BECOME WHAT YOU HATED MOST IN OTHERS?!
DO NOT DARE COMPARE ME TO ANY HUMAN, CHARLES! I SEEK TO RESCUE MY-- OUR-- PEOPLE! AND IF OTHERS MUST SUFFER BECAUSE OF THAT, I AM NOT RESPONSIBLE!
BISHOP-- WHAT'S HAPPENING?
WHAT'S WITH THE WALKING LITE BRITE?
MY MUTANT ABILITY DOES NOT INCLUDE AN ON-OFF SWITCH, ROBERT.
I AUTOMATICALLY ABSORB ANY ENERGY DIRECTED AT ME, CHANNELING IT THROUGH ME--
...ANY ENERGY INCLUDING APPARENTLY MAGNETO'S.
WE BOTH NOW MUTANTS ARE NOT LONG FOR THIS WORLD.
WHILE RECOVERING TOO, LEARNED OF STRYFE'S LEGACY. HAVE BORNE SILENT WITNESS TO THE PASSING OF ALL WHO HAVE FALLEN FOR NO OTHER REASON THAN THEY ARE OF MUTANT BLOOD.
HAVE WEPT FOR THOSE WHO HAVE DIED, AND WITH THOSE TEARS AN UNSPEAKABLE, UN-SHAKABLE TRUTH WAS REVEALED TO ME.
AND I KNOW THAT IN YOUR HEART, YOU SHARE THE KNOWLEDGE--
-- THAT UNLESS WE, AS A RACE, TAKE ACTION THIS MOMENT...
"... ILLYANA WILL BE BUT THE FIRST OF SCORES OF INNOCENT VICTIMS TO DIE!"

HE SENSES AN ELECTRO-MAGNETIC RUPTURE...
...THE INSTANT BEFORE IT HAPPENS...
EH?
AS A LIVING STORAGE CELL, EVEN I HAVE MY LIMITS!
ALL THE TIME YOU KEPT ME IMMOBILE--YOU WERE PROVIDING ME WITH THE VERY ENERGY I NEEDED TO FREE MYSELF...
STAND DOWN, PEOPLE! BISHOP'S ACTIONS MAY HAVE CUT US LOOSE, BUT--
IN YER ONE EYE, YA'--
CYCLOPS HAS A POINT, GENTLEMEN. THE CLOSER WE GET, THE MORE LIKELY MAGNETO WILL ONCE AGAIN ASSERT HIMSELF UPON OUR BODILY FUNCTIONS.
NEAR AS I KNOW THAT'S ILLEGAL IN MOST STATES.

"... ENERGY I'M RETURNING TO YOU IN KIND!"
KRUNCHT!
MM, PROF...CAN YOU MISE ME WE'RE GONNA' VE THROUGH THIS?
I MEAN, WE'RE TALKING THE BIG M HERE...
I CAN PROMISE IT WILL NOT BE FOR LACK OF TRYING, CHILD.
I HATE TO DO THIS, BISHOP--BUT THAT "AVALON" IS FILLED WITH FANATICS, AND ARMED TO THE TEETH WITH ENOUGH WEAPONS TO REDUCE NEW YORK TO A CINDER.
IN... DEED.
DO WHAT... YOU... MUST...

THIS--?!
THIS IS HOW YOU REPAY THE COURTESY I'VE EXTENDED TO YOU?!
RABOOM!
HAVE YOU ALL BECOME SO BLIND TO THE HATRED IN THE EYES OF THE HUMANS--
HAVE YOU BECOME DEAF THAT YOU NNOT HEAR THE AINTIVE PLEA OF UR BRETHREN YING FOR SALVATION?
IS WORLD IS NO NGER SAFE FOR TANTS WHILE STRYFE'S GACY COULD STRIKE Y OF US AT ANY MOMENT!
DO THESE GENETIC DEAD-ENDS--THESE HUMANS--WHO LIVE IN RIGHTEOUS FEAR OF OUR GENETIC BIRTHRIGHT MEAN SO MUCH TO YOU--
--THAT YOU ARE WILLING TO FORFEIT YOUR OWN LIVES TO SAVE THEIRS?
FOR MAKE NO MISTAKE, X-MEN--ALL THOSE WHO REFUSE TO JOIN ME...
...DIE HERE AND NOW WITH THESE WORTHLESS HERDS OF HUMAN CATTLE GRAZING UPON A LAND THAT IS RIGHTFULLY OURS!
BISHOP, ARE YOU CERTAIN YOU ARE UP TO THIS?!
WHAT IS YOUR LIMIT REGARDING THE NUMBER OF ENERGY SIGNATURES YOU CAN ABSORB AT ONE TIME?
AFRAID HAVOK... HAVE TO FIND OUT... T'GETHER!
THEN WE BETTER HURRY AND TAKE DOWN THE BIG M--
--'CAUSE, JUDGING BY THE WAY HOME BASE THERE IS GLOWING, HE'S ABOUT TO TURN ALL O' WESTCHESTER COUNTY INT'ONE BIG WARMED-OVER BURRITO!
ACTUALLY, IT WILL BE NOTHING MORE THAN A SMOLDERING CRATER--A TESTAMENT TO THE WORLD THAT FOR EVERY LIFE CLAIMED BY STRYFE'S LEGACY...
...I WILL TAKE TEN THOUSAND HUMANS AS PENANCE.

MAGNETO-- LISTEN TO YOURSELF!
STRYFE WAS A MUTANT SAME AS US--YA CAIN'T BLAME HUMANITY FOR HIS DISEASE!
CAN'T I, ROGUE?
IT IS THAT VERY HUMANITY WHICH IS ALL THAT STANDS BETWEEN MUTANTS AND OUR DIVINE RIGHT TO LIVE AS WE PLEASE.
NONE OF THE MUTANT FACTIONS WOULD BE FIGHTING AMONGST OURSELVES--
--IF NOT FOR THE FACT WE MUST DEFEND OUR VERY EXISTENCE FROM THOSE WHO WOULD SEE US DEAD!
AH'M SORRY AH HAVE TO DO THIS, SUGAH--
--BUT NEAR'S AH CAN TELL, IT MAY BE THE ONLY WAY T'KISS SOME SENSE INTO YA!
?!
WHAT HAPPENED? AH WAS SUPPOSED TO ABSORB YOUR POWER!
YOU DID, AFTER A FASHION.
YOU ACTUALLY MANAGED TO STEAL A BIT--
--THE DIFFERENCE BEING, IT WAS NOT ENOUGH!
AS THE LINGERING MEMORIES THAT FLOAT UNBIDDEN THROUGH YOUR MIND--AT LEAST FOR THE MOMENT--SHOULD REVEAL TO YOU... I AM NO LONGER THE MAN I WAS!
I AM STRONGER THAN I HAVE EVER BEEN--EVER HAVE IMAGINED I WOULD ONE DAY BECOME.

BUT THANK YOU FOR THE KISS, NONETHELESS.
WOK
IT SERVED AS THE BRIEFEST-- THE SWEETEST REMINDER OF WHAT MIGHT HAVE BEEN...
... WHAT MAY YET BE IF ANY OF YOU WOULD ALL ACCEPT THE TRUTH...
... IF YOU WOULD AT LAST SEE THE WORLD THE WAY IT IS, RATHER THAN THAT WHICH YOU WOULD SO DESPERATELY LIKE IT TO BECOME!
UNTIL THEN, YOU ARE ALL BOUND BY YOUR OWN ARCHAIC MORAL CODE OF PEACEFUL CO-EXISTENCE BETWEEN HUMANS AND MUTANTS.
UNTIL THEN YOU ARE RE-STRAINED BY YOUR CONFUSED BELIEF THAT ALL YOUR HARD WORK, ALL YOUR SACRIFICE WILL MAKE A BIT OF DIFFERENCE.
DO NOT WORRY ABOUT US, MAGNETO--
--FOR THE TRUTH HAS SET US FREE LONG AGO...!

AND AT THE HEART OF THAT TRUTH LIES A BITTER IRONY.
FOR YOU AND PROFESSOR XAVIER --AND BY EXTENSION ALL WHO WEAR THE COLORS OF THE X-MEN-- ARE ALL FIGHTING FOR THE SAME CAUSE.
IT IS ONLY THE METHODS WE'VE CHOSEN TO ADOPT, IT APPEARS, THAT WILL SEPARATE US FROM YOUR ACOLYTES FOREVER.
IT WILL BE FAR SHORTER THAN "FOREVER," CHILD!
FOR WITHIN THE HOUR THERE WILL BE NO "X-MEN," NO HUMANS TO PROTECT...
...THERE WILL BE ONLY A MASS GRAVE FOR WHICH ONLY A WORLD OF WALKING CORPSES SHALL MOURN!
LOFTY AMBITIONS, SIR.
THOUGH I'M AFRAID WE'RE NOT WITHOUT OUR OWN GAME PLAN.
IT'S CALLED SURVIVING, MAGNETO.
IT'S WHAT WE DO!

E'RE IN A
UBLE BIND
ERE, PEOPLE!
MAGNETO IS HOLDING HIS BASE TOGETHER BY SHEER FORCE OF WILL!
THE GREATER THE STRAIN HE IS PLACED UNDER, THE MORE THE INTEGRITY OF THIS STRUCTURE SUFFERS!
IF IT CRASHES...
...IF WE CAN'T KEEP IT TOGETHER...
...THE DEVASTATION WILL BE UNTHINK-ABLE!
YET, IF WE DO NOT TAKE THE RISK... IF WE DO NOT STOP MAGNETO...
...AND DO NOT DISMANTLE THIS ORBITING FORTRESS...
"...HOW MANY MORE LIVES WILL BE LOST IF WE DO NOT END IT HERE AND NOW?!"

PERHAPS WE OWE IT TO THOSE PEOPLE-- TO OURSELVES--TO FIND AN ALTERNATIVE TO THAT FATE?
I'VE KNOWN THIS MAN FOR YEARS-- AND WITNESSED THE COUNTLESS INDIGNITIES HEAPED UPON HIM....
...HAVE BEEN PRIVY TO EVERY AGONIZING STEP OF HIS STRUGGLE...
MUCH LIKE THE PROFESSOR, HIS COMMITMENT TO HIS GOAL HAS NEVER FALTERED.
PERHAPS, HAD I HAD THE STRENGTH OF CONVICTION TO JOIN HIM EARLIER--
DEAR GOD, PETER...
NO!
TELL ME SOMEBODY'S CONTROLLING HIS MIND!
FOR THE FIRST TIME IN MONTHS, LOGAN-- I FEEL I AM IN CONTROL!
TAKE YOUR PLACE AMONG THE OTHERS, COLOSSUS.

...A STRUGGLE WHICH, AS YOU POINTED OUT, IS SIMILAR TO OUR OWN IN CONTENT IF NOT IN EXECUTION!
WHAT I'M SAYING, MAGNETO, IS THAT IF YOU WILL HAVE ME--
--I WOULD LIKE TO JOIN YOU IN YOUR CHOSEN PLIGHT.
THERE IS NOTHING LEFT FOR ME HERE.
THERE IS... NOTHING LEFT HERE... FOR ANY OF US.
--FOUGHT MORE AGGRESSIVELY FOR THE RIGHTS OF MUTANTS--
--I WOULD NOT BE HERE AT THE GRAVE OF MY SISTER.
WELCOME TO THE FOLD, PETER.
WELCOME TO... THE FUTURE.
I WILL JOIN YOU SHORTLY.
I AM GLAD YOU WERE ALIVE TO WITNESS THIS FINAL HUMILIATION, CHARLES.
PERHAPS, BEFORE YOU DIE, YOU WILL REALIZE WHAT I HAVE ALWAYS KNOWN...
...THAT THE WEAK HAVE VIRTUALLY NO CHANCE OF EVER INHERITING THE EARTH!
WEAKNESS, ERIC-- HAS ALWAYS BEEN A MATTER OF PERSPECTIVE.

FOR ALL YOUR TALK OF "RULING" THE WORLD-- YOU'VE LOST SIGHT OF THE REALITY THAT IT IS THE WORLD THAT HAS ALWAYS RULED YOU!
IN YOUR YOUTH, IT TOOK AWAY THE FAMILY IN WHICH YOU WERE BORN!
AS A MAN, IT ROBBED YOU OF THE FAMILY YOU CREATED!
YOU COULD HAVE BEEN A FORCE FOR GOOD IN THIS WORLD...
... AND AS YOUR FRIEND, MAYBE THE ONLY FRIEND YOU'VE EVER ALLOWED INSIDE YOUR HEART...
... I CAN ATTEST TO THE INHERENT GOODNESS OF THE MAN YOU ONCE WERE!
BUT YOU LACKED COURAGE, ERIC. THE FORTITUDE TO RISE ABOVE THE CHALLENGES LIFE SET YOU. INSTEAD YOU BECAME THE ANGRY, BITTER MAN I SEE BEFORE ME!
ARRGH!
DON'T YOU PRESUME TO PITY ME, CHARLES
SIR, YOU'VE GOT TO ACT QUICKLY--JEAN CAN'T HOLD THAT VES-SEL TOGETHER MUCH LONGER!

EN IT IS CLEAR
WILL HAVE TO
ELP HER--
--BY USING MY MENTAL POWERS TO COMANDEER MAGNETO'S OWN!
THOUGH HE REALIZES THE RESULTING BIO-ELECTRIC FEEDBACK IS AGONIZING TO HIS STUDENTS...
...XAVIER ALSO KNOWS HE HAS NO CHOICE IF HE IS TO SAVE HIS CHARGES...
...AS WELL AS ALL THOSE PEOPLE THREATENED BY AVALON'S PRESENCE.
E ARE THOSE
CONSIDER US
G THE STRONGEST
NTS ON THE FACE
HE PLANET...
...BUT WE BOTH KNOW BETTER THAN THAT, DON'T WE?
YOU AND
TH STARTED
E SAME
T IN OUR
ES...
...BOTH BELIEVED WE COULD MAKE A DIFFERENCE IN THE LIVES OF THOSE AROUND US.
DO YOU REMEMBER WHAT HAPPENED THEN, ERIC?
DO YOU RECALL HOW ONE OF US KEPT THE PROMISE WE'D MADE TO THE OTHER?
THE PROMISE THAT OUR DREAM WOULD SURVIVE!

ONLY ONE OF US WAS TRUE TO OUR WORD.
FOR YEARS I CONVINCED MYSELF YOU WEREN'T TO BLAME FOR YOUR ACTIONS!
EACH CONFRONTATION, I HOPED WOULD BE
--BECAUSE I WAS SURE YOU WOULD COME TO
I HAD TO BELIEVE IN YOU...
...IN ORDER THAT I COULD BELIEVE IN THE DREAM TO WHICH WE'D DEDICATED
THEN YOU'VE WASTED YOUR TIME, CHARLES-- FOR THE MAN WHO MADE THAT PROMISE
THE MAN WHO SHARED YOUR HOPES OF A BETTER WORLD
HASN'T EXISTED IN YEARS
IF HE EVER
I REFUSE TO ACCEPT THAT!
JUST AS I REFUSE TO ALLOW YOU TO CONTINUE VENTING YOUR ANGER--YOUR GRIEF--YOUR DISILLUSIONMENT...
...ON THE WEAK AND
IF YOU WILL NOT TAKE RESPONSIBILITY FOR YOURSELF, MAGNETO...
...THEN GOD HELP ME I WILL!

MANDEERING MAGNETO'S
WERS WITH HIS OWN, THESE
MEN RISE ABOVE THE
TH WITH AVALON IN THEIR
ONIC THRALL.
GENETIC
CAIN AND
BEL...
...LOCKED FOREVER IN AN ETERNAL CONFLICT AS OLD AS THE FORCES OF GOOD AND EVIL.
AND WHEREAS MAGNUS WAS OFTEN GIVEN TO DISPLAYING THE FULL RANGE OF HIS POWERS--
--PROFESSOR CHARLES XAVIER WAS ALWAYS LESS INCLINED.
UNTIL THIS MOMENT.
FORGIVE ME--
--FOR WHAT I AM ABOUT TO DO.
AND WITH THAT,
XAVIER MAG-
ETICALLY HURLS
AVALON INTO
SPACE...
LACKING THE
URAGE, THE
SOLVE, TO
KE THE LIFE
THE MAN
O HE KNOWS...
...WILL CERTAINLY RETURN...
...AND ONCE MORE THREATEN THE ENTIRE WORLD...

FOR A FRACTION OF A MOMENT--
--HE'D LIKE TO BELIEVE IT IS ALL OVER.

THE STRUGGLE.
THE CONFLICT.
THE MOTIVATION TO CONTINUE A FIGHT THAT IS HIS...
...AND MUCH MORE THAN HIS.

BUT HE KNOWS BETTER.
I'M HERE, CHARLES.

OF COURSE YOU ARE, WARREN.

I'D EXPECT NOTHING LESS--
--FROM ANY OF MY X-MEN.

THE BATTLE CONTINUES IN X-MEN #2..

DREAMS DIE!

A STAN LEE PRESENTATION

...FOR WHAT I HAVE DONE

SCOTT LOBDELL
WRITER

JOHN ROMITA, Jr
jae lee
chris sprouse
brandon peterson
paul smith
PENCILERS

DAN GREEN
dan panosian
terry austin
tom palmer
keith williams
INKERS

MIKE THOMAS
COLORIST

CHRIS ELIOPOULOS
LETTERER

lisa patrick
ASSITANT EDITOR

bob harras
EDITOR

tom defalco
EDITOR IN CHIEF

On this, our 30th anniversary, we'd like to especially thank the following very talented gentlemen...Stan Lee, Jack Kirby, Len Wein, Dave Cockrum, John Byrne and Chris Claremont.

MARVEL® COMICS

$3.95 US
$4.95 CAN
2
SEPT
CC 01406

APPROVED BY THE COMICS CODE AUTHORITY

X-MEN UNLIMITED™

DUURSEMA–PANOSIAN

POINT BLANK

STAN LEE PRESENTS:

POINT BLANK

WRITER FABIAN NICIEZA PENCILER JAN DUURSEMA

INKERS DAN PANOSIAN KEITH WILLIAMS JIMMY PALMIOTTI JOE RUBINSTEIN

COLORIST MARIE JAVINS LETTERER RICHARD STARKINGS

EDITOR KELLY CORVESE ASST. EDITOR JAYE GARDNER

GROUP EDITOR BOB HARRAS EDITOR IN CHIEF TOM DeFALCO

WHEN I FIRST SAW HIM, IT WAS LIKE LOOKING DIRECTLY INTO THE SUN AT HIGH NOON.
SIMPLY OVERWHELMING IN HIS BRILLIANCE --
--DOMINEERING IN HIS SUPERIORITY--
--PROSTRATING IN HIS ARROGANCE--
--HE WAS EVERYTHING I WAS LED TO BELIEVE HE WOULD BE --
--MAGNETO, ONE OF THE MOST POWERFUL MUTANTS ON THE FACE OF THE PLANET--

--ESPOUSER OF THE DOMINANT RIGHTS OF **HOMO SUPERIOR** OVER NORMAL HUMANS--
--AND HE WAS **MORE** --HE WAS **COLD**, CLINICAL, METHODICAL--
--NONE OF WHICH I EXPECTED FROM A MAN WHOSE PSYCHE PROFILE INDICATED AN AVERSION TO THE MILITARY MINDSET.
YET, THERE WE WERE-- SOLDIERS IN THE **EAST GERMAN ARMY**, BEING BUFFETED ABOUT LIKE TOYS.

HIS CONTROL OVER THE ELECTRO-MAGNETIC FIELD WAS FRIGHTENING IN ITS APPLICATIONS.
BULLETS AIMED AT HIS HEART FOUND THEIR WAY BACK TO THE TRIGGER MEN.
THE IRON IN OUR BLOOD WAS USED TO CAUSE SEIZURES AND STROKES.
TANKS WHICH I HAD SEEN CRUSH MORTAR AND BONE ALIKE WERE RENT ASUNDER, AS IF MADE OF TISSUE PAPER.
THE AIR BURNED, THE WIND SCREAMED, AND THROUGH THE DIN, HIS VOICE COULD BE HEARD LIKE THE SNARLING OF A RABID WOLF...
"YOU WILL NOT TAKE WUNDAGORE MOUNTAIN FOR YOUR OWN!
"I WILL NOT ALLOW YOU TO TREAD SO CALLOUSL UPON CONSECRATED GROUND," I HEARD HIM BELLOW AS OUR COMMA ER CRIED FOR A STRATEGIC WITHDRA

IT WASN'T AN ORDER WE HAD TO THINK TWICE ABOUT.
WHAT COULD POSSESS A MAN SO, I THOUGHT THEN?
AS UTË AND I FLED THE SCENE OF THE CARNAGE, I WONDERED WHAT MADE WUNDAGORE MOUNTAIN WORTHY OF MAGNETO'S ATTENTIONS.
I ASKED UTË WHERE HE WAS GOING, BUT HE, PANICKING, RAN BLINDLY THROUGH THE HEAVY WOODS.
HE DID NOT ANSWER. "WHERE ARE WE?" I ASKED.
HE DID NOT KNOW.
WE HAD REACHED A CLEARING IN THE FOREST -- WE HAD COME UPON A SMALL CABIN.
"COULD THIS BE THE MADMAN'S HOME?" UTË ASKED DESPERATELY.
I KNEW THAT NO ONE AS SUPERIOR AS MAGNETO COULD LIVE IN SUCH A HOVEL, AND WHEN I SAW IT, I KNEW WHO DID LIVE HERE.

THAT CREATURE DID.
THAT HIDEOUS WOMAN THAT WAS CERTAINLY NOT HUMAN -- AND YET NOT ANIMAL. THE COW-LIKE THING.
SHE LOOKED AS TERRIFIED AS WE MUST HAVE.
THEN, IN A COARSE, DRY VOICE, SHE SAID, "RUN-- SAVE YOURSELVES!"
UTË MUTTERED SOMETHING ABOUT A TOMBSTONE, I'M NOT SURE WHAT.
I WAS WATCHING THE COW-WOMAN FLEE INTO THE DARKNESS.
I WAS LOOKING WITH DETACHED CURIOSITY AS THE LEAVES AND BRANCHES ABOVE MY HEAD WHIPPED TO AND FRO' --
--I WAS WATCHING THE MONSTER FROM HELL CALMLY ALIGHT ON THE SNOW-SWEPT GROUND.
I WAS STARING AT MY OWN IMPENDING DEATH WITH AN ALMOST BEMUSED INDIFFERENCE.
"YOU HAVE DISTURBED MY WIFE'S ETERNAL SLEEP," HE SAID WITH A VOICE NOW CHOKING IN CONTAINED FURY.
"HAVE YOU NO RESPECT?"

UTË THREW HIS ARMS UP, SURRENDERING IMMEDIATELY.
A PART OF ME WAS FURIOUS WITH HIM, THE REST ASHAMEDLY GRATEFUL THAT IT WAS HE --
--AND NOT I -- WHO SO QUICKLY GAVE IN TO THE FEAR WHICH SWEPT THROUGH US BOTH.
MAGNETO LOOKED AT US WITH THOSE EYES-- THEY WERE BEYOND INHUMAN --
-- THEY WERE DROWNING POOLS DEVOID OF REASON OR HOPE.
AND HE BELLOWED: "SURRENDER YOURSELVES? ISN'T THAT WHAT MY FAMILY DID? WHAT MY WIFE DID? WHAT I DID TIME AND AGAIN?
"SURRENDER MYSELF TO YOUR TENDER MERCIES --
" -- ONLY TO HAVE THAT THROWN BACK INTO MY FACE THROUGH THE PAIN, MISERY AND DEATH YOUR KIND HAS INFLICTED ON ME AND MINE?!!!"
UTË EXPLODED. THERE IS NO OTHER WAY TO DESCRIBE IT.
HIS ENTIRE BODY SIMPLY RUPTURED.

I WATCHED AS HIS MUTILATED BODY FELL BEFORE ME. I WAS BEYOND FEAR, BEYOND COMPREHENSION.
WHEN I LOOKED DOWN AT THE SMOLDERING REMAINS OF UTË, THE MONSTER'S VOICE SOFTENED.
"SHE ALWAYS DID SAY I WOULD BRING VIOLENCE TO HER," HE WHISPERED.
"WHEN I LEARNED THAT THIS WAS THE LAST PLACE SHE MAY HAVE KNOWN HOPE -- WHERE OUR TWIN CHILDREN WERE BORN -- I BUILT A MONUMENT TO HER.
"I SWORE NEVER TO ALLOW BLOOD TO BE SPILLED HERE.
"IT IS TOO LATE FOR THAT NOW, BECAUSE OF YOUR CORRUPT GOVERNMENT'S DESIRE FOR THIS MOUNTAIN'S MARVELS, IT IS TOO LATE...
"GO NOW," HE MUTTERED, HIS RAGE BUILDING AGAIN. "TAKE YOUR FELLOW SOLDIER WITH YOU AND GO."
"HE WAS MORE THAN MY TROOP-MATE," I CRIED, MY ANGER AT THIS BUTCHER SUPER-SEDING MY SENSE OF SURVIVAL.
"HE WAS MY BROTHER!"
AND WHAT HE SAID NEXT, I'LL NEVER FORGET... HE SAID, "SO THEN YOU NOW KNOW THE PAIN OF LOSS AS SHARPLY AS DO I.
"NOT MUCH DIFFERENCE BETWEEN HUMAN PAIN AND MUTANT PAIN IS THERE?"
AND HE LEFT.

<THAT WAS OVER SEVEN YEARS AGO.>*
<YOU LIVE IN THAT MOMENT, ADRIAN.>
<WHY CAN'T YOU LET IT GO?>
<I-- I WOULD PREFER NOT TO, DOCTOR HEISEN-BERG.>
PREIS 1982
PSYC
PSYCHIATE
ANSLATED OM GERMAN -- K.C.
<KEEPING THE ANGERS-- THE HATREDS-- CONSTANTLY STOKED-->
<--PROVIDES THE FUEL I NEED TO KEEP ON LIVING.>
OOK AROUND, ADRIAN. HE BERLIN WALL IS DOWN.>
OR BETTER R WORSE, OUR OUNTRY IS NOW NITED -- HOULDN'T YOUR ODY AND MIND E AS WELL?>
YOU RE FREE F YOUR BLIGATIONS O STATE ERVICE NOW-->
<ISN'T IT TIME TO BEGIN YOUR LIFE AGAIN?>
<DON'T YOU OWE UTE MORE THAN THIS?>
<PERHAPS I DO.>

<IT'S JUST SUCH A CLEANSING FIRE INSIDE ME, DOCTOR.>
<IT SIMPLIFIES THINGS -- IT PROVIDES ME WITH AN IMPETUS, A CLARITY OF VISION...>
<THEN WHY CONTINUE TO SEE ME, MISTER EISKALT ¿?¡>
<IT IS BECOMING QUITE OBVIOUS THAT YOU DO NOT WANT TO MOVE BEYOND THAT WHICH EMOTIONALLY CRIPPLES YOU.>
<I COME -- BECAUSE I STILL WANT TO FIND A BETTER WAY -- TO SAVE MYSELF...>
<A BETTER WAY THAN WHAT, ADRIAN ?>
<A BETTER WAY THAN WHAT--?>

EMPIRE STATE UNIVERSITY, MANHATTAN, NEW YORK.
CLAP CLAP CLAP CLAP CLAP CLAP
I WOULD KE TO ASK U TO JOIN IN WELCOMING UR SPECIAL GUEST-ECTURER--
SRAEL'S ORMER BASSADOR GREAT RITAIN, OCTOR BRIELLE HALLER--
THANK YOU, PROFESSOR FELDER.
QUITE AN INTERESTING APPROACH YOU'VE CHOSEN FOR A CLASS ENTITLED: "PRACTICAL APPLICATIONS OF INTERNATIONAL LAW," ISN'T IT?
"DEMAGOGUES OF THE TWENTIETH CENTURY -- A WEEKLY SEMINAR SERIES"--?
A TOPIC, I'M SAD TO SAY WITH FAR TOO MANY EXAMPLES TO CITE, AS IS EVIDENT FROM YOUR ROSTER OF PREVIOUS GUEST-SPEAKERS.
THE MAN WE ARE HERE TO DISCUSS TODAY IS UNIQUE IN HIS OWN RIGHT, A MAN WE KNOW PRECIOUS LITTLE ABOUT -- WITH THE OFFICIAL RECORD HAVING PRECIOUS LITTLE TO SAY.
WE BELIEVE THE MAN WHO WOULD BECOME MAGNETO WAS BORN ERIK MAGNUS LEHNSHERR, TO A GYPSY FAMILY OF SINTE DESCENT--
-- OUTSIDE GDANSK, POLAND, THEN KNOWN AS DANZIG, AROUND 1928.

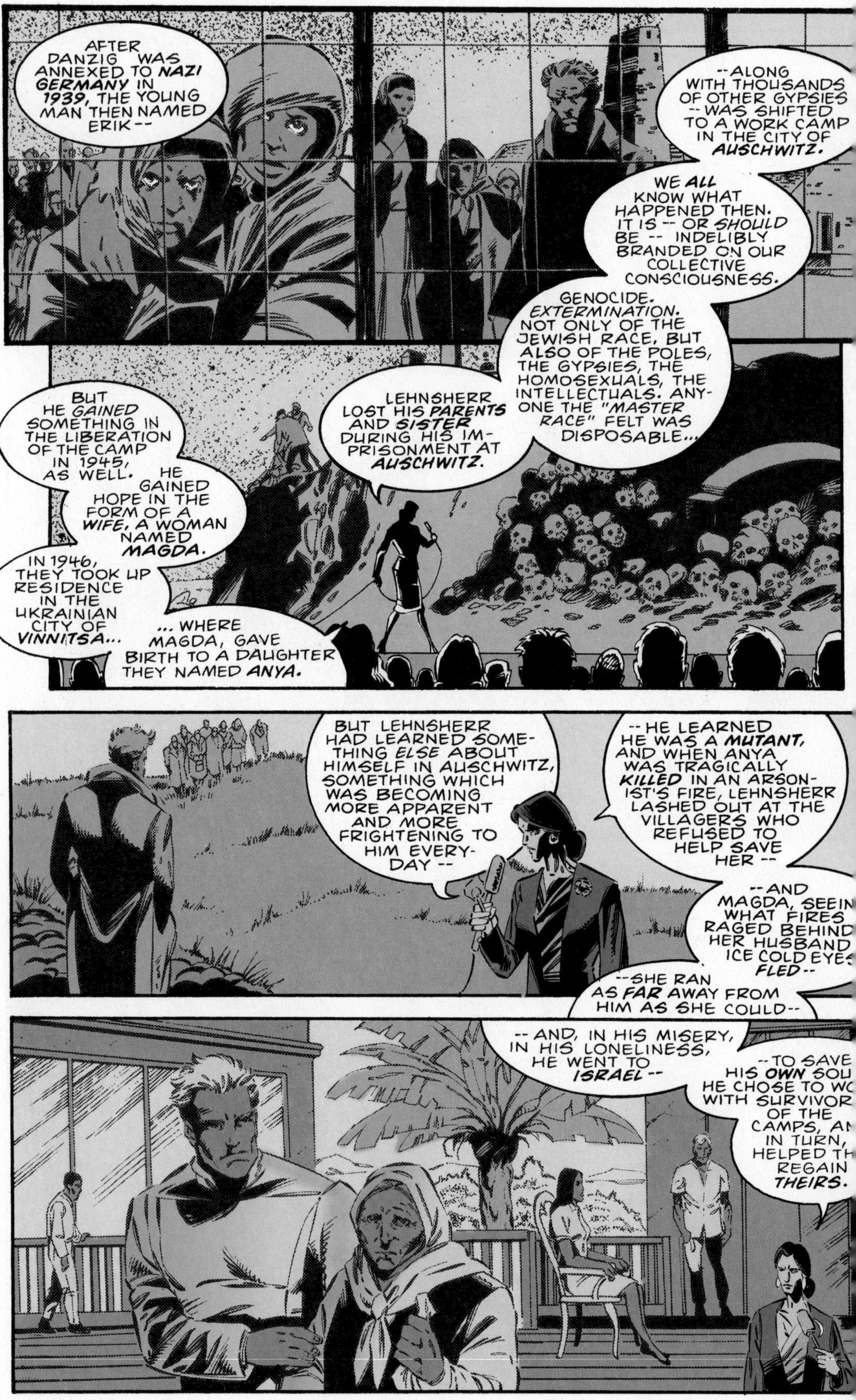

AFTER DANZIG WAS ANNEXED TO ***NAZI GERMANY*** IN ***1939***, THE YOUNG MAN THEN NAMED ERIK--

--ALONG WITH THOUSANDS OF OTHER GYPSIES --WAS SHIFTED TO A WORK CAMP IN THE CITY OF ***AUSCHWITZ.***

WE ***ALL*** KNOW WHAT HAPPENED THEN. IT IS -- OR *SHOULD* BE -- INDELIBLY BRANDED ON OUR COLLECTIVE CONSCIOUSNESS.

GENOCIDE. *EXTERMINATION.* NOT ONLY OF THE JEWISH RACE, BUT ALSO OF THE POLES, THE GYPSIES, THE HOMOSEXUALS, THE INTELLECTUALS. ANYONE THE *"MASTER RACE"* FELT WAS DISPOSABLE...

LEHNSHERR LOST HIS ***PARENTS*** AND ***SISTER*** DURING HIS IMPRISONMENT AT ***AUSCHWITZ.***

BUT HE *GAINED* SOMETHING IN THE LIBERATION OF THE CAMP IN 1945, AS WELL. HE GAINED HOPE IN THE FORM OF A ***WIFE***, A WOMAN NAMED ***MAGDA.***

IN 1946, THEY TOOK UP RESIDENCE IN THE UKRAINIAN CITY OF ***VINNITSA...***

... WHERE MAGDA, GAVE BIRTH TO A DAUGHTER THEY NAMED ***ANYA.***

BUT LEHNSHERR HAD LEARNED SOMETHING *ELSE* ABOUT HIMSELF IN AUSCHWITZ, SOMETHING WHICH WAS BECOMING MORE APPARENT AND MORE FRIGHTENING TO HIM EVERYDAY --

--HE LEARNED HE WAS A ***MUTANT,*** AND WHEN ANYA WAS TRAGICALLY ***KILLED*** IN AN ARSONIST'S FIRE, LEHNSHERR LASHED OUT AT THE VILLAGERS WHO REFUSED TO HELP *SAVE* HER --

--AND MAGDA, SEEIN WHAT FIRES RAGED BEHIND HER HUSBAND ICE COLD EYES ***FLED--***

--SHE RAN AS ***FAR*** AWAY FROM HIM AS SHE COULD--

-- AND, IN HIS MISERY, IN HIS LONELINESS, HE WENT TO ***ISRAEL --***

--TO SAVE HIS ***OWN*** SOU HE CHOSE TO WO WITH SURVIVOR OF THE CAMPS, AN IN TURN, HELPED TH REGAIN ***THEIRS.***

AND THAT IS WHERE I MET HIM, FOR I WAS A PATIENT AT THAT HOSPITAL IN HAIFA.
LEHNSHERR HAD TAKEN TO CALLING HIMSELF MAGNUS...
...AS IF BY CHOOSING HIS MIDDLE NAME, HE COULD BRING SOME SEMBLANCE OF BALANCE AND SIMPLICITY TO HIS HAUNTED LIFE.
MAGNUS HELPED NURSE ME BACK TO HEALTH. DOES THAT MAKE ME AN OBJECTIVE LECTURER, YOU MAY WELL WONDER?
FOR THE MOST PART, I CAN SEPARATE MAGNUS THE MAN FROM MAGNETO THE MUTANT CRUSADER.
AND PLEASE NOTE MY CHOICE OF WORDS, FOR I HAVE VALID REASONS TO LABEL MAGNETO CRUSADER AND NOT DICTATOR.
FIRSTLY: HE HAS NO COUNTRY TO CALL HIS OWN.
SECONDLY: HE HAS FOUGHT FOR A SPECIFIC CAUSE, NOT FOR PERSONAL POWER.
WHICH BEGS THE QUESTION THEN, BEFORE HE DIED IN A BATTLE ABOVE EARTH--
--WAS MAGNETO A DEMAGOGUE OR AN IDEALOGUE?
WAS HE A TYRRANNICAL MADMAN PLACING HIM-SELF ABOVE THE RIGHTS OF HUMANITY OR A RIGHTEOUS ZEALOT FIGHTING FOR A NOBLE CAUSE -- EQUALITY FOR MUTANTS?
CAN ANY ONE OF US TRULY ANSWER SUCH A QUESTION?

I'VE ALWAYS HATED THE FEELING WHEN THE WHEELS FIRST LEAVE THE GROUND.
YOU GET A PALPABLE SENSE THAT CONTROL OVER YOUR LIFE HAS BEEN PLACED IN THE HANDS OF OTHERS.
IRONIC THOUGH CONSIDERING HOW I HAVE LIVED MY LIFE ON LAND, THAT THIS SHOULD WORRY ME IN THE AIR.
I LEAVE BERLIN IN ORDER TO REGAIN THAT LOST SENSE OF CONTROL.
FATAL ATTRACTION MUTANTS & MEN J.B. CHAME
FATAL ATTRACTIONS MUTANTS & MEN
AND IN NEW YORK LIES THE BEGINNING OF THE END.
EXCUSE ME, SON, MAY I GET BY--?
EITHER FOR MYSELF, OR FOR THE BUTCHER WHO FLAYS MY NIGHTMARES.
THANK YOU, SON.
MAGNUS!
Oh.
PRECISE. ANALYTICAL. CLINICAL. DISPASSIONATE.
BE THE MONSTER HE WAS. KILL HIM AS HE KILLED UTE.
PRECISE. A NEEDLE CONCEALED IN A PEN.
ANALYTICAL. A NEEDLE TIPPED WITH POISON.

MAGNUS--!
ENT-
HULDI-
N SIE--?
CLINICAL. A POISON COURSING THROUGH HIS VEINS.
Uhm--
ES TUT
MIR
LEID--
IT'S ALL RIGHT--
I MISTAKE
MAN FOR SOME-
ONE ELSE.
ORRY.
DISPASSIONATE. A RAGING POISON BURNING THROUGH HIS VEINS.
FIRES RAGING INSIDE HIM.
AS THEY RAGE INSIDE OF ME.
AS THEY RAGED THROUGH MY BROTHER
AS THEY CLEANSE AND PURIFY ALL THAT IS WRONG
WITH MUTANTS
AND WITH ME

MANHATTAN. TWO DAYS LATER.
THAT IS EXACTLY WHAT I AM CLAIMING, MISTER KOPPEL.
AS I STATED QUITE THOROUGHLY IN MY NEW BOOK, MANKIND MUST ULTIMATELY BEAR THE RESPONSIBILITY FOR THE PROLIF-ERATION OF THE MUTANT GENE THROUGHOUT THE PLANET.
OVER THE LAST SEVERAL DECADES, WE HAVE INTRO-DUCED SO MANY CONTAGIONS INTO THE ENVIRON-MENT--
--WHICH HAVE SIMPLY MADE THEIR INEVITABLE WAY INTO THE HUMAN DNA STRUCTURE, THEREBY RESULTING IN MORE MUTANT OFFSPRING.
HOW CAN WE BLAME MUTANTS FOR THIS? IT IS ANALAGOUS TO BLAMING THE GRASS WHEN A WEED TAKES ROOT.
SO YOU COMPARE MUTANTS TO WEEDS THEN, MISTER CHAMBERS?
LIKE IVY GROWING OUT OF CONTROL ON A BRICK WALL?
YOUR ANALOGY ATTEMPTS TO PORTRAY MY ANALOGY AS SOMETHING --UGLY-- MISTER KOPPEL.
I MERELY COMPARE THEM FROM A VISUAL STAND-POINT--

--THE
IVY CLINGS
TO THE
SURFACE OF A
WALL, THRIVES
ON IT, GROWS
ON
IT--
--AND
EVENTUALLY
COMES TO
DOMINATE
THE VISUAL
PANO-
RAMA.
FAR BE
IT FROM ME
TO PLAY DUELING
ANALOGIES,
MISTER
CHAMBERS, BUT
IN YOUR OWN,
OBLIQUE,
WAY--
--ISN'T
YOUR BEST-
SELLING BOOK
SENDING A WARNING
SIGNAL THAT MUTANTS
ARE CLOSER THAN
EVER TO BECOMING
THIS PLANET'S
DOMINANT
SPECIES?
I SAY
TONIGHT, TED,
AS I SAY IN
MY BOOK,
FATAL
ATTRACTIONS--
--THAT
THEY EXIST
LIKE THE IVY ON
THE BRICK WALL,
THAT THE TWO CAN
MUTUALLY CO-
EXIST--
--AND, IN
SOME CASES
BECOME GREATER
THAN THE SUM
OF THEIR
PARTS.
ABC NEWS
JOINING
ME IN THE
STUDIO IS A MAN
WHO WOULD AGREE
WITH MUCH OF
WHAT YOU SAY,
MISTER
CHAMBERS--
--BUT
NOT WITH
YOUR
CONCLUSIONS.
WE BRING
BACK TO NIGHTLINE,
THE FOUNDER OF
A GROUP CALLED
FRIENDS OF HUMANITY,
MISTER GRAYDON
CREED.
MISTER
CREED, IN LIGHT
OF RECENT TERRORIST
ACTIVITIES BY FORMER
MEMBERS OF YOUR
ORGANIZATION* WHOM YOU
CLAIM WERE ACTING
ON THEIR OWN
WITHOUT YOUR
APPROVAL--
--HOW CAN
YOU SAY THAT
YOUR ORGANIZATION
IS ANY BETTER OR
WORSE THAN THE
MUTANTS YOU RAIL
AGAINST?
X-FORCE #24
--KELLY.

TED, YOU CITE ONE RADICAL FRINGE ELEMENT OF MY ORGANIZATION --
-- WHICH WAS PROTESTING THE FACT THAT TWO MUTANT TERRORISTS --
-- WERE NOT BEING CHARGED FOR THEIR CRIMES BY A UNITED STATES GOVERNMENT TOO AFRAID OF THE MUTANT LOBBY TO ACT DECISIVELY --
-- AND THEN BLOW THE INCIDENT OUT OF PROPORTION.
THE INCREASED AMOUNT OF MUTANT ACTIVITIES SINCE MY LAST APPEARANCE ALONE WHICH COULD BE CALLED INTO QUESTION --
-- FAR OUTNUMBER THE ACTS OF HUMANS DESPERATELY AND JUSTIFIABLY TERRIFIED FOR THEIR OWN WELL-BEING.
I CALL MISTER CREED'S REASONING INTO QUESTION! HE BANDIES THE PHRASE "MUTANT LOBBY" AS A BUZZ-WORD --
-- BUT THE TRUTH IS, THAT MUTANTS ARE NOT AN ORGANIZED CONGRESSIONAL LOBBY --
-- NOR DO THEY HAVE REPRESENTATION IN ANY OF THE WORLD'S GOVERNING BODIES --
-- INDEED, SINCE MAGNETO'S DISAPPEARANCE LAST YEAR --
-- THE MUTANT POPULATION DOES NOT EVEN HAVE A STRONG VOICE IN THEIR OWN AFFAIRS!
ARE YOU CALLING MAGNETO A "STATES-MAN"..?!
I AM SAYING THAT, JUST LIKE OUR FOUNDING FATHERS, OR MARTIN LUTHER KING --
-- MAGNETO'S WAS A VOICE RAISED TO BE HEARD ABOVE THE PROTESTS OF THE MAJORITY AND RULING CLASSES.
SO WAS HITLER'S!
KLIK
SO MANY SIDES TO ONE MAN.
HOW CAN THAT BE?
HOW CAN ANYONE SEE HIM FOR ANYTHING OTHER THAN WHAT HE TRULY IS -- A MURDERER?

THE GRAND HYATT HOTEL, GRAND CENTRAL STATION, MANHATTAN.
THIS WAY, MADAME.
FRAU HALLER.
HERR EISKALT. GUTEN MORGEN.
YOU ORDERED THE FRUIT AND GRAIN PLATTER, I SEE. GOOD CHOICE. IT IS ALWAYS WELL PREPARED HERE.
PERMIT ME TO BE BLUNT, HERR EISKALT.
I AM NOT COMFORTABLE WITH THIS MEETING.
I AM NOT COMFOR-TABLE WITH WHAT YOU REPRESENT.
I HAVE ONLY AGREED TO COME BECAUSE PEOPLE I RESPECT IN BOTH OUR RESPECTIVE GOVERN-MENTS--
--AS WELL AS THOSE IN THE UNITED STATES, ASKED ME TO.
FRAU HALLER -- WHAT MY COUNTRY WANTS, I DO -- PARDON MY ENGLISH -- YOU UNDERSTAND?
WE TALK ONLY OF THINGS WHO MIGHT BE, YES?
THINGS WE MIGHT NEED TO BE DOING IF MAGNETO IS ALIVE. WHO IS TO KNOW IT DO TO BE HAPPENING?
DO NOT PATRONIZE ME, SIR.
I KNOW WHAT YOU ARE -- AND SHOULD MAGNUS BE ALIVE AGAIN--
--I KNOW WHAT OUR COUNTRIES WOULD LIKE YOU TO DO.

THANK YOU, BUT I WON'T BE STAYING LONG ENOUGH TO EAT.
YOU DISAPPOINT ME.
HOW CAN YOU IGNORE THREAT OF MAGNETO?
MENU
YOU HAVE BEEN THROUGH MUCH PAIN IN LIFE, YES?
CAUSED, NO, BY ME WHO BE LIKE MAGNETO?
UNLIKE CERTAIN VOICES IN MY GOVERNMENT WHO WOULD RATIONALIZE THEIR OWN HISTORY --
-- IT IS BECAUSE OF MY BACKGROUND THAT I SUPPORTED MAGNUS'S GOALS.
HE WAS -- IS -- WHATEVER -- A MAN OF VISION, OF COURAGE AND OF HONOR.
WHAT HE SEEKS FOR MUTANTS, IS NOT SO DIFFERENT FROM WHAT MY PEOPLE BUILT FOR THEMSELVES AFTER THE HOLOCAUST, IS IT?
WHAT WOULD YOU CALL ISRAEL, IF NOT A PLACE WHERE PEOPLE OF LIKE MINDS AND GOALS CAN BE WHAT THEY WANT TO BE, FREE FROM THE PERSECUTION OF OTHERS.
SO YOU WILL NOT HELP ME? WE CANNOT BE WORKING TOGETHER? GERMANS AND ISRAELIS WITH SAME WANTINGS?
AH, RATHER SAD, ISN'T IT, THAT WHAT NOW UNITES OUR TWO COUNTRIES IS A THREAT WHICH IS GREATER THAN THE SUM OF ITS PARTS?
I WOULD SAY... NECESSARY... NOT SAD.

I WILL ONLY ASSIST YOU IF YOUR GOAL IS TO APPREHEND MAGNUS--
-- FOR THE SPECIFIC PURPOSE OF PUTTING HIM ON TRIAL FOR HIS ACTIONS--
-- AND THEREBY GRANTING HIM THE FORUM THROUGH WHICH HE CAN ONCE AGAIN EXPRESS HIS VIEWS.
IF YOUR FOOL'S MISSION IS TO KILL MAGNUS, THEN THIS CONVERSATION IS OVER.
KILL HIM?
I ASSURE YOU, MY EMPLOYERS WISH TO BE CAPTURING HIM ONLY.
TO KILL HIM IS TO MARTYR HIM.
TO MARTYR HIM IS TO BE ADVANCING HIS CAUSE.
I WILL MAKE SOME PHONE CALLS. I WILL GATHER SOME INFORMATION FOR YOU.
IT WOULD BE HELPFUL, FRAU HALLER.
BUT YOU DO NOT FOOL ME, HERR EISKALT.
I CAN SEE IT IN YOUR EYES. YOUR MOTIVES IN THIS MATTER ARE PERSONAL, NOT PROFESSIONAL.
IF YOU APPROACH THIS FROM A PERSONAL POSITION, YOU ARE DOOMED TO FAIL.
MAGNUS IS BEYOND SUCH THINGS.
GOOD DAY.
BUT IS YOUR PRECIOUS MAGNETO BEYOND LIFE AND DEATH?
I IMAGINE, WE SHALL SOON FIND OUT...

IN THE ATLANTIC, OFF THE KEY WEST ISLAND OF FLORIDA.
Y'SHOOR THIS IS WHERE WE'RE S'POSED T'BE, MATE?
YES, "I'M SHOOOR," JOHNNY -- JUST STEER THE BLOODY BOAT AND LEAVE THE THINKING TO ME.
I'M DAFT FER DOING THAT AS OFTEN AS I DO, MORTY.
AH, QUIT YER BELLY-ACHIN,' Y'AUSSIE TOOTH-PICK--
--I'M THE ONE WHOSE DELICATE SKIN'S GONNA BURN TO A CRISP OUT HERE.
ASTROPHYSICS
FRED, OL' BLUBBER-BOY, Y'SHOULDN'T BE TALKIN' T'ME ABOUT BURNIN' UP NOW, MATE, SHOULD YOU?
CHKT
ALL OF YOU, BE QUIET -- SOMEONE -- SOMETHING -- IS COMING --!
ARE YOU SURE, EILEEN?
OF COURSE I AM!

THE DISRUPTION OF THE ELECTROMAGNETIC FIELD IS LIKE A SLAP IN THE FACE!
I'M CERTAIN IT IS...
DON'T BELITTLE MY INTELLECT, MORTIMER, AND I WON'T BELITTLE YOUR GREED.
THEY ARE, AFTER ALL, OUR TWO BEST FEATURES.
NOT FROM WHERE I AM SQUATTING, MY DEAR.
SHZZFFRAKK ZZZKKKAAK
WHOEVER ARRANGED THIS MEETING-- HAS ARRIVED!
BROTHERHOOD OF MUTANTS-- MORTIMER TOYNBEE, KNOWN AS THE TOAD--
--FREDERICK DUKES, THE BLOB--
--SAINT JOHN ALLERDYCE, PYRO--
--AND EILEEN HARSAW, PHANTAZIA-- THANK YOU FOR MEETING ME HERE.
I AM CALLED EXODUS.
I AM THE FERRY MAN ASSIGNED TO TAKE MUTANTKIND ON A JOURNEY TO A BETTER PLACE.
Oh, I'M JUST SURE YOU ARE, MY GOOD MAN.

WHADDYOU WANT WITH US?
I? WITH YOU? NOTHING.
V2450
WHAT DOES HE WANT?
HE OFFERS A HAVEN. A REFUGE. A HOME.
HOW MANY BATH-ROOMS?
A SANCTUARY IS BEING BUILT -- GROWING, ACTUALLY -- FROM THE SEED OF FUTURE DECAY AND PAST SINS.
AN' YER TELLIN' ME HE WANTS US T'GO LIVE WITH HIM?
NOT ALL OF YOU, FRED.
JUST EILEEN.
ME?
WHY JUST ME?
BECAUSE YOU ARE THE ONLY ONE HE HAS DEEMED WORTHY.

THAT ARROGANT, SELF-RIGHTEOUS PIG!
ALL MY LIFE, HE HAS BEDEVILED ME WITH HIS CONCEIT!
WHY AREN'T WE ALL WORTHY OF "HIS HIGHNESS'S" KEEPING?
BECAUSE THERE IS SIMPLY NO PLACE IN AVALON FOR MUTANTS LIKE YOURSELF AND FREDERICK--PEOPLE WHO LACK VISION AND POTENTIAL.
WELL, WOT ABOUT ME, THEN? I GOT TWENTY-TWENTY HERE!
YOU MIGHT HAVE BEEN CONSIDERED, ST. JOHN... HAD YOU NOT BECOME TAINTED...
TAINTED? WHAT'RE YOU TALKING ABOUT?
EILEEN, YOUR ANSWER, PLEASE...
I --
-- I DON'T --
NO...
...NO -- I -- NO...

VERY WELL.
FARE YOU WELL, MUTANTS.
MAY YOUR COMING DEATHS BE PAIN-LESS.
ZZAAAK SHSHSH SSF

LORD, HE NEVER CHANGES, DOES HE?
HIS MONUMENTA SENSE OF SELF-IMPORTA NEVER CEAS TO AMAZE ME!
HOW DARE HE?
HOW DARE HE?!

SOD ON HIM.
TAINTED?
SOD ON THEM BOTH.
I'M TAKING US IN, MATES.
WE GOT A PRETTY GOOD RACKET GOING ON OUR OWN, ROIT?
WE STILL GOT AN AFTERNOON MEETING AT JIMMY BUFFET'S, ROIT?
GOOD.
LET'S MAKE US SOME NICE GIT WITH NO STRINGS ATTACHED.
WHO NEEDS MAGNETO, ANY-WAYS?

MET WITH THE
ROTHERHOOD OF
VIL MUTANTS
ARLIER TODAY.
THEY WERE IN QUITE THE MOOD.
NOTE TO SELF: NEVER TRY TO MATCH THE BLOB SHOT FOR SHOT.
ESPECIALLY TEQUILA.
TOYNBEE WAS MORE THAN HAPPY WITH MY OFFER. CASH FOR INFORMATION.
I ASSUME, SINCE HE LACKS THE COURAGE TO EXACT REVENGE ON MAGNETO HIMSELF...
...HE IS MORE THAN WILLING TO ASSIST ANYONE WHO DOES.
WHAT MUST IT HAVE BEEN LIKE FOR THE TOAD TO HAVE BEEN AN INDENTURED SERVANT TO SUCH A MONSTER?
SUCH A DICHOTOMY BETWEEN THE MAGNUS OF OLD AND THE MORE RECENT MAN.
FROM ABUSIVE, GENOCIDAL DEMAGOGUE TO TWEED-DRESSED SCHOOL HEAD-MASTER AND SYMPATHETIC SPOKESMAN FOR THE MUTANT CAUSE.
HOW DOES ONE PREDICT THE ACTIONS OF AN OPPONENT WHO IS SO ADEPT AT BEING UNPREDICTABLE?
XAVIER'S
SCHOOL
FOR
GIFTED

HE STARTED AS THE ANTITHESIS OF CHARLES XAVIER.
HE RECRUITED A BAND OF YOUNG MUTANTS WHO WOULD PURSUE THE ACHIEVEMENT OF HIS OWN DREAMS --
DREAMS OF CONQUEST.
DREAMS OF SUPERIORITY.
TIME AND AGAIN, HE ATTEMPTE TO FORCE WORLD VI DOWN TH COLLECTIV THROATS THIS PLAN PEOPL
--TO PRINCIPAL AND NURSEMAID TO THE CHILDREN OF XAVIER'S DREAM --
MAGNETO HAS FOUND EVERY WHICH WAY CONCEIVABLE TO ADVANCE HIS OWN POLITICAL AND GENETIC AGENDA.
WHEN HE FINALLY ALLOWED HIMSELF TO BE PLACED BEFORE A WORLD COURT, HE WAS FOUND NOT GUILTY OF CRIMES AGAINST HUMANITY.
AND THEN HE STARTED ALL OVER AGAIN.
XAVIER'S SCHOOL FOR GIFTED YOUNGSTERS

AND
, HE
STOPPED.
FROM THE DEPTHS OF THE SAVAGE LAND UNDERNEATH ANTARCTICA --
-- TO BEING REVERTED BACK TO CHILDHOOD BY ONE OF HIS OWN CREATIONS --
-- FROM SECRET BASES IN THE CARIBBEAN OF ANCIENT MYTH AND FANTASY --
TIME, THE NEXT
RATION OF PAWNS
E, IRONICALLY
IGH, HIS FIRST
ERATION AS WELL --
-- PIETRO AND WANDA MAXIMOFF -- QUICKSILVER AND SCARLET WITCH --
THE CHILDREN OF MAGNETO --
-- BOTH OF WHOM HAD SERVED THE CAUSE OF HUMANITY AS MEMBERS OF X-FACTOR AND THE AVENGERS.
WHEN MAGNETO ALLEGEDLY PERISHED, HE DIED A FAILURE IN THE GREATEST SENSE OF THE WORD --
-- FOR HE WAS A MAN UNABLE TO MAKE HIS OWN CHILDREN SEE THE JUSTNESS OF HIS CAUSE --
-- MUCH LESS A SPECIES OR AN ENTIRE PLANET.
HOW IRONIC, INDEED.

JACK DANIEL'S
HOW DID HE DO IT?
HOW COULD HE HAVE COME BACK TIME AND AGAIN --
--ALWAYS WITH A NEW METHOD OF CONQUEST.
ONE RIDICULOUS ATTEMPT AFTER ANOTHER.
AND WORST OF ALL -- HOW COULD ANYONE BELIEVE THAT SIMPLY HAVING HIS ASTEROID HOME INCINERATED WHILE ENTERING EARTH'S ATMOSPHERE COULD ACTUALLY KILL THIS MAN?
FOR GOD'S SAKE, HE WAS ONCE GENETICALLY REVERTED TO INFANCY AND STILL FOUND A WAY TO REGAIN HIS ADULTHOOD.
WHAT MAKES A MAN LIKE THAT CONTINUE TO BELIEVE IN HIMSELF?
KLIK
Oh, YES, OF COURSE I WAS FRIGHTENED OF HIM, MISTER EISKALT.
DID HE HIT YOU, MISTER TOYNBEE? DID HE ABUSE YOU?
Oh, CONSTANTLY. CONSTANTLY.

SO WHY DID YOU STAY WITH HIM FOR SO LONG?
I WAS YOUNGER THEN. YOU HAVE TO UNDERSTAND--
--HE HAD A WAY OF KEEPING YOU UNDER HIS CONTROL--
--AND NOT JUST THROUGH THE THREAT OF PHYSICAL PUNISHMENT, EITHER--
--HOW ELSE?
THROUGH SHEER FORCE OF WILL, MISTER EISKALT.
HE BELIEVED SO STRONGLY IN HIMSELF -- IN HIS GOALS -- IN HIS METHODS--
--THAT NO MATTER HOW LUDICROUS SOME OF THEM SOUNDED--
--YOU ACTUALLY BELIEVED HE WOULD ACCOMPLISH THEM!
HOW DID HITLER RALLY HIS COUNTRY AROUND HIM?
THROUGH THE INCREDIBLE ALLURE OF HIS CONFIDENCE--
--MAGNETO WAS MUCH THE SAME WAY, IN THAT REGARD.
FOR ALL HIS BLUSTER, FOR ALL HIS ILL-TEMPERED TREATMENT OF MYSELF AND MY COMRADES.
--WE STAYED WITH HIM BECAUSE HE MADE US BELIEVE WHAT HE STRONGLY BELIEVED HIMSELF--
--THAT HE WAS SUPERIOR TO US ALL--
--AND BY STAYING WITH HIM, WE WERE ENSURING OUR PLACE ALONGSIDE GREATNESS.

AND, FOR AS MUCH AS I HATE HIM, TO THIS DAY, I STILL BELIEVE HE MAY HAVE BEEN RIGHT...
KLIK
HOW?
HOW COULD HE DO IT?
TSSSS
HOW COULD ANY MAN REPEATEDLY FAIL IN HIS APPOINTED TASK--
--AND STILL HAVE THE SENSE OF SELF-CONFIDENCE, THE ENORMITY OF EGO--
--TO CONTINUE TO BELIEVE IN HIMSELF?
IT EITHER INDICATES A COMPLETELY DELUSIONAL SENSE OF SELF-WORTH...
...OR THE UNSHAKE-ABLE BELIEF IN THE CORRECT-NESS OF ONE'S WAYS.
KNOWING WHICH COULD MAKE ALL THE DIFFERENCE IN THE WORLD WHEN THE OPPOR-TUNITY TO KILL HIM ARRIVES...

THE ADMINISTRATIVE BUILDING WHICH HOUSES THE **MOSSAD**, ISRAEL'S SECURITY SERVICES.

I THANK YOU FOR TAKING THE TIME TO SPEAK WITH ME, **MOIRA**.

GABBY, WHEN YOU AND I CHAT, IT'S **NOT** AS GABRIELLE HALLER, AMBASSADOR-AT-LARGE AND DOCTOR **MOIRA MacTAGGERT**, BIOGENETICS EXPERT --

-- BUT AS TWO FRIENDS WHO'VE SHARED MUCH OF THE SAME THINGS IN THIS LIFE.

MUCH OF THE SAME **JOYS** -- AND THE SAME **PAINS**.

CHARLES XAVIER?

WOMEN WHO'VE LOVED **THAT** MAN ARE FEW AND FAR BETWEEN. WE SHARE THAT EXPERIENCE TOGETHER.

I THOUGHT
HAT LONELY
ARK OCEAN OF
OSS WAS
INE ALONE TO
DIVE INTO.

Ach, NO, GABBY--
--**BUT** LISTEN T'US-- YOU WANT TO TALK ABOUT MAGNUS, NO?
I NEED HELP... IN FINDING WAYS TO **NEUTRALIZE** HIM?

NEUTRAL-IZE--? BUT --HE'S DEAD-- **ISN'T HE?**

RECENT EVIDENCE CALLS THAT INTO QUESTION.

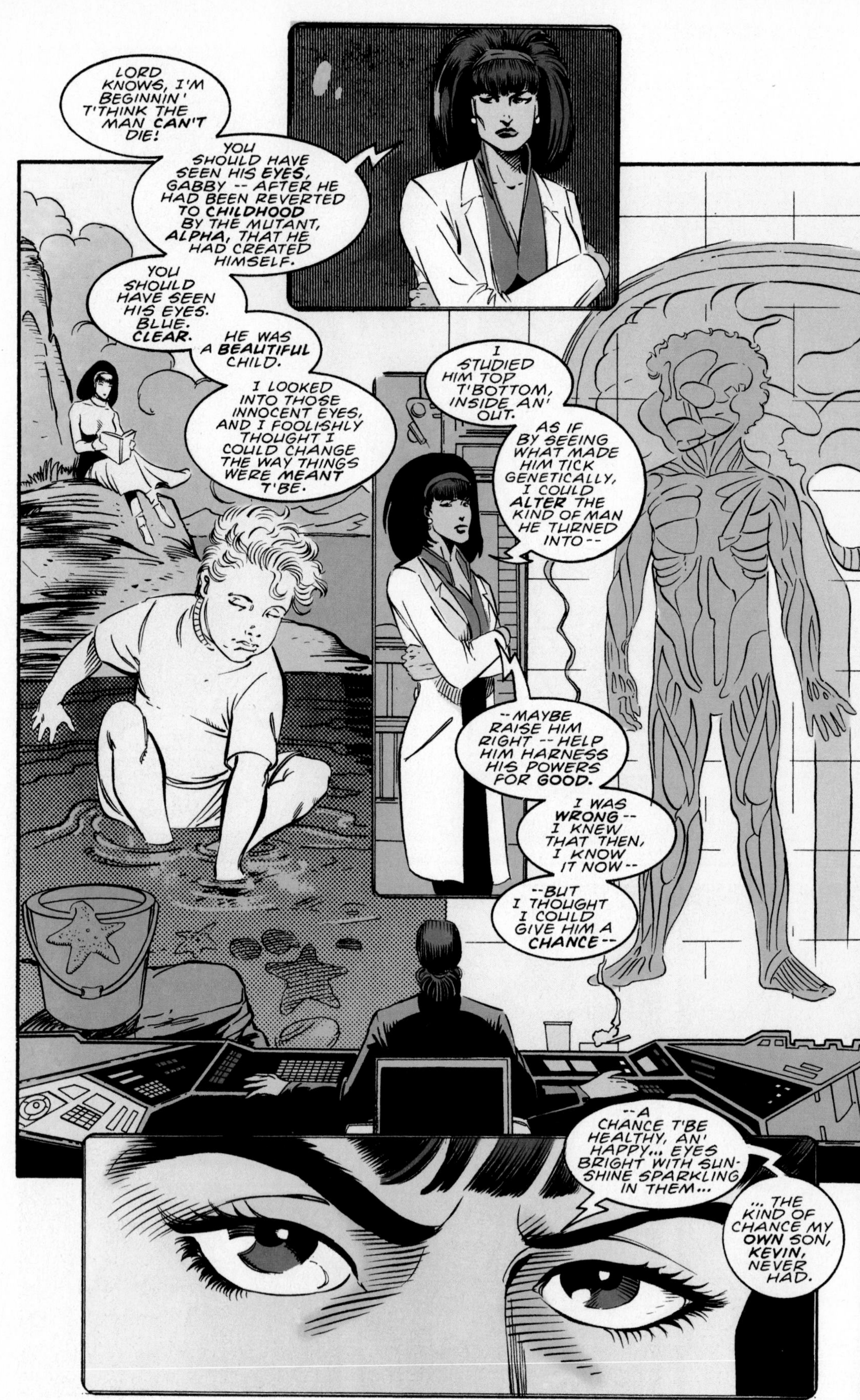
LORD KNOWS, I'M BEGINNIN' T'THINK THE MAN CAN'T DIE!
YOU SHOULD HAVE SEEN HIS EYES, GABBY -- AFTER HE HAD BEEN REVERTED TO CHILDHOOD BY THE MUTANT, ALPHA, THAT HE HAD CREATED HIMSELF.
YOU SHOULD HAVE SEEN HIS EYES. BLUE. CLEAR.
HE WAS A BEAUTIFUL CHILD.
I LOOKED INTO THOSE INNOCENT EYES, AND I FOOLISHLY THOUGHT I COULD CHANGE THE WAY THINGS WERE MEANT T'BE.
I STUDIED HIM TOP T'BOTTOM, INSIDE AN' OUT.
AS IF BY SEEING WHAT MADE HIM TICK GENETICALLY, I COULD ALTER THE KIND OF MAN HE TURNED INTO--
--MAYBE RAISE HIM RIGHT -- HELP HIM HARNESS HIS POWERS FOR GOOD.
I WAS WRONG -- I KNEW THAT THEN, I KNOW IT NOW--
--BUT I THOUGHT I COULD GIVE HIM A CHANCE--
--A CHANCE T'BE HEALTHY, AN' HAPPY... EYES BRIGHT WITH SUN-SHINE SPARKLING IN THEM...
...THE KIND OF CHANCE MY OWN SON, KEVIN, NEVER HAD.

OU NEEDN'T
PLAIN YOURSELF
O ME, MOIRA.
MY OWN SON, DAVID, LIES IN A VEGE-TATIVE STATE IN A HOSPI-TAL COT IN YOUR FACILITY.
I JUST WANTED T'HELP, GABBY... AND IF MAGNUS REALLY IS ALIVE --
-- HIS ANGERS, HIS FURY -- HIS RENEWED HATRED OF HUMANITY--
--THEY'LL BE MY FAULT!
THEN HELP US, MOIRA -- HELP US FIND A WAY TO STOP HIM BEFORE HE HAS THE CHANCE TO CARRY THROUGH ON THOSE PASSIONS!
I DON'T WANT HIM SANCTIONED ANY MORE THAN YOU, OR CHARLES, DO --
--BUT UNLESS I CAN PROVIDE THE PEOPLE WHO HAVE ASKED ME TO ORGANIZE THIS-- POSSE -- WITH AN ALTER-NATIVE --
-- WHAT CHOICE WILL THEY HAVE?
AND YOU'RE THE KEY, MOIRA -- YOU HAVE THE ANSWERS WE NEED...
...DON'T YOU--?

THE GENETECH BIO-RESEARCH FACILITY IN SAYVILLE, LONG ISLAND.
THREE WEEKS HAVE PASSED SINCE I LAST SAW GABRIELLE HALLER.
IN THAT TIME, IT WOULD APPEAR, WE HAVE BOTH BEEN VERY HARD AT WORK.
I HAVE PUT MYSELF INSIDE HIS MIND, DUG DEEP INTO HIS PSYCHE, STRIVING TO UNDERSTAND HIM -- PREDICT HIM --
-- WHILE HALLER HAS PUT TO TASK THE PEOPLE WHO WILL FIND A PHYSICAL WAY TO STOP THE MONSTER.
FOR THAT, WE HAVE SPENT THE LAST TWO DAYS AT THIS RESEARCH LAB, AS WALTER ROSEN, THE HEAD OF THE COMPANY, SHOWS US THE FRUITS OF HIS LABORS.
BELIEVE IT OR NOT --
-- AND I HARDLY DO MY-SELF --
-- I REALLY THINK THIS HAS A GOOD CHANCE OF SUCCEEDING.
IT IS ELEGANT IN ITS SIMPLICITY.
FROM OUR ORIGINAL CONVERSATIONS, I'D EXPECTED SOMETHING MECHANICAL -- SOMETHING BULKY --
-- BUT THIS DESIGN ROSEN IS SHOWING US --

--THIS WILL ALLOW ME TO KILL HIM AS A MAN.
MAN TO MAN. AS IT SHOULD BE.
I MEAN, FROM A THEORETICAL STANDPOINT, OF COURSE.
LITTLE MPLICATIONS ULD ALWAYS CUR DURING RACTICAL PPLICATIONS THINGS LIKE EALITY--
-I MEAN, HO CAN REDICT ALL THE RIABLES?
THAT IS TO BE MY CONCERN, MISTER ROSEN.
YOURS IS SIMPLY TO BE FULLY PREPARING ME.
TELL ME ALL I NEED TO STOP THIS... MAN.
OPERATIONS-- PLEASE CALL UP SUB-FILE LABELED TICK-TOCK.

NAME: ERIK MAGNUS LEHNSHERR
(EXTRAPOLATED FROM
PREVIOUSLY EXISTING DATA)
ALIAS: MAGNETO
HT: 6'2"
WT: 190
EYES: BLUE-GREY
HAIR: WHITE
PROPOSED SOURCE OF BIOGENETIC MUTATIVE ABILITIES:
ADDITIONAL NERVE FIBERS CONNECTING THE PONS TO THE
MEDULLA OBLONGATA
BIOELECTRIC ACTIVITY PROJECTED AT SEVENTEEN THOUSAND
PERCENT ABOVE NORMAL
ELECTROLYTE CONDUCTION THROUGHOUT NERVOUS
SYSTEM ENHANCED BY HIGH IRON COUNT (450% ABOVE
NORMAL) IN SUBJECT'S BLOOD SUPPLY
BIOELECTRIC FIELD READINGS ANALOGOUS TO
PLANETARY ELECTROMAGNETIC FIELD SYNCHRONOUS
ALIGNMENT TO .003%
SUBJECT'S NEURAL SYNAPTIC SPARKING ACCELERATED
TO 1450% ABOVE NORMAL.

MacTAGGERT PROVIDED YOU CAME IN HANDY?
WE COULDN'T HAVE MADE DO WITHOUT IT, MS. HALLER.
NO ONE ON THE PLANET HAS AS EXTENSIVE A BIOLOGICAL READING ON MAGNETO AS SHE DOES.
I'D LOVE A CRACK AT HER FILES SOMEDAY.
I WOULD LIKE A "CRACK" AT HIM, MISTER ROSEN --
-- CONTINUE IF YOU PLEASE.

YES, WELL--
--FROM WHAT WE HAVE BEEN ABLE TO GLEAN--
THE SUBJECT KNOWN AS MAGNETO IS QUITE SIMPLY THE SINGLE MOST POWERFUL BEING ON THE FACE OF THE EARTH.
AND IF ANYTHING, WE HAVE ONLY BORNE WITNES TO A FRACTION OF HIS TRUE POWERS.
THE MAN IS A FORCE OF NATURE, TIED, LITERALLY, TO THE PLANET'S ELECTROMAGNETIC FIELD.
WELL, HOW DID DAVID SLAY GOLIATH?
ONE MAN. COMPLETELY CLOAKED.
ONE CHANCE TO BRING HIM DOWN.
HE TALKS.
OF HOW WE WILL SLIP THROUGH MAGNETO'S IMPREGNABLE ELECTRO-MAGNETIC FIELD.
OF HOW WE WILL CAPTURE HIM BY REPOLARIZING THAT VERY FIELD FOR BUT A MOMENT--
--IN ESSENCE, SHORT-CIRCUITING HIS BATTERY.
SOME MORE.
BUT I STOP LISTENING.
I KNOW THE SPIRIT OF WHAT HE IS SAYING.
THAT THE CANCER CAN BE SURGICALLY EXCISED.
AND THAT I CAN BE THE SCALPEL...

WO MORE WEEKS PASS AS. HE TECHNICAL PREPARATIONS CONTINUE...
...RUMORS OF HIS RETURN CONTINUE TO INCREASE, AS MY PATIENCE CONTINUES TO DECREASE.
HERE IT IS--
THIS IS THE KEY TO CAPTURING HIM--
--THE BIOELECTRIC MASK -- YOU CAN SEE HIM, BUT HE CAN'T SEE YOU--
--AT LEAST IN AN ENERGY-WAVELENGTH SORT OF WAY.
HOW DOES IT WORK?
THE MASK WILL ALLOW THE WEARER TO PERCEIVE ALL BIO-ELECTRIC READINGS--
--WHILE THE COMPUTER REGISTERS ALL AMBIENT SIGNALS IN THE VICINITY--
--AND THE BAFFLES BUILT INTO THE MASK DISPERSE THE WAVE-LENGTHS AROUND THE RECEIVERS--
SO YOU SAY IF HE CAN-NOT SEE ME WITH HIS OWN EYES -- HE WILL NOT SEE ME AT ALL?

OVER THE COURSE OF THE NEXT TWO DAYS, MY BODY IS MEASURED SO THE MECHANICS CAN BETTER SERVE IT.
DOCTOR ROSEN, THIS SKIN-SHEATH HE WILL WEAR--?
A SKIN-TIGHT LYCRA SUIT, NO METAL OR IRONS IN IT AT ALL, PURELY SYNTHETIC FIBERS--
--A THIN PLASTIC VELLUM FILM ENVELOPS THE SUIT--
--BETWEEN WHICH WILL BE PUMPED A CLEAR RESIN GEL WHICH WILL BE INJECTED FULL OF STATIC ELECTROLYTES.
FOR ALL INTENTS AND PURPOSES, MISTER EISKALT WILL BE INVISIBLE!
AND THAT ONE ADVANTAGE IS THE ONLY HOPE WE HAVE OF BRINGING MAGNETO DOWN.
INDEED, MISTER ROSEN--PERHAPS IT WOULD BEST BE TIME TO WORK ON DAVID'S SLINGSHOT--?

HE "SLINGSHOT" WILL BE
N ENHANCED TASER GUN--
--ALL PARTS OF WHICH ARE COMPLETELY MADE OF PLASTIC--
--WITH A FIBERGLASS NEEDLE AND A NYLON TETHER-LINE FOR FIRING.
I FAMILIARIZE MYSELF WITH ITS INNER WORKINGS.
LIKE ALL GUNS, IT IS DESIGNED ON A BEAUTIFUL PATTERN OF LOGIC AND SIMPLICITY.
THE PARTS FIT TOGETHER. HOW OFTEN CAN ONE SAY THAT IN LIFE?
IRONIC, THAT I CAN ONLY SEEM TO FIND SUCH ORDER THROUGH A TOOL OF DEATH.
BUT THIS GUN IS MEANT ONLY TO STUN--
--AS ROSEN EXPLAINS, IF I CAN FIRE THE NEEDLE INTO THE BASE OF MAGNETO'S SKULL -- PIERCING THE MEDULLA OBLONGATA--
--THE TASER WILL DISRUPT MAGNETO'S BIOELECTRIC FIELD, SCRAMBLING HIS NEURAL SYNAPTIC INTERFACE WITH HIS POWERS FOR A TWO HOUR TIME PERIOD.
ENOUGH TIME FOR A SECURITY TEAM FROM THE AMERICAN VAULT PENITENTIARY TO CAPTURE HIM.
AS IF IT WILL COME TO THAT.
AS IF I WOULD ALLOW THE MONSTER TO WALK AWAY
I HOLD THE GUN, AND I HAVE BUT ONE THOUGHT -- YES... IT CAN BE MODIFIED...

WE ARE READY. NOW WE AWAIT HIS RETURN.
I SHOULD LEAVE HERE. THINGS HAVE GOTTEN UNCOMFORTABLE. TIME OBSCURES THE CLARITY OF MY MOTIVES.
TODAY, ROSEN BROUGHT IN A PUBLICITY CREW TO PHOTOGRAPH WHAT THEY HAVE BEEN CALLING THE FUGUE ARMOR.
HE FEELS GENE-TECH WILL PROSPER IF THE WORLD KNOWS THE EQUIPMENT THAT CAPTURED MAGNETO WAS DEVELOPED HERE.
I DO NOT CARE FOR THAT.
THIS IS NOT A GAME OF MONEY TO ME.
OR OF POLITICS.
OR OF PRESTIGE.
OR EVEN OF HEROISM.
TO ME, THIS ENTIRE OPERATION CAN BE READILY SIMPLIFIED.
THIS IS A GAME OF REVENGE.
FOR WHAT HE DID TO MY BROTHER -- FOR WHAT HE DID TO ME-- MAGNETO WILL DIE.
SIMPLE AS THAT.

DER THE REETS OF SHINGTON LIE THE FICES OF E COM- SSION ON ER HUMAN FFAIRS.
YESTERDAY, AN ELECTRO-MAGNETIC STORM RIPPED ACROSS THE EASTERN SEABOARD, SCRAMBLING ALL MECHANICAL AND ELECTRONIC SYSTEMS OVER AN EIGHT HUNDRED SQUARE MILE PERIMETER.
WE RECEIVED A CODE BLUE ALERT THIS MORNING. HALLER AND I IMMEDIATELY FLEW IN FROM KENNEDY AIRPORT.
WE WERE PICKED UP AT DULLES AND BROUGHT IN TO THE CSHA SITUATION ROOM.
FIVE MINUTES AGO WE WERE JOINED BY NATIONAL SECURITY LIAISON HENRY PETER GYRICH...
LADIES AND GENTLE-MEN...
MAGNETO HAS RETURNED!
...X-FACTOR ADMINISTRATOR DOCTOR VALERIE COOPER...
...AND ALEXI VAZHIN, THE HEAD OF MUTANT AFFAIRS FOR THE RUSSIAN STATE SERVICE.
I TENSE AT GYRICH'S WORDS. SWEAT SLIDES DOWN MY SPINAL COLUMN.
IS IT FEAR OR ANTICIPATION I FEEL?

"GYRICH TALKS.
MAGNETO MADE HIS RETURN IN RATHER DRAMATIC FASHION.
HAVING APPROPRIATED AND MODIFIED THE REMNANTS OF AN ORBITAL SPACE STATION FIRST DISCOVERED BY SHIELD A FEW MONTHS AGO --
-- MAGNETO BROUGHT HIS NEW HOME, DUBBED "AVALON," THROUGH EARTH'S ATMOSPHERE, TO INTERRUPT THE MEMORIAL SERVICE OF A SMALL MUTANT CHILD AFFILIATED WITH THE BROOD OF CHARLES XAVIER.
HE OFFERED THESE CHILDREN OF THE ATOM THE "OPPORTUNITY" TO PARTICIPATE IN HIS SELF-PROCLAIMED QUEST FOR "A HAVEN -- A HEAVEN -- WHERE MUTANTS CAN BE FREED FROM EARTH'S CHOKING HOLD."
CONVINCING ONLY ONE OF XAVIER'S BROOD TO ACCEPT HIS OFFER, MAGNETO RETURNED TO AVALON TO A GEO-SYNCHRONOUS ORBIT HIGH ABOVE THE PLANET.
AVALON'S CLOAKING SYSTEMS HAVE BEEN RE-ENGAGED. HE IS COMPLETELY HIDDEN FROM US.
HOW ARE WE EXPECTED TO REACH HIM THEN?

MAGNETO HAS USED AN EMISSARY NAMED EXODUS TO RECRUIT MUTANTS TO AVALON.
PERHAPS IF WE WERE ABLE TO CAPTURE OR FOLLOW HIM?
NEITHER EXODUS NOR MAGNETO HAS HARMED ANYONE YET --
--DO YOU HONESTLY BELIEVE ANY OF OUR SUPER-HUMAN OPERATIVES WILL HAPPILY ENGAGE EITHER IN BATTLE JUST BECAUSE WE ASK?
THAT'S A GOOD POINT, PETER...
...MAYBE WE SHOULDN'T BE DOING ANYTHING UNTIL MAGNETO DOES INSTIGATE OR INITIATE A PROBLEM.
THEY TALK.
AND TALK.
AND THEN THEY TALK SOME MORE.
THE VERY FACT HE EXISTS -- HOVERING ABOVE US --
--IS CAUSE ENOUGH FOR ANY ACTIONS WE TAKE.
ONE WAY OR THE OTHER, I BELIEVE WE ARE ALL IN AGREE-MENT--
--MAGNETO MUST BE STOPPED!
THEN E COME ACK AROUND TO THE HOW.
IF MAGNETO IS DIVORCING HIMSELF COMPLETELY FROM HUMANITY AS HE CLAIMS--
--AND WE CAN'T GET UP TO WHERE HE IS--
--HOW CAN WE TRULY EXPECT HIM TO COME TO US?
COME TO US? NO... BUT IF HE IS PREPARED TO ABAN-DON HIS PAST--
--THEN THERE MAY BE ONE PLACE HE WILL GO...

WUNDAGORE MOUNTAIN.
THIS WALKING FORCE OF NATURE--
--THIS FAILED MAN WHO WOULD STRIVE TO BE A GOD--
--RETURNS SEEKING ABSOLUTION--
--FROM THE ONE SOURCE LEFT TO REMIND HIM OF HIS LOST HUMANITY...
DO NOT BE AFRAID, GENTLE BOVA.
I AM MERELY HERE...
...TO SAY GOOD-BYE.

...MAGDA... MY WIFE...
...HOW DIFFERENT IT COULD HAVE BEEN --
--FOR BOTH OF US--
--PERHAPS FOR THE ENTIRE WORLD...
...IF ONLY YOU HAD STAYED BY MY SIDE...
...AND I HAD BEEN A MORE FORGIVING MAN...
...THAN A VENGEFUL MONSTER...
ONE CHANCE.
ONE BULLET.

MAGDA
POINT BLANK.

FOR ALL THE PAIN YOU HAVE CAUSED.
ALL THE MISERY.
ALL THE ANGUISH AND THE FEAR.
FOR MY BROTHER, UTË.
MY BROTHER YOU SO...
...CALLOUSLY...
...KILLED...
...MY BROTHER...

WHO DID NOT KNOW WHAT HE WAS DOING WHEN HE FELL OVER YOUR WIFE'S GRAVE...
WHO DID NOT LISTEN WHEN YOU ASKED US TO LEAVE THIS VERY PRIVATE PLACE YOU HELD SO DEAR...
WHO DID NOT CARE WHEN YOU TOLD HIM THIS WAS NOT A PLACE FOR VIOLENCE AND NEVER WOULD BE...
WHO SO STUPIDLY DREW HIS GUN, SPITTING OUT WORDS OF HATRED, OF RAGE, OF PREJUDICE...

WHO FIRED AT YOU WITH A MURDEROUS RAGE, POINT BLANK, RIGHT AT YOUR HEAD...
WHO WAS CAUGHT IN THE BACK-LASH AS YOU SIMPLY GESTURED TO PROTECT YOURSELF IN A MAGNETIC COCCOON...
...WHO DIED WHEN HIS OWN BULLET RICOCHETED AND PIERCED HIS THICK SKULL...
WHO FORCED YOU TO BREAK A VOW OF HONOR TO THE MEMORY OF YOUR WIFE...
WHO MAYBE, JUST MAYBE, MIGHT HAVE BEEN ULTIMATELY RESPONSIBLE, IN SOME SMALL WAY, FOR SETTING YOU UPON THE COURSE OF YOUR LIFE...
UTË... MY BROTHER... A SIMPLE, STUPID MAN... NOT A SYMBOL FOR A CAUSE...
...BUT A FRIGHT-ENED LAMB WHO SOUGHT TO STRIKE BACK AT THE WOLF...
...THE WOLF WHO WAS DOING WHAT IT WAS MEANT TO DO-- BEING WHAT IT WAS MEANT TO BE...
...NOT A MONSTER, NOT A VILLAIN, NOT LESS THAN HUMAN...
...BUT MORE...

...FOR HE DENIES HIMSELF A HUMAN LIFE IN ORDER TO MAKE THE LIVES OF OTHERS SAFE FROM THE KINDS OF PAIN AND HARDSHIP HE HAS SUFFERED.
HE IS MORE THAN ME...
THUP
...MORE THAN ALL OF US...
Eh--?
MAGDA

HE SAYS NOTHING.
HE KNOWS HE WAS JUST A WEAKNESS AWAY FROM DYING.
MY WEAKNESS.
AS I AM AWARE I WAS JUST AN ACT OF COMPASSION AWAY FROM BEING KILLED.
HIS ACT OF COMPASSION.
I LIVE BECAUSE OF AN ACT OF HUMANITY ON THE PART OF THE CREATURE I HAVE CALLED INHUMAN.

HOW COULD I HAVE SO UTTERLY FAILED?
FAILED MYSELF, FAILED UTË AND, ULTIMATELY, FAILED THE WORLD?
OR DID I FAIL IN SOMETHING MORE IMPORTANT?
FOR WANTING TO KILL THE MAN NAMED ERIK MAGNUS LEHNSHERR FOR ALL THE WRONG REASONS--
--COULD I HAVE FAILED HUMANITY ITSELF?
EITHER WAY, I HAVE LOST--
LOST EVERYTHING I WANTED AND EVERYTHING I BELIEVED IN--
--LOST NOT BECAUSE I WAS WEAK, BUT PERHAPS BECAUSE I WAS STRONG--
STRONG ENOUGH TO KNOW THAT, AFTER ALL IS SAID AND DONE--
--I LOST VERY LITTLE, BECAUSE I HAD VERY LITTLE TO LOSE IN THE FIRST PLACE--
--BECAUS ALL I EVE REALLY HAD...
...WAS HATE...
THE END

Fleer Ultra X-Men '96 "Fatal Atractions" trading-card art by Greg & Tim Hildebrandt

MARVEL COMICS

X-MEN

APPROVED BY THE COMICS CODE AUTHORITY

FATAL ATTRACTIONS

THE DEATH OF A DREAM

IN THIS...THE FINAL BATTLE!

X-Men #25 hologram original sketch by Andy Kubert, and inks by John Beatty

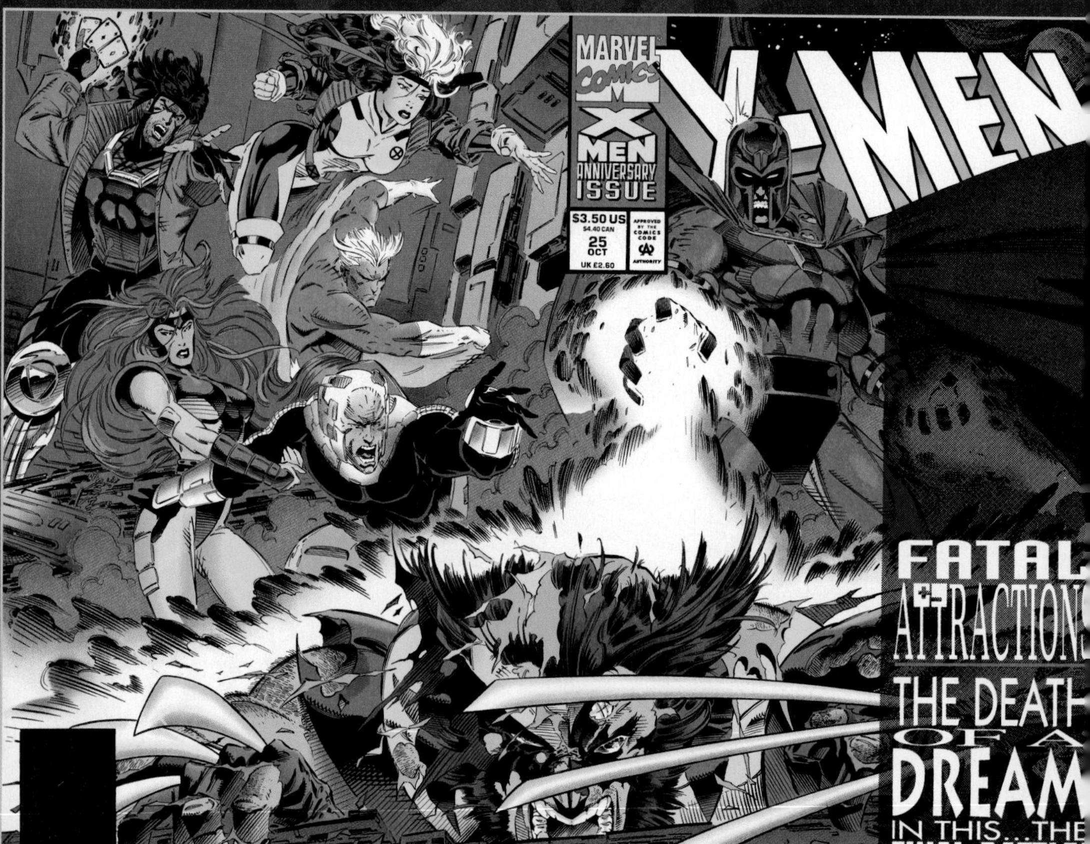

MARVEL COMICS
X-MEN
X MEN ANNIVERSARY ISSUE
$3.50 US
$4.40 CAN
25 OCT
UK £2.60
FATAL ATTRACTIONS
THE DEATH OF A DREAM
IN THIS...THE FINAL BATTLE

ATAL ATTRACTIONS
E HOUSE IS WHITE, THE FFICE IS OVAL, E MAN SITTING BEHIND THE ESK IS AFRAID.
NEVER PECTED BE THE ESIDENT HELPED RING OUT THE ND OF WORLD.
T NOW, HE KNOWS AT VERY WELL MAY THE EPITAPH ITTEN FOR HIM IN HISTORY BOOKS... ANYONE HAD A CHANCE SURVIVING WHAT S TO COME...
BORIS, I'M SORRY, I KNOW IT'S LATE--
--BUT THE UNITED NATIONS SECURITY COUNCIL JUST UNANIMOUSLY VOTED TO INITIATE THE ALPHA AND BETA PARAMETERS OF THE MAGNETO PROTOCOLS.
THE SQUARE IS RED, THE COUNTRY IS NEW, THE MAN RUBBING THE SLEEP OUT OF HIS EYES IS AFRAID.
HE NEVER EXPECTED TO PRESIDE OVER ONE DRAMATIC CHANGE IN THE WAY HIS COUNTRY EXISTED...
...MUCH LESS TWO...
< WHEN WILL THE ACTION BE INITIATED? >*
*TRANSLATED FROM RUSSIAN--BOB.
THE CIGAR IS CUBAN, THE ARMAMENT IS AMERICAN, AND THOUGH THE ATTITUDE IS PURE, HARD-EDGED STEEL...
...NICHOLAS FURY, DIRECTOR OF SHIELD, A MAN WHO HAS FOUGHT IN THREE WARS ACROSS FOUR DECADES...
--IS VERY MUCH AFRAID THAT HE IS PREPARING HIMSELF FOR THE FINAL BATTLE OF HIS LIFE...
THIS AIN'T GONNA WORK, IS IT, FORGE?
ONLY ONE WAY TO FIND OUT...

NEAR-EARTH SPACE, IN THE SHADOW OF THE TERMINATOR, RACING FROM DAY TO NIGHT...
...A COMMUNICATIONS RELAY TRIPS FROM ONE METICULOUSLY ALIGNED SATELLITE TO ANOTHER.
SYSTEMS WHICH HAD REMAINED SILENT FOR SEVERAL YEARS FIRE TO LIFE--
--LINKING ONE FLOATING SENTRY TO THE NEXT--
--UNTIL THE ENTIRE PLANET IS COVERED IN A PROTECTIVE MESH OF ELECTRO-MAGNETIC FIRE.

EFENSIVE ACTIONS TAKEN HE CITIZENS OF THE PLANET W DO NOT GO UNNOTICED NE WHO HAS PLACED HIMSELF FAR ABOVE THEM--
--BOTH BY ACCIDENT OF BIRTH, AND BY DINT OF CAREFULLY CRAFTED DESIGN...
I ARNED EM NOT TO THIS!
WHY DO EY SEEK PROVOKE ME?
WHAT WILL IT TAKE FOR THEM TO LEAVE US ALONE SO WE MAY FORGE OUR OWN UTOPIA, REMOVED FROM THEIR PETTY, PATHETIC LIVES?
...THE MASTER OF MAGNETISM, HAS TAKEN NOTICE...
...AND MAGNETO IS ANGRY!

MY ACOLYTES, I DID NOT GRANT YOU SAFE HAVEN HERE IN AVALON--
--IN ORDER TO SEE YOU ALL SLAUGHTERED BY THE HUMANS BELOW.
THIS ATTACK CANNOT BE IGNORED.
FOR TOO LONG, I HAVE PLAYED A FRUITLESS TÊTE-A-TÊTE WITH THOSE HUMANS IN POSITIONS OF POWER.
I HAD ALWAYS HOPED, THAT AS ADMINISTRATIONS CAME AND WENT--
--AS FIGUREHEADS CHANGED, ONE DAY, EVENTUALLY--
--THOSE WHO BELIEVED IN THE RIGHTS OF MUTANTS TO EXIST FREE FROM PERSECUTION, WOULD ATTAIN POWER.
IT WAS, I KNOW, A FOOLISH HOPE...
...BORN OUT OF MY DESIRE TO NEVER BECOME THAT WHICH I DESPISED IN MY YOUNGER DAYS...
...A DESPOT, A TYRANT--A HITLER.
YET, THERE MUST COME A TIME WHEN EVEN DEAF EARS MUST BE MADE TO LISTEN, LORD MAGNUS.
YOU ARE CORRECT, EXODUS.
INDEED, THAT TIME HAS COME AND GONE LONG BEFORE WE EVEN SOUGHT REFUGE HERE AMONG THE HEAVENS!

T IS TIME, THEN,
OR MY ACTIONS
O SPEAK FAR MORE
OUDLY THAN MY
ORDS EVER HAVE..."
HE LEAVES THEIR HAVEN, AVALON, BUILT FROM THE TECHNOLOGIES OF WORLDS LONG GONE AND THOSE STILL-TO-COME--
--AND SOARS ACROSS THE PLANET'S ELECTROMAGNETIC FIELD--
--DISTURBED BY THE EERIE DISRUPTION CAUSED BY THE ENERGY WAVELENGTH MESH SPANNING THE WORLD BELOW.
IMMEDIATELY, HE UNDERSTANDS WHAT THE HUMANS HAVE DONE.
HE IS SAFE HERE, FAR ABOVE THE PLANET, BUT TO GO HOME AGAIN COULD VERY WELL MEAN DEATH.
IN MANY WAYS, HE ADMIRES AND APPRECIATES THE INVENTIVENESS OF THE HUMANS' GAMBIT.
BUT ULTIMATELY, IT IS AN AFFRONT HE CANNOT ABIDE, FOR IT WILL DISRUPT HIS ABILITY TO RECRUIT NEW CONVERTS TO HIS FLOCK.
THE MESH HAS SKEWED THE PLANET'S E-M FIELD JUST ENOUGH TO DISRUPT MAGNETO'S MUTANT ABILITIES WITHIN THE PARAMETERS OF EARTH'S ATMOSPHERE.
SO MAGNETO CONCENTRATES, MUTTERING A SILENT PRAYER TO A GOD HE NO LONGER BELIEVES IN--
--AND CUTS A SWATH ACROSS EARTH'S ELECTROMAGNETIC FIELD LIKE A BATTLE-FORGED BLADE THROUGH SOFT FLESH.

MANHATTAN, NEW YORK. TEN SECONDS AFTER MAGNETO'S DETONATION... *
FASHAASHASHHH
WHAT THE--?
REED-- IS THAT YOU MESSIN' AROUND WITH ANOTHER FRAMISTAT OR SOMETHIN'--?
ALWAYS WHEN I'M TAKIN' A BUBBLE BATH, TOO!
HEY-- POWER'S NOT KICKIN' BACK IN! IS THIS FER REAL, STRETCHO?
TOO REAL, BEN-- AND APPALLINGLY FRIGHTENING IN ITS IMPLICATIONS. WE ARE COMPLETELY BLACKED-OUT!
A PULSE WAVE HIT US-- UNLIKE ANY I HAVE EVER ENCOUNTERED BEFORE. IT SWEPT RIGHT OVER US--
"--AND IT SHOWS NO SIGNS OF ABATING..."
LOS ANGELES, CALIFORNIA, TWO MINUTES AFTER DETONATION...
*THESE EVENTS TAKE PLACE BEFORE FF# 374-BOB.

TOKYO, JAPAN. FIVE MINUTES AFTER DETONATION...
FASHASH
--BUT HAS NO WAY TO PROTECT HIMSELF FROM IT--
HIRO YOSHIDA, THE MUTANT NAMED SUNFIRE, SEES THE COMING ONSLAUGHT--
THE KREMLIN, MOSCOW. SIX MINUTES AFTER DETONATION...
FSHAASHSHSH
BRADDOCK MANOR, ENGLAND. EIGHT MINUTES AFTER DETONATION...
unglaublich--!
BRIAN-- WHAT HAPPENED TO THE POWER?
I'M NOT CERTAIN, KURT.
BUT THE MANOR'S SECONDARY GENERATORS SHOULD FIRE UP MOMENTARILY.

ACROSS THE ATLANTIC OCEAN, ELEVEN MINUTES AFTER DETONATION...
...THE WAVE HAS COME FULL CIRCLE, WASHING BACK OVER THE NATION'S CAPITAL WITH AN ALMOST MOCKINGLY GENTLE EASE.
THE ENTIRE PLANET HAS BEEN CAST IN ITS PALL...
...AND WHERE THERE ARE NO SCREAMS OF PANIC AND FEAR, A CHILLING BLANKET OF SILENCE COVERS THE WORLD.
THIRTEEN MINUTES AFTER DETONATION...
SEAN, LET'S FIRE IT UP--
--SEE IF THE SHI'AR TECHNOLOGY CAN COMPENSATE FOR THE E-M PULSE WE WERE HIT WITH--

VMMMMMMM
ah-- THERE YE GO, HANK!
WUNDERBAR! WE'RE BACK ON-LINE!
BUT, METHINKS, THE TELL-TALE HUSH ACROSS THE BOARD DECLARES, THROUGH INCESSANT STATIC CRACKLE--
--THAT WE MAY BE THE ONLY ONES ANYWHERE WHO HAVE REGAINED ELECTRONIC CAPABILITIES!
I'M AFRAID YE MAY BE RIGHT, BOYO.
THIS IS REALLY BAD.
sigh
LET'S BE ON WITH IT... WE'D BEST TELL CHARLES...

Join
FABIAN NICIEZA WRITER
ANDY KUBERT PENCILER
MATT RYAN INKER
BILL OAKLEY LETTERER
JOE ROSAS COLORIST
BOB HARRAS EDITOR
TOM DEFALCO EDITOR IN CHIEF
In proudly presenting the 25th ISSUE of X-MEN!
DREAMS FADE
I HAVE CALLED YOU ALL HERE BECAUSE THERE IS SOME-THING I MUST TELL YOU.
IT BEGINS... WITH AN ENDING--AND PER-HAPS--THE BREAKING OF A MAN'S HEART. THIS MAN'S HEART.
THE HEART OF CHARLES XAVIER...
...AS HE FACES HIS STUDENTS--NEW AND OLD--FROM HIS SCHOOL FOR GIFTED YOUNGSTERS.
AMONG ONE OLD FRIEND, STAND FOURTEEN MUTANTS, BORN WITH FANTASTIC POWERS THAT SET THEM APART FROM THE REST OF HUMANITY.
THEY ARE THE X-MEN. AND ONCE AGAIN, THEY MUST SAVE A WORLD WHICH FEARS AND SHUNS THEM...
Dedicated to Stan & Jack, Roy & Neal, Len & Dave, Chris & John--to all those who have come before us and all those who will come in the NEXT 30 years!

OBVIOUSLY, MY X-MEN, WE HAVE A PROBLEM.
SCOTT WILL BRIEF YOU ALL.
THANK YOU, PROFESSOR.
OKAY, GUYS, HERE GOES-- AT TEN-THIRTY-THREE THIS MORNING-- EASTERN STANDARD TIME--
--THE UNITED STATES SECURITY COUNCIL VOTED TO INITIATE THE PRELIMINARY LEVELS OF DEFENSE IN THE MAGNETO PROTOCOLS.
THE ALPHA AND BETA OPTIONS OF THE PROTOCOLS INVOLVE THE ACTIVATING OF A DEFENSIVE SHIELD WHICH SPREADS ACROSS THE PLANET--
--AND PREVENTS MAGNETO FROM USING HIS POWERS WITHIN THE BOUNDARIES OF EARTH'S ATMOSPHERE.
THIS IS INTENDED TO PROTECT HUMANITY WITHOUT THE APPEARANCE OF INTENDED PROVOCATION.
WORKE LIKE A CHARM, E CYCLOP
AT ELEVEN FIFTY-FIVE P.M., AN ELECTRO-MAGNETIC EXPLOSION SENT A PULSE WAVE ACROSS THE PLANET.
IN RETALIATING, MAGNETO HAS EFFECTIVELY RENDERED THE MECHANICAL AND TECHNOLOGICAL RESOURCES OF THIS ENTIRE PLANET COMPLETELY USELESS.
WE BELIEVE THIS IS A TEMPORARY CONDITION, BUT EVEN SO, OUR SCATTERED INFORMATION LEADS US TO EXPECT--
--THAT THE PULSE WAVE WAS TERRIFYINGLY DEVASTATING IN ITS FEROCITY.
SCOTT--
HOW-- HOW BAD WAS IT?

WE CAN'T
ALLY KNOW
R CERTAIN,
OGUE.
WE'RE ONLY ON-LINE BECAUSE WE HAVE THE ADVANTAGE OF THE ALIEN SHI'AR TECHNOLOGY INCORPORATED INTO OUR SYSTEMS--
WE FEAR MANY HUNDREDS... PERHAPS THOUSANDS, HAVE DIED.
LORD.
THIS IS IN-SANE! WHY DIDN'T HE WARN US OR SOMETHIN'?
--WHICH
LOWS US TO
PERATE
EPENDENTLY OF
E PLANET'S E-M
IELD WAVE-
LENGTH.
MAGNUS WOULD CLAIM HIS ENTIRE LIFE HAS BEEN A WARNING. THIS WAS A VICIOUS ATTACK-- MEANT TO WOUND-- TO DEVASTATE.
BUT IF MAGNETO WAS ABLE TA DO THIS, DON'T YOU THINK HE COULDA JUST AS EASILY WIPED US ALL OUT?
FROM THE GARBLED STATIC WE HAVE BEEN ABLE TO PIECE TOGETHER, WE KNOW IT'S BAD.
REALLY BAD.
PLANE CRASHES... MEDICAL EQUIPMENT FAILURE.
INDEED. I KNOW HOW DIFFICULT THIS IS FOR YOU... HOW YOU FEEL ABOUT MAGNUS...
...BUT THE FACT THAT HE DID NOT KILL US ALL SHOULD BE VIEWED AS A MISTAKE ON HIS PART...
...AND WE HAVE TO MAKE
ERTAIN IT IS THE
AST MISTAKE HE
HAS THE OPPOR-
TUNITY TO
MAKE.
WHAT'RE YOU SAYIN', CHUCK?
YOU KNOW EXACTLY WHAT I AM SAYING, LOGAN...
...WE DO NOT HAVE THE LUXURY OF TIME, NOR THE OCCASION FOR NOBILITY...
...AT THIS POINT, WE ARE NOT FIGHTING FOR THE PHILOSOPHY OF A CAUSE, A HOPE, OR A DREAM--
--WE ARE FIGHTING FOR OUR VERY SURVIVAL--
--AND IF WE DO NOT FIGHT TO WIN, THIS PLANET WILL BE IRREVOCABLY LOST TO US!

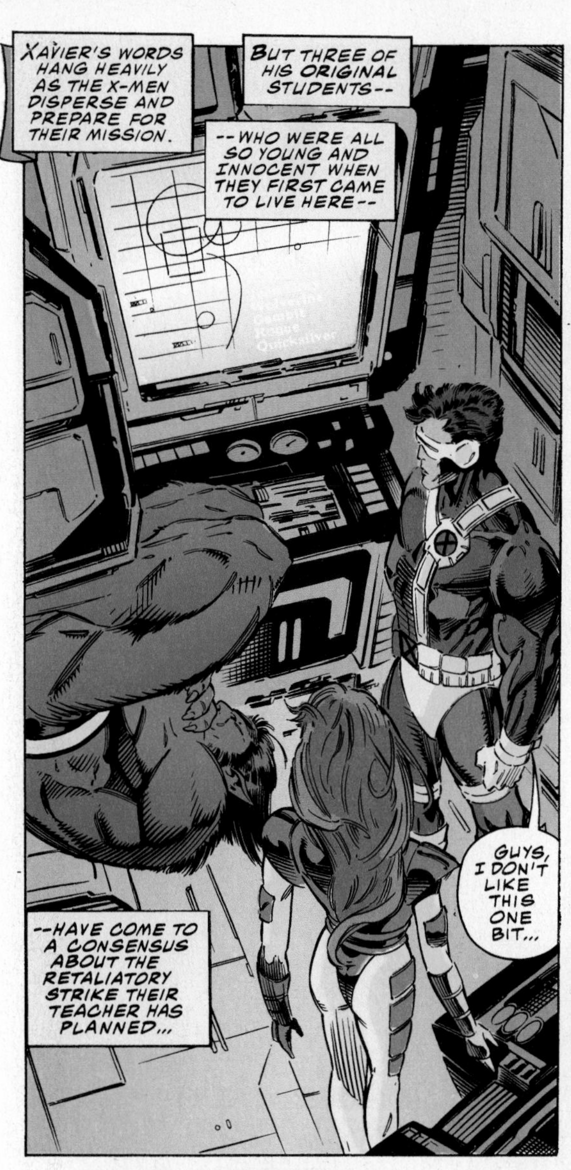
XAVIER'S WORDS HANG HEAVILY AS THE X-MEN DISPERSE AND PREPARE FOR THEIR MISSION.
BUT THREE OF HIS ORIGINAL STUDENTS--
--WHO WERE ALL SO YOUNG AND INNOCENT WHEN THEY FIRST CAME TO LIVE HERE--
--HAVE COME TO A CONSENSUS ABOUT THE RETALIATORY STRIKE THEIR TEACHER HAS PLANNED...
GUYS, I DON'T LIKE THIS ONE BIT...

IS IT BECAUSE, FEARLESS LEADER, YOU CONSIDER IT A PLAN WHICH IS STRATE-GICALLY UNSOUND--
--OR BECAUSE YOU WEREN'T INCLUDED IN IT?
NEITHER, HANK--OR MAYBE BOTH.
I JUST DON'T LIKE THE SOUND OF WHAT THE PROFESSOR HAS PLANNED.

HE'S UNDER A LOT OF STRAIN, SCOTT, AND I'M GOING WITH THEM. I WON'T ALLOW ANYTHING TO HAPPEN--
--OR BE A PARTY TO SOMETHING--WHICH GOES AGAINST EVERY-THING WE BELIEVE.
I KNOW, JEAN, BUT THOSE BELIEFS SEEM SO... I DON'T KNOW... OUTMODED LATELY.

DO THEY, SCOTT? A LITTLE CORNY, MAYBE...
"ALWAYS STRIVE TO HEAL THROUGH THE OPEN HAND, RATHER THAN HAMMER HOME SOLUTIONS THROUGH THE CLOSED FIST."
"SHOW THE WORLD THAT ONLY THROUGH RESPECT FOR OUR GEN-ETIC DIVERSITY CAN WE HOPE TO COME TOGETHER."
"BE WILLING TO FIGHT FOR THE BELIEFS AGAINST THOSE, BOTH HUMAN AND MUTANT, WHO WOULD TRY TO CRUSH THE DREAM."
MAYBE THEY DON'T SOUND SO OUTMODED AFTER ALL...
DID IT EVER OCCUR TO AN OF YOU, IN AL THE YEARS WE'VE BEEN TOGETHER--

--THAT PERHAPS I WAS WRONG?
HARLES--? YOU'RE-- ALKING?!
ONLY, I ASSURE YOU, THROUGH TREMENDOUS EXERTION.
THE SHI'AR EXOSKELETON OPERATES ON PSIONIC ENERGY, SO EVERY STEP I TAKE IS... A GIANT LEAP FOR MUTANTKIND.
CUTE. BUT, PROFESSOR, WHAT EXACTLY DO YOU THINK YOU ARE DOING?
I AM GOING TO LEAD THE STRIKE-FORCE AGAINST MAGNUS, HANK.
CHARLES... I DON'T KNOW WHERE YOU'VE BEEN HIDING THAT EXO-SKELETON...
...BUT EVEN WITH IT, WELL... THAT IS...
WHAT JEAN IS TRYING TO SAY, SIR, IS THAT EVEN WITH THE ABILITY TO WALK--
--YOU'VE NEVER REALLY BEEN MUCH OF A BATTLEFIELD OPERATIVE.

I WOULD TAKE GREAT INSULT AT THAT, SCOTT, IF I DIDN'T AGREE WITH YOU.
WHICH IS WHY I STRUCTURED THE ASSAULT TEAM AS A COMBINATION OF SKILLS AND ATTRIBUTES.
COMBINING THE BEST ELEMENTS OF STEALTH, SUBTERFUGE AND GUILE TO INFILTRATE MAGNETO'S BASE--
--WITH TELEPATHIC PROWESS TO ATTACK HIM AT HIS WEAKEST POINT--HIS TORTURED SOUL--
--AS WELL AS SPEED, STRENGTH AND THE STRONG DESIRE TO SETTLE UNRESOLVED EMOTIONAL CONFLICTS.
AND SINCE YOU'LL BE INSIDE A SPACE STATION--
--WE HIGH-OCTANE ENERGY WIELDERS DON'T COME IN TOO HANDY--
--BUT WHAT ABOUT SOME OF THE OTHERS?
WHY NOT INCLUDE MORE OF YOUR ORIGINAL STUDENTS WHO'VE FOUGHT THIS BATTLE WITH MAGNETO ALMOST AS LONG AS YOU?
BECAUSE YOU DON'T EXPECT TO COME BACK, DO YOU, CHARLES?
AND YOU NEED US DOWN HERE--TO STAY...
...TO CARRY ON...?

IF I HAD A CHOICE, SCOTT, JEAN WOULD STAY ALSO...
--I'LL NEED HER TELEPATHIC ABILITIES TO ASSIST ME AS WE EXECUTE MY PLANS.
AND WHAT EXACTLY IS YOUR PLAN, SIR?
YES, IT IS TIME. YOU DESERVE TO KNOW.
COMPUTER: BOOT UP MAGNETO MANEUVER NUMBER FOURTEEN-B; AMENDED AUGUST, NINETY-TWO.
UT WITH ALL OF MENTAL ENERGY M EXPENDING TO PERATE THIS OSKELETON--
OH, MY STARS AND GARTERS!
HE DOES MEAN TO PUT AN END TO THIS CYCLE OF VIOLENCE ONCE AND FOR ALL.
KEEPS ELLING MSELF HAT, IN SENCE, S JUST NOTHER OB.
REMY LEBEAU IS A THIEF AT HEART, AND IF RATIONALIZED PROPERLY, THIS IS NOTHING MORE THAN A NOBLE PINCH.
IT JUST SEEMS THAT THE LONGER HE STAYS WITH THESE PEOPLE, THE MORE HE BELIEVES IN THEIR CAUSE--
--AND THE HARDER IT GETS TO SIMPLY RATIONALIZE THE JOB.
THE TRUTH OF THE MATTER IS THAT, AS GAMBIT WELL KNOWS, HE IS FIGHTING FOR THE HOPE OF AN ENTIRE PLANET--
--AND MORE IMPORTANTLY THAN EVER TO HIM... HE IS ALSO FIGHTING FOR THE HEART OF THE WOMAN HE LOVES...
READY, CHERE?
AH GUESS.
I KNOW MAGNETO SAVED YOUR LIFE, ROGUE, AN' EVEN THOUGH I DON'T KNOW WHAT ELSE WENT ON 'TWEEN YOU TWO--
--WE STILL GOTTA DO THIS. Y'KNOW WE DO.
AH'M JUST AFRAID, REMY, WHEN PUSH COMES TA SHOVE--
--WHOSE SIDE AM AH GONNA BE ON?
THE SIDE Y'ALWAYS TRY T'BE ON... THE RIGHT SIDE...

"CHARLES, THE REST OF US HAVE BEEN DISCUSSING THIS, AND--
"--WE FEEL THAT YOU ARE TAKING AN UNNECESSARY RISK--
"--AS WELL AS PLACING THE X-MEN IN AN EXTREMELY HAZARDOUS POSITION--
"--BY GOING TO BATTLE MAGNETO WITH SUCH A SMALL CONTINGENT."
YOU TOOK THE WORDS RIGHT OUT OF HER MOUTH.
IF YOU CONSIDER SUICIDE THE ONLY OPTION LEFT TO YOU IN THIS STRUGGLE--
--I WOULD RESPECT YOUR DECISION, ALTHOUGH IN NO WAY WOULD I AGREE TO IT--
--BUT TO ASK IT OF THE OTHERS, AND NOT TO ASK IT OF US ALL--
FOR MY ENTIRE LIFE, I HAVE FOUGHT FOR THE SAKE OF A DREAM, ORORO, AND MAGNUS IS THE CAUSE OF WHAT I BELIEVE IS A NIGHTMARE.
"AT OUR LAST PARTING, ONE I HAD THOUGHT--AND FERVENTLY HOPED--WOULD BE OUR FINAL ONE--
"--MAGNUS SAID MY WILL WOULD BREAK AS I CAME TO REALIZE MY QUEST TO BE A FOOL'S HOPE.
"HE WAS WRONG. I HAVE NOT BEEN BROKEN.
"BUT I HAVE BEEN HARDENED. AS HAVE SOME OF YOU.
DREAMS FADE. DREAMERS COME AND GO--
--BUT THE HOPE WHICH FUELS THE FIRES OF OUR PASSION--OUR GOAL--MUST NOT DIE OUT!
BUT WHAT HAPPENS WHEN THE DREAM BECOMES THE NIGHTMARE?

D I, FOR ONE, I NOT ABOUT O LET IT.
ALL RIGHT, EN, ENOUGH WITH THE EECHES. I'M AFRAID I'VE MBARRASSED MYSELF.
MY X-MEN, IT IS TIME.
COMPUTER, ACTIVATE SHI'AR SECONDARY COMMAND PROGRAMMING LINK--
--OPTION: NERAMANI-OMEGA...
...COMMENCE AVALON SYSTEMS OVERRIDE SEQUENCE--
--ZED-ONE-ZERO-ONE--
--ZERO-ZERO-ZERO...
AVALON Systems Access: Defensive Scrambling: Grid Override Teleportation Sequence: Activated.
VSHYEERMM
"COME, WHY ARE YOU HOLDING BACK?
"WHY ARE YOU PITYING IN VAIN?
"WHY IS IT THAT YOU DO NOT HATE A GOD, WHOM THE GODS HATE MOST OF ALL?
"WHY IS IT THAT YOU DO NOT BETRAY HIM, SINCE IT WAS YOUR HONOR HE BETRAYED TO MEN?"
"OUR KINSHIP HAS STRANGE POWER; THAT AND OUR LIFE TOGETHER."
SHAKESPEARE?
AESCHYLUS. "PROMETHEUS UNBOUND."
GREEK TRAGEDIES, HANK?
UNFORTUNATELY, IT WOULD SEEM APROPOS, SLIM...

THE GATES OF "HEAVEN" OPEN...
...UNABLE TO PREVENT THE SERPENTS FROM ENTERING ONTO ITS HALLOWED HALLS.
WHICH RINGS RATH IRONIC, CONSIDE THAT THIS SUPPOS PARADISE...
...IS PRESIDED OVER BY A MAN HAUNTED BY THE DEVILS OF HIS OWN SCARRED LIFE...
...AND THOSE NOW RISING FROM THE HELL THAT EARTH HAS BECOME...
...COME AS DA ANGELS, SEEK TO CLEANSE, TO REDEEM
WE'RE IN. COAST IS CLEAR.
WE'D BEST BE PRUDENT, WOLVERINE.
THERE IS NO TELLING WHAT KIND OF SECURITY SYSTEMS MAGNUS HAS IN PLACE...
Internal Security Sensor Override Activated:
Paragenetic Biosignatures of Intruders No Longer Registering As Anomalous Presence, as per override command:
CHEK
SVISH
HOW GOES THE SECURITY WATCH, NIKOLEIVITCH?
HAS THERE BEEN ANY RETALIATORY ACTIVITY ON EARTH?
ON EARTH...? NO, JAVITZ...
...NOT ON EARTH.
THEY JUSTLY FEAR OUR LORD'S WRATH.
AND THE SHAME OF IT IS, KATU, THAT YOUR "LORD" HAS MOST CERTAINLY GIVEN THEM REASON TO...

SO MUCH OF THIS MATERIAL IS SHI'AR IN ORIGIN--
--STOLEN FROM US, NO DOUBT, WHILE I ENTRUSTED MAGNUS AS HEADMASTER OF MY SCHOOL!
Y'KNOW, IF WE SURVIVE THIS--
--I'M GON' TEACH ALL'A YOU--
--HOW TO BECOME BETTER, QUIETER THIEVES...
MY FATHER AS ALWAYS DONE VERY GOOD JOB USING THE HARD ORK OF OTHERS AGAINST THEM, XAVIER.
BUT WHAT AS HE EVER IVEN ANYONE WHICH HAS PRUNG FROM HIS OWN REATIVITY?
OTHER AN THE COLD, ITTER TASTE F HIS POWER ND THE BLEAK UTLOOK OF HIS VISION?
...IF IT'S THE LAST THING I DO!
THEN 'GAIN, LOOK WHO'S CALLIN' THE KETTLE BLACK...
WHO'S THERE--?!
UHM... AVON CALLIN'...
...HOW 'BOUT SOME MAKE-UP T'COVER UP THAT BLACK EYE?
WHAT BLACK EYE?
FWRRSHSH

THE ONE Y'GONNA HAVE FOR SURE IF YOU DON' GIVE UP RIGHT NOW, BOY.
EASY, GAMBIT. I KNOW THESE TWO. RUSTY COLLINS-- AND SKIDS.
CANNONBALL TOLD US THEY'D AGREED TO STAY UP HERE AFTER THEY WERE FREED FROM STRYFE'S MIND CONTROL.
THAT SO, JEAN? HOW DO WE KNOW THEY AIN'T BEEN FREED FROM ONE BRAINWASHIN'--
--JUST TO HAVE MAGNETO PLAY GAMES WITH THEIR HEADS ALL OVER AGAIN?
WE'RE HERE BY CHOICE, WOLVERINE!
FOR THE FIRST TIME SINCE WE MET ALL OF YOU--
--WE FEEL WE CAN ACHIEVE THE DREAM YOU X-MEN KEEP PREACHING ABOUT!
RUSTY... HOW? BY SEPARATING YOURSELVES FROM THE VERY PEOPLE WHO HAVE TO LEARN TO ACCEPT US BEFORE PEACE WILL EVER OCCUR?
I'M SORRY, CHILDREN--
--BUT WE SIMPLY DO NOT HAVE THE TIME--
--TO DEBATE THE MATTER.
CHARLES --YOU FORCED THEM TO FALL ASLEEP?!
I SCANNED THEIR MINDS, JEAN. I COULD NOT DETERMINE IF THEY WERE ACTING OF THEIR OWN FREE WILL OR NOT.
SO YOU ACTED FOR THEM?
HOW UNLIKE WHAT MAGNETO OR STRYFE DID TO THEM...
PIETRO, YOU KNOW WHAT TO DO.
I WILL REMAIN IN MENTAL CONTACT WITH YOU AS YOU GO.

BE WARY OF THE ACOLYTES WHO ROAM THE CORRIDORS, PIETRO.
AVIER, NSIDER- G THE OOD I'VE EEN IN NCE THE CIDENTS T CAMP AYDEN--
AND FIRST COUNTER TH THESE EMENTED SCIPLES OF MY ATHER--
--IT IS THEY WHO HAD BEST BE AFRAID OF ME!
FFWSHSH
THE DISC IS LOADED.
FFWSHSH
ALTHOUGH I STILL DO NOT FULLY UNDERSTAND HOW PLACING A PREPROGRAMMED DISC IN ONE TERMINAL WILL HELP US--?
THIS BASE MUST HAVE HUNDREDS OF INPUT OUTLETS!

THAT IT DOES, QUICKIE, BUT WE PLUGGED INTA THE ONE WITH A DIRECT ROUTE TA THE MAIN CONTROL BOARD.
THIS IS JUST LIKE OUR SYSTEM AT HOME, GANG. PIECEACAKE.
ALMOST TOO EASY, ISN'T IT?
YOU SUSPECT AN AMBUSH, JEANNIE?
JUST THE OPPOSITE, LOGAN.
I THINK WE'VE AMBUSHED THEM...
...AND THEY DON'T EVEN KNOW IT.
WHICH MAKES THE SIMPLICITY OF THIS MISSION VERY FRIGHT-ENING TO ME.
WOULDN'T YOU AGREE, PROFESSOR?
ACTUALLY, JEAN, I'M QUITE SATISFIED WITH OUR PROGRESS.
COMPUTER: LOCATE PARAGENETIC SIGNATURES OF ALL OCCUPANTS ABOARD THIS STATION.
THERE THEY ARE. HOW COM WE AIN'T SHOWIN'?
WE ARE BLIND TO AVALON'S SENSORS, ROGUE.
WE'VE HAD THE BENEFIT OF SOME INSIDE ASSISTANCE.
COMPUTER: ENGAGE PROCEDURE OVERRIDE TWO-ONE-ALPHA-ZED-ZERO.

VSHHYEEERRRRMMMMMMM
eh--?
WHAT'S GOING ON--?!
OH--
--CRUD--!
VSHHYEEERRRRMMMMMMM
MY LORD--?!
THE TELEPORTATION SYSTEMS HAVE BEEN ACTIVATED?
BY WHOM?
VSHHYEEERRRMMMMMM
Teleport transmission completed:.
SEAL AIR-LOCK HATCHES AND JETTISON AIR-LOCK PODS FOR STATIONARY ORBIT.
FIVE HUNDRED METER DISTANCE.
Acknowledged:.
PFFSSSTTT
WHAT
IS
GOING
ON--?
PSST
PSSTT
PFSSSTT
PFFSSSTT
PSST

FWATHAKROO
THAT ELIMINATES ANY MISCELLANEOUS OPPOSITION.
I BLAME NONE OF THEM FOR THIS, THOUGH.
FOR ALL WE KNOW, MAGNETO HAS--
HAS WHAT, CHARLES?
OFFERED THEM A BETTER OPTION THAN ANY YOU COULD EVER HOPE TO?
FOR THAT IS ALL I HAVE DONE!
I HAVE OFFERED THEM HOPE AND TRUTH, OPPORTUNITY AND ACCOMPLISH-MENT!
AND I WILL CONTINUE TO DO SO FOR ALL MUTANTS WHOM I DEEM WORTHY--
--AND I WILL NOT LET YOUR X-MEN STOP ME AGAIN!!

ouch
ouch
ouch
WELL, HERE GOES THE ONE THING WE DIDN'T WANT...
...A FULL-ON HEAD-TA-HEAD WITH THE BIG GUY!
THE PLAN WAS T'COME IN AN' NAIL HIM WHEN HE WASN'T READY! SO THE PLAN'S BEEN CHANGED A LITTLE, DARLIN'--
--ALL THAT MEANS IS WE IMPROVISE!
Ah, LOGAN... WE DANCE THE DANCE AGAIN AND AGAIN...
...AND YOU'VE NEVER LEARNED THE STEPS VERY WELL, HAVE YOU?
SHFWUM!
MAGNUS--WAIT!
DON'T YOU SEE, THIS TIME, YOU'VE GONE TOO FAR?
PEOPLE'RE DEAD DOWN ON EARTH 'CAUSE A' YOU! YOU SWORE THAT WOULD NEVER HAPPEN AGAIN!
SKRITCH
urk
I WAS MISTAKEN. THAT IS THE PRICE THEY MUST PAY, ROGUE.

PAY FOR WHAT? PAY SIMPLY FOR BEING HUMAN? SIMPLY FOR BEING ALIVE?
JEAN, DON'T WASTE YOUR ENERGIES IN SO FUTILE A MANNER!
LET THE OTHERS OCCUPY HIM--
--WE MUST CONCENTRATE, AS WE DISCUSSED--
--ON DEFEATING HIM FROM THE INSIDE. FROM WITHIN HIS MIND.
BUT THEY HAVE NO CHANCE WITHOUT US, PROFESSOR! WE--
THEIR ROLE IS TO PROVIDE THE CHANCE WE NEED, NOT THE OPPOSITE.
PSI-LINK WITH MY MIND, JEAN. I CANNOT BREAK THROUGH MAGNUS'S PSYCHIC DEFENSES ALONE. I NEED YOU--
--TO STRIKE AT HIS VERY CORE, WITH THE EXPECTATION THAT, AT THE ROOT OF HIS GOALS AND HIS OBSESSIONS--
--MAGNETO'S LIFE IS BUILT ON A FRAGILE SENSE OF FAILURE--
--THAT DEEP DOWN INSIDE, MAGNUS MUST KNOW THAT HIS WAY IS UTTERLY, UTTERLY WRONG!
BUT, PROFESSOR--THIS IS WRONG! IT GOES AGAINST EVERYTHING YOU EVER TAUGHT ME!
WONDERFUL, JEAN--WHAT D'YOU SUGGEST? WE SCOLD HIM AN' THAT'S THE END O' THAT?
FSHRAAKK!

FAKKK!
AAAH--!
"NOW, JEAN! GAMBIT'S PROVIDED US WITH THE OPPORTUNITY WE NEEDED!"
"WE'RE IN, CHARLES --INSIDE HIS MIND-- BUT HE'S FIGHTING US--"
"HE'S FIGHTING HIMSELF, JEAN--FIGHTING HIS PAST-- AND WE CAN USE THAT INNER TURMOIL AGAINST HIM!"
WHAT--? NO.
OH, CHARLES... HOW FAR YOU'VE FALLEN... HOW VERY FAR.
MAKE HIM FEEL HE PAIN OF LOSING IS FAMILY-- HIS OVED ONES--AGAIN IN ALL ITS INTENSITY!"
'CHARLES-- I CAN'T DO THIS--IT'S WRONG, IT'S--!"
"WE HAVE TO, JEAN! AS DISTASTEFUL AS IT IS--WE HAVE TO!"
YOU SURPRISE ME, CHARLES. I THOUGHT SUCH MANIPULATIONS ABHORRENT TO YOU.
ENOUGH!!
YOU ASK ME, X-MEN, WHY I DO WHAT I DO... AND I ASK IN RETURN, HOW CAN YOU NOT?
YOU SEE IT IN MY MIND, XAVIER! HOW CAN YOU ALLOW OUR RACE TO BE SYSTEMATICALLY ERADICATED BY HOMO SAPIENS--
--AS SO MANY INNOCENTS WERE BY THE NAZI BUTCHERS?!
FSIK
FSIK
FSIK
WELL, THEN, BUCKET-HEAD, SOUNDS LIKE KILLIN' EV'RYBODY WHO DON' AGREE WITH Y' POINT OF VIEW--
--SURE DON' MAKE YOU ANY BETTER THAN THEY WERE, HUH? MAKES YOU--
AAAK--!
SILENCE, X-MAN!!

REMY--!!
YOU HURT HIM!
AN' BECAUSE YOU KNOW HE WAS RIGHT, MAGNUS! YOU JUST COULDN'T FACE IT, COULD YA?
SURE THERE'S BEEN A MIGHTY FINE LINE BETWEEN THE ROAD WE WALK AND YOURS--
--BUT THE DIFFERENCE BETWEEN US, SUGAH, IS STILL SIMPLE AS RIGHT AN' WRONG--
AN' GOIN' T' WAR WITH HUMANS--
--KILLIN' 'EM--
--BECAUSE MAYBE THEY FEEL THE SAME WAY ABOUT YOU--
--DON' MAKE IT RIGHT!
AN' THAT'S A BELIEF WE'RE WILLIN' TA FIGHT--AN' DIE FOR!
"CHARLES, WHERE--?"
"AT THE GRAVESITE OF DOUG RAMSEY.
"THE YOUNG NEW MUTANT WHO DIED WHILE MAGNUS WAS HEADMASTER OF THE SCHOOL."
"IT HURT HIM DEEPLY, CHARLES.
"HIS FEELINGS ... HIS GRIEF... WERE GENUINE. IS THIS RIGHT? TO BRING THESE MEMORIES OUT? TO USE THEM IN THIS WAY...?"
--WHAT --CHARLES?! WHAT ARE YOU DOING--?
WHATEVER IT TAKES TO DEFEAT YOU, FATHER... AND END THIS MADNESS.
NNNRRRM--!
PIETRO! OUT OF ALL OF THEM--YOU --HAVE THE AUDACITY TO CONFRONT ME?!
OH, MY SON, MY SON... HOW SHARPER THAN A SERPENT'S TOOTH IS YOUR BETRAYAL!

E AND TIME
GAIN, UPON
RNING YOU AND
R SISTER, WANDA,
SCARLET WITCH,
RE MY CHILDREN--
CHILDREN OF
BELOVED LOST
AGDA--
--YOU HAVE BEEN OFFERED THE OPPORTUNITY TO STAND BY MY SIDE--AS WAS YOUR RIGHT--AS WOULD HAVE BEEN MY JOY.
AND WHAT A WONDERFUL FATHER YOU WOULD'VE MADE, MAGNUS--
--FORCING YOUR CHILDREN TO SIT SUBSERVIENT TO YOUR WHIMS... UNABLE TO EVEN THINK FOR THEMSELVES--
--AS YOU
CKED ONTO THE
RON IN THEIR
OODSTREAMS AND
OLDED THEIR VERY
THOUGHTS!
WE MISSED
T ON SO MUCH,
Y LOSING YOUR
RENTAL GUIDANCE,
DIDN'T WE?
"PROFESSOR... THIS MEMORY... IT DIDN'T HAPPEN THIS WAY--"
"WHEN MAGNUS'S WIFE, MAGDA, LEFT HIM, SHE WAS PREGNANT WITH WANDA AND PIETRO--
"--AND IT WAS THE FIRST TIME HE HAD USED HIS POWERS IN FRONT OF HER.
"HE WASN'T MAGNETO THEN--SIMPLY ERIK MAGNUS LEHNSHERR..."
"CHARLES, IF HIS MEMORIES ARE TWISTING--FRACTURING--
WHAT?
"--HIS CURRENT LIFE IMPOSING ITSELF ON HIS PAST, THEN THAT MEANS--"
"IT MEANS, JEAN, THAT WE ARE FORCING HIM TO QUESTION HIS OWN JUDGMENT, AT LAST!"
VERY DEVIOUS, CHARLES. BUT IN THE FACE OF YOUR SUBVERSION... YOUR BEFOULING OF MY MIND... I STAND --RESOLUTE.
NO,
ATHER,
OU DO
NOT!
LOOK AT ME! LOOK AT WHAT I HAVE BECOME BECAUSE OF YOU!
UNABLE TO LOVE FREELY, UNABLE TO TRUST WILLINGLY--AFRAID TO TRULY LIVE A LIFE WITH MY WIFE--MY DAUGHTER!
I AM TIRED OF RUNNING AWAY FROM MY PROBLEMS!
I AM TIRED OF RUNNING AWAY FROM YOU!
KRAKK!

PERHAPS I DID WRONG BY YOU AND YOUR SISTER, PIETRO...
...BUT I LOVED YOUR MOTHER MORE THAN LIFE ITSELF.
AND I DO NOT NEED YOU TO BLAME ME FOR THINGS I SO FREELY BLAME MYSELF!
AND I CANNOT ALLOW YOU TO DO THAT, PIETRO!
BUT CONSIDER THIS: YOU HAVE DONE EQUALLY WRONG BY ME AS WELL, MY SON!
BY REJECTING MY OFFER, YOU REJECT MY HOPES, MY DREAMS--
--MY CHANCE TO PASS ALONG AN INHERITANCE OF MUTANT FREEDOM ON TO YOU AND MY DESCENDANTS!
I CANNOT HAVE MY ONLY SON LEAVE THE PARADISE I HOPE TO CREATE HERE--
--AND SO, AS PAINFUL AS IT IS FOR ME, YOU MUST BE SACRIFICED FOR THE GOOD OF OF OUR PEOPLE--
--MY SON MUST BE SLAIN!
SORRY, MAGGIE--

--THAT JUST AIN'T GONNA HAPPEN!
WOLVERINE--?! NO!
TEAN, YOU UST SEIZE N THIS! IT THE KEY!--
--MAGNUS'S EELING THAT S 'CHILDREN' LWAYS BETRAY IM, ALWAYS FAIL HIM...
ROM PIETRO ND WANDA DOWN TO FABIAN CORTEZ, HO GATHERED THE COLYTES OF MAGNETO--
"--ONLY TO USE THEM IN HIS GRANDER SCHEME TO BETRAY MAGNETO AND KILL HIM!"
HESITATIN' AGAIN, MAGS?
BIG MISTAKE!
'CAUSE HERE'S WHERE I SHOW YOU HOW WELL I LEARNED OUR LITTLE DANCE!
SHREKK
ahh
oh, LOGAN, LOGAN, LOGAN
YOU HAVE--DONE THIS--?
THE GAME'S OVER, BUB. ANY MAN WHO'D TRY AN' KILL HIS OWN SON DESERVES NO LESS.
DON'T LOOK SO SURPRISED. AFTER ALL, AIN'T IT WHAT YOU WOULDA DONE?
LOGAN ...NO!
JEAN--YOU'VE SEVERED THE MIND-PROBE?!
I NEED YOU, JEAN--MY CONTROL OVER THIS ARMOR IS TAXING ME GREATLY!
NOW--WHILE HE IS GRAVELY INJURED--
--IS OUR BEST HOPE OF PIERCING THE FINAL BARRIERS IN MAGNETO'S MIND!

PRO-FESSOR! WHAT'S HAPPENED TO YOU? LOOK AT HIM! HE'S BLEEDING... BADLY!

HE'S SURVIVED WORSE.

IT'S IN OUR POWER TO PUT A PEACEFUL END TO THIS RIGHT NOW!

POWER IS NOTHING, JEAN. YOU HAVE IT. I HAVE IT.

WHAT MATTERS MOST ARE THE CHOICES WE MAKE ON HOW THAT POWER IS USED. AND MAGNUS HAS MADE HIS CHOICE ABUNDANTLY CLEAR. ASK THE MEN ON THE LENINGRAD. THE PEOPLE WHO DIED TODAY. ASK THEM ALL.

A PEACEFUL SOLUTION WAS LOST TO US LONG, LONG AGO. WE MUST ENTER HIS MIND AGAIN-- QUICKLY, BEFORE--

NO MORE, LOGAN. FOOLISH, FOOLISH MAN.

IT ENDS FOR US BOTH NOW.

OUR LONG ASSOCIATION, MY MOST VISCERAL ENEMY, MY MOST RESPECTED FOE--

--IS OVER!

MAGNETIC FIRE COURSES THROUGH WOLVERINE'S BODY.

AND IT BEGINS WITH A SMALL TUG--

--AN ALMOST GENTLE PULL--

--A HARDER YANK--

WHAT TH--?!

SPLUCH

--THEN A WRENCHING TEAR--

FLICHT!

LOGAN--? OH, LORD-- LOGAN!
NO! MAGNUS-- FOR THE LOVE OF GOD--DON'T DO THIS--
"NOW, PLAY THE INSOLENT; NOW, PLUNDER THE GOD'S PRIVILEGES AND GIVE THEM TO CREATURES OF A DAY.
"WHAT DROP OF YOUR SUFFERINGS CAN MORTALS SPARE YOU?"
WE ARE ALL BUT BIT PLAYERS IN A TRAGEDY FAR LARGER THAN ANY OF US...
...A TRAGEDY CALLED LIFE, LOGAN.
BUT TODAY, FOR YOU, PERHAPS FOR ME--
--THE CURTAIN FALLS...
...AND THE PLAY IS FINISHED!
SHREKKTTHH!
WOLVERINE DOESN'T SCREAM. INDEED, HE DOESN'T EVEN HAVE TIME, AS THE ADAMANTIUM WHICH LONG AGO WAS BONDED TO HIS VERY BONES--
--IS DESTABILIZED ON A MOLECULAR LEVEL, RIPPED FROM ITS MOORINGS, AND FORCED THROUGH HIS OPEN WOUNDS--
--ERUPTING OUTWARD LIKE WATER BURSTING THROUGH A DAM!
AS HE FALLS, THE STILLNESS OF PURE HORROR SURROUNDS THE KILLING GROUND--
--BROKEN ONLY BY THE VOICE OF ONE PERSON WHO HAS, SINCE THE DAY SHE FIRST MET HIM, AND PERHAPS ALWAYS WILL--
--LOVE HIM...

LOGAN!!
OH, LORD-- IS HE--?!
--HE'S STILL BREATHIN'--?!
STUBBORN TO THE LAST, eh--?
hack
WHAT OF YOU, CHARLES--
haurgh
--WHAT OF YOUR PART IN THIS FOOL'S FOLLY?
haff
haff
MINE IS THE DENOUEMENT, OLD FRIEND.
I HAVE HIDDEN BEHIND OUR PHILOSOPHICAL DIFFERENCES FOR TOO LONG, ALWAYS WILLING TO FORGIVE YOU FOR YOUR TRANS-GRESSIONS.
I CAN NO LONGER DO THAT-- YOU HAVE SHOWN AN INABILITY TO CHANGE YOUR WAYS, AND I, AN UNWILLING-NESS TO MAKE THE HARD DECISIONS!
MAYBE, IN OUR OWN WAYS, WE ARE BOTH FAILURES, MAGNUS!
DOUG RAMSEY
YOU, FOR FAILING TO RISE ABOVE THE HORRORS PERPETRATED ON YOU IN YOUR PAST--
--AND AS FOR ME, MAYBE I HAVE FAILED AS WELL... DENYING THE NEED TO STOP SUCH HORRORS --NO MATTER WHAT THE COST!

CHARLES, LOGAN IS STILL ***ALIVE*** --JUST BARELY--

--I'M ***TELE-KINETICALLY*** KEEPING HIS BODY TOGETHER--

--AND ***TELEPATHICALLY*** PREVENTING HIS MIND FROM UNDER-STANDING HOW MUCH DAMAGE WAS DONE TO HIM--

--BUT WE HAVE TO LEAVE ***NOW!***

HEAR THAT, CHARLES?

A LIFE NEEDS SAVING. SUCH AS ALWAYS BEEN YOUR BAILIWICK, YOUR CLARION CALL.

BILLIONS OF LIVES EED SAVING, MAGNUS.

WE CAME ERE TODAY O ***SACRIFICE*** UR ***OWN,*** SO THAT THOSE IVES MAY E SAVED ROM YOUR MISGUIDED ***WRATH!***

BY ***WHAT*** RIGHT DO YOU MAKE SUCH DECISIONS, CHARLES? BY ***WHAT RIGHT*** DO THE CHOICES ***YOU*** MAKE FOR THE LIVES OF HOMO SAPIENS AND SUPERIOR ALIKE...

...MAKE YOU ANY ***LESS*** MISGUIDED THAN I?

IT ALL BOILS DOWN, FINALLY, NO MATTER HOW ALIKE WE ARE, TO THE FUNDAMENTAL DIFFERENCE IN OUR VIEWS, MAGNUS!

MINE IS A ***DREAM*** TO LIVE IN ***HARMONY*** WITH THOSE WHO FEAR AND DESPISE US-- TO MAKE THEM SEE THE ***ERROR*** OF THEIR WAYS--

--NO ***MATTER*** THE ***HARDSHIPS*** WE MUST ENDURE, THE ***SACRIFICES*** WE MUST MAKE, TO ACHIEVE THAT GOAL--

--AND ***YOURS,*** QUITE SIMPLY, DEMANDS THAT WE ***RULE OVER*** THOSE WHO WOULD OPPOSE US... NO MATTER THE COST IN ***SUFFERING*** AND ***DEGRA-DATION!***

THE DIFFERENCE BETWEEN US IS THAT OF ***LIGHT*** AND ***DARK, LOVE*** AND ***HATE--***

--LIFE AND ***DEATH!!***

NO MORE, MAGNUS--
NO MORE!!
LOGAN SHALL BE THE LAST! NO ONE ELSE WILL EVER SUFFER!
YOU CAUSED THE DEATHS OF HUNDREDS TODAY, MAGNUS--DEATHS I COULD HAVE PREVENTED HAD I STOPPED YOU YEARS AGO!
YOU HAVE KILLED TOO MANY, MAGNUS--
--AND I HAVE HAD ENOUGH!!
I WILL MAKE SURE--HERE AND NOW--ONCE AND FOR ALL--THAT YOU NEVER KILL AGAIN!!
AHHHH...
CHAR--LES...
...I NEVER THOUGHT...
...YOU WOULD...
THWUMP!
NO!!
MAGNUS--?!!
PROFESSOR--WHAT DID YOU DO TO HIM?
...I TOOK HIS MIND AWAY FROM HIM... God forgive me...
I TOOK AWAY HIS GREATEST WEAPONS... HIS HATRED...
...HIS EGO, HIS NIGHT-MARES... I TOOK THEM ALL...
JEAN! HE'S BARELY BREATHIN'!!

Oh, LORD-- I CAN'T DO ANYTHING ABOUT IT RIGHT NOW--
--I'M BARELY ABLE TO KEEP LOGAN'S BODY FROM FALLING APART AS IT IS!
WE HAVE TA GET OUTTA HERE--WE HAVE TA GET BACK TA THE MANSION!
THE PROFESSOR--WOLVIE--EVEN MAGNETO NEED OUR HELP!
WE CAN TELEPORT BACK, RIGHT? CAN WE LEAVE NOW--?
YOU WILL NOT BE ABLE TO TELEPORT BACK HOME, ROGUE.
PETER--?
YOUR BATTLE HAS TAKEN MOST OF AVALON'S SYSTEMS OFF-LINE.
I HAVE SENT A SIGNAL TO THE MANSION. BISHOP IS COMING IN A MODIFIED BLACKBIRD.
FOR THE SAKE OF LOGAN ...AND EVEN OF THE PROFESSOR...
...I RECOMMEND YOU LEAVE QUICKLY--AS SOON AS HE ARRIVES.
PETEY--WHAT ABOUT MAGNUS? WHAT ABOUT YOU?
I AM STAYING, ROGUE. MAGNETO HAS BEEN LEFT IN A VEGETATIVE STATE. HE WILL NEED SOMEONE TO CARE FOR HIM.
WHAT I COULD NOT DO FOR MY SISTER, ILLYANA, PERHAPS I CAN FOR HIM.
THAT WILL BE, IN MANY WAYS, A MOST FITTING PENANCE FOR MY ROLE IN THIS SAD AFFAIR.

I PREVENTED AVALON'S SECURITY SYSTEMS FROM DETECTING YOU.
MY INDISCRETIONS ALLOWED ALL OF YOU FREE REIN OF THE STATION.
I AM, IN MANY WAYS, AS RESPONSIBLE FOR THIS AS MAGNETO IS--OR AS ARE ANY OF YOU...

THE STORY CONTINUES IN **WOLVERINE #75** --AS THE X-MEN FACE A STUNNING LOSS! AND NEXT MONTH YOU **MUST** READ **AVENGERS #368** BEFORE JOINING US HERE, AS **BLOODTIES** --THE X-MEN / AVENGERS CROSSOVER BEGINS!!

X-Men Series 2 (1993) trading-card art by Brandon Peterson, Mark Farmer & Paul Mounts

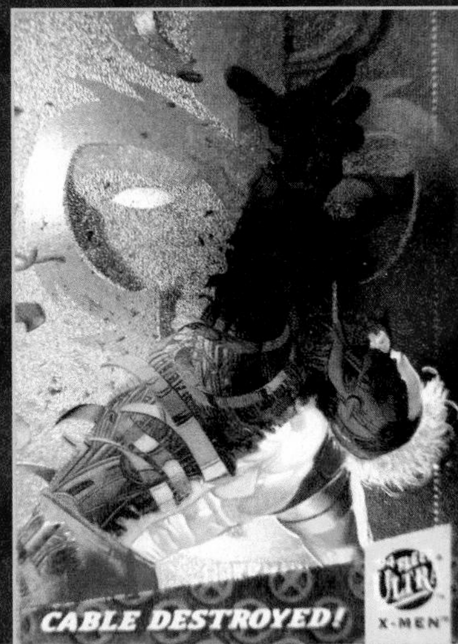

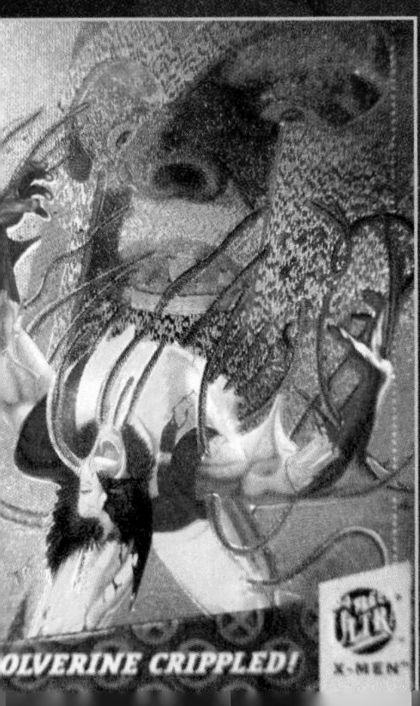

ADAM KUBERT
MARK FARMER

WOLVERINE
APPROVED BY THE COMICS CODE AUTHORITY
FATAL ATTRACTIONS
A NEW MYSTERY BEGINS AS A LIFE HANGS IN THE BALANCE!

Wolverine #75 hologram original pencils by Adam Kubert, and inks by Mark Farmer

YOU EVER BEEN HURT SO BAD, YOU COULDN'T HEAR ANYTHING BUT A HIGH-PITCHED ROAR...
Y'ALL HAVE TO DO SOMETHING FOR HIM, PROFESSOR...
--WE JUST CAN'T LET LOGAN DIE NOT AFTER ALL WE'VE JUST BEEN THROUGH!
HIS WOUNDS ARE SO GRAVE THAT EVEN HIS MUTANT HEALING FACTOR AND HIS INDOMITABLE WILL ARE TAXED TO THEIR VERY LIMITS!
THE MEDI-UNIT WE ENCASED HIM IN IS DOING ALL IT CAN TO STABILIZE HIS PHYSICAL TRAUMA...
...I AM AFRAID IT WILL REQUIRE A PSI-LINK INCURSION INTO THE CORE OF HIS SUBCONSCIOUS TO ALLEVIATE THE PSYCHIC TRAUMA.
JEAN...?
I'M READY, PROFESSOR. BUT ARE YOU SURE YOU'RE UP TO THIS?
...AND THEN YOU REALIZED THAT IT WAS THE SOUND O' YOURSELF SCREAMIN'?
TAKE MY SEAT, PIETRO.
THE COMMANDER'S SEAT? BUT, BISHOP--
JUST DO IT.

Stan Lee presents
NIGHTMARE
THERE'S A WORLD ON THE OTHER SIDE O' PAIN, FULL O' HORROR AND HOPE-LESSNESS AND CON-CENTRATED SUFFERIN'...
...BUT THERE'S NO FEAR THERE.
WHAT'S THERE TO FEAR WHEN YOU'RE IN THE MIDDLE O' THE WORST THAT CAN HAPPEN?
MY HEALTH IS UNIMPORTANT, JEAN. LOGAN NEEDS US... AND I WILL NOT FAIL HIM.
WE'RE AT THE EPICENTER OF LOGAN'S MOST SUPPRESSED CATACLYSMIC MEMORIES--
--SYNAPSES LONG DORMANT, NOW TRIGGERED BY THE BRUTAL ASSO-CIATION OF HIS TERRIBLE ORDEAL AT THE HANDS OF MAGNETO!
WHAT ARE WAITING FOR, PROFESSOR? WE HAVE TO GET RID OF ALL THESE--
NO!
YOU KNOW BETTER THAN THAT, JEAN. I REALIZE YOU'RE WORRIED ABOUT LOGAN, BUT WE MUST TREAD EVER SO CAUTIOUSLY HERE!
LARRY HAMA WRITER
ADAM KUBERT PENCILER
MARK FARMER DAN GREEN & MARK PENNINGTON INKERS
PAT BROSSEAU LETTERER
STEVE BUCCELLATO COLORIST
BOB HARRAS EDITOR
TOM DEFALCO EDITOR IN CHIEF

PERSIST

"...JUST AS THE ADAMANTIUM WAS BONDED TO WOLVERINE'S BONES!
" TO INDISCRIMINATELY EXCISE THESE MEMORIES WOULD BE AS DAMAGING TO HIS MIND AS MAGNETO'S FORCED EXTRACTION OF WOLVERINE'S ADAMANTIUM WAS TO HIS BODY!
"AS... DAMAGING AS WHAT I DID TO MAGNETO."
HOW CAN WE JUST STAND BY HERE AND DO NOTHING. WHAT WAS THE PURPOSE OF COMING IN HERE?
TO WAIT AND WATCH AND TO BE PREPARED TO COUNTER THE COLLAPSE OF THE MATRIX UPON WHICH THE WEB OF HIS PERSONALITY IS SPUN;
TO BE FRIENDS AT THE BRINK OF THE ULTIMATE LONELINESS.
TO BE ENCOURAGEMENT IN THE REALM OF DESPAIR;

LOGAN!
HE JUST PASSED THROUGH US, LIKE A PHANTOM--
--AND HE IGNORED US!
WE ARE NO MORE THAN A SERIES OF ELECTRICAL IMPULSES CHASING THOSE OTHER IMPULSES WHICH COMPRISE HIS MEMORY THROUGH THE NEURONS OF HIS BRAIN!
NO, JEAN-- HE IS SIMPLY IN TRANSITION FROM ONE TRIGGERED MEMORY TO ANOTHER. WE ARE THE PHANTOMS.
THERE'S SOMETHING IMMENSE COMING OVER THE HORIZON!
THERE'S NO HORIZON HERE!
REMEMBER, OUR POINT OF VIEW IS SKEWED BY THE FACT THAT WE ARE INADEQUATELY INTERPRETING ANOTHER PERSON'S VISUAL PERCEPTIONS--
THIS IS THE STUFF OF FEVER DREAMS!
BUT HAUNTINGLY FAMILIAR...
FAMILIAR? THIS ALIEN LANDSCAPE?
NOT FAMILIAR, MAYBE-- BUT DEFINITELY NOT ALIEN!
AH! I SEE! IT WAS THE SCALE!
SCALE? I DON'T--

--OH, LORD!
IT'S THE GENESIS TANK AT THE WEAPON X PROJECT!
WE'RE NOW PRIVY TO EVENTS THAT LOGAN HAS NEVER SEEN FIT TO SHARE WITH US!
WE'RE HERE TO HELP, HIM, PROFESSOR--BUT THIS--THIS IS A VIOLATION OF THE WORST ORDER!
IT WAS WRONG WITH MAGNETO, IT'S WRONG HERE!
I DID WHAT HAD TO BE DON WITH MAGNETO. A FOR LOGAN... TH TERMINATION OF PSI-LINK HAS READY BEEN NEC SITATED...

...BY THE PLIGHT OF OUR RE-ENTRY VEHICLE!
WE HAVE A TOTAL FAILURE IN THE MAIN HEAT SHIELD!
TELL GAMBIT TO SWITCH TO BACK-UPS FROM THE ENGINEER-ING CONSOLE!
I HEAR YOU, BISHOP! THERMOSTAT TO BACK-UP HEAT SHIELD IS DOWN! WE UP DAT CREEK, MON AMI!
CAN WE SCRUB THIS DESCENT AND REPLOT A SHALLOW-ER ANGLE? ON A QUINJET, SUCH A MANEUVER WOULD BE FAIRLY SIMPLE.
THE BLACKBIRD WAS NEVER DESIGNED TO FUNCTION AS AN ORBITAL SHUTTLE...
...WE DON'T HAVE ENOUGH FUEL TO REGAIN A STABILIZED ORBIT!
WE HAVE TO PLAY OUT THIS HAND AS IT WAS DEALT. USE THE MAIN COMPUTER TO BYPASS THE THERMOSTAT CON-TROLS...
...AND ADVISE THE OTHERS THAT THE RIDE QUALITY IS ON A DOWN CURVE!
DOWN CURVE?
YOU MEAN IT'S GOING TO GET WORSE?
LOOK OUT--!
--THE MEDI-UNIT SNAPPED LOOSE!

SKRAKKK!
HE'S CONSCIOUS!
ARRRRRRRRRRGGHH!
THE SHOCK HAS AWAKENED HIM!
RE-SECURE THE MEDI-UNIT!
HOLD HIM STEADY, WHILE I ADMINISTER ANOTHER INJECTION OF META-MORPHINE--
NO PAIN-KILLERS, CHARLES...
IT HURTS 'CAUSE... MY BODY IS... FIXIN' ITSELF.
I CAN... TAKE IT.
DON'T... WANNA BE... NUMB...
GONNA BE... NUMB FOREVER... AFTER I BUY THE... FARM!

OH, LORD... AH CAN SEE HIM KNITTIN' HIM-SELF BACK TO-GETHER!
IF THE TRAUMA WAS LOCALIZED AND NOT OF SUCH MAGNITUDE, HIS MUTANT HEALING FACTOR WOULD HAVE MADE HIM WHOLE ALREADY...
I'D BE... DANCIN' IN... THE AISLES, CHARLIE.
WE DON'T HAVE A CLUE ABOUT HOW THE HEALING FACTOR WORKS...
...AND THIS AMOUNT OF DAMAGE MAY BE TOO MUCH OF A STRAIN...
...ON AN OVERLOADED SYSTEM--
--JUST AS I FEARED! THE WOUNDS REOPEN! THE HEALING FACTOR CAN'T KEEP UP WITH ONGOING TISSUE DETERIORA-TION!
HE'S BURNING UP WITH FEVER! CAN THE MEDI-UNIT COOL HIS BODY TEMPERATURE DOWN ENOUGH TO KEEP HIM FROM GOING INTO SHOCK?
THE UNIT IS JUST AN INTERIM DEVICE. IT IS ONLY MEANT TO STABILIZE A PATIENT EN ROUTE TO A PROPER MEDICAL FACILITY!

I HAD THOUGHT THAT THE WORST WAS OVER WHEN I FLEW THE BLACK-BIRD UP TO AVALON TO BRING BACK THE ASSAULT TEAM!
WATCH THE PITCH INDICATOR!
CORRECT THE ANGLE OF ATTACK...
...ONE DEGREE OF DECLINATION CAN INCREASE OUR DRAG-FRICTION OVER THE RED-LINE!.
OVER?
OUR ALREADY VISIBLE INCAN-DESCENCE WOULD FLARE BRIEFLY AND FADE TO BLACK AS OUR MOLECULES DISPERSED OVER NEW JERSEY!
LOOK, DADDY! A SHOOTING STAR!
MAKE A WISH, SON...
THERE CAN NEVER BE A RESOLU-TION FOR PEOPLE LIKE US, BISHOP...
...FATE HAS NEVER BEEN THAT KIND.
DAD

YOU KNOW... WHAT I... WISH, JEAN, DARLIN'?
...I WISH... THINGS COULD'VE BEEN... DIFFERENT...
BUT I'M GLAD... YOU'RE FINALLY GONNA BE... HAPPY.
MOIRA... CAN YOU HEAR ME?
I'M STANDING BY =SKREEE!= THE COMMAND CENTER =SQUAWK!= AS PLANNED, CHARLES...!
...BUT CAN YE NOT USE A TELEPATHIC LINK? THE SIGNAL IS NAE GOOD AT ALL!
I AM ALREADY DEPLETED =SKREEEE!= FROM MY BATTLE WITH MAGNETO. I MUST CONSERVE MY PSI-STRENGTH TO =SQUAWK= HELP WOLVERINE IF HE NEEDS IT!
OH, WOLVIE!
WHAT I REQUIRE FROM YOU, MOIRA, IS =SHRRRRRRR!= FOR YOU TO TALK ME THROUGH THE =SKREE!= MEDICAL PROCEDURES TO KEEP LOGAN ALIVE UNTIL WE TOUCH DOWN!
MONITOR HIS TEMPERATURE CONSTANTLY! IF IT GOES ABOVE 108, HE CAN GO INTO CONVULSIVE SEIZURES!
OCH, AND KEEP HIM TALKING-- BUT DINNAE LET HIM GET SELF-ABSORBED AND MORBID!

WE HAVE A RED LIGHT ON THE CANOPY STRESS MONITOR!
HOLOGRAPHIC HEADS-UP-DISPLAYS AND LCD DIRECT SITUATION READ-OUTS ON LINE...!
...ACTIVATING BLAST SHIELDS!
SHOOOMP!
SHIELD
I 'SPOSE IT'S SEAT-O' THE PANTS FLYIN' FROM HERE ON IN--
LORDY! A WHOLE INSTRUMENT PANEL WENT BALLISTIC!
THAT WAS THE FLY-BY-WIRE INTER-FACE!
WITHOUT THE INTERFACE AND THE COMPUTER MAKING CONSTANT LIGHTNING FAST ATTITUDE COR-RECTIONS WE'LL WOBBL INTO AN UNCONTROL-LABLE SPIN!
PROFESSOR! LOGAN CAN'T TAKE THIS! HIS HEART-VALVE TIMING IS FLUC-TUATING!
GAMBIT, DO WE HAVE A BACK-UP ON THE ENGINEERING CONSOLE?
WHOOMP!
WHAT WE HAVE, IS CIRCUIT BOARDS EN FLAMBE'!
QUICK-SILVER! BY PASS THE COMPUTER. DO THE CONTR CORRECTIONS MANUALLY!

OL' PIETRO'S MORE'N A MATCH FOR ANY OL' FLY-BY-WIRE INTER-FACE, WHATEVER THAT IS!
WHY DIDN'T WE THINK O' THAT?
BISHOP DID.
HE HAD ME TAKE THE COMMANDER'S SHIP BECAUSE ALL THE MANUAL OVERRIDE CONTROLS ARE HERE BEFORE THE SITUATION DETERIORATED!
GAMBIT!
ICI!
ROGUE'S NEEDED UP ON THE FLIGHT DECK, SO WE NEED AN EXTRA PAIR OF HANDS TO HELP WITH LOGAN!
CHARLIE--
--I GOTTA... TALK TO YA, CHARLIE--
YOU GOTTA PROMISE ME YOU'LL TAKE CARE O' THINGS FOR ME AND ESPECIALLY, YA GOTTA WATCH OUT FOR JUBILEE--
WHAT'S HE TALKING ABOUT??
HE'S TALKING LIKE HE'S NOT GOING TO MAKE IT! HE'S NEVER SAID ANYTHING LIKE THAT BEFORE!!!!
YE CANNAE STAY HERE IF YE CANNAE CONTROL YOURSELF, YOUNG LADY!
THIS IS A TWO-WAY COMMUNICATIONS LINK!

SCHRRRRRIIIPPP!

WE JUST LOST THE RIGHT AILERON AND FLAPS!

WE HAVE A STRESS CRACK IN THE WING SKIN...

...AND IT'S *WIDENING* TOWARDS THE *CABIN!!*

QUICKSILVER-- CAN YOU CORRECT ALTITUDE WITH ONLY THE *LEFT WING* CONTROL SURFACES?

IMPOSSIBLE! ALTITUDE IS DECAYING INTO A *WOBBLE* THAT IS GENERATING *RESONATING WAVES*...
...THAT WILL *TEAR US APART* IN 5.247 *SECONDS!*

JEAN! I'M GOING TO CONCENTRATE ON KEEPING *LOGAN* ALIVE! IT IS UP TO *YOU*...

"...TO KEEP THE *BLACKBIRD TOGETHER*--

"--WITH YOUR *TELEKINETIC POWER!*"

SHE DID IT! WE'RE STABILIZ-ING!
BUT HOW LONG CAN SHE KEEP UP THE INTENSE CONCENTRATION NEEDED TO HOLD THE AIRFRAME TOGETHER?
IN SALEM CENTER...
MOIRA! WHAT'S GOING ON UP THERE...?
...WE WERE OUT PREPPING THE LANDING DOCK AND WE HEARD--
THEY'VE FIXED THINGS FOR THE TIME BEING, BUT THEY'RE NAE OOT O' THE WOODS YET!
IS HARLES--
WOLVIE...
ARE THEY--?
LOGAN! WHAT ABOUT LOGAN??
WHY ISN'T JEAN SAYING ANYTHING??
QUIET! ALL O' YE! I CANNAE HEAR!
I HAVE TO KEEP THIS CHANNEL OPEN TO RELAY MEDICAL INFORMATION TO PROFESSOR XAVIER--
HANK AND SCOTT-- IT IS UP TO YOU TO TRACK THE BLACKBIRD-- AND RECOMPUTE THE ENTRY TRAJECTORY!
ALREADY THOUGHT OF THAT! IT'S RUNNING THROUGH THE COMPUTER RIGHT NOW!

THE LIFE SYSTEMS ARE SPIKING! WE'RE LOSING HIM!
GAMBIT, YOU'RE TAKING OVER FOR ME! PLEASE MONITOR THE METERS CLOSELY!
STEPPING OUT FOR A PROMENADE, PROFESSEUR?
STEPPING IN, MORE APTLY.
IT IS NECESSARY FOR ME TO RE-ENTER WOLVERINE'S MIND AND FLATTEN OUT THE BRAIN-WAVE SPIKES!
PLEASE BEAR IN MIND THAT IF LOGAN SHOULD EXPIRE WHILE MY CONSCIOUSNESS IS RESIDENT IN HIS MIND...
...THE SHOCK WILL PROVE LETHAL TO ME, AS WELL!
CHARLES!
I CAN'T TAKE IT! FIRST ILLYANA, AND NOW LOGAN--!
DON'T YOU GIVE UP ON HIM!
HE WOULD NEVER GIVE UP ON YOU...
...HE WOULD NEVER WRITE YOU OFF!
IT'S HAPPENING ALL OVER AGAIN!
JUST LIKE THE SHUTTLE PLUMMETING THROUGH THE RADIATION STORM...
...BACK WHEN JEAN TURNED INTO PHOENIX!

IT'S WORSE THAN I IMAGINED.
...AND BEEN NULLIFIED.
HERE, THE LAME MAY WALK, LEAP AND RUN.
THE SILENCE VIBRATES WITH THE BRITTLE OF SCREAMS.
...HERE, THE BLIND MAY SEE WITH ELECTRIC EYES...
...AND RIP WITH CLAWS OF MYTHIC METAL.
THIS IS THE BLOODY SHILOH OF LOGAN'S VITAL ESSENCE.
HERE, IS RE-ENACTED THE PERSONAL RAGNORAK OF A SHATTERED SOUL...
...STAGED WITH ACCUMULATED PROPS AND BAGGAGE OF TRAUMAS PAST.
I'M COMIN' FOR YA, MAGS!
I'M GONNA RIP YER GUTS OUT!
HERE, THE PURE LINE OF LOGIC HAS BEEN INTERSECTED BY THE VARIABLE WAVE OF PAIN...
SCHRRIJKKK!
I KNOW WHERE YOU LIVE...!!

...IT'S THE PLACE WHERE THE LIGHTNING CONVERGES!
AHH
OH, LOGAN, LOGAN, LOGAN...
IT ENDS FOR US BOTH, NOW.
OUR LONG ASSOCIATION, MY MOST VISCERAL ENEMY, MY MOST RESPECTED FOE...
...IS OVER!
SO REAL.
THE OZONE SEARS MY NOSTRILS.
THE LINES OF FORCE THAT MOVE PLANETS ARE BENT, CHANNELED AND AMPLIFIED.
NO.
IT IS NOT REAL.
IT IS ONE MAN'S PERCEPTION...
...AND I AM WALKING, EVEN RUNNING THROUGH IT--
LOGAN!!!
--AND I HAVE POWER HERE!

THOOOM
I CAN SURRENDER MYSELF TO THIS REALITY AND AFFECT IT!
I CAN STOP LOGAN FROM BEING SUCKED INTO THAT AWFUL LIGHT!
LET ME GO, CHARLIE!
LET ME GO INTO THAT WONDERFUL WARMTH!
HEAR THAT MUSIC?
IT'S ALL THE VOICES O' EVERY-ONE I EVER LOVED, SINGIN' THE END TO LONELI-NESS AND SORROW!
IT'S THE BRILLIANT, SHININ' CHORD O' REDEMP-TION!
AWW, CHARLIE...
...DON'T YA THINK I KNOW THAT?
LOGAN! IT'S DEATH!!
BRACE YOUR-SELVES!
WE'RE HITTING A STORM FRONT!!!

BISHOP! I'M LOSING THE SKIN ON THE RIGHT WING!
LET IT GO! CONCENTRATE ON PRESERVING THE STRUCTURAL INTEGRITY OF THE AIR FRAME!
SCHOOOOM!
WE HAVE TO LEVEL THE SHIP OUT MANUALLY!
WHAT NOW, BISHOP?
FAPP!
FOOM!
THE POWER ASSISTS TO THE MAIN FLIGHT CONTROLS JUST DIED!
GAMBIT!
I NEED YOUR HELP!
TE BILE PAS, MEC!*
* DON'T SWEAT IT! --FRANCOPHILE BOB.
...UN PIECE DE GATEAU!
I'M GLAD YOU THINK SO!
THAT WAS THE MAIN HATCH!!
THE CABIN IS GOING TO DE-PRESSURIZE!!
EVERYTHING THAT ISN'T STRAPPED DOWN...
BA-DOOOOM!

"...IS GOING TO GET SUCKED OUT!"
GOODBYE, CHARLIE!
THE LIGHT IS CALLIN' ME--
...ILLYANA!
... THE LIGHT!
WHO...?
I KNOW YOU...
I'M READY TO GO, DARLIN'--
--WHU?
DON'T PUSH ME AWAY, DARLIN'--!
DON'T--!

JEAN! FORGET ABOUT THE WING AND SECURE THE HATCH!
WHAT HAPPENED TO LOGAN, PROFESSOR?
THERE'S NOTHING MORE I CAN DO FOR HIM!
WHY DID YOU COME OUT OF HIS MIND? IS HE--
CONCENTRATE ON THE HATCH, JEAN!
THE HATCH IS NOT GOING TO MOVE!!
I'M NOT GOING TO LET IT!!
I NEED A SITUATION REPORT!
JEAN HELD THAT OL' WING TOGETHER LONG ENOUGH!
WE'VE GOT THE AIRSPEED DOWN TO BELOW THE RESONATIN' LEVEL!
THE WING WON'T SHAKE ITSELF APART ANYMORE...
...NOW, ALL JEAN HAS TO WORRY ABOUT IS THE HATCH!
OH, LORD-- HE'S GOING INTO CARDIAC ARREST!
PULMONARY STIMULATION IS INEFFECTIVE!
VITAL SIGNS GRAPHS ARE FADING!!

I NEED TO RE-PLACE THE HATCH...!

...BUT WITH WHAT??

I CAN'T MAINTAIN CONTROL BY MYSELF!!

CAN'T HOLD ON!!

HELP ME, REMY!

WATCH OUT, JEAN! GAMBIT AND ROGUE ARE BEING SUCKED OUT TOWARDS THE HATCH!

NO! I'M NOT GOING TO LET IT HAPPEN!

CAN'T GO INTO THE LIGHT!

GOTTA GO BACK!

BUT, HOW?

GET BACK UP TO THE CONTROLS! I'M USING ALL MY PSI-STRENGTH TO PUSH YOU BACK UP THERE!

GET THE BLACKBIRD UNDER CONTROL!

JEAN!

DON'T LOOK BACK!

SAVE THE OTHERS!

HOW DO I PULL MYSELF BACK?

AM I OUT HERE ALL ALONE?

OHH, JEAN ...
SOMEBODY'S CALLIN' FOR YA, JEAN ...
--IS THAT ME?
AM I CALLIN' YOU, JEAN?
I NEED YOUR HELP.
CAN YOU HEAR ME, DARLIN'?
GIVE ME YOUR HAND, JEAN.
BRING ME--

...BACK!
LOGAN!
WE THOUGHT YOU WERE--
PROFESSOR XAVIER SAID YOU WERE--
I COULDN'T LET IT HAPPEN TO YOU AGAIN, DARLIN'!
LOGAN, YOUR LIFE-GRAPHS HAD BOTTOMED OUT ON THE MEDI-UNIT SCANNERS...
...Y-YOU CAME BACK--? FOR ME.
YOU GOT IT THE OTHER WAY AROUND, JEAN...
...IT WAS YOU WHO REACHED OUT AND TOOK MY HAND.

...AS YOUR PHYSICIAN, I CANNAE ABIDE IT!

WITH YOUR HEALING FACTOR SO WEAKENED AND YOUR BONES LEECHED O' THEIR ADAMANTIUM...

...THERE'S NAE TELLIN' WHAT HORRIBLE AND PERMA-NENT INJURY YE CAN INFLICT UPON YOUR THICK HEAD IN THE DANGER ROOM! IT'S ONLY BEEN TWO WEEKS, MAN. YE'VE GOT TO GIVE YE'SELF TIME!

I APPRECIATE YOUR CONCERN, MOIRA...

...BUT I NEED TO PROVE THAT I STILL DESERVE A PLACE ON THE TEAM--

YOU'LL ALWAYS HAVE A PLACE WITH THE X-MEN-- DON'T YOU KNOW THAT BY NOW?

ONLY IF I CAN PULL MY OWN WEIGHT, JEANIE.
DO I GET MY SHOT, CHARLIE?
AM I A CONTENDER?
VERY WELL...
LET'S SEE HOW WELL YOU PERFORM...
...AGAINST THE BATTLE DROIDS!
BE WARNED, LOGAN -- THESE ARE NOT INTER-ACTIVE HOLOGRAMS LIKE THE ONES YOUR TEAM-MATES WERE JUST SPARRING WITH--
--THESE BATTLE DROIDS ARE QUITE SOLID!
ONLY TWO O' THE WALKIN' CAN OPENERS?
I CAN EAT 'EM FOR BREAK-FAST!

SKRRAACKK!
-HE BARELY
-OT OUT OF
-HE WAY IN
TIME!
THAT LOOK ON HIS FACE-- IT WAS--
-FEAR.
THOOMP
YOU HAVE TO PUT A STOP TO THIS, CHARLES--
NO, MOIRA. I CANNOT. LOGAN HAS TO KNOW THIS ABOUT HIM-SELF...
"...HE HAS TO EXPERIENCE IT."
ZZZACK!
THOOM!
UNNNGH!

FWAMMMMM!
THAT'S ENOUGH!
GET HIM OUT OF THERE!
HASN'T HE SUFFERED ENOUGH?
HE DON'T GIVE UP, THIS ONE! C'EST HÓMME EST UN LION!
HE'S GETTING UP--
LOGAN, IT'S UP TO YOU...
OH, WOLVIE--!
...SHALL I TERMINATE THE EXERCISE?
I'M JUST GETTIN' WARMED UP, CHARLIE!
THESE PILES O' SCRAP METAL AND CIRCUIT BOARDS AIN'T GOT NOTHIN' ON THE OL' CANUCKLE-HEAD!
TURN IT OFF, PROFES-SOR!
DON'T LISTEN TO HER, CHARLIE--
I MAY BE DOWN, BUT I AIN'T OUT AND I'M STILL--
--THE BEST AT WHAT I DO!
SCHUKK
OCH!!!
MY GOD.

AARRRRGGHH
--HIS CLAWS--
--THEY'RE BONE!!? HOW CAN THAT BE!?
GET DOWN THERE!
GET HIM TO RETRACT THEM!
--STOP THE BLEEDING!
SHUT DOWN THOSE BATTLE DROIDS!
WOLVIE!!!
OCH! I NEED THE MEDI-CART!
I SHOULD HAVE SUSPECTED--!
NUMBER TWO SUTURES!
OF COURSE! IF THE ADAMANTIUM WAS LEECHED--
HIS HEALING FACTOR USED TO CLOSE THE WOUNDS!
--COAGULANT!
--WHAT ABOUT HIS HEALING FACTOR!?
YOU MEAN, EVERY TIME HE--
WOLLLLVIE!
WHEEL IN THE AUTO-CLAVE!
--AND TWO UNITS OF WHOLE BLOOD!
GET OUTTA MY WAY! I GOTTA GO TO HIM!!!!

...YOU HAVE TO RELAX AND LET YOUR BODY HEAL ITSELF.
MOIRA SAID, "JUBILEE, IT'S UP TO YOU TO SEE THAT LOGAN DOESN'T EXERRRRRT HIM-SELF AND GET ...
"...OVERWRRRROUGHT."

I SAID, WOLVIE DOESN'T GET OVERRRWRROUGHT, HE GETS EVEN!
THAT'S WHAT I--

CHOMP CRUNCH --THED.
WHAT'S BUGGIN' YA, DARLIN'?

NUFFINK.
DON'T WANNA CHOMP DUMP ANYFING HEAFFY ON YOU WHEN YOU'RE 'SPOSSED TO BE CHOMP CRUNCH 'CUPEWATING.
S'NOTHIN'.
FO'GEDDID.
WILLY. CHOMP
S'AWRITE. CRUNCH
SUIT YERSELF DARLIN

CHOMP CRUNCH
CHOMP CRUNCH
PAF!
HUH?
WHAT WAS THAT FER???
I CAN CONTROL MY PAFS BETTER NOW.
F I PLACE THEM JUST RIGHT AND JICE THEM UP THE MAX, CAN DO A LOT F DAMAGE...
...EVEN KILL.
I NEVER THOUGHT THAT MY HATE FOR THOSE TWO CREEPS WHO KILLED MY PARENTS COULD AMPLIFY MY POWERS...
...IT WAS LIKE WAKING UP WITH A LOADED GUN IN MY HAND!
SCHLIKK!
AND YA CHOSE THE OL' CANUCKLE-HEAD TO HAVE A HEART-TO-HEART WITH ABOUT IT?
DARLIN', THERE'S THINGS ABOUT MYSELF I AIN'T GOT CLUE ONE ABOUT...

...LIKE, IF THESE *CLAWS* O' MINE ARE *BONE*--
--THEN, I MUST'VE BEEN *BORN* WITH 'EM!
SHUKK!
HOW CAN YOUR HANDS *HEAL* IF YOU KEEP--?
I POP 'EM OUT A FEW TIMES A DAY NOW.
KEEPS THE CHANNEL OPEN.
LIKE PIERCED EARS.
SO IT STOPPED HURTING?
NOPE.
OH.
HOW COME I CAN'T REMEMBER THEM BEFORE THEY WAS BONDED WITH *ADAMANTIUM?* HOW COME I ALWAYS *THOUGHT* THEY WERE IMPLANTS?
I GUESS *MY* PROBLEMS AREN'T VERY IMPORTANT COMPARED TO--
THEY ARE TO *ME*, DARLIN'.
BEFORE I CAME TO THIS PLACE, I WAS LIKE WALKIN' IN A RED HAZE ALL THE TIME.
THERE WAS STUFF ROLLIN' AROUND INSIDE O' ME, I DON'T KNOW *WHAT* IT WAS OR WHERE IT CAME FROM AND I WAS *ANGRY* ALL THE TIME, LIKE SOME HUNGRY, HURT ANIMAL STALKIN' THROUGH THE WOODS...

...THEN I CAME TO SALEM CENTER--
--AND IT WAS LIKE COMIN' HOME.
'CAUSE HOME IS WHERE YA DON'T HAVE TO EXPLAIN YOURSELF. 'CAUSE EVERYBODY KNOWS WHAT YOU'RE ALL ABOUT.
ALL US MOTHERLESS CHILDREN WANDERIN' THROUGH THE STORM, AND ALL OF A SUDDEN THERE'S A LIGHT IN A WINDOW AN' SOMEBODY TO TAKE US IN AND CLOSE THE DOOR AGAINST THE WIND.
OL' CHARLIE XAVIER.
YOU STICK WITH THE PROFESSOR, DARLIN'. HE CAN HELP YOU DEAL WITH YOUR POWERS.
HE CAN SHOW YOU HOW TO LIVE WITH IT. TO HAVE MEANIN'. THAT'S THE TICKET.
PAF!
FOOOT!
WHAT ABOUT YOU, WOLVIE? YOU SOUND LIKE YOU'RE NOT GONNA BE AROUND TO HELP ME OUT...
PUFF PUFF PUFF PUFF
GACK! KOF KOF
HACKKKK!
YOU STICK WITH CHARLIE XAVIER, AND HE'LL SET YOU STRAIGHT.
YOU GOT A LIGHT, DARLIN'?
GACK! TIME I QUIT THESE NASTY OL' THINGS, ANYWAY!

Dear Jubilee,
This is just to say that I am going away because it is the best thing I can do.
Without my adamantium-laced skeleton, and my healing factor not being what it used to be, I ain't hardly the best any longer.
I am just a liability to the rest of the team. I should retire my pinstripes before I get traded to the minors.
I understand that you are going through a difficult time right now. I wish I could stay here for you, but it just cannot be.
Jubilee

I am not going to tell you that you have to be strong, because you are one of the strongest people I have ever met.
You have the strength to go on being happy and have fun, despite the bad things that happened to you and the horrors you have seen.
Professor C. Xavier
Jean and Scott

LIVE TO RIDE
RIDE TO LIVE
HARLEY-DAVIDSON
You don't have a callus on your soul like some folks who have had it half as bad as you.

So, you go on laughing, darling.
Hold on to your wonder--
--Aww, here I go getting preachy!

You just stick to professor Xavier like glue, do you hear me? He did all right by this old Canuckle-Head and he will do good by you!

Do not be sad for me, Jubilee. I am starting a whole new phase in my life! A new adventure!

So, think of me sometimes, and smile, because that is how I will always remember you.

And remember that I will always miss you...

...more than you will ever know.

Love,
Logan

Marvel Universe: Flair '94 trading-card art by Greg Capullo, Richard Bennett, Adam Kubert, John Romita Jr. & Joe Quesada

ARVEL®
MICS

IEN
IVERSARY
SUE

5 US
CAN
2530

APPROVED BY THE COMICS CODE AUTHORITY

EXCALIBUR

FATAL
ATTRACTIONS
FINALE

A COMRADE'S
RETURN...
A FRIENDSHIP
LOST!

Excalibur #71 hologram
original pencils by Joe Madureira,
and inks by Harry Candelario

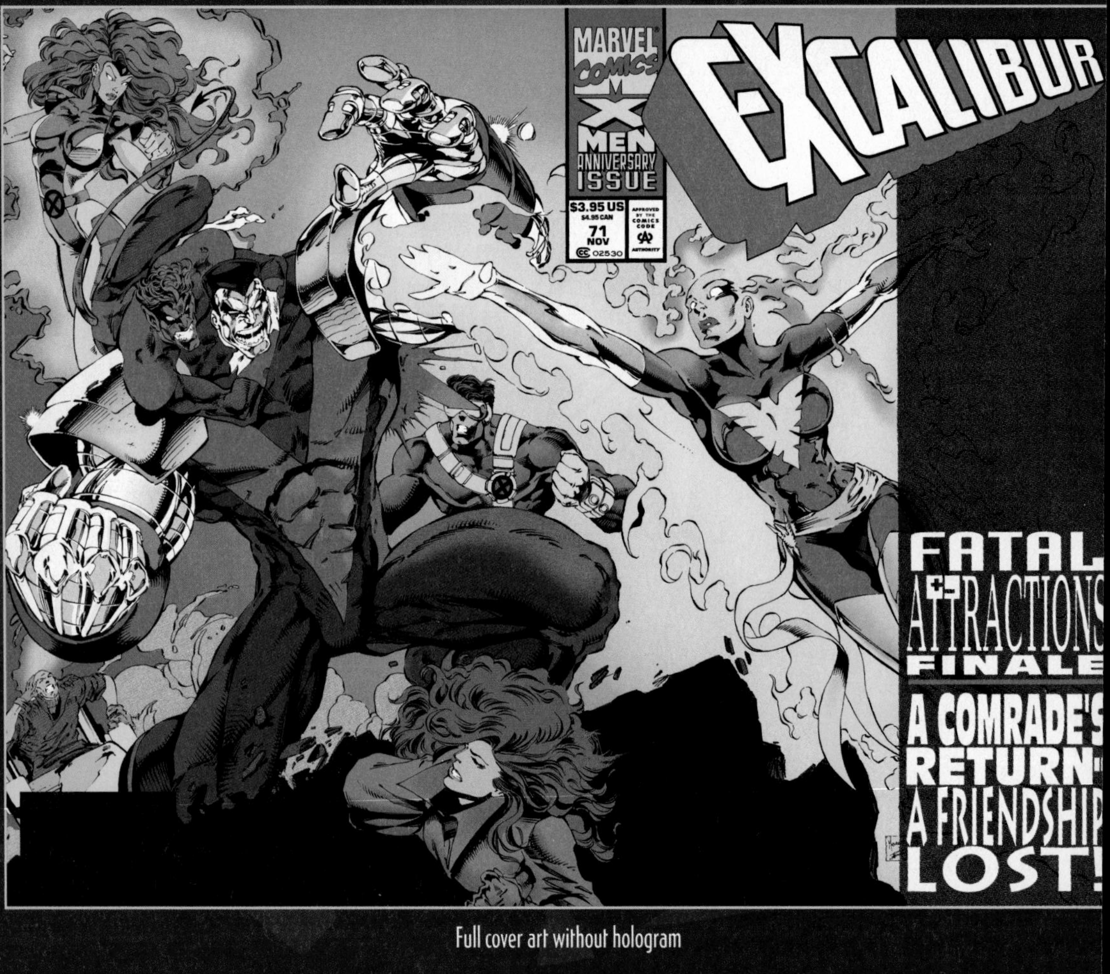

Full cover art without hologram

MUIR ISLE.
SOMEWHERE OFF THE COAST OF SCOTLAND.
I HAVE TO SAY, LAD-- I'M MORE THAN A WEE BIT DIS-APPOINTED!
THE FLATSCANS I SLAUGHTERED PUT UP MORE OF A FIGHT-- *
--AND MOST OF THEM WAS IN A COMA!
OVER ONE HUNDRED HUMANS DIED IN YOUR "GENETIC CLEANSING," SPOOR--
--AND YOU DARE TO MAKE LIGHT OF IT?!
I'M AN ACOLYTE, NIGHTCRAWLER--
--THERE ISNAE MUCH WE DON'T DARE!
*X-FACTOR #92.--SUDS

CROSSING SWORDS
SCOTT LOBDELL WRITER KEN LASHLEY, DARICK ROBERTSON, MATTHEW RYAN PENCILERS CAM SMITH, RANDY ELLIOTT, RANDY EMBERLIN, MARK NELSON INKERS BILL OAKLEY/ PAT BROSSEAU/DAVE SHARPE LETTERERS JOE ROSAS COLORIST SUZANNE GAFFNEY EDITOR BOB HARRAS GROUP EDITOR TOM DEFALCO EDITOR IN CHIEF
IF'N YE HAD HALF A BRAIN--
ENOUGH!
TWAP!
¡URNK¡ YUIR TAIL--?!
--YE'D JOIN US INSTEAD OF FIGHTIN' US!
EVEN YUIR BUDDY COLOSSUS HAD ENOUGH SENSE TO--
DESPITE THE STRAIN OF THE PAST SEVERAL MONTHS--
--PETER RASPUTIN HAS NO TASTE FOR BLOOD, HUMAN OR OTHER-WISE!
?!
ACTUALLY
...I AM TIRED OF PUTTING UP...
...WITH HOMICIDAL ZEALOTS LIKE YOU!
NOW, YOU ANSWER ME THIS--
--ARE YOU WILLING TO MARTYR YOURSELF FOR MAG-NETO'S CAUSE?!
ARE YOU PREPARED TO DIE AT THE HANDS OF YOUR ENEMY?!
TRUTH TO TELL, LAD...

WHOULMPH!
PUH-LEAZE, KURT-- ARE YE TRYIN' TO TELL ME YE NEVER HAD THE URGE--
--T'STOP MODDLE-CODDLING EVERY JOE WHAT ANNOYS YE?
KRAK!
ONCE HE SEES, CLEARLY, THAT THE ACOLYTES ARE NOTHING MORE THAN GENETIC TERRORISTS--
--HE WILL RETURN TO THE X-MEN!*
* IT ALL HAPPENED IN UNCANNY X-MEN #304.--SUZE
NEIN!
VAS--?! WHAT AM I DOING?
IT IS AS IF I CANNOT CONTROL MYSELF!
...NUTHIN' WOULD MAKE ME HAPPIER!
YE'SEE, JUST BECAUSE I KILLED THOSE HUMANS--
--DOESN'T MEAN I DINNAE UNDERSTAND IT WAS WRONG!
ANYMORE THAN IT IS WRONG... TO MURDER A MURDERER, NO?
THUD!

PHEWWW.
THAT WAS CLOSE.
PHOENIX? SHADOWCAT? I...
...I WANTED TO KILL HIM.
I-I DO NOT KNOW WHAT CAME OVER ME.
HE DID, KURT-- SPOOR'S POWER IS TO EMIT A PSYCHO-STIMULATORY PHEROMONE.
ACCORDING TO DR MACTAGGERT'S STUDIES... THIS PARTICULAR ACOLYT HAS A DEATH WISH.
WHEN HE RECOVERS FROM THE PSIONIC SHOCK TO HIS SYSTEM...?
...HE'LL BE LESS THAN ELATED THAT I MANAGED TO PHASE HIM INTO AN EPHEMERAL STATE--
--AN INSTANT BEFORE PHOENIX BROUGHT YOU BACK TO YOUR SENSES.
AREN'T WE WASTING AN AWFUL LOT OF COMPASSION--
--ON A GENETIC SUPREMACIST?
"THERE BUT FOR THE GRACE OF GOD..." RACHEL.
NU-UNH. I DON'T BUY THAT, KURT. THERE ARE GOOD GUYS--
--LIKE US...
...AND THEN THERE'S EVERYBODY ELSE.
SURELY, MEIN FREUND YOU DO NOT BELIEVE IT IS THAT SIMPLE A DISTINCTION?

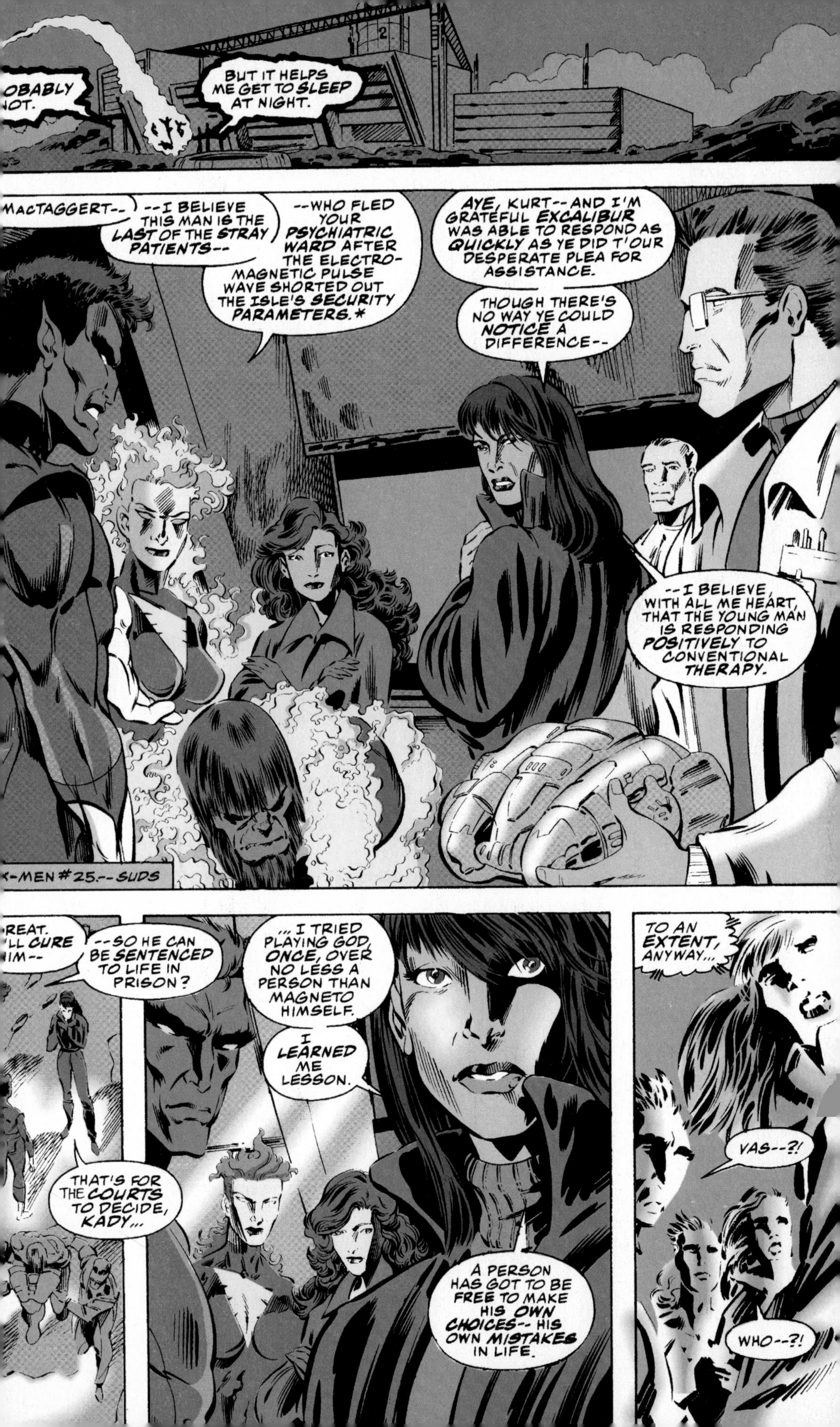

MACTAGGERT--
--I BELIEVE THIS MAN IS THE LAST OF THE STRAY PATIENTS--
--WHO FLED YOUR PSYCHIATRIC WARD AFTER THE ELECTRO-MAGNETIC PULSE WAVE SHORTED OUT THE ISLE'S SECURITY PARAMETERS.*
AYE, KURT--AND I'M GRATEFUL EXCALIBUR WAS ABLE TO RESPOND AS QUICKLY AS YE DID T'OUR DESPERATE PLEA FOR ASSISTANCE.
THOUGH THERE'S NO WAY YE COULD NOTICE A DIFFERENCE--
--I BELIEVE, WITH ALL ME HEART, THAT THE YOUNG MAN IS RESPONDING POSITIVELY TO CONVENTIONAL THERAPY.
X-MEN #25.--SUDS

AFTER ALL-- THERE'S STILL SOMETHING TO BE SAID FOR DOING THE RIGHT THING.
WOULDN'T YOU AGREE, PROFESSOR?
CERTAINLY-- IT'S FOR THAT VERY REASON WE'VE COME ALL THE WAY FROM THE UNITED STATES--
--TO ENLIST EXCALIBUR'S AID IN REDRESSING A MOST GREIVIOUS ERROR ON THE X-MEN'S PART.
WE WOULD'VE CALLED AHEAD, PEOPLE--BUT AS YOU'LL DISCOVER, WE COULDN'T RISK ANYONE LEARNING WHAT WE HAVE PLANNED.
IF WE COULD STEP INSIDE AND DISCUSS THIS...? TIME IS OF THE ESSENCE!
WHEN PROFESSOR XAVIER, JEAN GREY AND CYCLOPS COME KNOCKING--
--YOUR WISH IS OUR ETC., ETC., ETC. ...
I SINCERELY HOPE YOU FEEL THAT WAY, KATHERINE...
--WHAT WE MUST--
--DO IN ORDER TO SAVE ONE OF OUR OWN.

FIVE MINUTES LATER...
YOU CAN'T BE SERIOUS?!
KATZEN, PLEASE. WE SHOULD HEAR THEM OUT.
I'M AFRAID NOT, KURT. TIME IS OF THE ESSENCE, AND WE CAN ILL AFFORD THE LUXURY OF AN OPEN DEBATE.
IF WE STAND ANY CHANCE AT ALL OF HEALING PETER'S HEAD WOUND...
...AND, BY EXTENSION, RECLAIMING HIM FROM THE ACOLYTES...
...WE MUST ACT IMMEDIATELY!

AND TO DO THAT --YOU NEED ME TO SET HIM UP? TO BETRAY HIM?!
NOT EVEN AN OPTION, SIR!
WITH A THOUGHT, KITTY PRYDE PHASES HER BODY IN SYNC WITH THE CHAIR...
...AND DROPS THROUGH TO THE FLOOR BELOW.

I CAN'T BELIEVE...
...BE-LIEVE...
...THIS PLACE?! THE TECHNOLOGY IS SO... BIZARRE, ALIEN EVEN BY SHI'AR STANDARDS!
A MYSTERY FOR ANOTHER TIME, PERHAPS...

FOR THE MOMENT... I NEED YOU, KATHERINE--
--FIRST AND FOREMOST, TO STOP CARRYING ON LIKE A SPOILED CHILD WHO CLAMPS HER HANDS OVER HER EARS WHEN SHE DOESN'T WISH TO HEAR SOMETHING!
unh-uh, PROFESSOR...
...WE'VE HAD THIS CONVERSATION ONCE TOO OFTEN, WHEN I WAS STILL A MINOR, LIVING AT THE MANSION.
THE WHOLE STERN-BUT-BENEVOLENT PATRIARCH RIFF ISN'T GOING TO WORK ANYMORE.
YOU HAVE A CASE TO MAKE--MAKE IT AS AN ADULT, ONE-ON-ONE.

YOU ARE RIGHT, OF COURSE, AND I... APOLOGIZE, KATHERINE.
I'VE BEEN UNDER A BIT OF A STRAIN AS OF LATE, AND I FEAR I MAY BE TAKING IT OUT ON THOSE CLOSEST TO ME.
hmmph. FUNNY YOU SHOULD PUT IT THAT WAY.
I HAVEN'T FELT PARTICULARLY CLOSE TO YOU SINCE KURT, RACHEL AND I LEFT THE X-MEN TO HELP CREATE EXCALIBUR...
...AND IT DIDN'T SEEM TO BOTHER YOU AT ALL AFTER YOU RETURNED FROM THE SHI'AR AND DISCOVERED WE WERE GONE.
ON THE CONTRARY...
...IT HURT ME DEEPLY.
EVERY TIME I LOSE A STUDENT, WHETHER TO GRADUATION--
--TO ANOTHER TEAM SUCH AS YOURS, X-FACTOR AND X-FORCE--
--THAT LOSS TEARS AT A PART OF MY VERY SOUL. BUT I WOULD NOT BE MUCH OF A TEACHER...
...A "FATHER, IF YOU WOULD...
...IF I DID NOT LET EACH AND EVERY ONE OF YOU FIND YOUR OWN PATH.
EVERYONE, APPARENTLY, BUT PETER.
THAT IS DIFFERENT.
WHY?
BECAUSE HE'S THE FIRST ONE TO OPT TO JOIN MAGNETO?
BECAUSE HE IS SUFFERING FROM A SEVERE HEAD TRAUMA--*
*INFLICTED IN X-MEN ANN. #17.--SUZ.
--WHICH, IN AN EFFORT TO HELP HIS SISTER, I ADMIT I NEGLECTED TO ATTEND TO.
I AM NOT ABOVE MAKING MISTAKES, SHADOWCAT--
--ANY MORE THAN I AM ABOVE ASKING FOR HELP IN CORRECTING THEM.
YOUR HELP, KATHERINE...
...PLEASE?

IT WAS CREATED AS A "HEAVEN" FOR MUTANTS--
--AND SITUATED, ACCORDINGLY, AMONG THE STARS.
AND WHILE THE WOULD-BE MESSIAH KNOWN AS MAGNETO IS NOT CURRENTLY IN A STATE WHERE HE MIGHT LEAD HIS FOLLOWERS...
...THERE IS ANOTHER WHO HAS STEPPED FORWARD FROM THE FLOCK IN ORDER TO CARRY OUT THE WORD OF MAGNUS.
FOR THE THREATS TO THE MIGHTY FORTRESS THAT IS AVALON COME FROM MANY QUARTERS. SOME OBVIOUS...
...AND SOME LESS SO.
--CAN YOU HEAR ME, PETER?--
--AGNETIC INTERFERENCE--
--WANT TO BE BY YOUR SIDE... TO JOIN YOU AMONG--
BRRZZRT!
--FIND ANOTHER WAY! AN ALTERNATIVE TO THE--
SQUARRK!
I'LL BE WAITING --ALONE-- HERE ON MUIR ISLE. PLEASE DON'T LEAVE ME HERE, PETER...
WHAT DO YOU THINK, RASPUTIN?
I THINK THE KATYA I KNEW WOULD NEVER BETRAY ME.
IF SHE SAYS SHE WANTS TO JOIN ME HERE AMONG MAGNETO'S CHOSEN...
...THEN I BELIEVE HER WITH ALL MY HEART.
A HEART, I SHOULD ADD, YOU HAVE PLEDGED TO MAGNUS.
THAT SHOULD GO WITHOUT SAYING.
BY YOUR LEAVE, EXODUS?

I GRANT YOU ONE HOUR.
BUT GO WITH THE UNDERSTANDING THAT THIS WILL BE YOUR FINAL CONNECTION TO THE LIFE YOU ONCE KNEW.
THAT, ALSO, GOES WITHOUT SAYING. KITTY IS THE ONLY CONNECTION I HAVE LEFT TO MY FORMER EXISTENCE.
I DO NOT TRUST THIS SCION OF XAVIER, EXODUS.
YOU WOULD BE A FOOL IF YOU DID, VOGHT.
PETER RASPUTIN POSSESSES A TORTURED SOUL-- ONE RAVAGED BY THE LOSS OF HIS FAMILY...
...PEOPLE WHO MEANT MORE TO HIM THAN XAVIER AND HIS BROOD EVER WOULD --EVER COULD.
HE IS SUFFERING A CRISIS OF FAITH AT THIS MO-MENT. MAGNETO KNEW THIS WHEN HE INVITED COLOSSUS TO JOIN US.
WHETHER HE WILL EVER TRULY EMBRACE OUR WAY IS SOMETHING WE WILL NOT KNOW UNTIL HE SEVERS HIS TIES WITH THE X-MEN IN GENERAL...
...AND KITTY PRYDE IN PARTICULAR.
ONE HOUR, AMELIA... THEN BRING HIM BACK, ALIVE OR NOT.

ELSEWHERE...
THERE YOU GO, PROFESSOR.
NOW, WILL YOU BE HANDING ME MY THIRTY PIECES OF SILVER--
--OR DEPOSITING IT DIRECTLY INTO MY ACCOUNT?
YOU'RE BEING A BIT HARSH, KITTY-- ON BOTH PROFESSOR XAVIER AND YOURSELF.
IF IT'S OF ANY COMFORT, WE KNOW HOW MUCH OF A HARD DECISION THIS WAS FOR YOU-- ANY ADULT WOULD HAVE HAD A HARD TIME MAKING IT.
AND YOU PEOPLE SEEM TO HAVE A HARD TIME ACCEPTING ANY DECISION--
--THAT DOESN'T AGREE COMPLETELY WITH YOUR POINT OF VIEW.
THAT'S HARDLY A FAIR--
I DON'T FEEL VERY FAIR JUST NOW.
ACTUALLY, KITTY, I THINK YOU'RE SCARED... LIKE THE REST OF US.
SCARED, RAY?
SCARED THAT PETER MIGHT NOT CHANGE HIS MIND-- EVEN AFTER WE'VE HELPED HIM.
TELL ME, CYCLOPS... WHAT DO WE DO THEN?
I... DON'T KNOW, RACHEL.
I HONESTLY DON'T KNOW.

ELSEWHERE...
(CAMP VERDE, ARIZONA, TO BE EXACT...)
I have pinpointed the origination point, Nathan.
Muir Isle, Scotland.
I trust I should mobilize the rest of X-Force?
YOU TRUST WRONG, PROFESSOR!
I HAVE UNFINISHED BUSINESS WITH THE ACOLYTES--
K-CHIK!
--ON ACCOUNT OF THEIR ERSATZ LEADER REDUCING ME TO A CENTER-FOLD IN SPARE PARTS QUARTERLY.*
IN ALL LIKELIHOOD, COLOSSUS IS BEING SET UP. XAVIER ENGENDERS TOO MUCH LOYALTY FOR ME TO BELIEVE HIS FORMER STUDENTS ARE DEFECTING IN DROVES.
But according to the cross referents, there exists a very strong interpersonal relationship between Katherine Pryde and Peter Rasputin —
— on a MULTITUDE of different time continuim variants.
TRUST ME, PROFESSOR--HE'S BEING SET UP, AS SURE AS MY NAME IS CABLE.
Technically, your name is Nathaniel Day Spring Askani.
WHEN YOU'RE THROUGH PERFORMING FOR YOUR AUDIENCE OF ONE, I WANT TO BODYSLIDE AS CLOSE AS YOU CAN GET ME TO MUIR ISLE--
--COMPENSATING FOR THE ELECTRO-MAGNETIC INTER-FERENCE, OF COURSE.
*X-FORCE #25--THAT WAS THE LAST FOOTNOTE!

AMAZING, IS IT NOT...?
...THE AMOUNT OF TECHNOLOGY DR. MacTAGGERT HAS AMASSED IN AN EFFORT TO HELP UNDER-STAND--
--IN SOME CASES TREAT--
--THE MUTANT POPULATION OF THE WORLD.
REMEMBER, KURT-- MOIRA GAVE BIRTH TO ARGUABLY THE MOST DANGEROUS HOMO SUPERIOR IN RECORDED HISTORY.
SHE DEDICATED THE FIRST TWENTY YEARS OF KEVIN'S LIFE TO FINDING A WAY TO CURE HIM OF HIS GENETIC ABILITIES.
THIS SURGICAL PLATFORM-- AND THE FACT IT CAN WITHSTAND THE FULL BRUNT OF MY OPTIC BLAST--IS A TESTIMONY TO HER DEDICATION TO THE IMPACT PROTEUS' EXISTENCE HAD OVER HER.
ODD HOW EVEN IN THE FACE OF TRAGEDY, THERE ARE OFTEN SUCH WONDERS--SUCH MIRACLES--TO BE FOUND.
WE FIND THEM WHERE WE MAKE THEM
I DON'T THINK ANYONE KNOWS THAT BETTER THAN YOU AND I.
BUT TELL ME-- HOW ARE THE OTHER MEMBERS OF EXCALIBUR?
TRUTH TO TELL, MEIN FREUND--
--I DO NOT KNOW IF THERE ARE ANY OTHER MEMBERS OF EXCALIBUR!
KLIK!

CAPTAIN BRITAIN AND WIDGET, I FEAR, WERE LOST TO A CHRONOLOGICAL WAVE--
--WHEN WE WERE EN ROUTE FROM RACHEL'S FUTURE.
CERISE HAS OPTED TO SERVE THE SHI'AR EMPIRE, DESPITE THE TRUMPED UP CHARGES OF WAR CRIMES FILED AGAINST HER.
MEGGAN HAS BECOME LITTLE MORE THAN A CATATONIC WATER NYMPH SINCE BRIAN'S ABRUPT DEPARTURE--
--WITH THE LESS THAN MAGICALLY ADEPT FERON JOINING HER, FOR THE MOMENT, IN HER NEAR MINDLESS STATE...
DO NOT ASK...
KYLUN HAS SINCE RETURNED TO HIS SEARCH FOR HIS PARENTS--
--WHILE MICROMAX IS CURRENTLY IN THE STATES, WEIGHING A JOB OPTION...
...AS HEAD OF SECURITY OF A PLACE KNOW AS THE BRAN CORPORATI
"MUTANT" IS ANOTHER WORD FOR CHANGE, KURT--IT'S OUR ABILITY TO DO SO THAT KEEPS US GOING.
THAT IS KIND OF YOU TO SAY, SCOTT...
...BUT AS LEADER OF THE X-MEN, YOU HAVE NEVER HAD TO DEAL WITH YOUR TEAM DISSOLVING OUT FROM UNDER YOU.
YOU'D BE SURPRISED.
THERE WAS MORE THAN ONE TIME THE BOTTOM NEARLY DROPPED OUT FROM UNDER US--
--ONCE, EACH OF US CHOOSING TO GO OUR SEPARATE WAYS.
WITH YOU AS THEIR LEADER, NIGHTCRAWLER --I'M SURE EXCALIBUR IS MORE RESILIENT THAN EVEN YOU MIGHT REALIZE.

MEANWHILE, OUTSIDE...
I'D LIKE TO BELIEVE KURT PUT ME ON PERIMETER WATCH BECAUSE OF MY AWE-INSPIRING PHOENIX POWER.
BUT I KNOW BETTER.
THE ELF REALIZES I START ACTING LIKE AN EIGHT-YEAR-OLD EVERY TIME I'M ANYWHERE NEAR MY PARE--
--ANYWHERE NEAR SCOTT AND JEAN.
WHEN ARE YOU GOING TO GROW UP, RACHEL?
MY PARENTS WERE FROM ANOTHER TIME-LINE ALTOGETHER. THESE TWO OWE ME NOTHING!
YOU CAN KEEP THE RAIN OFF YOU, RACHEL--BUT YOU'RE STILL GOING TO CATCH YOUR DEATH IN THIS WEATHER.
YEAH.
SO?
WHAT DO YOU CARE?
YOU DON'T LIKE ME VERY MUCH, DO YOU?
IN A WAY, YOU'RE THE CLOSEST THING I HAVE TO A MOTHER.
I ALWAYS FIGURED YOU DIDN'T LIKE ME VERY MUCH.
"AFTER MY "RESURRECTION," I'LL ADMIT I WASN'T THRILLED TO FIND I HAD A TEENAGED DAUGHTER FROM ANOTHER TIME-STREAM--
--BUT THAT WAS MY PROBLEM...
ACTUALLY...
...I LOVE YOU.
...AND I, SELFISHLY, MADE IT YOURS.
I'M SORRY.

BUT THAT'S NOT WHY I CAME UP HERE.
I'M ABOUT TO DO SOMETHING THAT MAY OR MAY NOT HAVE A PROFOUND EFFECT ON YOUR LIFE.
IF IT WORKS OUT, YOU STAND A REALLY GOOD CHANCE OF BEING BORN SOMETIME IN THE IMMEDIATE FUTURE.
BUT HOW IS THAT POSSIBLE? THAT WOULD MEAN YOU AND SCOTT WOULD HAVE TO HAVE A KID.
AND THAT WOULD NEVER HAPPEN... UNLESS...
...UNLESS...
YOU MEAN--
THAT'S THE PLAN.
I THINK IT'S--
--BUT MOIRA'S SENSOR'S HAVE DETECTED PETER'S APPROACH!
WE MUST ACT IMMEDIATELY-- FOR WE WON'T GET ANOTHER CHANCE.
I'M ON MY WAY, SIR.
GO GET 'EM... MOM.
"MOM," HUH?

WITHIN THE MINUTE, EVERYONE HAS TAKEN HIS PLACE ...
HOW DID THIS HAPPEN?
WASN'T IT YESTERDAY I STEPPED OUT OF THE CAB IN FRONT OF THAT MASSIVE MANSION IN WESTCHESTER--
--DETERMINED I WAS NOT ONLY GOING TO BE AN X-MAN...
...BUT I WAS GOING TO BE MRS. PETER RASPUTIN?
OR MS. KATHERINE PRYDE-RASPUTIN?
OR KATYA ANNALOVITCH RASPUTIN?
CHARLES, YOU PROMISED ME YOU WOULD TAKE IT EASY AFTER YOU USED THE PSIONIC EXO-SKELETON TO CON-FRONT MAGNETO.
WHICH IS WHY YOU ARE HERE, JEAN -- NOW SHUSH, PLEASE.
KIDS.
I AM PICKING UP COLOSSUS' PSI-IMPRINT...
...HE IS HERE.
...PREPARE YOURSELVES, EVERYONE ...
JUST AS CYCLOPS FIGURED, THEY'RE TELE-PORTING HIM DOWN TO EARTH USING VOGHT'S TRAN-SUBSTANTIATION POWER!

KATYA?
OH, PETER-- I KNEW YOU'D COME! I KNEW YOU COULDN'T...
...POSSIBLY HAVE...
...CHANGED...
...THAT MUCH?
"CHANGED," KATYA? NO-- I DO NOT BELIEVE I HAVE CHANGED AT ALL.
RATHER IT WAS THE WORLD WHICH CHANGED AROUND ME.
CHANGED TO THE POINT WHERE I COULD--CAN-NOT--BELIEVE IN THE PROFESSOR'S METHODS ANYMORE.
MAGNETO AND THE ACOLYTES WHO FOLLOW HIM UNDERSTAND THAT WE CANNOT SIT PASSIVELY AS THE HUMANS SEEK TO SLAY US...
...TO KILL MUTANTS WITH THE SAME SAVAGE IGNORANCE WHICH TOOK THE LIVES OF MY PARENTS SIMPLY BECAUSE THEY GAVE BIRTH TO MUTANTS--
--ANYMORE THAN WE CAN CONTINUE TO ALLOW SUCH MADMEN AS MY BROTHER AND STRYFE TO VISIT DEATH UPON OUR GENETIC BRETHREN.
IMAGINE, KATYA, HOW HAPPY I AM--
--TO DISCOVER YOU HAVE COME TO THE SAME CONCLUSIONS!

'T THAT MOMENT, ON THE FAR SIDE OF MUIR ISLE...
gain, I apologize for the convenience.
YEAH, AND YOUR SINCERITY IS JUST ABOUT OOZING OUT OF EVERY ONE OF YOUR COMPUTER CHIPS.
FORGET IT, PROFESSOR. I'LL FIND THE ACOLYTES MY-SELF.
OR... YOU COULD ALWAYS ASK ME.
POLITELY.
YOU REALLY WANT TO MAKE IT UP TO ME?! SCAN THE AREA FOR HOSTILES AND TRY TO COME UP WITH SPECIFIC DIRECTIONS ONCE I GET TOPSIDE.
hat may not be possible at is moment.
gain, the electro-magnetic ulse makes it considerably fficult to —
WHAT'S GOING ON HERE, PROFESSOR?!
MY MIND HAS ALWAYS BEEN OUT OF REACH OF PSI-SENSITIVES IN THIS TIMELINE...
...SO TELL ME WHO'S PUSHING MY BUTTONS, AND HOW?!
Scanning...
SCAN FASTER!

ALLOW ME, CABLE.
I RECOGNIZE THIS ENERGY SIGNATURE, PROFESSOR ...WHICH MEANS THE PERSON RESPONSIBLE--
--IS PHOENIX!
SINCE WE'RE NO DOUBT GOING TO SPEND THE NEXT TWENTY MINUTES SLUGGING IT OUT, TO KEEP YOU FROM INTERFERING WITH OUR PLANS TO HELP COLOSSUS...
...THERE'S NO NEED TO BE SO FORMAL.
YOU CAN CALL ME RACHEL SUMMERS.
?!
Nathan—?
QUIET!
YOU ... SAY THAT--
--AS IF IT SHOULD MEAN SOMETHING TO ME.
MAYBE ... BECAUSE IT DOES?

THE ACOLYTES ARE FAR FROM PERFECT, KATYA--
--THE ATROCITIES THEY COMMITTED UNDER CORTEZ'S REIGN WERE UNFORGIVABLE.
BUT EXODUS, I AM CONVINCED, HAS A FIRMER GRASP OF MAGNETO'S COMMANDMENTS.
"COMMANDMENTS," PETER? L-LISTEN TO YOURSELF...
...YOU'RE TALKING AS IF MAGNETO WAS YOUR OWN PERSONAL SAVIOR.
I KNOW THAT HE IS A MAN OF FLESH AND BLOOD LIKE ANY OTHER--
-- JUST AS I KNOW HE HAS LIVED AN ENTIRE LIFE DEDICATED TO HIS IDEALS.
HAD I BEEN AS STRONG -- AS BRAVE AS HE -- PERHAPS MY SISTER, MY ENTIRE FAMILY, WOULD STILL BE SAFE ON OUR FARM ON THE UST-ORDANSKI COLLECTIVE.
NOW, JEAN-- GRAB HIM PSIONICALLY!
I WOULD... DO SO MYSELF...
...IF I COULD.
NO, CHARLES.
NOT YET.
WE TRIED IT THE PROFESSOR'S WAY, KATYA--
--NO ONE TRIED HARDER THAN I.
BUT DON'T YOU SEE, PETER...? IT WASN'T THE DREAM THAT FAILED YOU.
IT WAS THE REALITY.

JEAN, I INSIST!
EVERY INSTANT YOU REFUSE TO ACT, YOU PLACE KITTY IN GREATER JEOPARDY!
I DON'T THINK EITHER OF US BELIEVES THAT, CHARLES.
DESPITE EVERYTHING THAT HAS HAPPENED--
--EVERYTHING HE HAS ENDURED...
...PETER WOULD NEVER DO ANYTHING TO HURT KITTY.
YOU--
--YOU ARE NOT COMING WITH ME...
...ARE YOU?
NO.
AND I CAN'T LET YOU LEAVE.
NOT YET.

YOU -- YOU'VE PHASED ME...?!
...SO THAT I CAN'T MOVE-- CAN'T ESCAPE!
I HAD TO, PETER-- FOR YOUR OWN GOOD.
DON'T STRUGGLE, COLOSSUS--WE'RE NOT GOING TO DO ANYTHING TO HURT YOU!
THESE RESTRAINTS WILL ALLOW US TO HELP YOU.
NO! DON'T YOU PEOPLE UNDERSTAND?!
I DON'T WANT YOUR "HELP"!
NOT AT THIS MOMENT, PETER--BUT SOMEDAY, I TRUST...
KLIK
...YOU WILL APPRECIATE THE EFFORT.
WITH THE SHACKLES IN PLACE, COLOSSUS IS UNABLE TO MOVE...
...UNABLE EVEN TO UTTER A SOUND.
BUT HIS EXPRESSION OF RAGE--
--OF A MAN BETRAYED BY HIS LOVE--
--SPEAKS VOLUMES.
IT IS A SIGHT KITTY PRYDE WILL REMEMBER...
...EVERY DAY, FOR THE REST OF HER LIFE.

NOT FAR AWAY...
I DON'T SUPPOSE YOU'D CONSIDER LETTING US HANDLE THIS MESS "IN HOUSE"?
DON'T TRY TO CONFUSE THE ISSUE! PETER MADE HIS DECISION--
--I INTEND TO SEE THAT HE DEALS WITH THE CONSEQUENCES.
WOK
URNGH!
JUDGE?
JURY?
AND EXECUTIONER?
GOODGOLLY-GOODGOSH, CABLE--
--WHERE WOULD THE WORLD BE WITHOUT YOU?
TRUST ME...
...YOU DON'T WAN TO KNOW.
BRAKT!
ALL BETS WERE OFF THE MOMENT COLOSSUS LEFT THE X-MEN TO BECOME AN ACOLYTE.
GUILTY BY ASSOCIATION, IS IT?
OR HASN'T IT OCCURRED TO YOU PEOPLE THAT HE'S CAST HIS LOT WITH A GROUP OF HOMICIDAL RELIGIOUS ZEALOTS?
Burying her under a ton of rock?
SHE'S THE PHOENIX!
A COSMIC ENTITY!
WHY?
DID I OVER-REACT? I'M N BEIN' TOO TOUG ON HER. I JUST KNOW WHAT I'M AGAINST.
A tad.

MMP.
ALWAYS WONDERED IF THAT WOULD WORK.
HOW DID SHE DO THAT?
Apart from her responsibilities as vessel for the Phoenix power. . .
. . .it appears Ms. Summers is what will colloquially be referred to in our century as a "time tripper."
Possessed of the ability to propel herself along the chronological continuim —
--I PUSHED MYSELF TEN SECONDS INTO THE FUTURE, TO AVOID BEING CRUSHED BY THE ROCKS!
YOUR COMPUTER BUDDY IS PRETTY SMART, CABLE.
BUT...
...THE PROFESSOR WAS ON AN INTERNAL MODEM.
YOU SHOULDN'T HAVE BEEN ABLE TO HEAR HIM INSIDE MY HEAD!
THERE ARE A LOT OF THINGS I SHOULDN'T BE ABLE TO DO.
IN FACT I KIND OF PRIDE MYSELF ON BEING--
--UNPREDICTABLE?!
YEAH. SO I SEE.

THE LAB...
FUNNY.
FOR YEARS, I HAD THIS WHOLE "REUNION FANTASY" ALL PLANNED OUT.
ONE-PART, FOURTEEN YEAR OLD SCHOOL GIRL CRUSH--
--TWO-PARTS, WOMAN WITH AN AGENDA.
SO MUCH FOR THE POWER OF POSITIVE THINKING.
WHILE I DO NOT WISH TO CUT YOU SHOR KITTY--I DO NOT DOUBT FOR A MOMENT THAT PETER'S NEWFOUND ALLIE WILL BE SEARCHING FOR HIM SOON.
WITH YOU PHASING HIS OMNIUM ARMOR TO THE POIN IT IS MALLEABLE WITHOUT BEING IN-TANGIBLE--
AN ISLAND MEDICAL RE-SEARCH CENTER, PERHAPS IN NEED--
--OF PEOPLE DETERMINED TO SEE IT SURVIVE ANY EXTERNAL THREAT TO ITS CONTINUED EXISTENCE?
BEGIN, CYCLOPS. OPTIC BLASTS TO .933%.
CHANNEL THE REPULSOR SCALPEL TO THE PREARRANGED COORDINATES--
"...AND PRAY THAT ALL THIS GUESS WORK PAYS OFF."

READY WHEN YOU ARE, SIR.
THEN LET US BEGIN.
...I'M CONFIDENT CYCLOPS' OPTIC BLAST WILL SERVE AS THE "REPULSOR SCALPEL" NEEDED TO CORRECT COLOSSUS' CONDITION.
--IN TANDEM WITH MINE AND JEAN'S PSIONIC MONITORING OF HIS BIO-GENETIC PROCESSES...
THIS, THEN, IS THE ENTIRE PURPOSE OF MUIR ISLE--
--A FACILITY DEDICATED TO ADRESSING THE PROBLEMS UNIQUE TO AN ENTIRE RACE.
BING!
WHA--?!
THE MONITOR WE JURY-RIGGED TO REGISTER VOGHT'S POWER...
...HAS JUST BEEN TRIGGERED!
CONTINUE YOUR RESPECTIVE ERRANDS OF MERCY--
--I WILL ATTEND TO OUR VISITOR!
"VISITORS!" KURT-- THERE'S APPARENTLY MORE THAN ONE!
BUT HER WORDS ARE LOST...

...AS OPPOSED TO THE PROFESSOR, WHO--
--FOR THE MOMENT--
--IS AT A LOSS FOR WORDS.
01 00 00 11 01 01 01 00 11 00 11 00 11 00 11
I COULD REALLY USE A SENSOR READING HERE!
01 00 00 11 01 01 01
PROFESSOR-- SNAP OUT OF IT!
01 00! Oh — my apologies, Nathan.
the overlapping readings — compounded with her tenuous connection to our own symbiotic relationship — was disconcerting at the very least.
as near as i can discern, Rachel is. . ."co-opting" her personal space in the time continuim with. . .another entity.
AND JUDGING BY THE COSTUME...
...IT ISN'T TOO TERRIBLY DIFFICULT TO FIGURE OUT WHO THE "OTHER ENTITY" IS!
I'm here...
Askani' son!
Find me...
...Help... me...
WHA--?!
WHAT DID YOU CALL ME?!
WH-WHAT ARE YOU... TALKING ABOUT?
DIDN'T CALL YOU ANYTHING...
It appears, Nathan — she has no clear memory of what just happened.
NOT GOOD ENOUGH, PROFESSOR.
NOT GOOD ENOUGH BY HALF.
I'M NOT A BIG FAN OF ANY MYSTERY I'M NOT AT THE CENTER OF... RACHEL.
WHICH MEANS YOU AND I ARE GOING T HAVE OUR-SELVES A MA ATHON SIT-DOWN UNTI WE CAN FIGUR OUT WHAT JUST HAPPE ED.
FINE WITH ME... NATHAN.

FEEL
REE TO
OOK ME
UP...
...AFTER YOU STOP SEEING DOUBLE!
ORNMPH
SORRY ABOUT THE PSIONIC-SUCKER PUNCH, CABLE...
...BUT ACCORDING TO THE STRAY THOUGHTS I'M PICKING UP FROM NIGHTCRAWLER, A COUPLE OF UNINVITED GUESTS ARE ABOUT TO CHECK IN HERE AT THE MUIR HOTEL.
ALL OF WHICH PLACES YOU AND YOURS ON THE LAST RUNG OF THE UNSOLVED RIDDLE LADDER.
I am certain he will appreciate your priorities.
"PROFESSOR"-- YOU'RE STILL CONSCIOUS?
On-line actually... but that is merely an argument of semantics.
CAN YOU EXPLAIN TO ME THIS... CONNECTION... I FEEL FOR THIS MAN?
THERE IS A BOND BETWEEN US, I CAN FEEL IT... IN MY HEART.
IN MY SOUL.
There are too many variables along the time continuim that must be analyzed before I could answer that question, Ms. Summers.
"COULD" OR "WOULD"?
Either.
This can all wait for another day...

"— your teammate may not be as fortunate."
THAT DARN PAPER BOY.
IT IS NEARLY SIX, AND STILL NO PAPER!
GASP!
--ACOLYTES WHATEVER IS DEFENSELESS ELF LIKE MOI TO DO?
SARCASM, NIGHTCRAWLER
SOMEHOW I EXPECTED LEADER OF TO BE A BIT MATURE... WITH THE PROVE HIMSELF.
I AM VOGHT-- AN ANCESTOR, OF SORTS, TO ALL WHO CALL THEMSELVES XAVIER'S CHILDREN!
KATU IS INUIN, AS WELL AS BEING A LIVING CONDUIT FOR INTERATMOSPHERIC ANOMOLIES.
WHILE UNUSCIONE CAN PROJECT A PSIONIC EXO-SKIN.

YOU ARE THINKING OF X-FACTOR.
BUT YOU ARE THE LAST PEOPLE TO GO CASTING STONES IN THE GLASS HOUSE OF INTERCHANGEABLE PERSONALITIES.
I HAVE STUDIED THE FILES ON THE ACOLYTES--AND I STILL HAVE TROUBLE TELLING YOU PEOPLE APART.
DANKE.
"THANK YOU" FOR WHAT?
I ALWAYS FIND THESE THINGS GO MUCH BETTER...
... WHEN I KNOW EXACTLY WHO IT IS I AM BEATING INTO SUBMISSION.
NOW THEN--
--WHO IS FIRST?

PETER... SON... I NEED YOU TO RELAX--TO TRIGGER YOUR TRANSFORMATION INTO YOUR HUMAN FORM.
... BUT MY... WOUND...
...IS HEALED. BUT THE TRAUMA TO YOUR SYSTEM WAS SO GREAT--
--I DON'T DARE COMMANDEER YOUR THOUGHTS.
IT'S UP TO YOU, PETER.
TRUST ME.
FWABOOM
ALL THAT PENT-UP ENERGY WITHIN HIM--
--HAS BEEN RELEASED!
THESE READINGS ARE OFF THE SCALE!
KITTY--GET CLEAR!
I'M FINE, CYCLOPS!
THE ENERGY HAS NO EFFECT ON ME IN MY PHASED FORM.
EVEN IF IT DID--NOTHING COULD GET ME TO LEAVE PETER'S SIDE...
...NOT UNTIL I KNOW IF HE'S ALL RIGHT!

ALL RIGHT," KATYA?
I DO NOT HONESTLY FEEL I WILL EVER BE "ALL RIGHT" AGAIN.
FOR THOUGH MY BODY HAS BEEN MENDED...
...I BELIEVE MY HEART MAY BE BEYOND REPAIR.
AND IN TRUTH, I DON'T KNOW THAT I'D WANT IT ANY OTHER WAY.

YOU DON'T MEAN THAT, PETER--YOU CAN'T.
CAN'T I?
DON'T YOU SEE--DON'T ANY OF YOU REALIZE--THAT IF I LET MYSELF FEEL ANTHING...
...IF I AM ANYTHING LESS THAN THE COLD AND HARD ARMORED WARRIOR IN BOTH FORM AND FUNCTION...

...THAT I WILL HAVE NOTHING LEFT BUT THE REALIZATION THAT...
...I FAILED ILLYANA.
DON'T EVER THINK THAT, PETER--EVEN FOR A MOMENT!

YOU DID EVERYTHING HUMANLY POSSIBLE.
THE LEGACY VIRUS IS SOMETHING YOU COULDN'T CONTROL.

I'M HER BROTHER...
...I SHOULD HAVE BEEN THERE.

I SHOULD HAVE BEEN THERE.
YOU WERE THERE.
IN HER EVERY THOUGHT.
YOU WERE THE SMILE ON HER FACE--
--THE LIGHT IN HER EYES.
YOU WERE THERE, PETER-- IN EVERY WAY THAT TRULY MATTERED.

THE FRONT LAWN.
NIGHTCRAWLER?
AH, THE CAVALRY.
FEEL FREE TO GRAB AN ACOLYTE DU JOUR AND START SLUGGING.
I'VE WAITED A LONG TIME TO DEFEAT YOU IN PSIONIC COMBAT, PHOENIX!
YEAH, WELL...
:UORLP!:
...EVERYONE SHOULD HAVE A DREAM.
ONE OF THESE DAYS, KATU--
--I LOOK FORWARD TO SEEING YOU ACTUALLY USE YOUR MUTANT POWER.
ZAKT
NOT TODAY--
--BUT SOMEDAY.
WE CAME HERE FOR RASPUTIN-- NOT TO ENGAGE YOU PEOPLE IN BATTLE!
IF I HAVE TO, I'LL PULL EVERY ACOLYTE PLANET-SIDE, IF THAT'S WHAT IT TAKES TO RECLAIM ONE OF OUR NUMBER!
I DO NOT SUPPOSE YOU WOULD BE INTERESTED IN A TRADE?
SPOOR FOR COLOSSUS?
AMOS ALLOWED HIMSELF TO BE CAPTURED BY THE AUTHORITIES, AND DESERVES WHATEVER FATE HE GETS!
BUT RASPUTIN CAME HERE IN GOOD FAITH-- AND SHOULD BE ALLOWED TO LEAVE IF HE SO WISHES!
I FEEL THE SAME WAY.
VAS--?!

THERE IS NO NEED TO CONTINUE THIS FIGHT, VOGHT.
I HAVE EVERY INTENTION OF HONORING MY WORD TO EXODUS...
...AND WILL RETURN WITH YOU TO AVALON.
BUT YOU SHOULD KNOW THIS-- I AM DOING SO BECAUSE I GENUINELY BELIEVE MY PRESENCE MIGHT MAKE A DIFFERENCE...
...THAT I CAN CONVINCE YOU THAT THE MAN WHO WAS MAGNETO STOOD FOR MUCH MORE THAN BLOOD AND VIOLENCE AND DEATH.
THAT THE DIFFERENCE BETWEEN HIS GOAL AND THAT OF XAVIER'S IS NEARLY IDENTICAL IN INTENT--
--IF NOT IN EXECUTION.
ON BEHALF OF ALL OF US, RASPUTIN--
--WE LOOK FORWARD TO WHATEVER LIGHT YOU CAN SHINE UPON OUR LORD SAVIOR.
GOODBYE, GODSPODIN XAVIER.
FOR ALTHOUGH I DON'T BLAME YOU FOR MY SISTER'S DEATH--
--I DO NOT FEEL YOU, OR ANY OF US WHO PURSUE YOUR DREAM--
--HAVE DONE ALL WE CAN TO HELP OUR KIND.
WHEN YOU FOUND ME, I WAS AN ATHEIST... RAISED TO SERVE THE STATE. FOR BETTER OR FOR WORSE, YOU MADE ME BELIEVE IN SOMETHING--
--AND I CAN NEVER RETURN TO MY BELIEF IN "NOTHING."
FOR THAT AT LEAST, I WILL ALWAYS BE GRATEFUL.

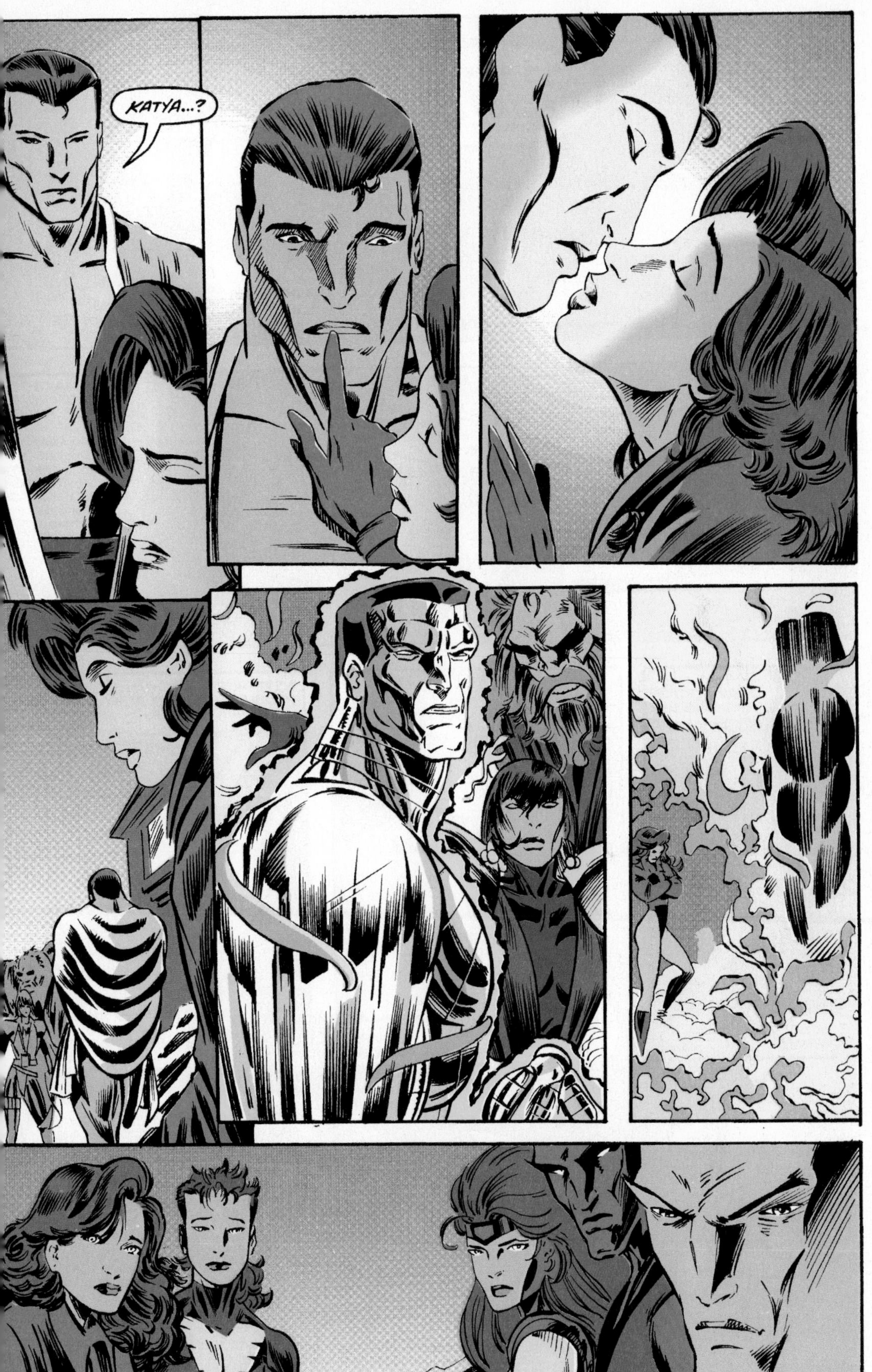
KATYA...?

SUNSET...

WE'RE ALL SET TO DEPART, KURT. OF COURSE WE'LL DROP YOU OFF IN **ENGLAND** ON OUR WAY.

DANKE, SCOTT-- BUT THAT WON'T BE **NECESSARY**.

KITTY, RACHEL AND I HAVE **DISCUSSED** IT, AND WE FEEL THAT EXCALIBUR MIGHT **FUNCTION BEST** AS AN **EXTENSION** OF MOIRA'S WORK HERE ON MUIR ISLE.

THE "ENCHANTED BLADE" SERVING AS **METAPHOR** FOR A **SCALPEL**, IF YOU WI --CUTTING **DEEP** INT THE PROBLEMS THA FALL BETWEEN TH CRACKS OF THE **X-MEN, X-FACTO** AND **X-FORCE**.

ASSUMING, OF COURSE--

--THAT THE **GOOD DOCTOR** WILL HAVE US?

I WOULD BE **HONORED**.

WHAT **PROMPTED** THIS DECISION?

BY **HELPING** PETER--

--INSTEAD OF **FIGHTING** HIM--

--WE REALIZED THEREIN LIES OUR **STRENGTH** AS A TEAM...

...PERHAPS, OUR **PURPOSE**.

WE'RE HOPING WE CAN **STOP** A PROBLEM **BEFORE** IT BECOMES A DISASTER--

--INSTEAD OF THE **CRISIS MANAGEMENT** FAVORED BY **EVERYON** **ELSE** WEARING AN "X" ON THEIR COSTUME.

THE WORLD IS GETTING **SMALLER**, SCOTT-- **EVERY** DAY.

THE **GLOBAL MAKE-UP** OF THE ACOLYTES ALONE SHOULD INDICATE THAT THERE ARE MUTANTS ACROSS THE PLANET WHO HAVE NEVER **HEARD** OF CHARLES XAVIER--

--AND HIS DREAM OF **GENETIC HARMONY** BETWEEN **HOMO SAPIEN** AND **HOMO SUPERIOR**.

IT FALLS TO **US** TO CUT A SWATH OF **TOLERANCE** AND **UNDER-STANDING** THROUGH THE BLANKET OF **IGNORANCE** AND **FEAR** THAT OFTEN **SEPARATES** OUR TWO RACES.

WHAT HE'S TRYING TO SAY IS, WE BELIEVE THAT NOW--
--MORE THAN EVER--
--THE WORLD NEEDS THE NEW EXCALIBUR!
SPECIAL THANKS TO CHRIS CLAREMONT AND ALAN DAVIS-- FORGERS OF THE SWORD.

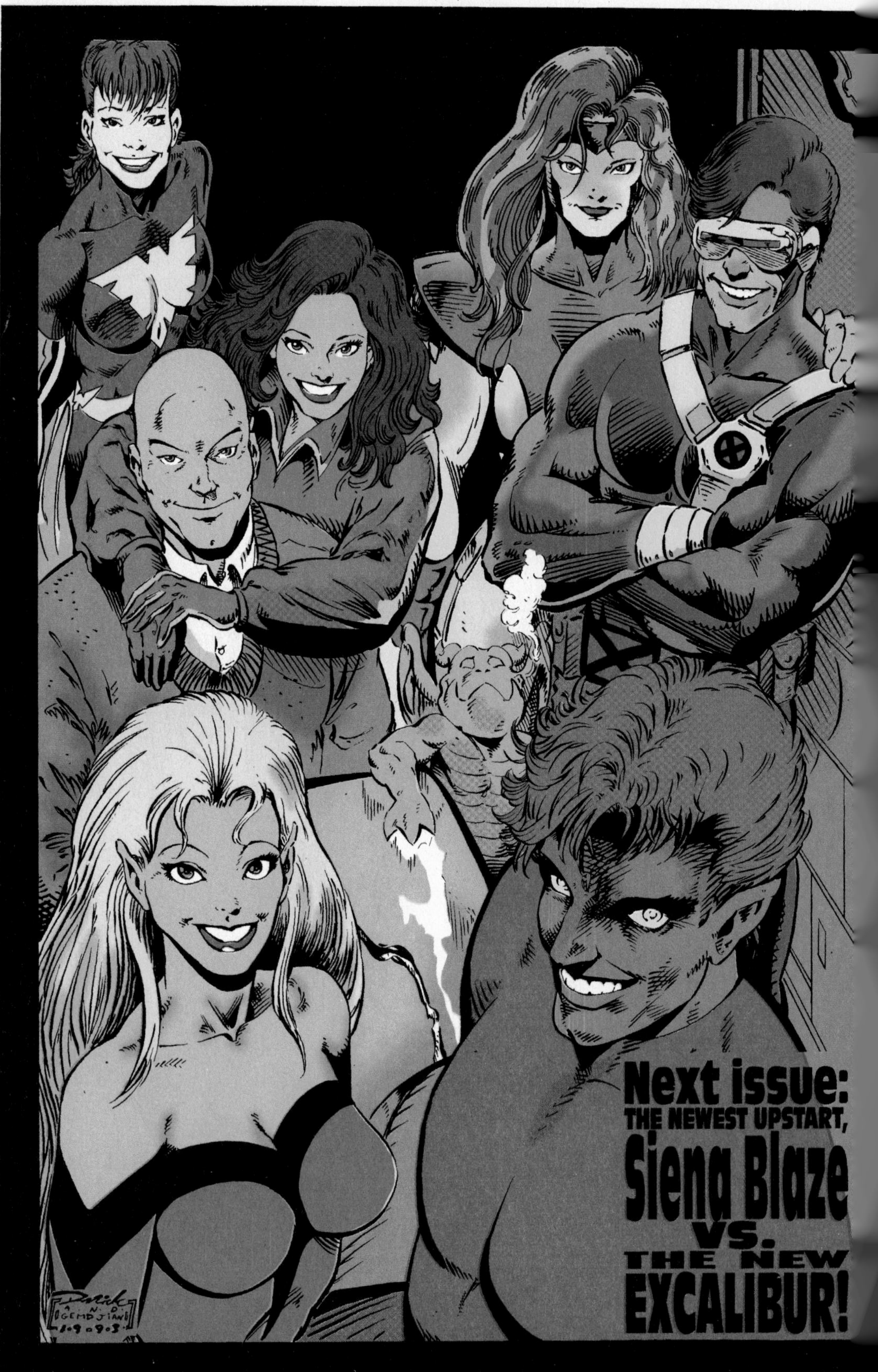
Next issue:
THE NEWEST UPSTART,
Siena Blaze
VS.
THE NEW
EXCALIBUR!

MARVEL COMICS
THE UNCANNY
X-MEN
50 US
AN/UK £1.25
315
AUG
02461
APPROVED BY THE COMICS CODE AUTHORITY
JUDGMENT AT AVALON!
R. CRUZ
KONRAD

WHERE DO DREAMS GO TO DIE?
FOR PETER RASPUTIN-- ONCE CALLED COLOSSUS OF THE X-MEN-- THAT PLACE IS HERE.
AVALON... A SPACE STATION CLOAKED IN ORBIT FAR ABOVE THE EARTH.
STAN LEE PRESENTS A TALE OF THE ACOLYTES
PEERS
SCOTT LOBDELL WRITER
ROGER CRUZ GUEST PENCILER
GREEN, RUBINSTEIN, LAROSA AND BARTA INKERS
CHRIS ELIOPOULOS LETTERER
BUCCELLATO/JAVINS COLORISTS
BOB HARRAS EDITOR
TOM DeFALCO EDITOR IN CHIEF

T DEEP
HIN THE
WELS...
...OF THIS PROFESSED HAVEN FOR THE DIS-ENFRANCHISED...
I KNOW THIS ALL SEEMS HOPE-LESS TO YOU--
--BUT YOU HAVE TO UNDERSTAND THIS ENTIRE COMPLEX WAS CREATED BY MAGNETO--
--TO OFFER HOPE OF A BETTER WORLD FOR ALL OF US.
...THE ONETIME FARMBOY-- THE WOULD-BE ARTIST... IS ABOUT TO REDISCOVER...
...SOMETHING HE'S ALWAYS KNOWN:
DREAMS DIE HARD.
I PETITIONED TO DEFEND YOU IN THIS TRIAL, BECAUSE I BELIEVE THE MAN I ONCE KNEW AS MAGNUS...
...WOULD ULTIMATELY HAVE FORGIVEN YOU YOUR TRANSGRESSION AGAINST HIS CAUSE.

T, THERE IS
OTHING I CAN
, TOVARISCH...
...IF YOU REFUSE TO HELP ME PREPARE MY DEFENSE.
WHY RISK YOUR STANDING AMONG THE ACOLYTES...
...TO DEFEND ME?
WHY... ?
BECAUSE I AM A FIRM BELIEVER IN SECOND CHANCES.
BECAUSE IF I DON'T--
--THE PUNISH-MENT FOR YOUR CRIME IS DEATH.
IS IT NOT POSSIBLE...
...THAT I DESERVE TO DIE?

WHEN I WAS LOST, ALONE, CONFUSED...
...THE ACOLYTES TOOK ME IN AND TAUGHT ME THE WORD OF MAG-NETO.
BY HELPING PROFESSOR XAVIER'S X-MEN DEFEAT THEM--*
--I BETRAYED MY BRETHREN'S TRUST IN ME.
HOW CAN A JURY OF MY PEERS FIND ME ANYTHING BUT GUILTY?
PEERS?
YOU AND I THE CLOSES THING TO THA ALL OF AVALC
WHILE THE RE OF THE ACOLY BLINDLY FOLL THE WORDS O THEIR CHOS MESSIAH-
--ONLY WE A BRAVE ENOUG SEEK OUT T TRUTH BEHIN THOSE WORDS AND ACT UPO WHAT WE FIND
IS THAT WHAT THIS IS ABOUT... PETER?
ARE YOU PLEADING MY CASE FOR BE-TRAYING THE ACO-LYTES...
...OR YOUR O FOR HAVING TURNED YO BACK ON T X-MEN?
*UNCANNY X-MEN #300.--BOB
KREEEAAK
YOU CANNOT BE SERIOUS-- WE HAVE HAD NO TIME TO PREPARE THE BOY'S DEFENSE!
DO YOU HONESTLY BELIEVE, RASPUTIN, THAT ANYTHING YOU HAVE TO SAY WILL CHANGE THE OUTCOME OF THE VERDICT?
AN INTERESTING QUESTION, NEOPHYTE.
COME WITH US, AND WE WILL NO DOUBT DISCOVER THE ANSWER TOGETHER.
OF COURSE I DO, VOGHT! HE HAS THE RIGHT TO--
PLEASE...
...I HAVE BEEN ON THE RUN FOR WEEKS, TRYING TO PUT DISTANCE BETWEEN MYSELF--
--AND MY DESTINY.
I'M TIRED OF RUNNING.
LET'S JUST GET THIS OVER WITH...

ONE MILE DIRECTLY ABOVE...
...AS FAR REMOVED PHYSICALLY FROM HIS FOLLOWERS AS HE IS SPIRITUALLY...
...SITS THE CHOSEN MESSIAH OF THE ACOLYTES.
BORN ERIC MAGNUS LENNSHERR, HE SPENT MANY YEARS OF HIS LIFE KNOWN AS THE MUTANT NAMED MAGNETO--
--SELF-PROCLAIMED MASTER OF MAGNETISM, AND SELF-APPOINTED SAVIOR OF THE MUTANT RACE.

THOSE DAYS ARE OVER.
THEY DOUBT, MY LORD.
THERE ARE THOSE AMONG YOUR FLOCK WHO FEEL THAT YOU-- THROUGH NO FAULT OF YOUR OWN--HAVE ABANDONED THEM.
THEY THINK SIMPLY BECAUSE CHARLES XAVIER SHUT DOWN YOUR MIND--*
--THAT YOU NO LONGER SEE, NO LONGER HEAR. THAT YOU NEITHER TASTE, NOR FEEL.
WHY, LORD?
WHY DO THEY DOUBT THAT I AM NOT ONLY YOUR MOST-FAVORED DISCIPLE--
--BUT THE EYES AND EARS AND VOICE OF MAGNETO AS WELL?
HOW DARE THEY DOUBT ME?
HOW DARE THEY DOUBT... US?
*IN THE NOW CLASSIC X-MEN #25. --BOB

BUT THERE COMES NO REPLY FROM THIS EMPTY VESSEL OF A MAN.
NO ANSWER--SAVE PERHAPS, THE WHISPERS THAT ECHO WITHIN THE HEAD OF THE MAN CALLED EXODUS.

ORGIVE E INTRUSION, XODUS...
TKNK
NOT AT ALL, SCANNER.
IS EVERYTHING PREPARED FOR THE TRIAL?
Y-YES, SIR.
THE NEOPHYTE IS BEING BROUGHT TO THE JUSTICE CHAMBER NOW...
LORD MAGNETO...?
IT HAS BEEN SO LONG SINCE ANY OF US HAVE SEEN HIM. HE LOOKS SO...
...SO... DIFFERENT!
SPLENDID. I WILL BE ALONG--
?
THAT WAS FOOLISH, CHILD...
...YOU SHOULD HAVE KNOWN BETTER.
WHAT...?
W-WHAT DID I DO?
SSWSS!
DO NOT TREAT ME LIKE A FOOL, WOMAN.
YOU DARED TO STARE UPON THE FACE OF MAGNETO--
--WHEN I HAVE MADE IT CLEAR THAT NONE BUT I SHALL KNOW THAT HONOR!
IT IS A PAIN UNLIKE ANY SHE HAS EVER KNOWN.
IN TRUTH, SCANNER'S MUTANT POWER TO PROJECT HER ASTRAL SELF INDEFINITELY--
--SHOULD PROTECT HER FROM SUCH PHYSICAL ASSAULTS.
IT IS A CRUEL TESTAMENT TO THE POWER OF THIS MAN--
--THAT HE ALMOST CASUALLY CRIPPLES BOTH HER BODY AND SPIRIT WITH SOMETHING LESS THAN A STRAY THOUGHT.
I-I AM SORRY, EXODUS.
I-I MEANT NOTHING BY...
EXACTLY.
YOU MEANT NOTHING--

-- BECAUSE YOU ARE NOTHING!
CHHACKK
P-PLEASE...
...FORGIVE M-ME...
NONE OF YOU ARE WORTHY TO GAZE UPON OUR LORD IN THIS HOUR OF HIS MOST IGNOBLE CONDITION.
CAN YOU NOT AFFORD HIM AT LEAST ENOUGH DIGNITY-- TO ALLOW HIM TO SUFFER FREE OF YOUR INSIPID CURIOSITY?
OF COURSE
THIS ONCE.
NOW, ON TO THE CHAMBE GIRL. I'LL BE ALONG SHORTLY
THANK YOU.
TRNK
ALONE AGAIN, MY LORD.
JUST YOU AND I.
JUST AS IT SHOULD BE.
TELL ME AGAIN HOW YOU SUFFERED SUCH FOOLS, MAGNETO.
FOR IN TRUTH, YOUR "ACOLYTES" ARE TRYING MY PATIENCE.

ND...
WE WERE PROMISED ENOUGH TIME TO MOUNT A PROPER DEFENSE!
AND WHAT ABOUT THE PROMISE THE NEOPHYTE MADE...
...WHEN HE PLEDGED HIS FEALTY TO OUR LORD MAGNUS?
FORGIVE RASPUTIN FOR HIS NAIVETE, JAVITZ.
AS A FORMER PUPIL OF XAVIER, PETER WAS NEVER ENCOURAGED TO THINK IN SUCH BROAD TERMS.
VOGHT, PLEASE--
--IT IS AN AFFRONT TO EVEN MENTION THAT HATED NAME IN THESE SACRED HALLS.
MOVE ALONG, CHILD... YOUR DESTINY AWAITS.
TELL ME, AMELIA. DOES YOUR UNFOUNDED HATRED OF THE PROFESSOR RUN SO DEEP--
--YOU ARE WILLING TO TAKE OUT YOUR HOSTILITIES ON THE MAN BY PROSECUTING THIS BOY IN HIS PLACE?
MY FEELINGS FOR CHARLES HAVE NOTHING TO DO WITH THIS, PETER..*
*SEE UNCANNY X-MEN #309 FOR A GLIMPSE AT THE HISTORY BETWEEN CHARLES XAVIER AND AMELIA VOGHT. --BOB
...I WAS ASKED TO ASSUME THIS ROLE BY EXODUS HIMSELF. JUST AS I SUSPECT YOU WERE.
I AM MERELY DOING AS I HAVE BEEN ASKED BY THE VOICE OF MAGNETO.
OUR CONVERSATIONS OF LATE HAVE CAUSED ME TO EXPECT MORE FROM YOU THAN MINDLESS OBEDIENCE, AMELIA.
HOW CAN YOU BE RESPONSIBLE FOR THE NEOPHYTE'S FATE WHEN YOU ARE NOT CONVINCED THAT HIS DEEDS NECESSITATE PUNISHMENT?
I LEARNED A LONG TIME AGO, RASPUTIN--THAT WHAT I BELIEVE OR DON'T BELIEVE IS INCONSEQUENTIAL.
I FOUND, WHEN LEFT TO MAKE MY OWN CHOICES IN LIFE, I INVARIABLY MAKE THE WRONG ONES.
SO INSTEAD--FOR BETTER OR FOR WORSE--I DO WHAT I AM TOLD.
BUT ISN'T THAT A CHOICE AS WELL?
CERTAINLY. BUT IT IS ONE WHICH, FOR THE MOMENT, I CAN LIVE WITH.

AT THE SIGHT OF THE MAIN CHAMBER --
-- FILLED WITH THE HOSTILE FACES OF HIS "PEERS" AND AT LEAST FOR THE MOMENT, HIS COMPATRIOTS --
-- PETER RASPUTIN QUESTIONS HIS OWN RECENT MAJOR LIFE DECISIONS.
WHEN HE FIRST CHOSE TO WALK AMONG THE ACOLYTES, FOR A TIME HE GENUINELY BELIEVED HE COULD DO SO...
... WITHOUT ABANDONING ALL THAT WAS GOOD ABOUT XAVIER'S DREAM FOR A BETTER WORLD.
HE SAW IN MAGNETO A MEANS TO ACCOMPLISH THE SAME GOALS BY EMPLOYING MORE AG-GRESSIVE TECHNIQUES.
BUT SINCE THE MOMENT EXODUS ASSUMED THE MANTLE OF LEADERSHIP...
... IT WAS CLEAR TO EVERYONE ASSEMBLED THAT A NEW DAY WAS DAWNING FOR THESE WAYWARD CHILDREN OF THE ATOM.
I... I... ACCEPT RE-SPONSIBIL--
SILENCE, CHILD.
WHAT YOU FEEL IS OF NO CONCERN TO THIS COURT.
ALL THAT MAT-TERS, NEOPHYTE, IS THAT JUSTICE IN THE NAME OF LORD MAGNUS BE DELIVERED.
JUSTICE?
NOTHING LESS THAN I DESERVE.

LET IT BE SHOWN THAT ON THIS DAY...
...SCANNER, MILAN. CARGIL--
--UNUSCIONE, THE KLEINSTOCKS, RUSTY COLLINS AND SKIDS BLEVINS--
--EACH A FAITHFUL FOLLOWER OF HE WHO IS FATHER TO US ALL...
... BEAR WITNESS TO THE CHARGES AGAINST HE WHO HAS BETRAYED US AND ALL WE HOLD SACRED.
VOGHT, ARE YOU PRE-PARED?
PREPARED AND HONORED, EXODUS--
--THAT I MIGHT BE OF SOME SMALL USE IN EXACTING VENGEANCE ON BEHALF OF MAGNETO.
THEN LET THE TRIAL OF THE NEOPHYTE BEGIN...
...AND LET IT SERVE AS AN EXAMPLE TO ALL AMONG US WHO ARE NOT COMPLETELY DEVOTED TO OUR MOST SACRED CRUSADE.
THIS "TRIAL" IS MORE THAN THE BOY DESERVES--
--ESPECIALLY CONSIDERING WHAT MAGNETO DID TO SENYAKA WHEN THAT MAN ACTED OF HIS OWN ACCORD.*
*UNCANNY #304. --BOB

WITHOUT OUR FAITH, WE HAVE NOTHING.
THIS IS AS TRUE HERE AMONG OURSELVES, THOUSANDS OF KILO-METERS ABOVE THE PLANET WHICH SPAWNED US...
... AS IT WAS WHEN WE LIVED AMONG A POPU-LATION THAT FEARED US SIMPLY FOR BEING BORN HOMO SUPERIOR.
FOR IF WE CANNOT TRUST OURSELVES, FELLOW ACOLYTES, WHO CAN WE TRUST?
I AM SPEAKING NOT ONLY OF A FAITH IN MAGNETO, HIS ULTIMATE WISDOM AND NEAR INFINITE POWER WHICH FIRST BROUGHT US HERE--
--BUT RATHER THE FAITH THAT WE MUST PLACE IN EACH OTHER IF WE ARE TO SURVIVE AS A RACE.
I AM SPEAKING ALSO OF THE BLIND FAITH WE HAVE WILLFULLY PLACED IN ONE WHO PURPORTS TO SPEAK THE WORD OF MAGNUS...
... AS WELL AS ONE WHO CLAIMS TO HAVE HEARD THAT WORD.
ON THE EVENING THE NEOPHYTE BETRAYED US TO THE X-MEN--
--HIS ACTIONS WENT A LONG WAY TO ERODING THES FAITHS THAT LAY AT THE HEART OF OUR MOVEMENT.
FOR THIS REASON ALONE, THE BOY SHOULD LOSE WHAT HE TOOK AWAY FROM US.
EVERYTHING.

GNORE EVERYTHING THE PROSECUTOR HAS JUST TOLD YOU.
FOR THIS HAS NOTHING TO DO WITH "FAITH" AND EVERYTHING TO DO WITH THE REALITY OF THE MAN BORN ERIC LENNSCHERR.
AND THEREIN LIES THE PROBLEM.
FOR MAGNETO HAS BEEN MANY THINGS TO MANY PEOPLE.
TO SOME, HE WAS CONSIDERED A BUTCHER HIMSELF WHEN HE EXACTED VENGEANCE FROM THE PEOPLE WHO PREVENTED HIM FROM SAVING HIS DAUGHTER...
...WHILE TO THE OTHERS HE HAS BEEN CONSIDERED A LIBERATOR.
TO THE X-MEN HE ALTERNATED, FOR A TIME, BETWEEN OUR-- CORRECTION, THEIR DEADLIEST ADVER-SARY...
...AND MOST POWERFUL ALLY.
MAGNETO ONCE SERVED AS HEAD-MASTER FOR XAVIER'S SCHOOL FOR GIFTED YOUNGSTERS WHEN MY OWN SISTER WAS... ALIVE.
THERE WERE MANY ASPECTS TO THE MAN'S LIFE-- HIS ACTIONS OPENED TO MANY DIFFERENT INTERPRETATIONS.
THAT IS THE REALITY OF THE MAN CALLED MAGNETO.
THAT IS WHAT THIS CASE IS ALL ABOUT.
TO THIS YOUNG MAN, HIS LORD AND CHOSEN MESSIAH WAS A MAN WHO WOULD NOT STAND BY--
--AND WATCH AS MOIRA MACTAGGERT WAS ABUSED-- TORTURED-- BECAUSE OF THE MERE FACT THAT HER GENETIC STRUCTURE WAS LESS EVOLVED THAN OURS.
IS IT OUR PLACE TO SAY HE WAS WRONG?
DOES HE NOT HAVE THE RIGHT-- THE RESPONSIBILITY-- TO HONOR THE MAN IN HIS OWN WAY?
YOU ARE GOOD, PETER RASPUTIN.
VERY GOOD.
WE CALL TO THE STAND BROTHER MILAN-- TO DISCUSS HOW THE YOUNG NEOPHYTE FIRST CAME TO SEE THE LIGHT.

BY USING MY MUTANT GIFT OF PROJECTING E.M. THOUGHT-WAVES INTO COGNITIVE ELEC-TRONIC IMAGERY--
--IT IS EASIER FOR ME TO SHOW YOU EXACTLY WHAT OC-CURRED THAT AUTUMN EVENING IN SWITZERLAND.
CARGIL, UNUSCIONE AND I WERE INVESTIGATING HUSHED RUMORS OF A MUTANT BOY WHO LIVED ALONE ATOP A MOUNTAIN RIDGE...
... HAVING SEQUESTERED HIMSELF IN AN ABANDONED CHURCH.
HAVING ALL OF US, AT ONE TIME OR ANOTHER, KNOWN THE NEED FOR SANCTUARY FROM A DISTRUSTFUL WORLD--
--WE TOOK OUR TIME IN DRAWING HIM OUT, SPEAKING OUR WORDS TO CLOSED DOORS FOR TWO DAYS.
BEFORE HE FINALLY RESPONDED.
AND RESPONDED WITH A VENGEANCE.
"TEACH ME," HE SAID. "TEACH ME OF THE MAN AND HIS LOVE, HIS DE-VOTION TOWARDS HIS PEOPLE!"
"GIVE ME SOMEONE TO BELIEVE IN," HE BEGGED.
"GIVE ME A HOME."
FOR MONTHS HE STUDIED THE HOLOGRAMS.
LISTENED TO THE FEW RECORDED WORDS OF OUR SAVIOR.
LEARNING AND-- SO WE THOUGHT, BELIEVING.
BUT WE WERE WRONG--PITIFULL PITIFULLY WRONG
THE ENTIRE TIME HE WAS WAITING, PLANNING TO DESTROY US FROM WITHIN!
N-NOT TRUE...

NO, CHILD?
THEN, PERHAPS, YOU WOULD SHARE WITH US--
--IN YOUR OWN WORDS--
--WHAT COULD POSSESS A PERSON TO TURN ONE'S BACK ON OUR FELLOWSHIP?
WHEN I FIRST ARRIVED AT THE MOUNT, IT IS TRUE...
... I FELT WITH ALL MY HEART THAT MAGNETO WAS A SAVIOR FOR US ALL.

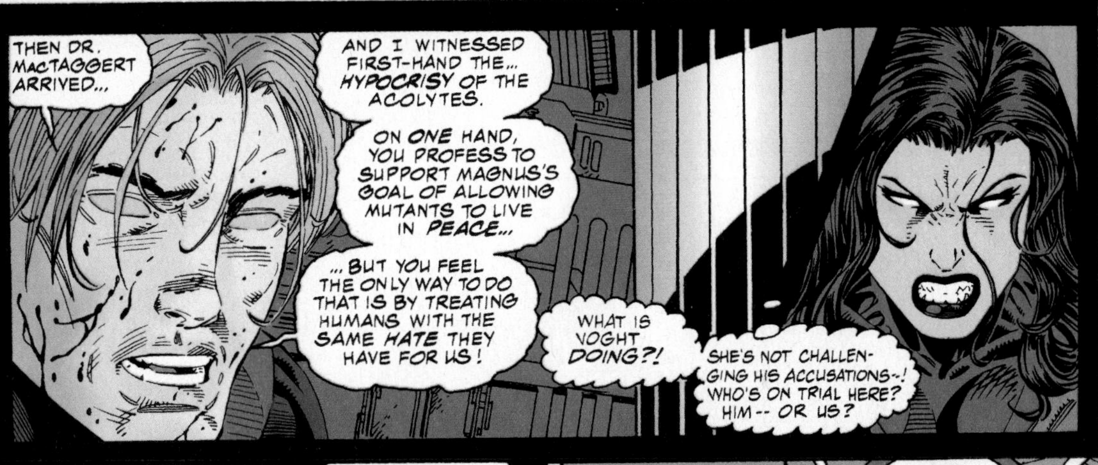

THEN DR. MACTAGGERT ARRIVED...
AND I WITNESSED FIRST-HAND THE... HYPOCRISY OF THE ACOLYTES.
ON ONE HAND, YOU PROFESS TO SUPPORT MAGNUS'S GOAL OF ALLOWING MUTANTS TO LIVE IN PEACE...
... BUT YOU FEEL THE ONLY WAY TO DO THAT IS BY TREATING HUMANS WITH THE SAME HATE THEY HAVE FOR US!
WHAT IS VOGHT DOING?!
SHE'S NOT CHALLENGING HIS ACCUSATIONS--! WHO'S ON TRIAL HERE? HIM-- OR US?

IN THE FACE OF YOUR... INHUMANITY TO THE WOMAN, I REALIZED THERE MUST BE ANOTHER WAY--
--AN ALTERNATIVE TO THE PAIN, SUFFERING AND DEADLY CONFRONTATIONS BETWEEN OUR TWO PEOPLE.
KNEE DEEP IN THE RAIN AND MUD OF MONT SAINT FRANCIS--I MET THAT ALTERNATIVE FACE-TO-FACE.
THIS OTHER WAY--DID IT HAVE A NAME?

Y-YES. CHARLES XAVIER!

BLASPHEMER!
IN THE NAME OF MAGNETO--
-- I WOULD SEE YOU CRUSHED IN MY PSIONIC EXO-SKELETON...
... BEFORE I ALLOW YOU TO SPEAK THAT NAME AGAIN WITH SUCH REVERENCE!
UNUSCIONE, NO!
DO NOT FORCE ME TO PIT MY OWN MUTANT ABILITY AGAINST YOURS!
WHA--?!
I'VE TRANSMUTED THE BOY TO SAFETY, RASPUTIN...
...FOR ALTHOUGH I'M CERTAIN HE WILL DIE THIS DAY--
-- THAT DEATH WILL COME ONLY AFTER THE VERDICT!
COUGH KAK
MY BROTHER AND I KNEW YOU WOULD EVENTUALLY SHOW YOUR TRUE COLORS, COLOSSUS!
THAT IS INSANITY! I WAS MERELY PROTECT--!
WHAM!
IDEALIST FOOLS SUCH AS YOU CAN NEVER BE EXPECTED TO CHANGE!
AFTER FABIAN CORTEZ DECEIVED US, WE LEARNED!

ENOUGH.

IT SEEMS I MISJUDGED THE AMOUNT OF TENSION THIS WOULD CREATE.
RATHER THAN RUN THE RISK OF FRAYING THE EDGES OF OUR DELICATE LITTLE TAPESTRY ANY FURTHER--
-- I WILL TAKE THIS MATTER BEFORE LORD MAGNUS HIMSELF. NOW.

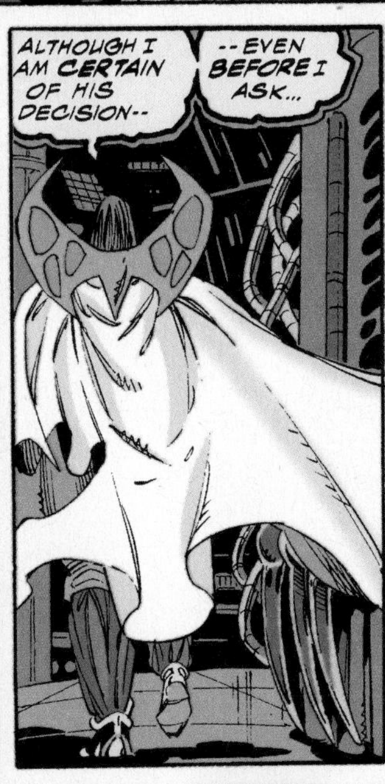
ALTHOUGH I AM CERTAIN OF HIS DECISION--
--EVEN BEFORE I ASK...

... I WILL RETURN SHORTLY.

THANK YOU, AMELIA... FOR SAVING WHAT LITTLE LIFE I HAVE LEFT.
IT WAS... NOTHING.

DON'T FOOL YOURSELF, VOGHT.
TO US, IT WAS A CLEAR SIGN AS TO WHERE YOUR LOYALTIES TRULY LIE HERE!

WHY, PETER? WHY DIDN'T YOU JUST LET ME PLEAD GUILTY FOR MY CRIMES?
AS A FORMER X-MAN, EVEN YOU ADMIT XAVIER'S WAY IS WRONG.
NO. I NEVER SAID IT WAS WRONG.
I SAID IT DIDN'T WORK... FOR ME.
NOT NOW... NOT IN THE WORLD AS IT EXISTS.
COULD IT BE, PETER, THAT YOU'VE COME TO UNDERSTAND WHAT I'VE SUSPECTED FOR SOME TIME.
THAT PERHAPS NEITHER XAVIER'S DREAMS NOR MAGNETO'S VISION IS ONE HUNDRED PERCENT CORRECT?
COULD IT BE THE ANSWER LIES SOMEWHERE IN THE MIDDLE OF THE TWO?
VOGHT, MY PRESENCE HERE ALONE IS TESTIMONY-- THAT ANYTHING IS POSSIBLE.
INCLUDING THE REALIZATION THAT IT WAS NOT GODSPOTIN XAVIER'S DREAM WHICH DIDN'T WORK--
--BUT THAT I DID NOT WORK HARD ENOUGH... DID NOT SACRIFICE ENOUGH TO MAKE THAT DREAM A REALITY.

I HAVE HEARD HIS WORD, AND NOW RETURN TO SPEAK IN HIS NAME.
STEP FORWARD, LAD...
...SO YOU MIGHT RECEIVE THE JUDGMENT OF MAGNETO.
KNOW THAT THIS DECISION WAS NOT MADE EASILY.
UNDERSTAND THAT, DESPITE HIS CURRENT CONDITION, OUR LORD'S HEART IS STILL FULL TO OVERFLOWING...
...WITH LOVE AND COMPASSION FOR ALL WHO FOLLOW HIM.
THAT IS, ALL WHO FOLLOW HIM FAITHFULLY.
I AM CALLED EXODUS, FOR IT IS MY SACRED DUTY TO FERRY HIS CHOSEN PEOPLE TO A BETTER PLACE...
...AS WELL AS DELIVER THE UNGRATEFUL AND THE UNFORGIVEN INTO THE DARK, COLD EMBRACE OF OBLIVION.
I DO THIS WITH NO MALICE IN MY HEART, NEOPHYTE, BUT KNOW THAT YOU ARE HEREBY SENTENCED TO--

NO!
THE BOY'S ONLY "CRIME" WAS THE STRENGTH OF HIS OWN CONVICTIONS!
SOMETHING MAGNETO, AS I KNEW HIM, WOULD HAVE RESPECTED AND HONORED.
FOR HE WAS A MAN WHOSE ENTIRE FAMILY WAS SLAUGHTERED BY AN ARMY OF SOLDIERS--MEN "FOLLOWING ORDERS." THOSE SAM MEN SENT MILLIONS OF THEIR FELLOW HUMAN BEINGS INTO A HOLOCAUST RAGING WITH THE HEAT OF STUPIDIT AND IGNORANCE.

I CAME HERE TO AVALON BECAUSE I BELIEVED WE WERE GOING TO BE BETTER THAN THAT.
IT IS THE VERY SAME REASON THIS BOY CAME TO YOU...
...TO US.

IS HE TO BE PUNISHED FOR REFUSING TO SIT BACK AND BLINDLY FOLLOW ORDERS?
IS HE TO BE CONDEMNED FOR THINKING DIFFERENTLY, FOR REFUSING TO STAND BACK AND WATCH AS ANOTHER LIVING BEING WAS BEATEN AND TORTURED?

IS THIS HOW FAR WE'VE COME SINCE MAGNETO'S OWN YOUTH--
--THAT WE ARE WILLING, SOME OF US EAGER, TO SEND ONE MORE BEING TO HIS DEATH BECAUSE HE IS "DIFFERENT" FROM US?
IF SO, THEN WE SHOULD ALL FOLLOW, BECAUS EVENTUALLY THA IS WHERE WE WILL ALL END U ANYONE WHO DISAGREES--
--WHO HAS THEIR OWN OPINION WILL SOON ENOUGH BE FODDER FOR THE FLAMES.

NO, EXODUS-- IF MAGNETO'S LIFE HAS TAUGHT US ANYTHING AT ALL...
...IT WAS HOW NOT TO FOLLOW THE ORDERS OF OTHERS--
--BUT TO FOLLOW, AS HE HAS DONE, THE DICTATES OF HIS OWN HEART.

THE ROOM IS SILENT, SAVE FOR THE ECHO OF COLOSSUS'S WORDS...
... BUT EXODUS NOTES THE FACES OF THE ACOLYTES... THE IMPRESSION THOSE WORDS HAVE MADE...
... AND, AS EVER, HE ADAPTS TO SURVIVE.
AS I WAS ABOUT TO SAY, PIOTR NIKOLAIEVITCH...
... I WOULD HAVE TAKEN HIS LIFE WITHOUT A SHRED OF REMORSE--
--BUT MAGNETO IS BY FAR A MORE COMPASSIONATE SOUL.
THAT IS WHY HE INSTRUCTED ME TO BANISH THIS WRETCH TO THE PLACE OF FOOLS KNOWN AS EARTH.
BEGONE, NEOPHYTE--KNOWING YOU ARE FOREVER BANNED FROM THE HEAVEN THAT IS AVALON.
AS FOR THE REST OF YOU...
...PEACE BE WITH YOU.

SO TELL ME, RASPUTIN... WAS IT WORTH IT?
TO WIN YOUR CASE, WHILE AT THE SAME TIME ALIENATING YOURSELF FROM THE REST OF US?
I DON'T THINK THAT IS WHAT HAPPENED, AMELIA.
IF NOTHING ELSE, I'M CONFIDENT THAT THE REST OF THE ACOLYTES HEARD MY WORDS.

HOW LONG, I WONDER, BEFORE THEY UNDERSTAND IN THEIR HEARTS THAT THESE ARE THE TRUE WORDS BY WHICH MEN SUCH AS PROFESSOR XAVIER AND MAGNETO LIVED THEIR LIVES?

IT IS THAT QUESTION WHICH HAUNTS EXODUS AS HE RETURNS TO HIS MASTER'S SIDE.

A DOUBT HE FEELS GNAWING AT THE VERY HEART OF HIS SOUL--

--A DOUBT THAT AFTER TODAY THE ACOLYTES WILL NO LONGER BELIEVE HE ALONE SPEAKS FOR HIS LORD.

A DOUBT THAT MIGHT WEAKEN HIM AS SURELY AS MAGNETO FELL BEFORE XAVIER.

WITHOUT THEIR FAITH, EXODUS HAS NOTHING.

RATHER THAN FACE MAGNUS, HE WANDERS THE HALLS OF AVALON... EVER ALONE.

AND THUS HE IS NOT ON HAND TO WITNESS THE FAINTEST OF A SMILE WHICH APPEARS LIKE A FADED MEMORY ACROSS THE FACE OF A MAN...

...AN ENIGMATIC SMILE THAT SIGNALS, PERHAPS ...THE RETURN OF A MESSIAH?

FINI.

MARVEL Age

127

AUGUST 1993

$1.00 US $1.25 CAN 80p UK

APPROVED BY THE COMICS CODE AUTHORITY

Making the Mutant Holograms

Cover art by Greg Capullo, Kevin Conrad & George Roussos; sculpture by Dario Grangroth; photography by Christopher Ebel

3-D Mu

The making of the X-Men anniversary holograms

Less than a year ago, Marvel commemorated the 30th anniversary of Spider-Man with holograms on each of the four Spider-Man titles, in an event that was described as "hard to top." The upcoming X-Men anniversary celebration, featuring state-of-the-art holograms on all of the X-Men titles, just might top the web-slinger's celebration. While both events feature holograms made from three-dimensional models, the X-Men holograms will be produced by Polaroid Corporation with an exclusive technology that yields the best and brightest three-dimensional images currently available.

The anniversary storyline focuses on Magneto's return to Earth, and each hologram will feature a key player in the struggle. Each anniversary issue will feature a different hologram and a wrap-around cover.

The first hologram (featuring Havok by Joe Quesada) appeared on X-FACTOR #92. Holograms will appear on X-FORCE #25 (Cable by Greg Capullo), available in June; UNCANNY X-MEN #304 (Magneto by Greg Capullo), on sale in July; X-MEN #25 (Gambit by Andy Kubert), set for August; WOLVERINE #75 (Wolverine by Adam Kubert) out in September; and on EXCALIBUR #71 (Nightcrawler by Joe Maduriera), slated for September. Each of these books will be 48-page issues priced at $3.50, except for UNCANNY X-MEN #304 and WOLVERINE #75, which will be special, oversized issues priced at $3.95 each.

As with the Spider-Man holograms, the X-Men holograms start out as specially commissioned flat artwork that is given to a sculptor/painter who will translate each piece as a three-dimensional statue. The hologram won't be full-color, so th sculptor uses various shades of gr for the greatest possible detail wh painting the statue.

Photographs by Christopher Ebel

The Havok statue for X-FACTOR #92, based on artwork by Joe Quesada, was the first to be sculpted.

ants

These views of the Gambit sculpture, based on Andy Kubert artwork, show how the sculptor has to *imply* depth despite how narrow the pieces have to be.

Since these holographic images are made by reflecting a laser beam off of an object and onto a glass photographic plate, and no lenses are involved in focusing the laser, the image cannot be reduced or enlarged. The holographic model must be made the exact same height and width as the finished hologram appearing on the books — 2¼" × 3½". Since keeping a three-dimensional model in sharp focus without lenses is very difficult, the model cannot exceed one-half inch in *depth*. Because of this restriction, most of the appearance of depth in a model must be convincingly *implied*, and the model-maker must perform his work without having any way of previewing how it will look in the final holographic image.

These requirements call for a very talented and experienced sculptor, and since the painting of the model is also very tricky work, a very skilled painter, as well. Enter Dario Grangroth, the artist who will be doing all of the models for the X-Men Anniversary holograms (see sidebar).

After a model is finished, it is sent to Marvel, where Dario's vision of how the art should look in three dimensions must meet the approval of the editors. For example, the Cable model appearing on X-FORCE #25 first came to Marvel with the character grinning from ear to ear; he looked like a game show host getting ready to introduce his next contestant. It had to go back to Dario to be given the serious, hard-edge look that is associated with Cable.

Once final editorial approval is given, the model and all of the additional two-dimensional artwork that will be used for backgrounds and special effects are shipped off to the Polaroid lab in Cambridge, MA, for the "origination" of the hologram. The flat art layers and the model are shot individually onto a special silver halide photographic glass plate to form a single hologram viewable only under laser lighting, called the H-1. These glass plates are commercially available, super-high resolution photographic plates usually used for astrophotography and/ or micro-lithography, and the plates are developed with fairly standard black-and-white film developing chemistry.

Shooting an H-1 is a very time-consuming task that requires a great deal of skill, experience, and patience in order to create a workable lighting and exposure set-up, and any number of things can go wrong. All of the various mirrors, beam-splitters, prisms, and other optical devices that you see bolted down on the the holography table must be very precisely aligned and arranged for every hologram. The model is lit from four directions at once by a single laser beam that is being split five times. The set-up can take days to perfect. There can be absolutely no vibration whatsoever during the exposure of a holographic plate. The table on which the holography set-up rests weighs 2 *tons* and is suspended on multiple air cushions to insulate it from the normal vibration found in a city, but since the Polaroid holography studio is located within 250 yards of a Boston subway tunnel, when a train is runs close to the building, any holography exposure must be shut down. If everything goes well with the overall set-up, the only other snag that can occur is laser trouble.

The main engine of any holography studio is a high-power laser — a very high-tech piece of equipment that requires elaborate control and monitoring gear, consumes an enormous amount of power, and requires a large cooling system to keep it at operating temperature. Invented in the mid-Sixties, laser technology is quite young, and while the small lasers that are found in CD players and optical fiber networks have achieved a high degree of reliability, high-power lasers used for very exacting work such as holography do not have the same reliability. The holographer's laser must produce a beam of light of an *exact*

The Cable statue (X-FORCE #25) under the vivid red laser beam at the Poloroid holographic studios.

The Polaroid holographic studio in Cambridge, MA–this table weighs two tons and is suspended on air cushions to protect against the slightest vibrations.

frequency at an exact intensity th is perfectly collimated (all light ra being emitted by the laser must b exactly parallel to each other). Because of this collimation, a las beam can theoretically travel for a almost infinite distance without increasing in diameter or losing intensity. If the laser frequency drifts during exposure, or if there any variation in intensity or colli tion, the hologram is ruined.

Once shot, the H-1 plate is dev oped. An H-1 glass plate, when se in normal light, appears to have nothing more than a thin grey fil on it. If, however, a laser beam is projected through this glass plat the glowing image of the original model appears suspended in spa several inches in front of the plat and can be viewed from any angl The laser-projected H-1 hologram while not very practical for mass distribution, is holography at its most breathtaking. The image lo solid-until you try to touch it and your fingers pass right through Each level of background art appe to be a glowing piece of flat art su pended in mid-air. (If you ever ge opportunity to see an exhibit of holography, it is definitely worth your time.)

Polaroid technician checks the equency of the laser beam to make rtain it remains consistent.

Magneto statue (from Greg Capullo ork) for UNCANNY X-MEN #304.

Photograph by Stephen F. Hanson

When the H-1 holograms are made from all of the art and the model, these images are projected onto a single photographic plate in a series of exposures that form an H-2 hologram. This is often likened to making a photographic print from a negative, or several negatives in this case. It is the H-2 hologram that forms a multi-level holographic image that is viewable in normal light.

Once the H-2 image is generated and approved by the Marvel editors, plates are made for the production of the H-2 images that will be applied to the comic books. It is in the production of the finished holograms that the Polaroid process is unique. Rather than emboss the hologram pattern (which is really an immensely complex structure of pits and ridges) into an aluminum foil film, the hologram image is transferred to a photographic film. This allows for the sharpest and most vivid image available.

While the holograms are being produced, other work is being done to create the rest of the book. The actual covers are printed at Seiple Litho of Canton, Ohio, on a high-speed mini-web press. This press prints onto a 14-inch roll (or web) of paper, and cuts the web into sheets — two covers to a sheet. Printing covers at a rate of 19,000 sheets per hour, this press is producing more than 10 covers per second. Once the covers are printed, they are shipped to one of Marvel's printers, where the books are manufactured. The text of the book is printed on a much larger full-bed web press standing two-stories high. These presses print on rolls of paper that are up to five feet wide and can weigh 1,400 pounds each. Running flat out, these presses will produce 60,000 folded text sections per hour, just over 16 per second. Then the covers and texts are bound together into books, which are then packed and shipped to stores.

Unlike any other special cover that Marvel has done, the holograms themselves will not be applied until the books are bound. Polaroid holograms must be hand applied because of the thickness of the image, and this adds weeks to the already tight schedule for these books.

These special covers are only one part of the 30th anniversary celebration of the X-Men, as there are many other events scheduled for this summer. However, the holograms will undoubtedly be among the most *memorable* aspects of the X-Men summer of 1993, and who knows how Marvel will top this one!

Model making & the Modelmaker

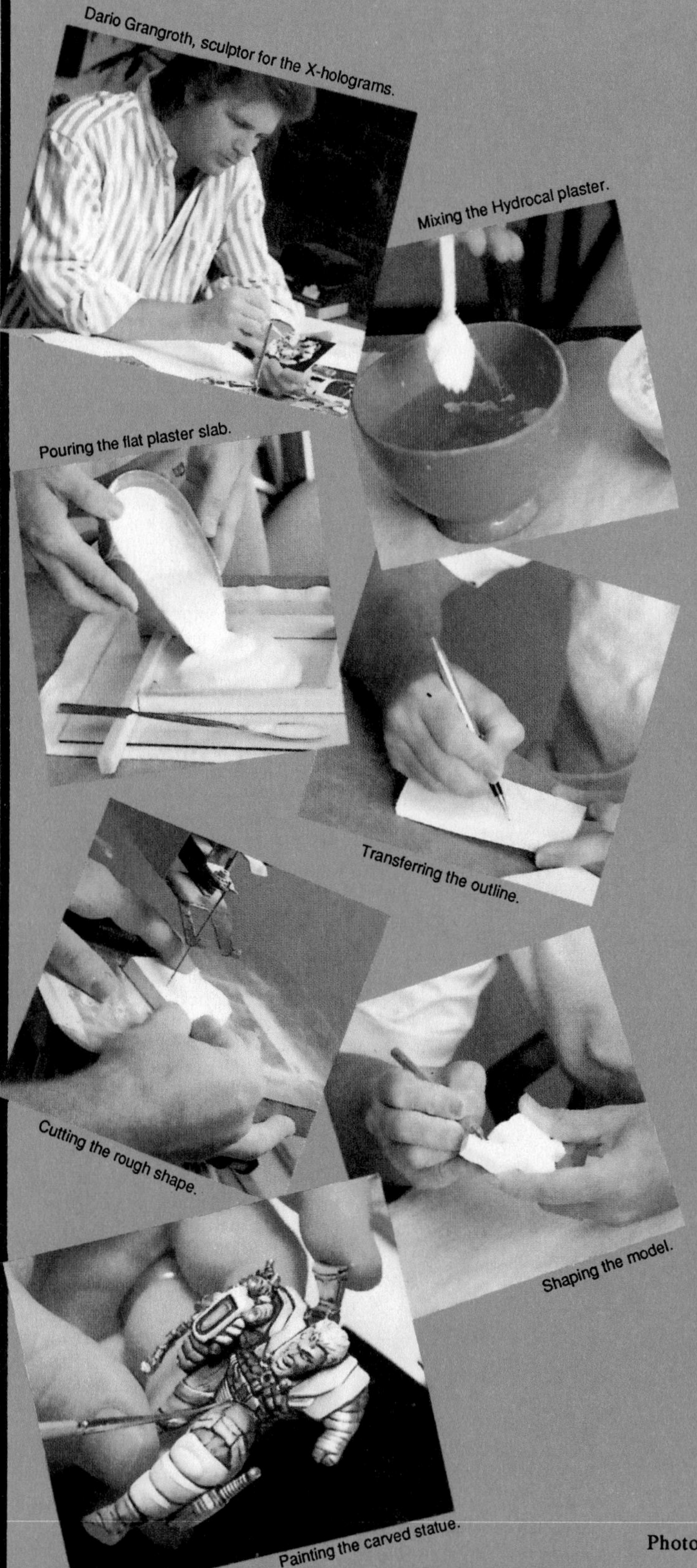

Dario Grangroth, sculptor for the X-holograms.

Mixing the Hydrocal plaster.

Pouring the flat plaster slab.

Transferring the outline.

Cutting the rough shape.

Shaping the model.

Painting the carved statue.

Currently based in Salt Lake City, UT, Dario Grangroth was born and raised in Minneapolis, MN. He started doing sculpture in high school, and knew then that it was his calling. He then attended Minneapolis College of Art & Design and graduated in 1970 with a fine arts degree in sculpture, then moved to Salt Lake City in 1979. Dario usually goes by his first name only, and has been working with Polaroid regularly for several years. He has been a commercial sculptor for almost 25 years and has been creating models for holography for the last five. His previous clients include Tonka, General Mills, Disney, and Hanna-Barbera, for which he has created prototypes of action figures and other toys.

Dario is finding his work for Marvel to be challenging and enjoyable because of the exciting nature of the artwork and the fact that there "are no straight lines" to these models, he noted. What Dario likes most about his work is the flexibility he has in setting his own hours, the professionalism that he runs into in his field, and the opportunity that he has to use his talents every day. His least favorite aspects are the intense pressure to get jobs done on tight deadlines, and the fact that not all of the jobs that he takes are as visually stimulating as the X-Men hologram models.

It takes Dario three to five full days to create something like the Havok model that appeared on the cover of X-FACTOR #92. The first thing he does is to mix up a batch of Hydrocal (a hard plaster) and pour it into a mold to form a flat slab. After this has thoroughly set, he transfers the outlines from the flat art (at final size) to the face of the slab and uses a jigsaw to cut the rough shape of the model out of the slab. Then the time-consuming process of carving the details into the model can begin. He frequently refers back to the original art as the model slowly emerges. Once all of the shaping is done, several coats of sealer are applied until the plaster is smooth. Once the surface of the plaster has been finished, the details are painted on in muted shades of grey using *very* fine brushes, as no color can be used or is visible in the final hologram. The finished model is then attached to its background and is ready to be sent to Marvel for editorial approval.

—Christopher Ebel

Photographs by Charmaine Grangroth

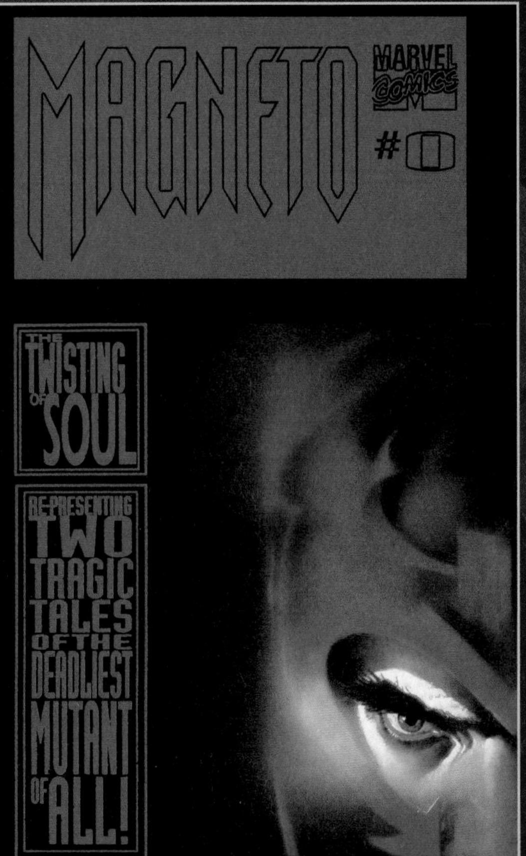

he promotional one-shot *Magneto #0* reprinted Magneto stories from *Classic X-Men #12* and *#19*, and an excerpt from *X-Men Unlimited #2*. Cover art by Bill Sienkiewicz.

Magneto #0 pinup by John Byrne, Terry Austin & Carlos Lopez

Magneto #0 pinup by Jan Duursema, Chris Ivy & Carlos Lopez

Magneto #0 pinup by Steve Epting, Tom Palmer & Carlos Lopez

Marvel Collectible Classics: X-Men #4 reprinted *X-Men* #25. Cover art by Adam Kubert, Jesse Delperdang & Liquid!

Wizard: X-Men Turn Thirty cover art by Andy Kubert & Mark McNabb

X-Men: Fatal Attractions poster by Bob Larkin

X-Men 30th anniversary poster by Greg Capullo & Tom Smit

X-Men 30th anniversary poster by Greg Capullo, Harry Candelario & Tom Smith

Exodus character design sketch by Joe Quesada

Illyana Rasputin pinup pencils by Dwayne Turner

Magneto #0 gold variant

Uncanny X-Men #303 gold variant

X-Men #25 B&W variant, with Magneto hologram

X-Men #25 gold variant

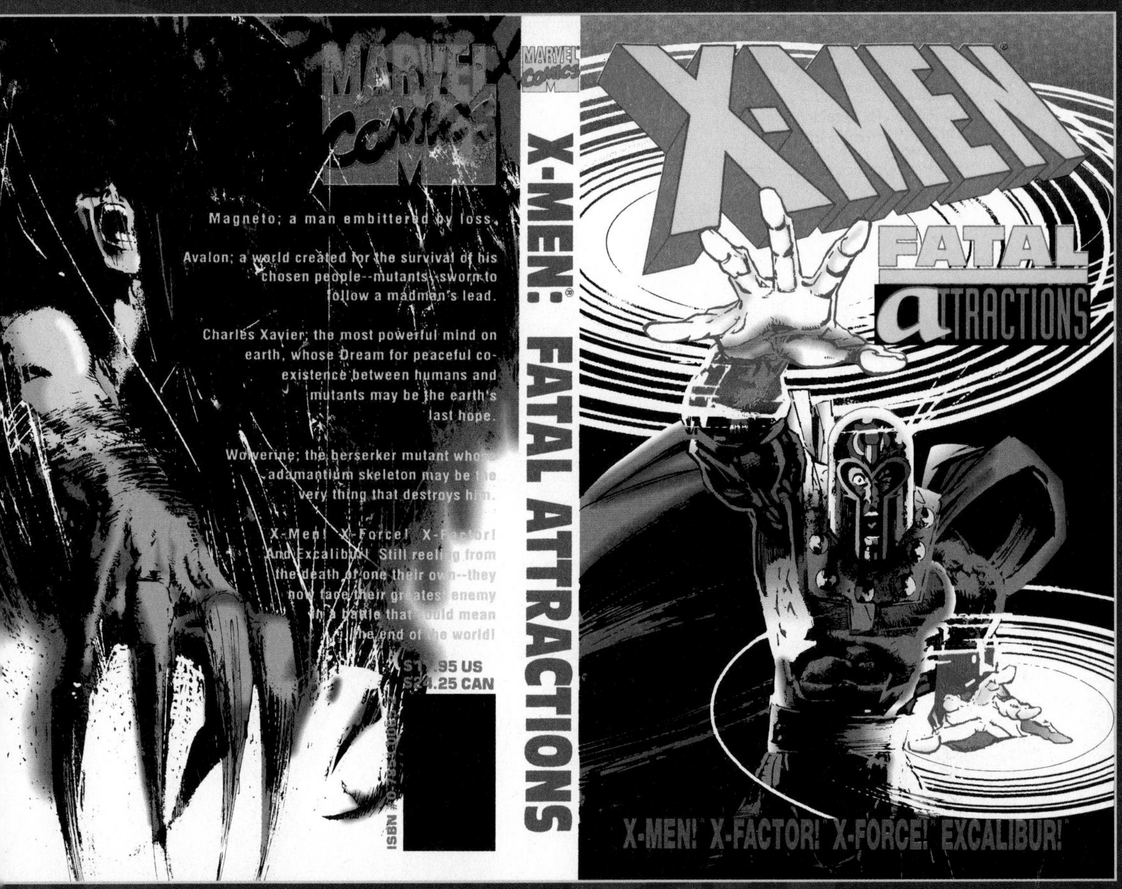

X-Men: Fatal Attractions TPB (1994) cover art by Bill Sienkiewicz

ᴾB introduction by SCOTT LOBDELL

at's that old saying about "always expect the unexpected?"

a kid, I regarded it as one of the Great Paradoxes...ranking right up there with "If you don't know how to spell the word, look it up in the ionary." If you expect something, how could it possibly be unexpected? It was about this time I was going to stuff all my worldly belongings my otherwise empty gym bag and head for the wisdom-infested mountains of Tibet, when suddenly...I discovered the "All New, All Different len" (circa 1975).

d at that moment, all was made clear.

, for as long as they've been around, everyone's favorite misunderstood mutants have been delivering the unexpected. Whether it was the first ath" of Professor X (courtesy of the Changeling), the subsequent dissolution of the X-Men, the rise and fall of the Phoenix, or the unannounced h forward into the "Days of Future Past," one of the canons of X-Men law is...you never know what's going to happen from one issue to the t — sometimes, from one panel to the next.

"Fatal Attractions" story you are about to read may be the most dramatic example of all. Colossus's sister Illyana has passed away as a victim of fe's Legacy Virus. Magneto's sect of mutant Acolytes, who have been missing, gather together to stage a big ole' welcome home party. Senator y has been publicly debating the merits of Project Wideawake, when all of a sudden...whoooops.

ess if I tell you, you'll expect it.

oy!

cott Lobdell

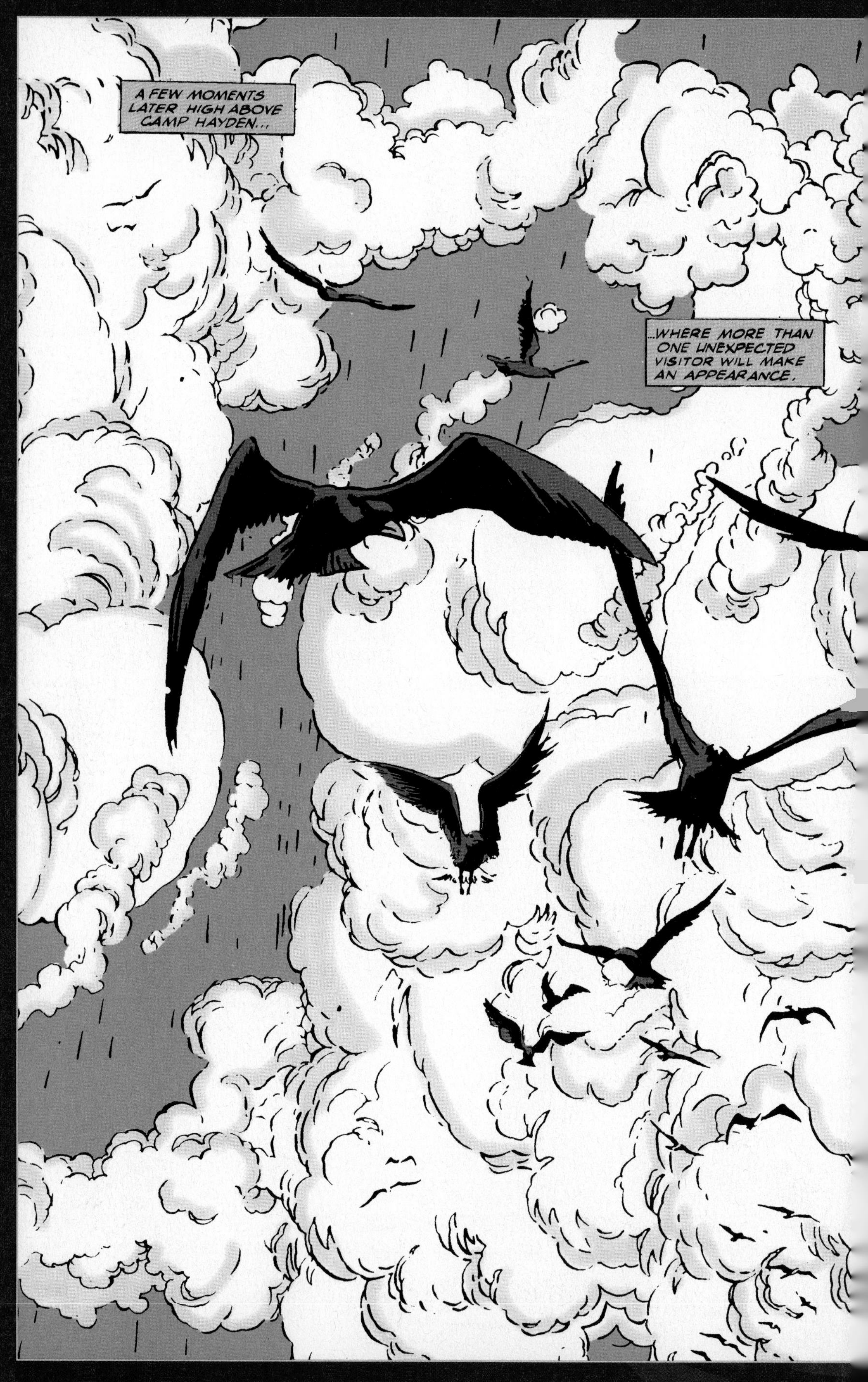

A FEW MOMENTS LATER HIGH ABOVE CAMP HAYDEN...
...WHERE MORE THAN ONE UNEXPECTED VISITOR WILL MAKE AN APPEARANCE.

The 1994 *X-Men: Fatal Attractions TPB* created two new story pages to balance double-page spreads. This page, using art by Joe Quesada & Al Milgrom, fit between *X-Factor #92* pages 12-13 (pages 151-152 in this TPB).

This page, using art by John Romita Jr., fit between *Uncanny X-Men #304* pages 44-45 (pages 271-272 in this TPB).